MW01035336

Visual Basic® 6
in Plain English

Brian Overland

IDG Books Worldwide, Inc.
An International Data Group Company

Foster City, CA • Chicago, IL • Indianapolis, IN • New York, NY

Visual Basic® 6 in Plain English

Published by
M&T Books
An imprint of IDG Books Worldwide, Inc.
919 E. Hillsdale Blvd., Suite 400
Foster City, CA 94404
www.idgbooks.com (IDG Books Worldwide Web site)

Library of Congress Catalog Card Number: 98-75150

ISBN: 0-7645-7007-2

Printed in the United States of America

10 9 8 7 6 5 4 3

1P/QU/QS/ZY/FC-IN

Distributed in the United States by IDG Books Worldwide, Inc.

Distributed by Macmillan Canada for Canada; by Transworld Publishers Limited in the United Kingdom; by IDG Norge Books for Norway; by IDG Sweden Books for Sweden; by Woodslane Pty. Ltd. for Australia; by Woodslane (NZ) Ltd. for New Zealand; by Addison Wesley Longman Singapore Pte Ltd. for Singapore, Malaysia, Thailand, Indonesia, and Korea; by Norma Comunicaciones S.A. for Colombia; by Intersoft for South Africa; by International Thomson Publishing for Germany, Austria, and Switzerland; by Toppan Company Ltd. for Japan; by Distribuidora Cuspide for Argentina; by Livraria Cultura for Brazil; by Ediciencia S.A. for Ecuador; by Ediciones ZETA S.C.R. Ltda. for Peru; by WS Computer Publishing Corporation, Inc., for the Philippines; by Unalis Corporation for Taiwan; by Contemporanea de Ediciones for Venezuela; by Computer Book & Magazine Store for Puerto Rico; by Express Computer Distributors for the Caribbean and West Indies. Authorized Sales Agent: Anthony Rudkin Associates for the Middle East and North Africa.

For general information on IDG Books Worldwide's books in the U.S., please call our Consumer Customer Service department at 800-762-2974. For reseller information, including discounts and premium sales, please call our Reseller Customer Service department at 800-434-3422.

For information on where to purchase IDG Books Worldwide's books outside the U.S., please contact our International Sales department at 317-596-5530 or fax 317-596-5692.

For consumer information on foreign language translations, please contact our Customer Service department at 1-800-434-3422, fax 317-596-5692, or e-mail rights@idgbooks.com.

For information on licensing foreign or domestic rights, please phone + 1-650-655-3109.

For sales inquiries and special prices for bulk quantities, please contact our Sales department at 650-655-3200 or write to the address above.

For information on using IDG Books Worldwide's books in the classroom or for ordering examination copies, please contact our Educational Sales department at 800-434-2086 or fax 317-596-5499.

For press review copies, author interviews, or other publicity information, please contact our Public Relations department at 650-655-3000 or fax 650-655-3299.

For authorization to photocopy items for corporate, personal, or educational use, please contact Copyright Clearance Center, 222 Rosewood Drive, Danvers, MA 01923, or fax 978-750-4470.

ABOUT IDG BOOKS WORLDWIDE

Welcome to the world of IDG Books Worldwide.

IDG Books Worldwide, Inc., is a subsidiary of International Data Group, the world's largest publisher of computer-related information and the leading global provider of information services on information technology. IDG was founded more than 25 years ago and now employs more than 8,500 people worldwide. IDG publishes more than 275 computer publications in over 75 countries (see listing below). More than 90 million people read one or more IDG publications each month.

Launched in 1990, IDG Books Worldwide is today the #1 publisher of best-selling computer books in the United States. We are proud to have received eight awards from the Computer Press Association in recognition of editorial excellence and three from *Computer Currents*' First Annual Readers' Choice Awards. Our best-selling *...For Dummies*® series has more than 50 million copies in print with translations in 38 languages. IDG Books Worldwide, through a joint venture with IDG's Hi-Tech Beijing, became the first U.S. publisher to publish a computer book in the People's Republic of China. In record time, IDG Books Worldwide has become the first choice for millions of readers around the world who want to learn how to better manage their businesses.

Our mission is simple: Every one of our books is designed to bring extra value and skill-building instructions to the reader. Our books are written by experts who understand and care about our readers. The knowledge base of our editorial staff comes from years of experience in publishing, education, and journalism — experience we use to produce books for the '90s. In short, we care about books, so we attract the best people. We devote special attention to details such as audience, interior design, use of icons, and illustrations. And because we use an efficient process of authoring, editing, and desktop publishing our books electronically, we can spend more time ensuring superior content and spend less time on the technicalities of making books.

You can count on our commitment to deliver high-quality books at competitive prices on topics you want to read about. At IDG Books Worldwide, we continue in the IDG tradition of delivering quality for more than 25 years. You'll find no better book on a subject than one from IDG Books Worldwide.

John Kilcullen
CEO
IDG Books Worldwide, Inc.

Steven Berkowitz
President and Publisher
IDG Books Worldwide, Inc.

Eighth Annual
Computer Press
Awards ≥1992

Ninth Annual
Computer Press
Awards ≥1993

Tenth Annual
Computer Press
Awards ≥1994

Eleventh Annual
Computer Press
Awards ≥1995

IDG Books Worldwide, Inc., is a subsidiary of International Data Group, the world's largest publisher of computer-related information and the leading global provider of information services on information technology. International Data Group publishes over 275 computer publications in over 75 countries. More than 90 million people read one or more International Data Group publications each month. International Data Group's publications include: ARGENTINA: Buyer's Guide, Computerworld Argentina, PC World Argentina; AUSTRALIA: Australian Macworld, Australian PC World, Australian Reseller News, Computerworld, IT Casebook, Network World, Publish, Webmaster; AUSTRIA: Computerwelt Oesterreich, Networks Austria, PC Tip Austria; BANGLADESH: PC World Bangladesh; BELARUS: PC World Belarus; BELGIUM: Data News; BRAZIL: Annuário de Informática, Computerworld, Connections, Macworld, PC Player, PC World, Publish, Reseller News, Supergamepower; BULGARIA: Computerworld Bulgaria, Network World Bulgaria, PC & MacWorld Bulgaria; CANADA: CIO Canada, Client/Server World, ComputerWorld Canada, InfoWorld Canada, NetworkWorld Canada, WebWorld; CHILE: Computerworld Chile, PC World Chile; COLOMBIA: Computerworld Colombia, PC World Colombia; COSTA RICA: PC World Centro America; THE CZECH AND SLOVAK REPUBLICS: Computerworld Czechoslovakia, Macworld Czech Republic, PC World Czechoslovakia; DENMARK: Communications World Danmark, Computerworld Danmark, Macworld Danmark, PC World Danmark, Techworld Denmark; DOMINICAN REPUBLIC: PC World Republica Dominicana; ECUADOR: PC World Ecuador; EGYPT: Computerworld Middle East, PC World Middle East; EL SALVADOR: PC World Centro America; FINLAND: MikroPC, Tietoverkko, Tietoviikko; FRANCE: Distributique, Hebdo, Info PC, Le Monde Informatique, Macworld, Reseaux & Telecoms, WebMaster France; GERMANY: Computer Partner, Computerwoche, Computerwoche Extra, Computerwoche FOCUS, Global Online, Macwelt, PC Welt; GREECE: Amiga Computing, GamePro Greece, Multimedia World; GUATEMALA: PC World Centro America; HONDURAS: PC World Centro America; HONG KONG: Computerworld Hong Kong, PC World Hong Kong, Publish in Asia; HUNGARY: ABCD CD-ROM, Computerworld Szamitastechnika, Internetto online Magazine, PC World Hungary, PC-X Magazin Hungary; ICELAND: Tolvuheimur PC World Island; INDIA: Information Communications World, Information Systems Computerworld, PC World India, Publish in Asia; INDONESIA: InfoKomputer PC World, Komputek Computerworld, Publish in Asia; IRELAND: ComputerScope, PC Live!; ISRAEL: Macworld Israel, People & Computers/Computerworld; ITALY: Computerworld Italia, Macworld Italia, Networking Italia, PC World Italia; JAPAN: DTP World, Macworld Japan, Nikkei Personal Computing, OS/2 World Japan, SunWorld Japan, Windows NT World, Windows World Japan; KENYA: PC World East African; KOREA: Hi-Tech Information, Macworld Korea, PC World Korea; MACEDONIA: PC World Macedonia; MALAYSIA: Computerworld Malaysia, PC World Malaysia, Publish in Asia; MALTA: PC World Malta; MEXICO: Computerworld Mexico, PC World Mexico; MYANMAR: PC World Myanmar; NETHERLANDS: Computer! Totaal, LAN Internetworking Magazine, LAN World Buyers Guide, Macworld Netherlands, Net, WebWeld; NEW ZEALAND: Absolute Beginners Guide and Plain & Simple Series, Computer Buyer, Computer Industry Directory, Computerworld New Zealand, MTB, Network World, PC World New Zealand; NICARAGUA: PC World Centro America; NORWAY: Computerworld Norge, CW Rapport, Datamagasinet, Financial Rapport, Kursguide Norge, Macworld Norge, Multimediaworld Norge, PC World Ekspress Norge, PC World Network, PC World Norge, PC World ProduktGuide Norge; PAKISTAN: Computerworld Pakistan; PANAMA: PC World Panama; PEOPLE'S REPUBLIC OF CHINA: China Computer Users, China Computerworld, China InfoWorld, China Telecom World Weekly, Computer & Communication, Electronic Design China, Electronics Today, Electronics World, Information Networks World, Information Systems Computerworld, PC Advisor, PC Home, PSX Pro, The WEB, UNITED STATES: Cable in the Classroom, CIO Magazine, Computerworld, DOS World, Federal Computer Week, GamePro Magazine, InfoWorld, I-Way, Macworld, Network World, PC Games, PC World, Publish, Video Event, THE WEB Magazine, and WebMaster; online webzines: JavaWorld, NetscapeWorld, and SunWorld Online; URUGUAY: InfoWorld Uruguay; VENEZUELA: Computerworld Venezuela, PC World Venezuela; and VIETNAM: PC World Vietnam. 5/7/98

Credits

Acquisitions Editor
Laura Lewin

Development Editor
Matthew E. Lusher

Technical Editor
Chris Stone

Copy Editor
Ami Knox

Project Coordinator
Susan Parini

Cover Coordinator
Annie Romanowitz

Book Designer
London Road Design

Graphics and Production Specialists
Mario Amador
Hector Mendoza
Dina F Quan

Quality Control Specialists
Mick Arellano
Mark Schumann

Proofreader
Arielle Carole Mennelle

Indexer
York Production Services

About the Author

Brian Overland worked as programmer/writer, tester, and manager for Microsoft for ten years and played an important role in the development of Visual Basic (he wrote the first-ever sample Visual Basic program). He was documentation project lead for Visual Basic 1.0 and sole author of the *Control Development Guide*, which played an important role in VB's success. He is the author of *C in Plain English*, *C++ in Plain English*, and *Java in Plain English*.

To everyone at Microsoft I worked with
on Visual Basic 1.0.
Thanks, it was a great ride.

Preface

Welcome to *Visual Basic 6 in Plain English,* an insider's guide to the language as well as a common-sense handbook. This is two books in one: a survey of intermediate topics as well as a compact reference book that can be used by beginning, intermediate, and advanced programmers alike. It provides many ways to look things up, and it gives simple, direct answers to common questions. If there's one programming book that you'll want to keep next to your keyboard or read on the bus, this is it.

As the *Plain English* part of the title implies, this book has a special mission: to de-mystify some of the more baffling concepts of programming. There's a heavy emphasis on challenging ideas such as object-oriented programming, ActiveX controls, low-level graphics, and advanced file operations. The goal is to explain not only how to use these features, but also how to make them work for you . . . that is, why they matter.

As the *Visual Basic 6* part of the title implies, brand new features of Version 6.0 get a lot of attention. Many chapters start with a "What's New in VB 6.0" section so that you get a quick rundown of what's new in each subject area.

Visual Basic and I go back a long way together. Though I've worked on many other languages, I was one of the project leads of the original VB 1.0 and retain a lot of affection for it. You'll get some hints as to the "whys" and "hows" of the product's design and evolution. Above all, Visual Basic is designed to be fun to use, and I wasn't above having some fun with this book! I trust you'll have as much fun as I do every time I sit down to write a program.

Who Can Use This Book

As previously mentioned, the book includes intermediate topics, as well as reference material useful to all VB programmers. It does, however, start with a review of the basics, and even advanced programmers may benefit from the discussion of new features.

Although the book reviews fundamentals, it's perhaps best used as your next book after reading an absolute-beginner book like those in the . . . *For Dummies* series. But if you have any background in a previous version of Basic or another language such as C++, *Visual Basic 6 in Plain English* will take you by the hand and get you quickly up to speed.

To enter and run the examples, you'll need a copy of Visual Basic 6.0. Visual Basic 5.0 supports most, but not all, of these examples; some are written to exploit new features in Version 6.0.

How to Use This Book

The book is divided into two main parts that reinforce and cross reference each other.

Part I: Getting to Know VB6

This is the place to get the big picture on a general subject area, such as controls, files, object orientation, or database operations. It's also where to go to get a summary of the new features that Visual Basic 6.0 brings to each area. Most chapters are tutorial in nature, first describing general techniques and then leading you through simple but useful examples. The text analyzes each example, explaining how and why each part of the code works. This part is also rich in pictures and conceptual drawings, in keeping with the attitude that Visual Basic should be visual.

Part I ends with a special task summary chapter that encapsulates techniques from earlier chapters as well as a few additional ones. This is your guide to how to get things done in Visual Basic, with short, direct, step-by-step instructions.

Part II: Tables and Reference Data

Although it's not possible to summarize all of Visual Basic in this small a space, Part II summarizes the core of the language itself, including object-oriented features and debugging commands. Part II also pays close attention to the new intrinsic functions in Visual Basic 6.0. I give a summary of each standard control in the Toolbox, pointing out the key properties, methods, and events. Using this summary can save you hours of plodding through the long list of properties supported for each control to find what you need.

Part II begins with two special sections — *Visual Basic in Plain English* and *Visual Basic Elements A to Z* — which help you look up information by task or by keyword.

Conventions

A number of conventions are used throughout the book as a kind of shorthand. These conventions are intended to explain more in less time and space.

Source Code

Example code uses a specific font to set it off from ordinary text:

```
pi = Atn(1) * 4
angle1 = 135 * pi / 180
angle2 = 45 * pi / 180
Circle (2000, 2000), 1000, , angle1, angle2
```

Keywords and Examples in Text

Keywords, command names, and code fragments inside of regular text all use a special font: Keyword. To take but one example, use of this font helps distinguish the keyword If from the ordinary English word "if."

Syntax Displays

This book often summarizes everything (or almost everything) you can do with a particular statement or function. To communicate this information succinctly and clearly, it uses a syntax similar to that used in the Visual Basic environment itself. Keywords and required punctuation are in bold, and placeholders (items where you supply the value) are in italic.

For example, the following syntax implies that you must enter Dim exactly as shown, but you supply your own name for *variable_name*:

```
Dim variable_name
```

Brackets indicate an optional item — you can choose to include it or not include it. A more complete version of the syntax above is as follows:

```
Dim variable_name [As type]
```

This implies that you can optionally include As, a keyword, and *type*, a placeholder. Because they are inside the same pair of brackets, you must use both if you use either.

Finally, every once in a while you will see the use of ellipses (...) to show that an item can be repeated any number of times. For example, in the If...Then syntax, you can include any number of ElseIf clauses. Each occurrence of ElseIf must include its own *condition*, *statements*, and Then keyword:

```
If condition Then
    statements
[ElseIf condition Then
    statements]...
[Else
    statements]
End If
```

Note Icons

To keep things simple, I've included just one special icon: the Note icon. Material placed in notes includes ideas that are separate from the main discussion but require your attention sooner or later. Often, a note gives an important warning or a tip you may have forgotten. Sometimes a note points out that a feature is new to Visual Basic 6.0.

●—**NOTE**────────────────────────────

Here's an example of what a Note looks like.

Contacting the Author

I welcome your comments and feedback. I can't always reply immediately with the technical answer that someone wants, but I will try. I especially welcome feedback on your experience with the book and suggestions as to how to improve any future edition. You can contact me at `Briano2u@aol.com`.

Acknowledgments

This book exists because of the efforts of a number of people working in different parts of the country. Despite the distances involved, I worked with several of them fairly closely, thanks to the miracles of e-mail and file attachments.

The book exists because of Laura Lewin, who got me to write it and never failed to be a source of optimism and encouragement. It also exists because of the project's development editor, Matt Lusher, who kept everything moving and was flexible and responsive at all times. The technical editor, Chris Stone, was important to the project not only for the excellent suggestions (many of which were incorporated into the book), but also for his general encouragement and positive feedback.

I'd like to extend a special thanks to Ami Knox, the copy editor, for promptly and patiently answering all my queries, and being open to discussing all aspects of completing the book. In addition, Ami went above and beyond the call of duty by correcting misspellings even when they appeared in comments in example code.

Finally, I'd like to thank the project coordinator, Susan Parini, as well as the graphic artists involved, for supporting a book with an unusually high number of screen shots and figures compared to text. Visual Basic is meant to be a straightforward language, but there are a number of tricky concepts; the richness of the figures, I hope, will be an important aid to the reader.

Contents at a Glance

Contents

Visual Basic® 6
in Plain English

Getting to Know VB6

A Historical Introduction to VB

> *"In the future, everyone will be a*
> *programmer for 15 minutes."*
>
> — Andy Peacenik, pop artist

No language ever developed has yet succeeded in turning everyone who uses it into a programmer, but Visual Basic has possibly come the closest. As I've looked at features added to Visual Basic in recent years, I've sometimes found myself mumbling, "But it can't be that *easy!*"

Of course, it seems easy to me because I've been acquainted with Visual Basic from the beginning, back when one of my own programs was one of the first ever to run in the then-new language. I didn't have to worry what the strange *object.property* syntax was, because I learned it from the lead developer. But for more than a few people — some very intelligent people — this was a bit of a hurdle at first.

Later, there was much more of this object business, the goal being in part to make Visual Basic a state-of-the-art computer language. More important still was the goal of supporting Microsoft's emerging systems architecture. This architecture aimed at creating a world in which applications

1

talk to each other, and Visual Basic runs them all. This takes us back to the original vision for the project.

In the Beginning

In the beginning, there was Bill Gates and a language called Basic (or BASIC, as it was known then). Now, Gates didn't invent Basic any more than Henry Ford invented the automobile. What he did do was produce Basic in a form that could be used by millions of people. Although Microsoft has had many other landmark products, Basic was in a sense the foundation of the company. It brought in revenue to help the young partnership take its first steps toward expansion, which in turn led to other projects.

Years rolled by, and then came Windows. Not everyone remembers how long the company had to stand behind this product before it could be called even a moderate success. In one of my initial jobs for Microsoft, I provided phone support. People would call in and ask about Windows: What in the world ran on it? Other than the mini-apps that came in the package, I could only mention a couple of applications.

Windows took so long to catch on for many reasons. One reason was that the early versions were so inferior to what came later. But another had to be that few people outside of those at Microsoft were successfully developing applications to run on Windows in the early days. This, in turn, was because Windows programs were notoriously difficult for the average programmer to write.

To be fair, this difficulty isn't exclusive to Windows. Windows is an event-driven, graphical user interface (GUI), as is the Macintosh, to name one example. And such systems, though easier for the end user, plunk the programmer down into a world of getting and receiving messages, allocating resources, and asking for something called a handle before sending any kind of output to the screen. In short, GUI programming is difficult because one can't start with a simple application. The programmer has to start with a rather sophisticated model in which he or she cooperates closely with a complex system.

A language was needed that would be to Windows what Basic had always been to DOS: programming for the masses. One of the factors behind the success of both Basic and DOS was that Basic was easy to use, and it could be used to write acceptable pro-

1

grams in the DOS environment — not remarkably fast or efficient programs, but programs that could get the job done. Even experienced programmers with engineering degrees (I remember working for some of them in the early '80s) would condescend to writing commercial programs in Basic. Although clunky and sometimes inelegant, Basic made it possible to finish projects much faster than if everything were written in machine language.

Perhaps this is why Bill Gates talked about a hypothetical business-application language to be developed in the future. He envisioned it would be a language accessible to people programming in Basic, and it would use high-level commands to drive Windows applications, therefore leading to fast development. It would also be visual, making available to programmers some of the graphical tools end users enjoyed under Windows.

However, several years ticked by before Visual Basic became much more than an idea.

The Ideal Becomes Real

The first time I heard the name *Visual Basic,* I had been working (too long, really) on assembler documentation and was looking around for a new project. I spoke to a guy named John Fine, probably the most energetic program manager in the history of Microsoft (other than Steve Balmer, of course), and the person I'd worked with a couple of years earlier on my first assembler product.

John had recently received a mandate from Bill Gates, he told me. Microsoft had acquired technology from a company called Cooper Software, which had prototyping software for Windows. (*Prototyping* refers to a way of quickly creating a user interface.) In later years, I've come across books that give Cooper Software the credit for inventing Visual Basic, but I don't believe this is accurate. It was Gates' idea that the interface-drawing software from Cooper be married to another existing technology — that of Basic's threaded p-code — to produce Visual Basic.

Another bit of background is necessary here. Basic didn't always have the *threaded p-code,* or *pseudo-code,* technology. This technology came about as a response to both the compiler/interpreter problem and the challenge mounted to Basic's supremacy by a successful product called TurboPascal back in the early-to-mid '80s. TurboPascal translated and executed programs very fast for its day and had a growing cult following.

1

QuickBasic was Microsoft's hope for regaining and holding the programming-for-the-masses market, and it succeeded. It offered a user-friendly environment, much as TurboPascal did, but it went much further: QuickBasic not only compiled and executed programs quickly, it also enabled programmers to stop execution, fix an error, and *continue to execute the program* — an unheard-of luxury for most programmers. Part of what made this possible was threaded p-code. After a programmer entered each statement, QuickBasic compiled it into an intermediate binary form. Pressing the Run key caused the QuickBasic engine to execute these binary commands with reasonably good performance. Because the binary commands were threaded, new commands could be inserted into the program without necessarily having to restart everything.

In essence, QuickBasic was already an unrivaled tool for fast creation of programs under DOS. The technology from Cooper Software constituted a tool for fast creation of graphical objects under Windows. What the latter lacked was a true programming language — a way of giving those objects elaborate, customized, complex behavior. In retrospect, it's easy to see these two as made for each other. I don't know if just anyone could have made the connection, however. Gates not only wrote the original code for Basic, but also deserves credit for later acquiring technology and visualizing what could be done with it.

Creating a Marriage That Worked

Even starting with a great UI design tool and a great (or at least popular) computer language, the Visual Basic design team still had a big job ahead of them: How could they integrate these two components so they act as one?

The design team came up with a solution by borrowing syntax from the *object-oriented* model, which even back then was seen as the future of programming. Skeptics might argue that Basic was far too unstructured to ever support an object-oriented model, but as far as Microsoft was concerned, it was inevitable. For years, "Object Basic" was considered destiny, the holy grail for which Visual Basic was just an intermediate step. Now objects are just another aspect of VB.

The essence of object-based syntax is this: A language is based on objects, which are sophisticated packets of data, and their members, which include data fields and functions. There's a universal way to express this relationship:

```
object.member
```

Building on this idea, the Visual Basic design team went a little further and came up with *properties,* a special kind of data member. A property refers to some general attribute of an object: width, height, color, contents, and so on. When a new value is assigned to a property, Visual Basic does everything necessary to reflect the change. Change the height, for example, and — like magic! — the object is redrawn with the new size.

Let's take a purely imaginary example. Suppose you have an object named Bill. For such an object, certain properties apply: Height, Age, and EarningPower, for example. You could use object syntax to set Bill's properties:

```
Bill.Age = 43
Bill.Height = 6.1
Bill.EarningPower = ASTRONOMICAL
```

Bill's properties are now correctly set. You don't have to remember any function names or quirky syntax. This one syntax works for all situations. If you want to set properties for another object — say, an object named SteveB — you can do that, too:

```
SteveB.Age = 44
SteveB.Height = 6.3
SteveB.EarningPower = EXCEPTIONAL
```

Of course, these are imaginary examples. Now suppose you have a text box named Readout. You can use the name to set a number of properties. For example, the following statement makes the text box temporarily invisible:

```
Readout.Visible = False
```

Another statement makes it visible again:

```
Readout.Visible = True
```

And the following statement, which both gets and sets a property value, doubles the height of the text box:

```
Readout.Height = Readout.Height * 2
```

1

The main purpose of text boxes, of course, is to contain text. Not surprisingly, a specific property refers to this data, and its name is `Text`. Therefore, to place new text into the control, just set this property:

```
Readout.Text = "Hello, world, it's Visual Basic!"
```

The syntax is simple, elegant, and more than a little ingenious. The beauty of this system is if something needs to be done to reflect a change (redrawing the control, for example) it's all taken care of behind the scenes, as it were. The VB programmer is only concerned with results. Properties became the core of how Visual Basic worked — and still works, to this day.

Beyond the invention of properties (and the event-driven model, which I discuss in the next chapter), another novel aspect of Visual Basic was it presented the Basic team with the first — and last — chance to purge the ugliest, most troublesome features of the Basic language itself. Years earlier, Bill Gates had to cram the original version of Basic into a few kilobytes of memory. It was remarkable how much Basic did, considering the constraints, but it was not an elegant, academically pure language like Pascal, Ada, or C++. Nor could it have been.

Each subsequent version of Basic added new features that made it possible to write better code. However, Basic was haunted by the specter of *backward compatibility*, which meant that all the code that users wrote using earlier versions had to continue to work when they updated their development systems. This made it impossible to drop anything ugly from the Basic language. All the development team could do was provide a better alternative and then de-emphasize the old feature in the documentation.

But for one brief, shining moment, backward compatibility could be violated. It was a unique, never-to-be-repeated situation. The theory was that when the transition from the DOS to Windows applications was made, programmers were going to have to rewrite large amounts of code anyway (a safe assumption). Furthermore, a number of keywords had to be dropped because they violated restrictions under Windows. Prime culprits of non-Windows-like behavior included `PEEK` and `POKE`, among others.

It therefore made sense to drop the more problematic syntax. This could be done just once. Subsequent versions of Visual Basic would have to support everything in VB 1.0. Anything that made

1

the transition from DOS to VB was in for good. One of the major pieces of syntax to be purged was the so-called (and in my opinion misnamed) *module-level code*, which was code that floated outside of any procedure. Module-level code was annoying to Pascal and C++ programmers, because it was like a "main" procedure except that it followed its own strange rules. With the exclusion of module-level code, Visual Basic was given a better structure.

You will still on occasion see things that are odd about Visual Basic when compared to more structured, "pure" languages, such as Pascal. In spite of this, the new features in the Visual Basic model, combined with elimination of some of Basic's less elegant features, gave Basic a whole new look. In the early days of VB 1.0, people were often brought in for usability testing without being told the name of the (as yet unreleased) product. They consistently said, "This looks a lot like C or Pascal," but never "Oh, this is Basic."

Those were heady times, designing a new language like that. I was lucky to be in on some of it, meeting with two of the driving forces — Scott Ferguson, the lead developer, and Adam Rauch, the program manager working under John Fine. Each of them was a great talent, leading a team of other very talented people.

On the Naming of Names

Most people now probably think of the name *Visual Basic* as carved in stone, but that wasn't always the case. At the very beginning of the project, Visual Basic was never anything more than a working title. The code name for the project (long since leaked to the public) was *Thunder*, and those of us working on it were led to believe that eventually Thunder would be replaced by some exciting name. Other software prototyping tools had appealing names such as HyperCard and ToolBook, and we thought our project would get one, too.

Everyone connected to the project suggested names. One by one, they were struck down either because they didn't sufficiently describe the product or because they had already been taken. (It's still tough to come up with good names for new software packages, because so many thousands of them are already out there.) In the end, we stayed with Visual Basic, Gates' original working title — and the term would refer not only to the language, but also to the entire product.

1

For me personally, it came as a relief that no separate names existed for the language and the environment. Trying to write about the language and the environment as though they were two separate entities was incredibly difficult, even if it made sense in theory. Recently, as I've gone back to focus on Visual Basic, I am convinced of this more than ever: The programming language is so tightly integrated with the graphical tools that it's tough to separate them. This fact remains a defining characteristic of Visual Basic, even when compared to other Windows languages, such as Visual C++.

Never Fear, Custom Controls Are Here

Custom-control technology has often been cited as one of the keys to the success of Visual Basic. Here's what it enables you to do: If you could also program in C, you could create an entirely new class of graphical object (a *control*). In effect, you could extend the capabilities of what Visual Basic could do, with few limits. In addition, you could sell your custom controls to other VB programmers. Microsoft's product marketing, in fact, always lent support to this secondary market.

Yet in Version 1.0, custom-control technology was added very late in the game. It seemed to me almost an afterthought, although I learned later that Bill Gates had seen the value of this technology early on.

Custom controls represent my own strongest involvement with the project. Though worn out from working on the *Programmer's Guide*, I took an assignment to put together custom-control documentation less than two months before the ship date. Scott Ferguson gave me some samples, several pages of notes, and unlimited access to his doorway when I had questions. I decided what was needed was an example that was simple but that did a little bit of everything. The sample I came up with, the Circle control, might be sneered at for its simplicity, but I found (almost to my amusement) that later Visual Basic teams continued to use it for years.

Programmers, it turned out, loved custom-control technology. They loved the idea of extending Visual Basic itself; if it didn't do something you needed, you just came up with your own control. The beauty of it was the new control would fit neatly into the existing programming model. A user of the control could get and set property values, for example, just as they could with standard controls.

The one disappointment fans of Basic experienced was they couldn't write controls in Visual Basic itself. They had to use C and Windows-programming techniques, employing all those intimidating Windows API calls. This is one reason why Visual Basic Version 5.0 was such a breakthrough: It finally enabled Visual Basic programmers to create new types of controls without leaving the environment. Version 6.0, of course, continues this support.

Onward and Upward

This is what Microsoft had when it launched the first version of Visual Basic: a programming language known and loved by millions; a set of tools for quickly drawing objects on the screen (such as text boxes, buttons, and scrollbars); a reasonably simple syntax that connected the language to the objects; an environment that made development of programs lightning fast; and above all, the custom-control architecture.

Even with all this, there was the potential to get lost among competitors. More than one company had foreseen the need to address the same issue, *how to create Windows applications real fast,* and everybody seemed to be coming out with their solution at about the same time. Fortunately, not all of those companies were direct competitors. For example, a couple of months before Visual Basic was released, Paul Allen's company, Asymetrix, had gone to market with a very good product called ToolBook. This development system was well suited to creating certain kinds of applications: slide slows and multimedia presentations. Visual Basic, however, still could fulfill a niche for people who needed a more general-purpose programming language. The slogan of Visual Basic soon became "to create *real* Windows applications real fast."

Sales of Visual Basic were good from the beginning, and they grew over time. More than one magazine out there now is devoted to the subject, which is certainly a sign of success. But even today, you still can't compare Visual Basic sales numbers to those for, say, Microsoft Word. Nor should that be surprising. By far the largest number of people who've bought new computers in the

1

last 15 years have been those who've wanted to use them to get actual work done, rather than to learn to become hackers.

Yet if a user did enjoy working in Windows and wanted to try his or her hand at writing applications, Visual Basic provided an enjoyable, user-friendly learning path. It also became the tool of choice for countless business programmers — people who needed to get some customized utility working fast for their small business or department. This orientation toward business programming would help influence future directions of the product.

In general, Visual Basic's greatest impact on the world was in helping to change the way people related to Windows. It was now *easier* to create an application in Windows than DOS. This was a complete reversal of the way things had been.

Visual Basic, the Next Version

Always seeking to work on new products, I moved over to Visual C++ Version 1.0, while continuing to stay interested in Visual Basic and use it for most of my own programming (writing games and utilities such as my own daily To Do list program).

The first update was an interim release: a custom-control edition. It packaged a number of controls contributed from both inside and outside Microsoft. If anything in particular surprised people within Microsoft about Visual Basic's reception, it was the amount of interest sparked by custom controls.

For the last 10 or 15 years, the big issues in computer languages have been *object-orientation* and *reusability*. A creeping fog of jargon and mysticism surrounds these ideas, but if you can get through the fog, you can see the light: the idea that computer software should profit from division of labor, just as hardware has. Let one group of people build standardized, reusable parts. Let another group of people connect these parts to form powerful systems. This is what's happened in hardware, leading to stunning, thousand-fold increases in efficiency. Although this sounds good in theory, it has always been hard to find cases where people really made these advances in software, despite all the new concepts.

Ironically, even though Visual Basic did not come close to a pure object-oriented language, custom-control technology fulfilled some of the greatest hopes of object orientation. Graphical controls provided much of Visual Basic's appeal: A programmer could draw the control on the screen to see how it worked before writing the first line of code. Custom controls let C programmers put any idea they wanted into this same appealing model, selling their components to many thousands of VB programmers who could then see, feel, and touch all the things the component did. For the first time, software components seemed nearly as real as hardware.

Visual Basic 2.0 started to take object orientation more seriously, although new custom-control classes still couldn't be created from within Visual Basic. One of the new features was the availability of *object variables*, which could refer to different objects at different times.

Object variables were difficult to explain, however, especially to people who had never used C++. If you look at object variables closely, you can see they act suspiciously like pointers. (They are actually reference variables, taken right out of C++.) But to most Basic people, *pointers* is a nasty word. Pointers are dangerous, sharp, painful instruments borrowed from that ill-mannered systems language, C. So, in VB documentation, object variables had to be described without alluding to pointers. I felt the documentation team had a difficult job in this area. My take on this subject is in Chapter 8, where I try to clear up some of the conceptual difficulties.

Other improvements in Visual Basic 2.0 included some useful conveniences. The `Variant` type was introduced and made the default type. Although it can encourage lazy programming, this type has the virtue of making it even easier to get simple programs running fast. Version 2.0 also included the predefined `True` and `False` constants, something I had lobbied for in Version 1.0.

And the Beat Goes On: Versions 3.0 to 5.0

The next two versions, 3.0 and 4.0, came out fairly quickly on the heels of Version 2.0. By then Visual C++ had been released. I noted with some chagrin that in Visual C++ we adopted part of the name of Visual Basic, but little of its simplicity. (However, Visual C++ still had graphical-design tools, as well as a feature called Wizards, which wrote part of the application for the programmer.) As Visual Basic and Visual C++ each found their own niche, it was clear that Visual Basic was the more business-oriented language. Visual Basic's strength was that it minimized — even

1

more than Visual C++ — the amount of attention the programmer had to pay to low-level details. When using VB, programmers could spend most of their time thinking about interface design and managing data.

Versions 3.0 and 4.0 capitalized heavily on the business orientation of Visual Basic. A new built-in control type, the `Data` control, made it amazingly easy to create applications that interacted with a database. And changes were being made in other Microsoft applications, such as Word, Excel, and Access, that enabled them to work with Visual Basic. This new technology was called Visual Basic for Applications, and it helped realize the original vision for VB. In theory, one could always have Windows applications talk to each other through something called Dynamic Data Exchange (DDE). But that is slow and cumbersome. The beauty of Visual Basic is it enables programmers to grab a big chunk of data — a spreadsheet, for example — and treat it as just another Visual Basic object. The goal is to make everything in Windows support the same easy-to-use, high-level language.

This scheme is all part of an open architecture that Microsoft publishes and proselytizes as *OLE Automation.* The drawback for programmers using VB versions 3.0 and 4.0 was they had to use C or C++ if they wanted to create an OLE Automation Server — the same problem they faced with custom controls.

When Version 5.0 came out, it was in some ways the biggest breakthrough of all. It gave programmers the long-awaited ability to create new classes of custom controls without leaving Visual Basic, as well as the ability to create other kinds of projects. In addition to regular applications, programmers could create documents, DLLs, OLE Servers, and ActiveX controls. As Visual Basic was gaining sophistication, so was the world around it. The proliferation of project types was there not to confuse the programmer, but to provide flexibility. Windows has grown into an exceptionally rich environment, enabling applications to talk to each other and share data. Visual Basic now supports every aspect of this process.

In general, Version 5.0 answered the calls of VB programmers who had long asked for advances in the core language itself. In Versions 3.0 and 4.0, Visual Basic development had become a part of the Microsoft Office group, and its features were if anything too often dictated by its position as a business-application language. With Version 5.0, the pendulum finally began to swing back the other way.

The New Version: 6.0

Visual Basic 6.0 might almost be called the network version of
VB. It seems a certain amount of effort went into supporting
Microsoft's increased emphasis on the Internet and on distributed
(network) computing. If you're not involved with this kind of
computing, the new features will probably not seem as dramatic
as the ones introduced in Version 5.0. Yet there are a number of
miscellaneous, useful improvements.

From Microsoft's point of view, possibly the most important
addition is the availability of an ADO Data control, which mini-
mizes the difference between local and remote data objects. In
other words, a programmer can interact with a database, for the
most part, without worrying about who on a network is providing
it. This supports Microsoft's distributed-computing strategy.

If you're not currently doing database operations using distributed computing, this feature is unlikely to be useful to you right
away. Other new features are available, though, some of which
are potentially very useful. The following is a partial list, but it
covers most of the principal items:

- You can allocate an object whose class is supplied by a
  remote location on a network. (`CreateObject`)

- The new ADO family of classes (which includes the ADO
  Data control previously mentioned) provides a better
  model for both local and remote database applications.

- You can select Web-document-creation as a project type. The
  Professional and Enterprise editions (which I don't focus on
  in this book) have a number of other Internet-related
  enhancements, such as the ability to respond to browser
  requests. The Setup Wizard — or rather, its replacement —
  enables you to publish applications to the Web.

- Function syntax has been extended, so you can define
  `Function` procedures returning arrays or user-defined
  types.

- From within Visual Basic, you can now create lightweight
  custom controls. Such controls sacrifice some capabilities
  in exchange for being much less taxing on system
  resources. (They lack an `hWnd` property.) They also can be
  made transparent, just like `Line` and `Shape` controls.

1

- A new class, `FileSystemObject`, makes certain high-level file operations much easier. You can use an object of this class, for example, to move or delete entire directories. (Of course, you can continue to use the old file-system statements, as well.) This class also works with a number of other new classes — `Drive`, `Folder`, and `File` — that together give you structured access to the entire file system.

- Another new class, `Dictionary`, offers some advantages over the old collection class, `Collection`. You can add any number of different objects of different types to a `Dictionary` object. Each object must have a unique key for retrieving it.

- A large number of string functions have been added. Most of these are related in some way to formatting and are easier to use than the old `Format` function. They also have an important advantage: The new formatting functions automatically observe regional settings, in keeping with Microsoft's philosophy that internationalization should be supported at all levels.

- For standard controls, the new `Validate` event is better to work with than `LostFocus`, because `Validate` is called when the form closes.

- In addition to the new ADO control, there are updated versions of many of the extended controls. In some cases, the completely new versions are similar to old controls, but better. For example, the `DataGrid`, `DataList`, and `DataCombo` controls are improved versions of `DBGrid`, `DBList`, and `DBCombo` controls. These are not covered here due to size restrictions, but you can go to online Help to get more information on them.

- A new control function, `CallByName`, enables programs to construct a string at run time and use it to access a property or method. This opens up some new possibilities.

- A new math function, `Round`, produces rounded numbers to any degree of precision. It can be useful in working with currency that needs to be rounded to cents or tenths of a cent, prior to use in calculations.

The new string functions are important because they support Microsoft's philosophy of encouraging applications for an international market. The *regional settings* on each user's computer include information on how numbers and dates are displayed in the end user's own country.

You've Come a Long Way, Basic

Visual Basic originally started as a way to create standard Window applications quickly. It was basically QuickBasic with graphical objects. The addition of custom controls, although almost an afterthought at the time, helped VB make a deep impact on programmers everywhere. Custom controls took concepts such as *extensibility*, *reusability*, and *object orientation* and made them work in a concrete way even Basic programmers could see and appreciate.

Over the years, Visual Basic became much more sophisticated, particularly in the kinds of projects it could create. Advances were almost always made with an overreaching vision in mind: to support the emerging Windows architecture, a system in which data and functions are shared with existing applications. No one should ever have to rewrite the major applications (word processor, spreadsheet, database) from scratch. I tend to dislike jargon and vague marketing mantras, but there's a word here that really does apply: *leveraging* — the idea that you can take advantage of what people have done before you. Our entire industrial society, if you think about it, is based on leveraging.

One of the running questions in the history of Visual Basic has been, "But is it object oriented?" From the beginning, VB adopted a good deal of object syntax, but the answer was still no. In writing manuals and Help topics, we were admonished to use the term *object based* rather than *object oriented*. This policy anticipated objections by all the object-oriented devotees, people who spend their time developing long lists of features that a language must have to be considered truly object oriented.

It's worth asking, "Does it matter?" I think the answer is yes, but it's not the most important thing. Is it more important to have all the object-oriented features of, for example, C++, or is it more important to get large amounts of work done in a short time? The designers of Visual Basic have always laid more stress on the latter.

1

At the same time, object orientation is a good thing in general, because it offers programmers a superior model for reusing, adapting, and refining bits of software, and then passing on their work to others. Over the years, Visual Basic has become more and more object oriented. In Version 6.0, it now lacks just one major feature: derived classes (inheritance). This is actually not as big an omission as it might seem, because Visual Basic provides alternative techniques for getting the same results. (Even polymorphism is supported, but not in a way that depends on derived classes.)

The advances in Visual Basic raise a more pressing question than object-orientation, however: Because the language and environment are now so vast, how does one approach it all? To be honest, it would now take several thousand pages to cover everything that can now be done in Visual Basic, particularly if widely distributed custom controls are thrown into the mix. Depending on what you're doing, though, you don't *need* to learn all these features. The core ideas in Visual Basic are still relatively simple, and would-be programmers can use it to create simple programs now just as they could with VB 1.0. In fact, the beginner level got some attention, so the simplest programs are *even simpler* to write than when Visual Basic was first released.

So, bear with me, if you would, if I don't cover all the thousands of capabilities of Visual Basic in this limited space. The purpose of this book is to cover the core Visual Basic features, paying special attention to intermediate features that are central to the language but haven't always been clearly explained. (Object variables are a good example.) Having spent some time with the different versions of Visual Basic has made me aware of some features of the environment a new user might otherwise overlook, so I also point these out.

I've written about many languages over the years. But for a number of reasons, I retain a special fondness for Visual Basic. More than anything else, I never go to create a utility, demo, game, or sample program — indeed, use Visual Basic for anything at all — without rediscovering all over again that it's just plain fun.

2

A VB Survival Guide

> *"The goal of Visual Basic: not merely to*
> *survive but to prevail."*
>
> —*Billg Ates, ace programmer*

For a programming environment so easy to use, Visual Basic 6.0 can be intimidating at first. It has so many capabilities, it's a vast ocean. The range of things you can do with it is just short of astounding. The only problem is that if you're approaching Visual Basic for the first time, where do you start? How do you catch that first small fish?

In this chapter, I'm going to focus on a few simple features and techniques to get you started doing some productive work with Visual Basic.

What's New in VB 6.0

In terms of the basic application-writing environment, little is new in Visual Basic 6.0. If you've used Visual Basic 5.0, this will be review to you, so you might want to skip the chapter. But if you haven't used Visual Basic before or are

familiar only with early versions of the language, stick around.
I'm going to point out some fairly up-to-date features.

2 Starting Up Visual Basic

When you start Visual Basic 6.0 for the first time, the dialog box
shown in Figure 2-1 appears. If this dialog box does not appear,
open the File menu, and choose the New Project command.

Figure 2-1 *The initial Visual Basic dialog box*

Click the Open button or press Enter to accept the default
project type, Standard EXE.

One thing you may notice right away is Visual Basic supports
a wide variety of project types; this means you can produce many
kinds of programs and objects. This step also shows how much
work is automated for you. You don't have to worry about changing a bunch of settings for each kind of project. Just select the
project type you want.

Visual Basic has a number of different windows (see Figure
2-2). One of these is the Form Layout window, in the lower-right
corner. You can use this window to position the form on the
screen. After using it once, I find it isn't that helpful for simple
applications. So I recommend closing this window for now. (You
can always reopen the Form Layout window later by using the
View menu.) The goal here is to give the Properties window more
space. The Properties window is also on the right side of the

screen. You can also grab the divider between the Properties and Project windows and move it to provide even more space for the Properties window.

Form Layout window

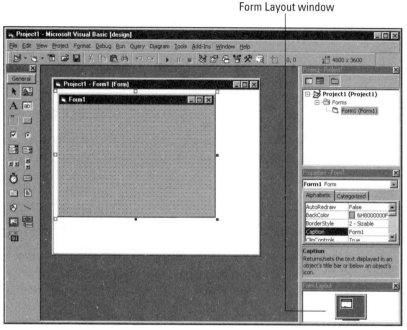

Figure 2-2   *The Visual Basic development environment*

The large window in the middle of the screen is the main window where you design a form. If you're new to Visual Basic, you may be asking, "What the heck is a form?"

A *form* is a general-purpose window that can contain graphics and input/output devices, called *controls*. What I call a form is very close to what the user perceives as a window. Technically, *form* and *window* are not exactly synonymous, because the system considers other kinds of objects to be windows.

For now, it may be most helpful to think of a form as the basic workspace area of an application. As applications become more complex, you can add other forms. You can even create multiple document interface (MDI) applications, in which several forms are contained inside one larger form.

The Visual Basic environment itself, by the way, uses neither single document interface (SDI) nor MDI, strictly speaking, but is closest to the Explorer model, which uses adjustable panes. Within the main window area, Visual Basic uses MDI, supporting any number of overlapping windows. The environment used to be a classic SDI application, consisting of several windows floating next to each other on the desktop. This organization was okay unless you had other applications peering through the gaps between Visual Basic windows, in which case it was a mess.

Getting Started: Drawing Controls

Let's get started. Follow along with me if you like. This first application will do something mildly amusing: display a shape that the user can change with the click of a button. The purpose here is to show off the Shape control.

You'll need to locate the shape control tool if you don't know where it already is. Like all control-drawing tools, this one is located in the Toolbox (see Figure 2-3), which is the panel on the left of the screen.

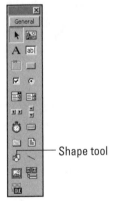 ——— Shape tool

Figure 2-3   *The Shape icon in the Toolbox*

The whole Toolbox resembles the toolbox or palette for a paint program. From the very beginning, Visual Basic was meant to be an application writing tool where programmers drew the structure of a program as much as they wrote it.

There are two basic ways of drawing a control:

- Click the appropriate Toolbox icon once, move the mouse pointer to the form area, click where you want the object's top-left corner to go, and then drag to size the control.

- Double-click the icon. The control appears in the middle of the form. Use the mouse to move and size the control as desired.

When double-clicking the Shape icon, a rectangle appears in the middle of the screen. Admittedly, this is not that exciting yet, but the end user will eventually have the ability to change shapes as he or she wishes.

You're still in the control-drawing phase — a good time to consider what the user interface should look like. The purpose of this application is to let the user choose a shape. For simple selection like this, a command button is sufficient. All a command button does, basically, is give the program a chance to respond when the user clicks it. That's all the functionality needed here, with one button per shape.

You'll need six command buttons. Figure 2-4 shows the location of the CommandButton tool in the Toolbox.

— Command Button tool

Figure 2-4   *The CommandButton icon in the Toolbox*

It's both quick and easy to create six command buttons. First, double-click the CommandButton icon. A command button appears in the middle of the form; drag this command button to a position on the right side of the form. (There's no need to resize in this case; the default size is fine.) Repeat for each button. Look at Figure 2-5 for guidance in placing the buttons.

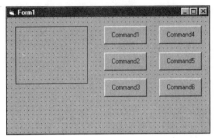

Figure 2-5 *The ShapesDemo application, first view*

Before you're done, you may run out of space on the form. In this case, you'll need to resize the form by doing the following:

1. Select the form by clicking on any blank area.
2. Use the mouse to grab one of the sizing handles.
3. Drag the mouse.

Setting Initial Property Values

Now it's time to backtrack a bit. When I was leading the Visual Basic 1.0 documentation team, I came up with three steps that summarized the development process:

1. Draw controls
2. Set properties (to determine initial attributes)
3. Write code (to determine behavior)

These three steps still apply. The only thing to add is that both Steps 2 and 3 involve setting properties, as discussed later.

A *property* is an attribute of a control or form; it's some basic quality, such as a control's color, height, or width. Far beyond being passive pieces of data, properties can seem almost magical at times. If you set the value of a property that is an obvious visual attribute, you see the changes happen immediately. You don't have to worry how the changes are carried out.

Every property has a unique name, which is fixed. However, a property can take on different values (or *settings*) at different times.

Setting a property at design time is easy, because all you do is select a control (by clicking on it *once*) and then use the Properties window to make changes. Figure 2-6 shows the Properties window, which appears on the right side of the screen.

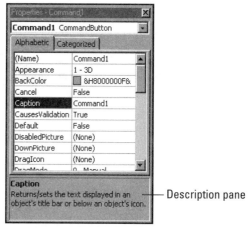

Description pane

Figure 2-6   *The Properties window. The Description pane provides a description of the selected property.*

Right now, the command buttons have the captions Command1, Command2, and so on. Clearly, these aren't adequate: The buttons should have descriptive names like Rectangle, Square, Oval, and Circle. You can change all the captions by doing the following:

1. Click the first command button once.

2. The Properties window should have the Caption property selected. If it isn't, use the Properties window to select Caption.

3. Type the new caption: **Rectangle**.

4. Click the next command button and type **Square**.

5. Click the next command button and type **Oval**.

6. Click the next command button and type **Circle**.

7. Click the next command button and type **Rounded Rectangle**.

8. Click the next command button and type: **Rounded Square**. Press Enter to realize the last change, or click in another window.

You can, if you want, press Enter after each change to have the new value accepted. This isn't necessary, though; simply clicking in a new location has the same effect.

● **NOTE**

If you make the mistake of double-clicking a control or form, Visual Basic brings up the Code window. If this happens, press Shift+F7 to bring back the form designer. You can also display the form by using the Project window in the top-right corner (double-click Form1) or choosing the Object command near the top of the View menu.

Figure 2-7 shows what the application should look like.

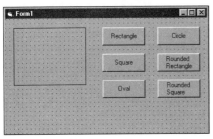

Figure 2-7 *The ShapesDemo application, final view*

You're almost done with setting initial property values, but not quite. Another important property is the Name property, which will become critical when you proceed to the next step: writing code. Regardless of the captions, the internal names are still Command1, Command2, Command3, and so on. Retaining these names would make writing the code difficult.

You can set new names by clicking a command button and selecting the Name property in the Properties window. The Properties window can be organized in two ways, alphabetically or by category, depending on which of two tabs is selected: If the Alphabetic tab is selected, the Name property appears at the top of the list; if the Categorized tab is selected, you'll have to scroll down to the Misc category to find the property. In either case, click on (Name).

● **NOTE**

If you're perplexed as to why Name should come first in an alphabetic list, that's understandable. Name is one of a very few special properties that appears in parentheses in the Properties window: (Name). The parentheses move it to the head of the list.

Type the new name. Because (Name) is selected, all you have to do for the remaining command buttons is click the button and enter the new name.

Here are the names I suggest for each button.

For the Button with This Caption	Enter This Name Setting
Rectangle	Rectangle
Square	Square
Oval	Oval
Circle	Circle
Rounded Rectangle	RRect
Rounded Square	RSquare

The distinction here is important. The Caption property controls what word or words the user sees at run time. The Name property determines how the control is referred to in code. (Note that a setting for the Name property cannot include spaces.) Once you start to write application code, you'll appreciate these more descriptive names.

Writing the Code: Getting into Events

In the traditional DOS world, programmers had to expend lots of effort prompting the user for input, deciding what to do, and then prompting the user again. The event-driven world of Visual Basic makes things easier.

In this application, all you should care about is writing code that responds to button clicks. What the user chooses to do between clicks is of no concern.

Figure 2-8 illustrates this point. On the lowest level, Windows manages user interaction. When an event happens — such as the user clicking a control — Windows calls a special procedure you've written, known as an *event procedure*, and then resumes control when the procedure is finished. The only thing you have to do is respond to a mouse click.

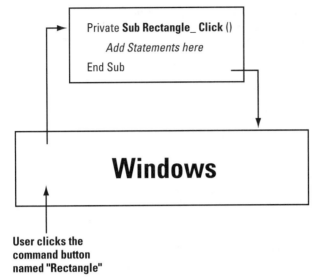

Private **Sub Rectangle_ Click** ()
Add Statements here
End Sub

Windows

User clicks the
command button
named "Rectangle"

Figure 2-8 *How an event procedure works*

Writing the event procedure is easy. Visual Basic even writes some of the code for you. Just do the following:

1. Double-click the control you want to write code for. (Let's start with the first control, Rectangle.)

2. The Code window appears with an event procedure for that control. You can select a different event by using the drop-down list at the top right of the window. Right now, it shows Click, which is what you want.

Each event procedure has a unique name, which is a combination of the name of the control and the name of the event — in this case, Click. Figure 2-9 shows the Code window with a Click event procedure for the Rectangle control.

Object list box   Event list box

Figure 2-9   *The Code window. Click the Object list box to select the control you want to affect, and click the Event list box to select the event you want to write code for. (The Event list box is also called the Procedure list box.)*

When you open the event procedure, Visual Basic thoughtfully positions the cursor for you, between the Sub and End Sub statements. Now all you have to do is write the statements that respond to the mouse click.

Writing the Code: Setting Properties

The code tells the application how to respond to each event. Many events won't have an event procedure; that's fine. You only need to write code for events you care about.

Here, as before, the issue is how to set properties. This has to be done from within code; you don't have access to the Properties window at run time. Nor would you want to. The point is to use a statement to automate a response.

To set a property, from within code, use the following syntax:

```
object.propname = new_setting
```

To take a purely imaginary example, say you could make someone grow to seven feet by simply saying "Bill's height is seven." Here's how you'd say that with Visual Basic syntax:

```
Bill.Height = 7
```

If you wanted to make Bill a teenager again, you could say that with Visual Basic syntax as well:

```
Bill.Age = 19
```

Now, what you want to do with this application is make the Shape control change to a different shape. It turns out that a particular property controls this attribute. But first, you need to recall the name of the Shape control.

To look at a list of all the objects (controls and forms) in the application, use the drop-down list in the Properties window. Clicking the down arrow displays this list, as shown in Figure 2-10.

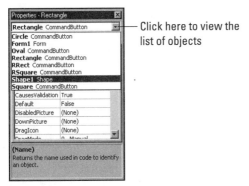

Click here to view the list of objects

Figure 2-10   *Viewing the list of objects in the Properties window*

As you can see in Figure 2-10, the name of the control is Shape1, the next-to-last item on the list. You can replace *object* with the name Shape1:

Shape1.*propname* = *new_setting*

Now you need to know what the name of the relevant property is. Again, you can find this out by using the Properties window. Select Shape1 from the drop-down list at the top of the window, click the Categorized tab if not already selected, and look at the list of properties in the Appearance category. One of these is the Shape property, which is obviously what you want. (Remember also that if you select the property, a description appears at the bottom of the Properties window, although admittedly not all these descriptions are equally helpful.)

The name of the relevant property here is Shape, so the syntax
for the desired statement becomes

```
Shape1.Shape = new_setting
```

Now you need to know just one more thing: how to specify a
specific shape by supplying a new setting. Once again, the
Properties window comes to the rescue. Make sure the Shape1
control and the Shape property are selected, and then click the
drop-down list to the right of the property name, Shape.

Figure 2-11 shows the Properties window used to view Shape
property settings.

Figure 2-11   *Viewing property settings in the Properties window. The drop-
down list shows possible settings for each property.*

If you can't see the settings on your screen this well, you can
increase the width of the Properties window by grabbing the left
edge (the divider bar) and moving it left.

The drop-down list shows you that 0 corresponds to
Rectangle, 1 corresponds to Square, 2 corresponds to Oval, and so
on. You can, if you choose, enter these numbers directly into
code. For example, to set the shape to that of a rectangle, you
would enter the following:

```
Shape1.Shape = 0
```

But this is hard to read. Fortunately, Visual Basic provides
symbolic constants for property settings like this. To get this information, just type **Shape** in the Code window, put the cursor over
the word "Shape", and press F1. Up comes the Help topic for the
Shape property. If you scroll through this Help topic, it shows you
all the constants and their corresponding values, as follows.

Symbolic Constant	Value
vbShapeRectangle	0
vbShapeSquare	1
vbShapeOval	2
vbShapeCircle	3
vbShapeRoundedRectangle	4
vbShapeRoundedSquare	5

The event procedure should therefore look as follows (add the middle line if you haven't already):

```
Private Sub Rectangle_Click ()
    Shape1.Shape = vbShapeRectangle
End Sub
```

To write the next procedure, click the drop-down list at the top left of the Code window (refer back to Figure 2-9). This displays a list of all controls that can receive events. (Note that the Shape control does not appear here; this is because shapes receive no events.) Select another command button: for example, Square. Then write a statement for it.

```
Private Sub Square_Click ()
    Shape1.Shape = vbShapeSquare
End Sub
```

After you've added a statement to each of the six command button Click procedures, the code for the application should look as follows:

```
Private Sub Rectangle_Click ()
    Shape1.Shape = vbShapeRectangle
End Sub


Private Sub Square_Click ()
    Shape1.Shape = vbShapeSquare
End Sub
```

```
Private Sub Oval_Click ()
   Shape1.Shape = vbShapeOval
End Sub

Private Sub Circle_Click ()
   Shape1.Shape = vbShapeCircle
End Sub

Private Sub RRect_Click ()
   Shape1.Shape = vbShapeRoundedRectangle
End Sub

Private Sub RSquare_Click ()
   Shape1.Shape = vbShapeRoundedSquare
End Sub
```

Now, you're done. To run the application, just press F5. It's that easy! To close the application, close the form by clicking the Close button (the X in the top-right corner of the window).

Saving and Managing the Project

All the code and design elements for a given application are part of a *project*. The final output, an EXE file, is not part of the project, although there is a one-to-one relationship between a project and an EXE. To go back and change the application, you'll need to find the project files again. You can always re-create the EXE from the project-related files, but you can't generate those files from the EXE.

By default, Visual Basic saves your project under the helpful name Project1. The next project would be named Project2, the next one after that Project3, and so on. Before you know it, you'll have a number of projects with dull, meaningless names.

To avoid this situation, give your files meaningful names. In this case, two files need to be saved. Each is vital to the project.

2

File (and Default Name)	Description
project (Project1.vbp)	Contains information about what other files are in the project and which is the start-up form. In a multiple-form application, this file would contain a list of all the forms and how they were stored.
form (Form1.frm)	Contains all visual data and code for a single form, in a human-readable format. No matter how many controls are on a form, all the information for those controls is combined in this one file.

To save and rename project-related files, open the File menu and choose the Save Project As command. Visual Basic responds by prompting you for a name for each project file. In this case there are two.

1. The Save Project As command first prompts for a name for the form file. For this example, I recommend the name ShapesForm. (A .frm extension is added automatically.)

2. The Save Project As command then prompts you for a name for the project file itself. I recommend the name ShapesDemo. (A .vbp extension is added automatically.)

You can also save or rename the current form without having to save other project-related files. Just open the File menu and choose Save Form1 As.

Saving the Project in the Future

After the project and form files are given reasonable names, it's incredibly easy to save the project from then on. (It's a good idea to save periodically, by the way, if you work for any length of time. You never know when a power outage will occur or when a pixie will come along and make Windows mysteriously crash.) Just click the Save button on the toolbar (Figure 2-12). Visual Basic saves any and all project-related files that are out of date — meaning they've been changed since the last save.

Save button

Figure 2-12   *Click the Save button on the main*
Toolbar to save your project files.

Opening the Project in the Future

When, after closing Visual Basic, you want to work on the application again, all you have to do is reload the project (.vbp) file. This is why project files are so helpful: Even if there were many different forms in the application, simply reloading the project file would cause reloading of everything you need.

If you want to return to an existing project after closing Visual Basic, open the File menu and choose the Open Project command. Also, when Visual Basic starts up, it offers you an opportunity to start an existing project. Click the Existing tab (as shown in Figure 2-1).

Creating an EXE File

Running an application inside Visual Basic is one thing; creating an application that others can use is quite another. Once you are reasonably sure the application runs correctly, you'll want to generate an independent EXE file. This is easy to do: Just open the File menu and choose the Make EXE command.

Visual Basic displays the EXE name as part of this command. If the project name is ShapesDemo, the Make command is Make ShapesDemo.exe.

By default, Visual Basic 6.0 generates a stand-alone EXE, which means end users don't need to have any special DLL to run the application; they merely need to be running a current version of Windows (Windows 95 or later or Windows NT). You can modify the kind of application file Visual Basic produces, as well as what the build process optimizes for. Open the Project menu and choose the *projectname* Properties command, which is located at the bottom of the menu. (In this case, the name of the command is ShapesDemo Properties.) Then click the Compile tab.

Managing the Project

Once you start thinking about project files, you can see why the Project window is so useful. It becomes even more useful as you add forms and other kinds of files (such as class modules). As you can see in Figure 2-13, a line in the Project window displays two pieces of information. First, it shows the internal name of the form or module. Then, in parentheses, it shows the filename under which the item was saved.

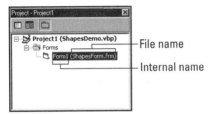

Figure 2-13   *Each line in the Project window shows the internal name of a form or module and its filename.*

Both names are important, each in a different way. The internal name is used in code to refer to a specific form or module. (In simple applications, you may never need to refer to a form, but complex applications need ways of letting different forms and modules refer to each other.) Form and module names need to be unique within a project, but these names can be reused in different projects. The filename of a form should be unique not only within a project, but also across all projects in the same directory — unless you want to share code between projects. Such a decision should be made carefully. Certain kinds of files are often intended to contain reusable code (especially class modules), but you should reuse them only after you've set their basic structure. This structure includes the names of public procedures, methods, and properties.

●—NOTE

You can use the Properties window to change the internal name of the form or the project itself (these are names that appear only during development). To change the internal project name, click the first line in the Project window, and then set the Name property.

You can, if you want, move all the files for a given project to a separate directory. Doing so after the fact used to be difficult, because it required the forms and modules (if any) to be added all over again. However, Visual Basic has become more intelligent in this regard. If all the project files are moved, Visual Basic will look for existing forms and modules in the new directory if it can't find them in the old directory.

Another Application:
The Swami Knows

When the ShapesDemo project has been saved, you can proceed to creating a new application. Just choose New Project from the File menu.

This application will involve a little more code, and, I hope, offer some amusement. This new application will have mystical powers. The end user will ask a yes/no question, click a button, and then magically get one of several answers. Little will the poor user suspect that a random-number generator was responsible for picking the answer!

Now that I've got your attention, I'm sure you can't wait to create this application. First, start a new project if you haven't already. Next, draw a label, text box, and command button on the form, as shown in Figure 2-14. Remember to create a control by double-clicking its Toolbox icon; or by clicking the icon and then clicking on the form, dragging to size the control, and releasing.

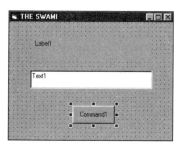

Figure 2-14 *The Swami application, first view*

2

If you're not sure which Toolbox icons are used to create these three types of controls, move the mouse pointer over one of the icons. The name of the control type appears just below the mouse pointer. Hint: label, text box, and command-button icons are all in the top three rows of the Toolbox.

Next, set initial property values for each of the three controls, as shown below. You can accept the default object names, Label1, Text1, and Command1, because there's only one of each in this application, so it's easy to know which is which. Only three properties really need to be set.

Object (Control)	Property	Set to
Label1	Caption	**The Swami knows all. Say your question and click ANSWER.**
Command1	Caption	**ANSWER**
Text1	Text	(blank)

If you're not sure how to set property values, you might need to review the earlier material in the chapter. But basically, all you do is click the control *once*, make sure the desired property is selected in the Properties window, and type the new value.

The form should now look like Figure 2-15.

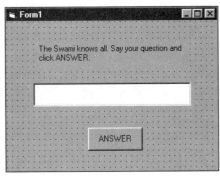

Figure 2-15 *The Swami application, second view*

Writing the Code

With the user interface in place, Swami needs only one event procedure to do his thing. All this application does is respond to the user clicking the command button, Command1. The event procedure is therefore Command1_Click.

```
Private Sub Command1_Click ()

End Sub
```

To get to this procedure, just double-click the button, Command1, and then enter statements between Sub and End Sub, so that the resulting code is as follows:

```
Private Sub Command1_Click ()
    answers = Array("I'm afraid so.", _
                "I sincerely hope not.", _
                "I haven't the foggiest.", _
                "You've got to be kidding.", _
                "Thanks, I needed a good laugh.")
    Randomize
    n = Int(5 * Rnd)
    Text1.Text = answers(n)
End Sub
```

Now, press F5 to run the application. If you entered a typo while writing the code, Visual Basic will complain of a syntax error. Check the code carefully. If you entered everything correctly, the application will run smoothly, and the Swami will give you entertaining answers.

Understanding the Code

Let's start with the last line inside the event procedure. (Forgive me for working in reverse order here.)

```
Text1.Text = answers(n)
```

This is the statement that actually changes something in the interface — in this case, the text that appears in Text1, the text-box control. For the record, you can use similar syntax to change a number of different attributes of Text1. For example:

```
Text1.Height = 100     ' Set height to 100 twips
Text1.Width = 500      ' Set width to 500 twips
Text1.ForeColor = vbRed ' Set color to red
```

Here I've used the single-quotation mark (') to place a comment on each line. Visual Basic ignores each of these to the end of the line.

You could also change the label. As it happens, text in a label control is determined by the Caption, not the Text, property:

```
Label1.Caption = "Swami not gonna answer no more."
```

Now let's return to the statement that sets a new value for Text1.Text. The text is taken from the array, answers, which contains five strings. The variable n selects one of the five strings. To see how the array is set up, look at the first statement:

```
answers = Array("I'm afraid so.", _
                "I sincerely hope not.", _
                "I haven't the foggiest.", _
                "You've got to be kidding.", _
                "Thanks, I needed a good laugh.")
```

This is actually one statement. The underscore (_) at the end of each line is a line-continuation character, and it appears in this book anywhere I couldn't get a single statement to fit on one line. The statement is the same as if it were one long line.

●—TIP

When you use the line continuation character (_), make sure you precede it by at least one blank space. Otherwise, Visual Basic will misinterpret it.

Another feature of this statement is that it calls the Array function, which creates and initializes an array. As demonstrated in Chapter 5, there are other, more rigorous ways of creating an array. Even so, calling this function is faster. This function returns an array of type Variant, which can contain numbers, strings, date/time values, or even other arrays. In this case, each member of the new array contains string data.

If you come from the more disciplined worlds of C, C++, or Pascal, you may be wondering, "What is the variable named answers, and when did it get declared?" It isn't declared at all, except implicitly. This variable gets the Visual Basic default type,

Variant, which can contain an array as well as other data. Visual Basic is remarkably free-wheeling in this regard. This behavior is incredibly convenient, but it can get you into trouble in long and complex programs. In the next chapter, I show you how to turn off implicit variables by using Option Explicit.

The following table shows the structure of the array. Note that the lowest index (or *lower bound*) is 0.

Array/Index Number	String Contained in This Element
answers(0)	I'm afraid so.
answers(1)	I sincerely hope not.
answers(2)	I haven't the foggiest.
answers(3)	You've got to be kidding.
answers(4)	Thanks, I needed a good laugh.

The trick now is to select a random number from 0 to 4. This is done with the following statements:

```
Randomize
n = Int(5 * Rnd)
```

You don't need to understand how this works, because most applications don't use random numbers at all — the principal exception being game programs. But if you're interested, here's what these statements do: First, they use Randomize to set a seed for generating random numbers. Calling the Rnd function then returns a random number between 0.0 and 1.0. Multiplying by 5 and using the Int function (which always rounds downward) produces one of the numbers 0, 1, 2, 3, or 4 with equal frequency.

Figure 2-16 shows a sample run. Assume that a call to Rnd generates the number 0.43556. Multiplying this by 5 and rounding down produces the number 2, which results in the selection of the string stored in answers(2). The selected string then gets displayed.

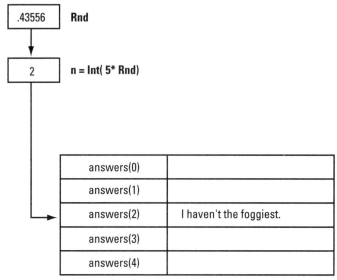

Figure 2-16 *How Swami selects a string*

Enhancing the Code

If you've tried running the Swami application, you may have noticed that its behavior is less than optimal. Swami always displays a string. If the same string is selected twice in a row (which is always possible with random selection like this), it appears as if Swami didn't answer at all. The customers will want their money back.

One solution would be to create a button with Clear as its caption. You'd need to add only one line of code to its Click event procedure. Assuming the name of the control is Command2, it would need the following code:

```
Private Sub Command2_Click()
    Text1.Text = ""
End Sub
```

A more economical solution, in terms of the interface, is to let the ANSWER button (Command1) serve double duty: Every other click clears the text box (Text1). The way to code this behavior is to write an `If` statement block. Add these statements to the beginning of the `Command1_Click` procedure, just after the line that begins with `Private Sub`, but before any other lines.

```
If Text1.Text <> "" Then
    Text1.Text = ""
    Exit Sub
End If
```

This code says, "If the text in Text1 is *not* empty, then set it to the empty string and exit." Otherwise, the event procedure continues with the rest of the code.

This code fragment illustrates a number of important features of Visual Basic. First, you can get the value of a property such as `Text1.Text`, as well as set it. Getting `Text1.Text` returns a string. Second, notice how easy it is to compare strings in Basic. You can use comparison operators such as = (test for equality when used in a condition) and <> (test for inequality). Finally, you can use `Exit Sub` to get out of a `Sub` procedure early.

Setting a Caption for the Form

You can set properties for the form itself as well as for its controls. One of the more useful form properties in almost any application is the `Caption` property. By default, this is the same as the default name of the form, `Form1`. To set a more meaningful caption, follow these steps:

1. Click any blank area of the form. This causes the Properties window to display the form's property settings. If the form is not currently visible, you can use the drop-down list box at the top of the Properties window to select `Form1`.

2. Within the Properties window, select the `Caption` property.

3. Type the new caption. In this case, I recommend the name THE SWAMI. Press Enter.

Figure 2-17 shows an example of the application running, given this new form caption. Note how the form's caption is displayed in the window's title bar.

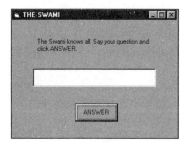

Figure 2-17   *The Swami application with caption*

Optimizing: More About Events

Notice that the code for Command1_Click creates an array at the beginning of the procedure. This wastes processor time and resources. The procedure dynamically generates the array every time the user clicks the button; at the end of the procedure, the array is released from memory.

It's not at all necessary to keep creating and destroying the array all the time. The array only needs to be created once, when the application is first loaded. Each call to Command1_Click should be able to reuse this same array.

The solution is to find an event that only occurs once. The following table summarizes some commonly used Visual Basic events.

Event Procedure	Description
Form_Load	Called just once, when the form is loaded into memory. This is the logical place to do any initialization in code for any part of the form, including its controls and variables.
Form_Paint	Called every time the form needs to be repainted. (Repainting is the process of updating the form's image on screen. This happens, for example, when the form is minimized and then restored.)
Form_Click	Called when the user clicks an area of the form not covered by a control.
*buttonname*_Click	Called when the user clicks a button.

Clearly, the Form_Load procedure is the place to create and initialize the array answers. For this to work, however, answers needs to be shared between procedures. You can do this by declaring it in the form's Declaration section. Open the Code window, select (General) in the left list box, select (Declarations) in the right list box, and type the following in the Code window:

```
Dim answers
```

Next, move the call to the Array function to the Form_Load procedure. (Select Form in the left list box and Load in the list box on the right.)

```
Private Sub Form_Load()
    answers = Array("I'm afraid so.", _
                "I sincerely hope not.", _
                "I haven't the foggiest.", _
                "You've got to be kidding.", _
                "Thanks, I needed a good laugh.")
End Sub
```

You probably won't notice any significant difference in performance speed by doing this, but it's good programming practice. If you were writing a program where use of CPU time was a factor, these kinds of optimizations could make a difference.

Summary of Visual Basic Development

Although the applications in this chapter are conceptually simple, they've helped you explore all the principal windows of the Visual Basic environment. There are a number of other windows, all of which have more specialized uses. (Some of these windows are discussed in Chapters 16 and 22.) However, the windows in this chapter are the ones you'll probably use the most.

The following table summarizes the location and purpose of each window.

Window	Description
main window: Form designer (Object)	Main window in the center of the screen, except when the window is being used as the Code window. Here is where you draw forms and controls. If the Code window is currently being displayed, you can bring back the Form designer by pressing Shift+F7, choosing Object from the View menu, or double-clicking in the Project window.
main window: Code	Window you use to view and edit code — the set of statements that define behavior. To display the Code window, double-click any form or control. Use the two drop-down lists at the top to navigate to different procedures.
Toolbox	Set of control-drawing icons on the left of the screen. You can see the function of each icon by moving the mouse pointer over that icon. To draw a control, click or double-click its icon.
Properties window	Window on the right that shows property names and settings for a selected object. You can view settings for another object by single-clicking that object in the main window, or by using the Properties window's drop-down list. As this chapter has shown, the Properties window can be used to reveal a great deal of information without having to resort to reading documentation, including the list of objects, properties supported, and valid settings.
Project window	Window on the upper-right side of the screen. This window shows a list of all the forms and modules in the application, by internal name and by filename. Doubling-clicking a form here causes the main window to display the form.
Form Layout window	Window in the bottom-right corner. I recommend closing the window for simple applications. You can, however, use it to position the form on the screen, which otherwise would require setting form properties Top and Left.

Just as a reminder, here is an overview of the three basic steps of development:

1. **Draw controls.**

   Use the Toolbox icons to draw different kinds of controls. Single-click a Toolbox icon, and then use the click-and-drag method to draw the control directly onto the form; or else double-click an icon to get a control to appear in the middle of the form, and then move and resize the control later.

2. **Set initial property values.**

   To set properties at design time, first select an object by single-clicking it or using the drop-down list at the top of the Properties window. An important property to set at this time is the Name property. The Name setting of a control determines how you'll refer to it in code during Step 3. If there are multiple controls of the same type, it's important to give them meaningful names. Name is different from the Caption property, which only affects what the user sees.

3. **Write code to determine behavior.**

   Nearly all Visual Basic application code is concerned, directly or indirectly, with responding to events. To write an event procedure for an object, start by double-clicking it; this brings up the Code window. Next, use the two list boxes at the top of the Code window to navigate to different objects and events as needed.

Remember that each combination of object and event has a unique name.

```
Private Sub object_event ()

End Sub
```

The exception here is that event procedures for the form itself always use Form as the object name in this context, regardless of the form's actual name.

To set a property in code, use the following syntax:

```
object.property = new_setting
```

As you'll see in later chapters, if you want to refer to a property of the form itself, drop the *object* reference:

```
property = new_setting
```

Coding Tips and Tricks

*"It's not coding, it's just typing
(or the lack thereof)."*

— *Truman Capacity, C programmer*

You can use Visual Basic for years without knowing all the shortcuts and tools for writing code. In this chapter, I point some of these out so you can be more productive more quickly. With ease and convenience as major design goals, Visual Basic has lots of techniques for getting around and getting fast information.

I also spend some time on data variables and procedures later in the chapter. This is mostly review, unless you haven't updated Visual Basic for several versions.

What's New in VB 6.0

There isn't much that's new in basic code-writing techniques, except in the area of arrays and user-defined types. Functions can now return both of these types. Variants can hold arrays, as well. I cover how the new features affect arrays in much more depth in Chapter 5.

Most of the timesaving features in this chapter have been around for some time, although many of them will be new to you if you haven't updated your copy of Visual Basic since Version 1.0 or 2.0.

Code Window Management

Get used to the Code window — you'll probably be spending a lot of time there. Fortunately, over the years it's been continually improved and refined, so it's not a bad place to hang out.

Viewing One Procedure at a Time

All the event procedures for everything on a form, as well as other code and variables, are stored together in the form file. By default, you view all of this code together, scrolling through it as needed. This way of viewing code is called *full-module view*, and it's convenient when you're scanning through a lot of code.

But you may also prefer to view only one procedure at a time. This way of viewing code is called *procedure view*.

You can use the two buttons in the bottom-left corner of the window to switch between these two views. Figure 3-1 shows these two buttons in an example of the Code window in full-module view.

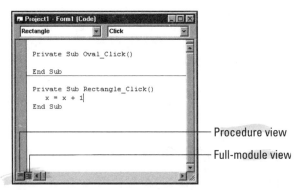

Figure 3-1 *Switching between views in the Code window*

Sizing and Tiling the Window

Programming is usually easier if you give the Code window as much room as possible. To maximize the Code window, click the Maximize button in the upper-right corner of the window. (This is the standard Windows button — Maximize actually looks like a little square.) Doing this does not block out the Toolbox, Properties window, or other elements; it just gives the Code window all the space in the main window area.

If the Code window is currently maximized, you won't see a Maximize or Close button in the upper-right corner.

Sometimes, you may not want the Code window to take up the entire main window area. To return the Code window to its smaller size, open the Windows menu and choose the Cascade command. (You can also use the Tile command.) The effect of this command makes it possible to switch quickly between different form designers and form code, as well as windows such as the Object Browser — all of which is sometimes useful in large projects (see Figure 3-2).

Figure 3-2   *Cascading windows in the main window area*

Navigating Quickly to a Definition

In a project of any size, you'll have lots of procedures calling each other. (I cover how to write procedures at the end of the chapter.) In such a situation, you might spend lots of your time just trying to get around.

You can quickly get to the definition of a procedure you're looking at by pressing Shift + F2. For example, assume you have the following code:

```
Private Sub Form_Click()
    a = 1
    b = 4
    c = 4
    Print "Equation root is " & _
    Quadratic(a, b, c)
End Sub
```

Now, suppose you want to see the definition of Quadratic, a procedure you've written. All you have to do is place the cursor on the word "Quadratic" and press Shift + F2, which invokes the Definition command.

You'll then see the definition of the procedure. To get back to the code you were looking at before, press Ctrl + Shift + F2. This invokes the Last Position command, which transfers you to the last position you were viewing. This command works even if you've moved around in the window, because it ignores small movements.

In case you forget these keystroke combinations, you can bring up the View menu, which displays the keystrokes as well as providing the commands themselves.

Finally, suppose you are viewing a procedure definition and you want to see all the other places in the code that call that procedure. Highlight the procedure name and press Ctrl + F3. This invokes the Find command.

Using Bookmarks

Another way to get around in a big project is to use bookmarks. The bookmark mechanism is simple:

- The Toggle Bookmark command sets a bookmark at the cursor line if there isn't one already; otherwise it clears it. Visual Basic shows a bookmark by displaying a blue square just to the left of the line of code that was marked.

- To cycle through bookmark positions, use the Next Bookmark or Last Bookmark command.

- To remove all bookmarks, choose the Clear All Bookmarks command.

It's possible to get at these commands by using the Bookmarks submenu of the Edit menu. This is cumbersome, however. If you're going to be using bookmarks, the best thing to do is to bring up the Edit toolbar. You can do this by opening the View menu, selecting the Toolbar submenu, and then selecting Edit.

Figure 3-3 shows the Edit toolbar, with bookmark commands pointed out. The Edit toolbar is extremely useful, so you might consider displaying it all the time. It's also *dockable*, which means you can attach it to the other toolbars at the top of the screen by dragging and dropping it.

Bookmark commands

Figure 3-3   *The Edit toolbar*

Shortcuts in Entering Code

The next few sections cover some timesaving features you might not be familiar with.

The Print Shortcut

For some reason, the designers of recent versions of Visual Basic don't want you to use the Print method. They've deleted most references to it in the documentation. This may well be because of a specific pitfall; Print method output, like all graphics-statement output, gets erased if you place it in a Form_Load procedure. To avoid this problem, use the Print method only in other procedures, such as Form_Click, Form_Paint, and Command1_Click.

In any case, there's a trick to using the Print method that's been around forever, but that most people have forgotten about. To quickly create a Print statement, you can type a question mark (?), as shown in this example:

```
? amount
```

As soon as you leave the line, Visual Basic translates ? into the word `Print`:

```
Print amount
```

This technique is particularly useful within the Immediate window for getting quick responses (see Chapter 22). `Print` output goes directly to the current form, except within the Immediate window or where another object is specified.

The Finish-the-Word Feature (Auto List Member)

When you type the name of an object or method and then start to type an *object.member* reference, Visual Basic shows you all the possible method and property references in a pop-up list. As you continue to type, it shows methods and properties most closely matching the letters.

For example, assume that `Command1` is a command button and that you type the following in the Code window:

```
Command1.H
```

Visual Basic responds by displaying the first property or method beginning with "H", as shown in Figure 3-4.

Figure 3-4   *The Code window aids in selecting properties*

If `Height`, in this case, happens to be the name you were going to type, press the spacebar. Like magic, Visual Basic finishes the word by inserting the remaining characters.

If the name selected in the list is not what you want, continue typing. You can also use arrow keys to select the desired name from the list and then press the spacebar.

The Options Editor tab that controls this feature is Auto List Members.

Getting Argument Information (Auto Quick Info)

Visual Basic automatically displays formal argument (parameter) information for intrinsic functions and statements. It also does this for any procedure you define in your project. For example, suppose you type the following reference to the Mid statement:

```
Mid (
```

As soon as you type the opening parenthesis, Visual Basic displays the complete argument list, as shown in Figure 3-5.

Figure 3-5 *Argument list information in the Code window*

The use of this information is almost self-explanatory, but there are a few subtleties:

- The current argument — the one you're about to type — is in bold.

- Optional arguments (such as Length in this case) are in brackets.

- The equal sign (=), if used, shows a default value.

- The As clause shows what kind of data is expected. If no type is given, the default type is Variant. However, usually only one kind of data makes sense. In Figure 3-5, String should be a string and Length a number. The argument name should make the type clear.

If you start to type a reference to the StrComp function, you'll see an example of some of the features mentioned above. The third argument is optional and has a default value.

[Compare As VbCompareMethod = vbBinaryCompare]

This merits a little explanation. VbCompareMethod is a subtype of integer. It indicates that this field accepts one of several constants. As you reach this field (after entering the first two arguments), a pop-up list of accepted constants appears. You can use arrow keys and the spacebar to select one of these constants. In this case, one of the values is vbBinaryCompare, the default.

The Options Editor tab that controls this feature is Auto Quick Info.

Controlling Code Window Behavior

As convenient as some of the Code Window automated features are (finish-the-word, argument list, syntax checking), you may want to selectively turn them on or off.

To control Code Window editor behavior, open the Tools menu and choose Options. Click the Editor tab, if it's not selected already. To get more information about each of the editor options, click the Help button.

One feature you might want to turn off sometimes is Auto Syntax Check. This feature causes the Code Window editor to check each line of code for syntax errors, as soon as you leave the line. When writing complex code, I sometimes find myself typing part of a line, moving to another line to look at something else, and then moving back to finish typing. Auto Syntax Check can be annoying in this situation, because it insists you enter a complete line of code before moving the cursor away.

In any case, Visual Basic always checks syntax before running the application. If Auto Syntax Check is on, it checks the current line as soon as you press Enter or move the cursor off the line. This is mostly useful, but as I suggested, you might sometimes find it annoying.

Comments and the Comment Block Command

Like most (if not all) modern programming languages, Visual Basic has a comment symbol ('). Visual Basic supports only a line-comment syntax, meaning that everything from an apostrophe (') to the end of a line is ignored by the compiler. Such text is retained when you save the project, but only so that you and other programmers can read it.

```
x = y     ' This is a comment; Visual Basic ignores.
```

Although Visual Basic doesn't have a multiline comment symbol, it does support the Comment Block command. This command allows you to prevent an entire section of code from being executed without having to delete it. Another command, Uncomment Block, lets you to make the code active again. This can be very useful during debugging.

The command works by inserting a comment symbol (') at the front of every line that's part of the current selection. If no text is selected, it inserts the symbol at the front of the line containing the cursor. In either case, every line selected gets commented out.

For example, if you highlight any portion of four lines and then choose the Comment Block command, it inserts a comment symbol (') in front of each of those four lines.

```
'If Text1.Text <> "" Then
'    Text1.Text = ""
'    Exit Sub
'End If
```

To use this command, first highlight every line of code you want to comment out, and then choose the command. The Comment Block command is available on the Edit toolbar, as shown in Figure 3-6. (To display this toolbar, use the Toolbar submenu of the View menu.)

Comment Block   Uncomment Block

Figure 3-6   *Comment Block and Uncomment Block*
commands on the Edit toolbar

The Uncomment Block command works the same way as the block-comment command. First highlight any set of lines. The command then removes a comment symbol from the beginning of each line that has one.

Getting Quick Input and Output

In a finished Visual Basic application, you tend to get most input and output through controls such as a text box. While you're developing, however, many times you will want to get quick input and output from the user, to help test a particular feature.

The following language features help get input or display a result quickly.

- Print method
- String concatenation (&)
- InputBox function
- MsgBox statement
- MsgBox function

In Chapter 19 I give the complete syntax for each of the keywords.

The Print method is one of the most useful, but it appears to be discouraged. Many references to it in the documentation have been removed. The reason for the deletions is likely because of a particular pitfall: If you use Print in the Form_Load procedure, the output gets erased before you ever see it! But this isn't the fault of Print; all graphics-method output (of which Print is an example) gets erased if used in Form_Load.

There are several ways to effectively use Print. One is to use it from within the Immediate window during debugging. Another is to send output to the Immediate window from within code, by using Debug.Print.

```
Debug.Print "The value of x is " & x
```

Another way to use Print is to use it in a Form_Paint procedure, which is where it most properly belongs. And finally, you can use it almost any place (except Form_Load!) simply as a way of getting quick feedback while you're developing an application.

```
Print "The value of x is " & x
```

Remember that anywhere you use Print, you can use ? as shorthand.

```
? "The value of x is " & x
```

In each of the last three examples, I used the string-concatenation operator (&). (Use of + to concatenate strings is less flexible, but still supported for backward compatibility.) The virtue of & is it takes any kind of operand and always produces a string representation of each.

The InputBox and MsgBox functions provide a quick means for getting and displaying a string through a standardized dialog box. InputBox includes a prompt string.

```
aString = InputBox("Enter a string")
? "The string entered was " & aString
```

```
n = MsgBox("You committed a grave error.")
```

MsgBox is both a function and a statement. In its function version (as used in the preceding example), it returns a number indicating what button the user clicked to close the dialog box. See Chapter 19 for the interpretation of this value. In its statement version, MsgBox doesn't bother to return this button value.

```
MsgBox "You committed a grave error."
```

● **NOTE**

Function calls require parentheses around the argument list, while statement and Sub procedure calls cause an error unless you *omit* those same parentheses. (Exception: You can place parentheses around a single argument to force passing by value.) This quirk in Visual Basic syntax may be annoying, but it's one you have to live with. And it's why I take pains to point out that MsgBox is both a function and a statement, even though the official documentation glosses over this fact.

Declaring and Using Variables

A variable — as you already know if you've used any programming language — is a named location for storing data. As with
properties, the name of a variable (such as i, x, amount, myName)
stays fixed, but the data it holds can change over time. Each variable corresponds to a specific address in RAM, but with rare
exceptions, you never have to worry what that address is.

Implicit Variables and Variant Type

Visual Basic has always made it possible to get applications, especially simple applications, running with a minimum of fuss. This
is true almost to a fault. Unlike other languages such as C and
Pascal, Visual Basic doesn't even ask you to declare variables.

For example, take the Swami example from the previous chapter. Several variables are declared *implicitly* here — meaning I did-
n't declare them, I just put variable names I liked directly into
executable code. See if you can find the variables I'm referring to:

```
Private Sub Command1_Click ()
    answers = Array("I'm afraid so.", _
               "I sincerely hope not.", _
               "I haven't the foggiest.", _
               "You've got to be kidding.", _
               "Thanks, I needed a good laugh.")
    Randomize
    n = Int(5 * Rnd)
    Text1.Text = answers(n)
End Sub
```

There are two variables: n and answers. The way you know
this is simple: Any name that is not a keyword is either a procedure name, a visual-object name (such as Command1 or Text1), or a
variable. Quoted material and comments, of course, are exceptions.

●—NOTE

As a convention, I use names with initial lowercase letters for variables
and procedures. This is not required by Visual Basic, but it helps distinguish user-created names (*identifiers*) from keywords. Looking at the
example, you can see that Array, Randomize, Int, Rnd, Text, Text1,

and Command1 are names defined by Visual Basic. You know that n and answers are variable names because I made them lowercase.

Technically, Text1 and Command1 are identifiers, but Visual Basic generated the names. (I would have used initial lowercase.) The other words — Randomize, Int, Rnd, and Text — are keywords.

Also note that within the environment, Visual Basic uses color coding to distinguish keywords from other parts of syntax. Only the *core* keywords are color coded, however; for example, it doesn't distinguish intrinsic functions from user-defined ones.

3

Visual Basic determines that n and answers are variable names, because they are neither keywords, object names, or procedures. Because they weren't declared explicitly, they weren't given a type. Visual Basic therefore gives them the default type, Variant.

The Variant type, if you've never used it, is amazing in the convenience it lends. Because Variant is the default type, you can enter statements like the following without ever declaring a variable:

```
n = 5
? n
n = "The big Buba"
? n
n = Date + Time    ' Store current date and time
? n
n = Array(1, 2, 3, 15, 25)
? n(1)
```

You can store numbers, strings, object variables, and date/time values in a variable of type Variant. You can even store arrays. In fact, the only kind of data you can't store in a Variant is an instance of a user-defined type.

But there's at least one major problem with using this form of variable creation, called *implicit declaration*. It's primarily a problem for long, complex programs, and in most of the book, I ignore this problem for short examples. If you use many variables, there's always a chance that you'll accidentally use two different spellings for the same name. Typos are always possible. For example, you might spell a variable name this way one time:

```
employeesSalaryDeduct
```

And this way another time:

```
employeeSalaryDeductt
```

Visual Basic has no idea that you intended these two names to be the same, so it assumes you meant to create two different variables. This can generate some of the most elusive, frustrating bugs. You place input in `employeesSalaryDeduct` and then wonder why the value is mysteriously 0 at some later point in the program.

"If only declarations were required," you think, "the typo would have been flagged. Visual Basic would have complained as soon as I attempted to use the alternative spelling."

So for programs of any real length, you're often better off preventing Visual Basic from this automatic variable creation. `Option Explicit`, described in the next section, prevents this behavior.

Option Explicit and Declarations

The `Option Explicit` statement prevents implicit declaration of variables. When this statement is in force, all variables must be declared with statements such as `Dim`, `Public`, and `Private`. The statement restricts your own choices to an extent. But that isn't always bad; in long and complex programs, you can think of this as preventing you from shooting yourself in the foot.

The statement has no arguments or optional syntax:

```
Option Explicit
```

`Option Explicit` is different from the types of statements used so far. It cannot be placed inside a procedure; it must be placed inside the Declarations section of a form or module. This section contains certain statements — most of which are usually variable declarations — that apply to all the code for the form.

You can use the Code window to get to the Declarations section:

1. Open the Code window, if not open already, by double-clicking any object.

2. In the Object list box (the drop-down list at the top left) select (General).

3. In the Procedure list box (the drop-down list at the top right) select (Declarations).

If the Code window is currently open, an even faster way to place something in Declarations is to simply write it before all procedures.

1. Place the cursor at the very beginning of the first line of the Code window.

2. Press Enter, press the up arrow key, and then start typing.

Once Option Explicit is added to form code, all variables must be declared before being used, as shown in this example:

```
Option Explicit

Private Sub Command1_Click()
    Dim sString, n
    aString = Text1.Text    ' Ok: aString is declared
    n = 1                   ' Ok: n is declared
    x = n + 1               ' ERROR: x was not declared
End Sub
```

One thing you should notice about this example is references to Command1, Text1, and Text are fine, even though these were never declared. In the case of Command1 and Text1, this is because they were defined in the environment. In the case of Text, it's because Text is already defined as a property.

This example also illustrates simple use of the Dim statement to declare a couple of variables:

```
Dim aString, n
```

In its simplest usage, Dim declares one or more variables, separated by commas if there are more than one. However, Dim can potentially employ a much richer and more complex syntax. Other statements for declaring variables include Public, Private, Static, and ReDim, some of which appear in upcoming sections.

●—**NOTE**

You can have the Option Explicit statement automatically placed in every form and module, by using the Options command from the Tools menu. Click the Editor tab in the window and select Require Variable Declaration.

Using Specific Types in Declarations

Beyond simply declaring variables, you can give them more specific types, such as Integer, Long, Single, Double, Boolean, Date, Currency, and String. You can also explicitly declare them as Variant, although they have that type by default.

There are several advantages to using more specific types. First, specific types are more efficient. Each variable of Variant type uses an extra two bytes in memory to indicate what type of data (numeric, string, or other) is currently being stored. Second, situations will arise in which you need to be precise about what kinds of data you're using. In file operations — especially with binary files — use of the Variant type can cause errors if you're not extremely careful. Finally, it's good programming discipline to always be thinking about what kind of data you intend to store.

In a Dim statement or argument declaration, use the As keyword to declare a type:

Dim *varname* **As** *type*

Each variable name can be followed by As *type*. For example:

Dim n As Integer, s As String, aString As String

You can even mix variables with specific types and variables with the default type in the same Dim statement, as demonstrated here:

Dim a, b, c, n As Integer, total As Long

In this example, a, b, and c all have the default type, Variant, whereas n has type Integer and total has type Long.

The Integer and Long types are short and long integers, respectively. Single and Double are short and long floating-point types, which means they can hold amounts containing fractions (unlike integers). For exact information on range and precision, see Chapter 13.

Form Variables

All the variables used in all the examples so far — with one exception in Chapter 2 — have one thing in common: They are all local to some procedure. This means once the procedure is finished executing, the value is lost. It also means the value is not shared with other procedures.

The principal way of sharing information between procedures is to create form variables. (You can do the same thing for modules and class modules, in which case the variables are *module variables*.) Such variables must be declared in the Declarations section, described earlier. For example:

```
Dim answers       ' answers is shared by all procedures
Dim x As Integer ' So is x


Private Sub Form_Load()
    ' Initialize answers here
End Sub


Private Sub Command1_Click()
    ' Use answers values here
End Sub
```

Occasionally, you may want to create a variable that retains its value between calls to the same procedure, but is not shared with other procedures. The way to create such a variable is to use the Static keyword in place of Dim:

```
Sub myProcedure()
    Static n As Integer ' n retains value between calls
    '...
End Sub
```

Public and Private Variables

You can use the Public or Private keyword in place of Dim when declaring variables. For example, the following statements all declare variables:

```
Dim a, b, c
Public d, e, f
Private g, h, i
```

You can also use them to declare variables with specific types:

```
Dim i As Integer, j As Integer
Public x As Double, y As Double
Private myName As String
```

In the case of variables, Dim and Private declarations are the same. Public is the interesting case; if a variable is declared in the Declarations section and is declared Public, it is shared by the entire project. Right now, this might not seem important. But when you start adding other forms and modules, Public variables can become useful.

In general, Private, Public, and Static can be used wherever you would use Dim. As you can see in last few examples, each of these keywords replaces Dim when used. Private and Public also can be used in procedure declarations, but there the syntax is different. In that context, Private and Public act as modifiers to an existing keyword (Sub or Function) and do not replace it.

●—NOTE ─────────────────────────────────────

Visual Basic 1.0 supported the Global keyword, which is similar in some respects to Public, except that it can be used only in modules, not forms; and it can be used only to declare variables, not procedures. In general, Public is a much more generally useful keyword. I think the Visual Basic team felt embarrassed that there ever was a Global keyword, which is why they deleted all references to it in the documentation. It is supported, however, for backward compatibility.

Roll Your Own: Defining New Procedures

If you've followed this book so far, you've seen examples of Visual Basic event procedures. These have a special meaning to the application and are automatically called at run time in response to certain events. To respond to an event received by a control, the general syntax is as follows:

```
Private Sub control_event(args)
    statements
End Sub
```

To respond to an event received by the form itself (if, for example, the user clicks on a blank portion of the form rather than a control), the general syntax is this:

```
Private Sub Form_event(args)
    statements
End Sub
```

Note that the `Form` prefix is used in this context, regardless of the actual name of the form.

You can also write your own procedures, which, for lack of a better word, are sometimes called *general procedures*. These can include both `Function` and `Sub` procedures (`Function` procedures are sometimes referred to as simply *functions*.) Execution of code begins when an event procedure is called. This is the first port of call, in a sense. But event procedures can call general procedures, which in a long program usually do most of the work.

Writing Sub Procedures

A `Sub` procedure declaration (also called a *definition*) consists of `Sub` and `End Sub` statements, along with any number of statements in between that define what the procedure does. The `Sub` statement itself specifies the name of the procedure, as demonstrated here:

```
Sub showWarning
    MsgBox "Don't do that again."
End Sub
```

You can optionally include an argument list, in parentheses. Argument declarations are similar to variable declarations, except that they don't use `Dim`. For example, you can declare arguments with the default type:

```
Sub showWarning(n, msg)
    s = "Error " & n & ":" & msg
    MsgBox s
End Sub
```

You can also declare arguments with specific types, using the `As` clause just as you would in a `Dim` statement:

```
Sub showWarning(n As Integer, msg As String)
    Dim s As String
    s = "Error " & n & ":" & msg
    MsgBox s
End Sub
```

To actually enter a procedure, just start typing code outside of any existing procedure. (Visual Basic does not allow procedures to be nested.) Once you're in the Code window, the quickest way to start writing a new procedure is to do the following:

1. Place the cursor at the very beginning of the first line of any procedure.

2. Press Enter and then press the up arrow key. Then start typing.

Alternatively, you can go to the end of the last line of any procedure and then press Enter.

For example, you might move the cursor outside of the current procedure and then type the following:

```
Sub showWarning(n As Integer, msg As String)
```

As soon as you enter the first line, Visual Basic immediately recognizes the input as a new procedure and provides the corresponding End statement.

● **NOTE**

Another way to create a procedure declaration is to use the Add Procedure command in the Tools menu. Although this command provides some help, I usually find it faster just to move outside existing procedures as previously described and type the first line of a declaration. The Add Procedure command is limited; it does not automate entering of arguments or return-value type for functions, which you have to type yourself.

Eventually, you'll probably want to call your new procedure from inside some other procedure. Contrary to the practice of other programming languages, you don't place parentheses around a Sub procedure argument list during a call. For example:

```
showWarning 5, "Attempt to insert peg in round hole."
```

This is admittedly one of the more ugly features of Basic syntax, because it runs counter to the syntax for calling a function. (See the next section.) There's a historical explanation for the inconsistency, however. The statement syntax was fixed long before Function procedures were added to the language. It was easier at that time not to involve parentheses.

Some of the quirks in Visual Basic syntax can seem strange at times. But there's always an explanation if you know enough about its history. The reasons are out there. (Cue scary music.)

Writing Function Procedures

A Function procedure (sometimes just called a *function*) does everything that a Sub procedure does, with two important exceptions. First, a Function procedure returns a value. Second, calling a function requires parentheses around the argument list. (But note that in contrast to most other languages, the parentheses are needed only if there are one or more arguments.)

A function, unlike a Sub procedure, always has a return type. This type may be implicitly declared, just as variable types can be implicit. For example, the following function has the default type, Variant:

```
Function getRnd(n)
   Randomize
   getRnd = 1 + Int(n * Rnd)
End Function
```

The following declaration is the same, except that it defines the function's return type to be Long rather than Variant:

```
Function getRnd(n) As Long
   Randomize
   getRnd = 1 + Int(n * Rnd)
End Function
```

One thing you may notice in these two examples is the name itself is used to return a value. Having at least one such statement is required in a function.

```
function_name = return_value
```

Another basic rule of syntax is that when you call a function, the function call must appear as part of a larger statement. This is another area in which Visual Basic differs from C/C++, which allows a simple function call to form a complete statement by itself. Not so in Basic.

Here is an example of a call to getRnd. Notice the parentheses, which are required.

```
r = getRnd(5)   ' r gets a number from 1 to 5
```

As long as you have one or more arguments, you must use parentheses around the entire argument list when you call the function. The general syntax is as follows:

function_name(*arguments*)

If there are no arguments, you can omit the parentheses completely:

function_name

Shortcuts for Working with Controls and Objects

The techniques in the next two sections work with controls; in addition, the With . . . End With technique works with all types of objects. If you're not familiar with the concept of *object* yet, don't worry. As I explain in Chapter 8, if you're working with controls, you're already working with objects. In Chapter 8, you'll learn more about objects in general.

The techniques in these sections were added to Visual Basic some time after Version 1.0.

Default Properties (with a Small "d")

Each of the standard controls has a default property. (This term should not be confused with the Default property of a command button — which is Default with a capital "D".) You can refer to a control's default property by simply referring to the control itself.

In the case of text boxes, list boxes, and combo boxes, the default property is Text. This means instead of writing code like this:

```
txtAddress.Text = "123 Main Street"
txtName.Text = txtName.Text + ", Esq."
? List1.Text
```

You can write this:

```
txtAddress = "123 Main Street"
TxtName = txtName + ", Esq."
? List1
```

For other controls, the default property is usually the Value property. This is the case with check boxes, option buttons, and scrollbars. For example, instead of writing this code:

```
Option1.Value = True
Check1.Value = False
```

You can write this:

```
Option1 = True
Check1 = False
```

This technique is now no longer mentioned in the official documentation, if at all. Clearly, the development team has stopped encouraging people to use it. This may be for the same reason that I don't use it anywhere else in this book: It can lead to confusing and even misleading examples. After all, you never really assign a value to a control or other object directly. All that's really going on is you're implicitly referring to a certain property.

However, this is still a useful technique if you're clear about what you're actually doing, and you want to save some work when entering code.

The With . . . End With Shortcut

The previous section dealt with how to eliminate or imply the *property* part of the *object.property* syntax. This section deals with the converse: how to eliminate the *object* part of this syntax, at least temporarily.

When you're doing a large number of operations on a particular control, you can use a With . . . End With block to reduce the amount of code you write. The With statement identifies a control or other object. This object then becomes the object default for all property and method references.

For example, suppose you're setting a number of properties for a text box named txtReadout:

```
txtReadout.ForeColor = vbRed
txtReadout.Enabled = False
```

```
txtReadout.Text = "This is a text box."
txtReadout.Height = 800
txtReadout.Width = Text1.Width * 2
```

Five references to `txtReadout` appear in this example. By placing all these statements in a `With . . . End With` block, you need refer to `txtReadout` just once.

```
With txtReadout
    .ForeColor = vbRed
    .Enabled = False
    .Text = "This is a text box."
    .Height = 800
    .Width =.Width * 2
End With
```

Now, the net savings in the amount of code you have to type in here is not overwhelming, but the savings can be greater in longer examples. Perhaps even more important is that you reduce line length and even improve readability. The last line has two references to `Text1.Width`, so the line that replaces it in the `With . . . End With` version is substantially shorter.

(In writing this book, I had to deal with lines that couldn't get much wider than 50 characters, so I've become a fanatic about line length!)

One prime example of using `With` effectively is in the case of list boxes and combo boxes. These controls use the `AddItem` method to initialize contents. The following is a typical list box initialization (assume a list box named `lstPeople`):

```
lstPeople.AddItem "Groucho"
lstPeople.AddItem "Chico"
lstPeople.AddItem "Harpo"
lstPeople.AddItem "Larry"
lstPeople.AddItem "Moe"
lstPeople.AddItem "Curly"
```

You can save a little typing by placing all this inside a `With . . . End With` block:

```
With lstPeople
    .AddItem "Groucho"
    .AddItem "Chico"
    .AddItem "Harpo"
    .AddItem "Larry"
    .AddItem "Moe"
    .AddItem "Curly"
End With
```

Note that in a simple, single-form application, you would probably never have reason to place references to form properties and methods inside a `With` block, because when the object and the dot (.) are omitted, a property or method is assumed to refer to the form itself. For example:

```
Width = 5000     ' Set width of form to 5,000 units
```

I hope you've enjoyed this tour of Visual Basic coding techniques, or at least found it useful. I don't use all these techniques myself later in this book, but that's only because I try to keep things simple for the casual reader. I suggest you pick and choose the ones that work best for you. Visual Basic is your servant. Use it well. Use it wisely.

Graphical VB

"So many colors."

— Dr. Timothy Weary, pop guru

One of the design goals in Visual Basic is to make graphics programming as easy as possible. In particular, the lightweight graphics controls (`Line`, `Shape`, and `Image`) can minimize the amount of programming you need to do in many cases. They can even be used with no programming at all.

If you want to perform animation, this is easy to do with the `Image` and `Timer` controls. Some programming, however, is required.

Most of this chapter is intended for people who don't mind doing some programming when it comes to graphics. The more you depart from the simple model of drawing a static line and leaving it there, the more technical you need to get. There's a fair amount of hard-core technical stuff in this chapter; don't be afraid to wade through it to get what you need. And remember, graphics are supposed to be fun!

What's New in VB 6.0

Almost all of the graphics capabilities in Visual Basic 6.0 were present in Version 5.0, and a good majority of them have been around forever. If, however, you haven't used Visual Basic since Version 1.0, you'll find that the lightweight graphics controls (Image, Line, Shape) are new.

The only really new feature in Version 6.0 is that you can create a lightweight graphics control yourself, as an ActiveX control. But this is getting ahead of the story; I don't discuss how to create ActiveX controls until Chapters 9 and 10.

Some Graphics Fundamentals

If you're eager to write an application that displays some graphics, you might want to skip ahead to "Drawing Stuff with Methods." A number of important considerations apply to all graphics methods and drawing operations, however, and I discuss them here.

Drawing to Forms and Picture Boxes

Unlike most controls, forms and picture boxes allow you to display any image through the use of graphics methods and the Picture property. Picture boxes and forms actually have many of the same capabilities.

Forms and picture boxes support all the graphics methods — including Print. Here are several sample calls to graphics methods. In the first two cases, output goes to the form. In the third and fourth cases, it gets sent to a picture box named myPictureBox.

```
Form1.Circle (1000, 1000), 500
Form1.Print "This is a form."
myPicturebox.Circle (1000, 1000), 500
myPicturebox.Print "This is a picture box."
```

If no object is specified in a property or method call, the current form is implied. For example, the first and second statements from the previous example can be written as follows:

```
Circle (1000, 1000), 500
Print "This is a form."
```

Understanding Screen Measurements

Most graphics methods use a coordinate system to specify sizes
and coordinates on the screen. The default unit of measurement
is something called a *twip*, which stands for "twentieth of a printer's point." This is not terribly meaningful to most people. The
best way to get a feel for twips is by experimentation.

Monitor sizes vary from user to user, so the meaning of *twip* is
relative to the size of an object when sent to the printer. A twip is
$\frac{1}{1440}$ of an inch when printed. To verify this, you can use the
PrintForm method:

```
PrintForm    ' Send a picture of the form to the
             ' system printer
```

Coordinates run from the top-left corner — which by default
has the coordinates (0, 0) — to the bottom-right corner. Larger
numbers therefore take you toward the right and downward (see
Figure 4-1).

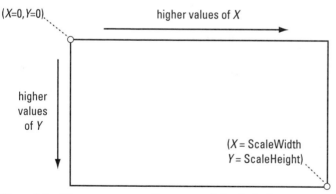

Figure 4-1 *How screen coordinates work by default*

There are several ways of changing the coordinate system.
The quickest way is to set the ScaleMode property of a form or
picture box. The values run from 0 to 7, with 3 selecting pixels as
the unit of measurement:

```
ScaleMode = 3    ' Use pixels for the form's
                 ' coordinate system.
```

The ScaleMode property returns the number corresponding to the current coordinate system. If you've set a custom scale, this property returns 0.

You can create a customized scale by setting the ScaleHeight and ScaleWidth properties of a form or picture box. Setting these properties sets the unit size in terms of the *current size of the object's internal display area*. For example, setting each of these properties to 100 means each unit in the coordinate system is $1/100$ of the height or width of the current size of the display area.

If the size of the object then changes, the size of each unit remains the same, although the number of units changes. Changing height changes the number that ScaleHeight returns as well. For example:

```
ScaleHeight = 100   ' 1 unit = 1/100 of form's height
Height = Height * 2 ' Double form's actual height
Print ScaleHeight   ' Print new ScaleHeight; will be
                    ' roughly 200 units
```

The most important thing to remember here is that changing Height and Width resizes an object, but changing ScaleHeight and ScaleWidth has no effect on actual size; it only affects the coordinate system. Remember also that Height and Width (unlike ScaleHeight and ScaleWidth) always use the *container's* coordinate system and refer to the object's total size, including borders (if any).

Setting negative values for ScaleHeight or ScaleWidth reverses directions. For example, the following code changes the coordinate system so that the bottom-left corner is (0, 0) and the x axis runs from left to right. Setting ScaleTop assigns a new y coordinate to the top-left corner.

```
ScaleHeight = -ScaleHeight
ScaleTop = -ScaleHeight
```

To do the same thing for a picture box, qualify the property references. For example:

```
myPicture.ScaleHeight = -myPicture.ScaleHeight
myPicture.ScaleTop = -myPicture.ScaleHeight
```

Getting Dimensions: Height, Width, Top, Left

With few exceptions, controls have Height and Width properties, as well as Top and Left. You can get or set a control's size by using Height and Width. You can set or get a control's position by using Top and Left, which specify the horizontal and vertical distance, respectively, from the top-left corner.

All four of these properties are relative to the object's container. There are several cases in which something can be a container:

- In the most obvious case, when a control is drawn onto a form at design time, the form is the container.

- You can create a picture box and then draw controls onto it, using the drag-and-draw approach. In this case, the picture box is the container.

- Similarly, you can draw controls onto frames. Although frames don't support graphics methods, they can serve as containers for controls.

- The form itself uses the Screen object as its container. You cannot change the screen's coordinate system, but you can get its dimensions.

There is also a special case: An MDI form can be the container of other forms. You probably won't use MDI for simple applications.

In all of these cases, the height, width, and position of an object are relative to its container's coordinate system. For example, if you draw a check box (Check1) onto a frame at design time, and then write the following procedure, clicking the control sends the button to the *frame's* top-left corner, not the form's.

```
' Move to top left corner when clicked.
'
Private Sub Check1_Click()
    Check1.Top = 0
    Check1.Left = 0
End Sub
```

The Top and Left properties can be used to move a certain distance as well as positioned absolutely. But no matter how far it moves, a control cannot appear outside its container. If it attempts to move outside the container's borders, it disappears from sight.

```
' Move downward and to the right when clicked.
'
Private Sub Check1_Click()
    Check1.Top = Check1.Top + 100
    Check1.Left = Check1.Left + 100
End Sub
```

Selecting Colors

A number of properties hold a color value. These properties include BackColor, which specifies the background color of a control; and ForeColor, which specifies the foreground, or "drawing" color. Specifically, if you set ForeColor to red and then use the Line or Print method, the graphics method outputs a red line. The Circle method also uses the ForeColor setting by default.

You can set color properties at design time or run time. At design time, it's easy to spot a color property because it usually has "Color" in its name, and for each color property, the Properties window displays a small square with a sample of the selected color.

If you double-click on the name of any color property in the Properties window, Visual Basic displays a color-selection pop-up window, letting you select from System colors or from a much wider range, the Palette. Figure 4-2 shows an example.

You can also assign color values at run time. The most versatile way of doing this is by using the RGB function.

Every color value is stored as a Long, a four-byte integer. The lowest three bytes correspond to red, green, and blue (red being in the lowest byte, then green, then blue), and each has a setting of 0 to 255. The RGB function provides a convenient way to assemble the bit values.

```
Dim colorRed As Long, colorLightRed As Long
Dim colorGreen As Long, colorYellow As Long

colorRed = RGB(255, 0, 0)
colorGreen = RGB(0, 255, 0)
colorLightRed = RGB(128, 0, 0)
colorYellow = RGB(255, 255, 0)
```

```
ForeColor = colorYellow   ' Set form's foreground
                          '   color to yellow.
```

The RGB function provides a way of creating your own colors to precise specifications. Note that Visual Basic predefines a number of color constants, so you usually don't need to use RGB, unless you need to create unusual colors.

The predefined RGB constants include the following:

vbBlack	vbBlue
vbRed	vbMagenta
vbGreen	vbCyan
vbYellow	vbWhite

To use a system color, set the high bit in the color value to 1, and add a number from 1 to 24 that designates one of the system color settings. (To set the high bit to 1, add hex value &H80000000.) Examples include Toolbars (0), Desktop (1), and Active Title Bar (2). The advantage of using these settings is that they are automatically customized appropriately for each user's desktop. If the user changes the desktop color configuration in the Control Panel, the meaning of all the system colors change as well.

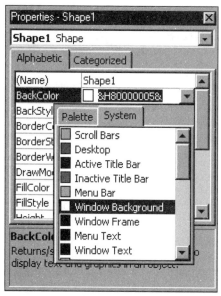

Figure 4-2 *Setting the BackColor property*

Visual Basic predefines constants corresponding to the system color settings:

vbScrollBars	vbHighlightText
vbDesktop	vbButtonFace
vbActiveTitleBar	vbButtonShadow
vbInactiveTitleBar	vbGrayText
vbMenuBar	vbButtonText
vbWindowBackground	vbInactiveCaptionText
vbWindowFrame	vb3DHighlight
vbMenuText	vb3DDKShadow
vbWindowText	vb3DLight
vbTitleBarText	vb3DFace
vbActiveBorder	vb3DShadow
vbInactiveBorder	vbInfoText
vbApplicationWorkspace	vbInfoBackground
vbHighlight	

The Properties window displays the hexadecimal value of each color value as well as showing a small square with the color. You can recognize system color settings very easily, because they begin with the characters &H8 rather than &H0. (The first two characters, &H, are the hexadecimal prefix; the 8 shows that the high bit is turned on.)

Working with Events

Once you get into working with graphics, you may find that you need to understand more about events. Table 4-1 describes some events that are useful for graphics programmers to understand.

Table 4-1 *Important Events in Graphics*

Event	Description
Form_Load	Called when the form is first loaded into memory but before any image is displayed. This is the logical place to initialize variables. If you use graphics methods here, such as Print, Line, and Circle, the output gets erased unless AutoRedraw is on.

Event	Description
Form_Paint	Called whenever the form, or any portion of it, needs to be repainted. This can happen, for example, when the form had been minimized but is getting restored. Unless AutoRedraw is on, this is the place to restore output of graphics methods.
Form_Resize	Called whenever the form is resized and when it's first displayed. Appropriate responses may include resetting property values in response to the new size, which is ScaleWidth * ScaleHeight.
Click events	Called when the user clicks anywhere within a given object. Click event procedures do not get mouse coordinates, so in some cases you may need to write code for an event such as MouseDown. (Note that a mouse click produces all three events: Click, MouseDown, and MouseUp.)
mouse events	Called in response to specific actions, including MouseDown, MouseUp, and MouseMove. All of these event procedures get passed information on mouse coordinates and mouse-button state.

Form events follow a predictable sequence. When both a Resize and a Paint event are generated (a common occurrence), Resize always occurs first. When a form is first loaded into memory, the order of the events is as follows:

1. Form_Load
2. Form_Resize
3. Form_Paint
4. Form_GotFocus

More About the Paint Event

You only need to concern yourself about Paint events when the following circumstances are all true:

- You use graphics methods (as opposed to lightweight controls or standard controls).
- You leave the AutoRedraw property off.
- You want a persistent image.

All forms and picture boxes have Paint events, although you can restrict yourself to responding to Form_Paint if you want. When you get down and dirty, using low-level graphics operations that the designers of Visual Basic didn't necessarily foresee, you need to know precisely what's going on with Paint events. Here's what happens:

4

1. Any of the obvious cases trigger a Paint event, such as the user restoring a minimized form. Note that if a portion of the object was already visible, that portion does not get repainted in Steps 3 through 6.

2. The following things also trigger a Paint event: changes to child controls and changes to certain properties, including Picture.

3. Once the Paint event is triggered, the object's display area is repainted with the background color (BackColor). This effectively erases graphics-method output.

4. The image in the Picture property, if any, is repainted.

5. The object's Paint event procedure is called.

6. Controls are redrawn. Most controls paint over their area, although Line and Shape are transparent.

One of the consequences of this sequence is that graphics-method output can easily get erased. In addition, you should be careful about what code you place in a Paint event procedure. For example, if you change the form's Picture setting from within Form_Paint, this causes an infinite regress, effectively hanging the application! (The Scribble example, at the end of the chapter, shows how to avoid this problem by using both a form and a picture box.)

Drawing Stuff with Graphics Methods

Graphics methods provide a way to draw text directly in the background area of a form or picture box. Table 4-2 summarizes the most common graphics methods.

Table 4-2 *Summary of Graphics Methods*

Method	Description
Print	Prints text at the current drawing coordinates (CurrentX, CurrentY properties), optionally advancing to the next line. The syntax is **Print** *items* [;|,]
Line	Draws a line segment between two points. It can also draw blocks. The basic syntax is shown below. Note that either point can be preceded by the Step keyword, and that commas are used only as argument separators. **Line** [(*x1*, *y1*)]–(*x2*, *y2*), [*color*], [**B**[**F**]] If the first point is omitted, the line is drawn from the current drawing coordinates.
Circle	Draws a circle, ellipse, arc (a segment of a line or ellipse), or pie-shaped wedge. The syntax is **Circle** [**Step**] (*x*, *y*), *radius*, [*color*],_ [*start*, *end*], [*aspect*]
Cls	Clears graphics by repainting the object's display area with background color. All controls and the object's Picture property are then restored. The syntax includes no arguments: **Cls**
Refresh	Forces a complete repaint. The syntax includes no arguments: **Refresh**
PSet	Sets an individual pixel at the specified location. The syntax is **PSet** [**Step**] (*x*, *y*) [*color*]
Point	Returns the value of an individual pixel at the specified location. The syntax is **Point** (*x*, *y*)
PaintPicture	Places an image at a specified location. This method is similar to the BitBlt functions in the Windows API. It has a complex syntax; for more information, see online Help for this method.

Remember that with all graphics methods, as well as all properties (such as CurrentX, CurrentY, BackColor, and ForeColor), you can optionally give an object reference. For example:

```
myPictBox.CurrentX = 0
myPictBox.CurrentY = 200
myPictBox.Line (0, 0) — (500, 500)
myPictBox.Circle (500, 500), 250
```

If you don't give any object reference, the current form is assumed.

The next several sections focus on the most commonly used methods, Line and Circle.

Drawing Lines

Drawing lines is straightforward. You just specify the two points you want to connect. The following sample application takes advantage of the ScaleWidth and ScaleHeight properties to draw an "X" in any size form. If the form is resized or repainted, a new "X" is drawn.

```
Private Sub Form_Paint()
    x = ScaleWidth
    y = ScaleHeight
    Line (0, 0)-(x, y)
    Line (0, y)-(x, 0)
End Sub

Private Sub Form_Resize()
    Refresh    ' Force complete repaint.
End Sub
```

Notice I use ScaleWidth and ScaleHeight to get the form's dimensions, not Width and Height. There are some good reasons for this. First, ScaleWidth and ScaleHeight are guaranteed to use the form's own dimensions. Second, they return the size of the internal display area, rather than the complete window including borders and title bar, which Width and Height would take into account.

Also notice I use the `Refresh` method in response to a resize. This, in turn, causes the entire form to be repainted, not just the newly visible portion. Without this code, parts of the previous "X" lines would still be present after a resize.

Figure 4-3 shows a sample of this application at work.

Figure 4-3   *Sample Line method output*

Drawing Blocks

You can use the `Line` method to draw blocks (rectangular regions) by including the optional `B` argument. If you include `B`, you can also include `F` to fill the block with the same color used to draw the rectangle. `F` can only be used if `B` is.

For example, the following code draws and fills a rectangle 1000 units by 1500 units. The upper-left corner is point (500, 500).

```
Line (500, 500) - Step (1000, 1500), , BF
```

If you omit the `F` argument, you can still choose to fill the block by setting the `FillStyle` and `FillColor` properties for the object into which the block is drawn. In this case, of course, that object is the current form.

Note the use of the `Step` keyword. In any use of the `Line` method, you can use `Step` before either point specification. If `Step` is used before the first point, then the first point specifies a distance from the current drawing coordinates (`CurrentX`, `CurrentY`).

Drawing Ordinary Circles

If all you want to do is draw an ordinary circle, the syntax is fairly simple. For example, the following statement draws a circle with center at (1000, 1000) and a radius of 500:

```
Circle (1000, 1000), 500
```

The optional Step argument makes the center relative to the drawing coordinates, (CurrentX, CurrentY), which specify the location of the last drawing operation.

```
Circle Step (1000, 1000), 500
```

The following sample application, which is a variation of the one in the previous section, draws a circle that is always inscribed within the limits of the form's display area.

```
Private Sub Form_Paint()
    x = ScaleWidth
    y = ScaleHeight
    minxy = x
    If minxy > y Then minxy = y
    Circle (x / 2, y / 2), minxy / 2
End Sub

Private Sub Form_Resize()
    Refresh    ' Force complete repaint.
End Sub
```

Figure 4-4 shows a sample of this application at work.

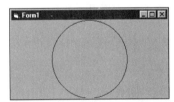

Figure 4-4   *Sample Circle method output*

Drawing Ellipses

To draw an ellipse (or *oval*) use the *aspect* argument of the Circle method. As is true with most Visual Basic statements and methods, commas are used to indicate skipped arguments. To use *aspect* but none of the other optional arguments — *color*, *start*, and *end* — you'd need four commas. For example:

```
Circle (x / 2, y / 2), 1200, , , , 3    ' aspect = 3
```

The *aspect* argument always specifies the ratio of the vertical (*y* dimension) over the horizontal (*x* dimension). An aspect value of 3 specifies an ellipse that is tall and narrow. Conversely, an aspect value of 0.33 would specify an ellipse that is wider than it is tall.

The meaning of the *radius* argument changes a bit with this version of the Circle method. The *radius* argument is always the length of the longer of the two dimensions. In this case, the ellipse will be 2400 units wide (twice the radius) and 800 units tall.

The following code inscribes an ellipse inside the form:

```
Private Sub Form_Paint()
    x = ScaleWidth
    y = ScaleHeight
    maxxy = x
    If maxxy < y Then maxxy = y
    Circle (x / 2, y / 2), maxxy / 2, , , , y / x
End Sub


Private Sub Form_Resize()
    Refresh      ' Force complete repaint.
End Sub
```

You can see what sample output looks like, of course, by typing in this code and running the application. You should find that the resulting ellipse is always just small enough to fit perfectly inside the form, no matter how it is resized.

Drawing Arcs

To draw an arc using the Circle method, you need to do several things:

1. Determine the circle or oval that the arc is taken from. This will enable you to get center, radius, and aspect values, as appropriate.

2. Using a separate sheet of paper, if necessary, draw the arc on top of its circle or oval.

3. Moving along the arc, determine which endpoint is the farthest you can go in a clockwise direction. This gives you the *start* value. The other endpoint is your *end* value.

4. Assign *start* and *end* values by using radians, considering angle zero to be the three o'clock position. (See Figure 4-5).

Use of radians may be less convenient than, oh, let's say maybe . . . *degrees*, but mathematicians like things that way. Fortunately, Visual Basic provides an easy way to get the value of pi, which you then use for conversion:

```
pi = Atn(1) * 4
```

To convert from degrees to radians, multiply by pi / 180:

```
angle1Rads = angle1Degrees * pi / 180
```

Figure 4-5 shows an example of how to determine *start* and *end* arguments. Notice that you get a completely different arc, depending on which angle is the *start* angle and which is the *end* angle. The Circle method always draws arcs in a counterclockwise (positive) direction.

The following code draws a long arc, three-quarters of the way around a circle; this is the second of the two arcs illustrated in Figure 4-5. If you reverse the two angles, the application draws the shorter of the two arcs in this case.

This code assumes that the form is big enough to handle these size coordinates. They are not unreasonably large if the coordinate system is using twips (the default).

```
Private Sub Form_Paint()
    pi = Atn(1) * 4
    angle1 = 135 * pi / 180
    angle2 = 45 * pi / 180
    Circle (2000, 2000), 1000, , angle1, angle2
End Sub
```

Drawing Pie Slices

The hardest thing about using Circle is determining points for an arc. Once you accomplish this task, it's easy to draw a pie slice. (You could alternatively think of this as a pizza slice, if it more suits your taste buds.)

When you assign a negative value to the *start* or *end* angle, the Circle method draws a line from the center to the corresponding endpoint. The Circle method then treats the value exactly as though it were positive.

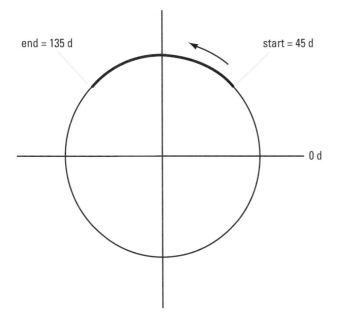

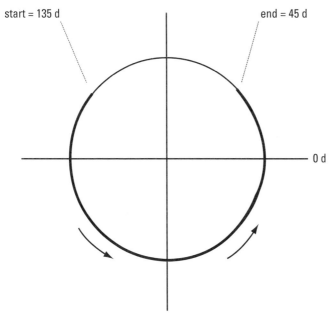

Figure 4-5 *How to get start and end values for arcs*

For example, to draw exactly the same arc as in the previous example, but add line segments from the center (thereby creating a pie slice), put a negative sign (-) in front of the *start* and *end* values:

```
Private Sub Form_Paint()
    pi = Atn(1) * 4
    angle1 = 135 * pi / 180
    angle2 = 45 * pi / 180
    Circle (2000, 2000), 1000, , -angle1, -angle2
End Sub
```

Figure 4-6 shows the resulting figure. In this case, the figure looks like a pie after you've taken out a slice. To get the slice itself, reverse the values assigned to angle1 and angle2. (As in the previous section, arcs are always drawn in a counterclockwise direction.)

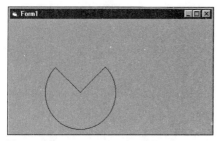

Figure 4-6 *Drawing a pie slice*

Filling Out Circles, Ellipses, and Slices

To draw a figure that has its interior filled with a particular color or a pattern, first set the FillColor and FillStyle properties for the form or picture box in which the item is drawn, and then use the Circle method. For example:

```
FillColor = RGB(255, 0, 0)   ' Set fill color to red
FillStyle = 0                ' Set style to Solid
Circle (2000, 2000), 1000
```

Lightweight Graphics Controls

The lightweight controls — Image, Line, and Shape — support a more visual way of doing graphics than the graphics methods. You can draw all these controls at design time. If they need to be resized later, you can do that by adjusting property settings.

There are some differences between lightweight controls and standard controls such as a text box. The lightweight controls aid performance by using fewer resources. (They don't have hWnd's.) Line and Shape controls do not recognize events, although the Image control recognizes the same set of events as a command button, including Click.

Figures created with lightweight controls are persistent. You never need to place code in Form_Paint to redraw them. Table 4-3 summarizes the relationship of different graphical techniques.

Table 4-3 *Relationship of Different Types of Images*

Type of Image Displayed	Blocks Out Other Images?	Needs to Be Redrawn?
Standard controls	Yes; everything	No
Image control	Yes; everything below	No
Line and Shape controls	No	No
Picture property setting	No	No
Graphics method output	No	Yes

The Line and Shape control, Picture property setting, and graphics methods all share part of the background graphics; they do not block out anything else in the background. Standard controls, however, block the view of anything underneath them. The Image control blocks out background graphics other than itself.

● **NOTE**

Making any change to a lightweight control or setting the Picture property of the container has a side effect: Doing either of these things triggers the Paint event for the container. Be careful, because infinite regresses are possible if you cause these changes from within a Paint event.

The following example uses a Shape control to inscribe an ellipse in a form, regardless of its size. To create this application, place a Shape control on a blank form. Don't worry about sizing it; the code does that. Just make sure the Shape property is set to 2 (Oval).

The application has just one event procedure:

```
Private Sub Form_Resize()
    Shape1.Height = ScaleHeight
    Shape1.Width = ScaleWidth
End Sub
```

Compare the simplicity of this application code to that used earlier in the section "Drawing Ellipses," which required several calculations to use the Circle method in achieving the same result.

Sample Application: Bubbles

Now it's time to put together some of the techniques in this chapter to write an entertaining application. This application, named Bubbles, displays a series of circles of different colors, locations, and sizes at random. Clicking on the form clears the bubbles.

The form has just one control: This is a timer control, and its icon should be fairly obvious when you see it on the Toolbox. Double-click the timer-control icon (Figure 4-7). It makes no difference where you position it on the form; it can never be visible at run time anyway.

Figure 4-7   *The Timer icon in the VB Toolbox*

After adding it to the form, set the Interval property of the timer control to 500. (This specifies an event every 500 milliseconds, or one-half second.)

The application has the following code:

```
Private Sub Form_Click()
    Cls
```

```
End Sub

Private Sub Timer1_Timer()
   Dim myColor As ColorConstants

   ' Select location
   Randomize
   x = ScaleWidth * Rnd
   y = ScaleHeight * Rnd

   ' Select size
   mySize = (ScaleHeight / 20) * randN(4)

   ' Select color
   n = randN(3)
   If n = 1 Then
      myColor = vbBlack
   ElseIf n = 2 Then
      myColor = vbBlue
   Else
      myColor = vbRed
   End If

   Circle (x, y), mySize, myColor
End Sub

Function randN(n As Integer) As Integer
   Randomize
   RandN = Int(n * Rnd) + 1
End Function
```

This application code contains one general procedure, a support function named randN. This function takes an integer n and randomly returns an integer from 1 to n. It uses Randomize, which prepares for random-number generation by setting a seed for a pseudo-random sequence, and Rnd, which generates a fractional number between 0 and 1. For more explanation of how random-number generation works, see Chapter 21.

Most of the work is done in the `Timer1_Timer` event. The event procedure is called at intervals of 500 microseconds.

The first thing this event does is utilize a coding trick in Visual Basic. The variable named `myColor` is declared as having type `ColorConstant`. Whenever you enter code and start to assign a value to such a variable, Visual Basic brings up a pop-up list box showing all color constants, such as `vbBlack`, `vbBlue`, and `vbRed`.

The `If...Then` statement chooses between these three constants, after randomly generating a number from 1 to 3:

```
' Select color
n = randN(3)
If n = 1 Then
    myColor = vbBlack
ElseIf n = 2 Then
    myColor = vbBlue
Else
    myColor = vbRed
End If
```

The location and size coordinates, x, y, and `mySize`, are all generated randomly, taking advantage of the fact that `Rnd` returns a random number from 0 to 1. To translate this number into a reasonable range, all you have to do is multiply it by the largest possible size:

```
' Select location
Randomize
x = ScaleHeight * Rnd
y = ScaleWidth * Rnd
```

When all the coordinates have been determined, all the application has to do is call the `Circle` method:

```
Circle (x, y), mySize, myColor
```

Figure 4-8 shows sample output.

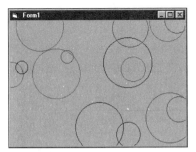

Figure 4-8 *The Bubbles application*

Animation with the Image Control

The Image control occupies a strange but useful place in the graphics hierarchy. On the one hand, it's more solid than graphics methods and the Line and Shape controls. On the other hand, it's less solid than a standard control such as a text box, because the Image control is part of the background graphics.

An Image control differs in several important ways from a PictureBox control, even though they have similar looking Toolbox icons. A picture box can display a composite image from many sources, and it can contain child controls. An Image control contains a single image downloaded from a graphics file.

On the Toolbox, the Image control icon is down at the bottom, near the Line and Shape icons (Figure 4-9).

Image controls are ideal for animation. At design time, load as many pictures as you need by creating Image controls and setting their Picture properties. You can then make these Image controls invisible if you need to (by setting their Visible properties to false).

Figure 4-10 shows a sample application containing one visible Image control with its name set to imgVisible and two controls, imgStored0 and imgStored1, that are invisible at run time. The Name and Visible properties should be set as shown.

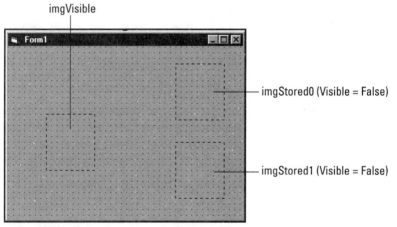

Figure 4-9 *The Image tool icon in the VB Toolbox*

imgVisible

imgStored0 (Visible = False)

imgStored1 (Visible = False)

Figure 4-10 *Use of several image controls in an application*

In Figure 4-10, no images are yet loaded. If you were to run this application, you would also need to first set the Picture property for both imgStored0 and imgStored1. When the Picture property of an Image control is set, Visual Basic displays the image and resizes the control as needed to perfectly fit the graphic.

It's possible to load graphics files dynamically by using the LoadPicture function at run time. But generally, it's better to load graphics files at design time if possible, because then all the images are stored together with executable code in one big, happy EXE file.

Once the images are loaded, you can copy a picture from one Image control to another, by using the Picture property. For example, the following statement copies a stored image (in imgStored1) to a visible control (imgVisible):

```
imgVisible.Picture = imgStored1.Picture
```

You can use an Image control in a way similar to a command button; they support the same events. To show the effect of a click, display a new picture. For example:

```
Private Sub Form_Load()
    imgVisible.Picture = imgStored0.Picture
End Sub


Private Sub imgVisible_Click()
    Static indicator As Integer

    If indicator = 0 Then
        imgVisible.Picture = imgStored0.Picture
        indicator = 1
    Else
        imgVisible.Picture = imgStored1.Picture
        indicator = 0
    End If
End Sub
```

This example uses a static variable, indicator. Because it is declared with Static rather than Dim, this variable retains its value between calls to the procedure.

You can use similar code in a Timer control to create an animation effect. Create a timer control and assign it an Interval property setting, as described in the previous section, "Sample Application: Bubbles." You also need to create a series of Image controls and set their Picture properties at design time. The following code then changes the image displayed at regular intervals.

```vb
Private Sub Timer1_Timer()
    Static indicator As Integer

    ' Use indicator to determine which image to
    '  display.
    '
    If indicator = 0 Then
        imgVisible.Picture = imgStored0.Picture
    ElseIf indicator = 1 Then
        imgVisible.Picture = imgStored1.Picture
    ElseIf indicator = 2 Then
        imgVisible.Picture = imgStored2.Picture
    ElseIf indicator = 3 Then
        imgVisible.Picture = imgStored3.Picture
    Else
        imgVisible.Picture = imgStored4.Picture
    End If

    ' Advance to the next image.
    '
    indicator = indicator + 1
    If indicator > 4 Then indicator = 0
End Sub
```

When working with a large number of images like this, certain development techniques can make your life easier. One such technique is to use the Select Case statement rather than If...Then. (See Chapter 17 for more information on Select Case.) An even slicker approach is to use a control array, as described in the next chapter. With a control array, you could replace the entire If...Then structure with a single statement:

```vb
imgVisible.Picture = imgStored(indicator).Picture
```

The Picture property contains a handle, or "magic number," that is meaningful only to Windows and Visual Basic. It is useful to compare Picture values, however. If two controls have the same Picture value, this means they refer to the exact same graphics data in memory.

Using comparisons of `Picture` values, you could rewrite the first example in this section as follows:

```
Private Sub Form_Load()
    imgVisible.Picture = imgStored0.Picture
End Sub


Private Sub imgVisible_Click()
    If imgVisible.Picture = imgStored0.Picture Then
        imgVisible.Picture = imgStored1.Picture
    Else
        imgVisible.Picture = imgStored0.Picture
    End If
End Sub
```

This version is a little shorter.

Loading and Saving Images: the Scribble Application

Now let's turn to one of my favorite applications, Scribble. This application has seen many incarnations in different computer languages, but its origin (so far as I know) goes back to Visual Basic 1.0.

In this section, I demonstrate a somewhat more refined version that highlights the ability to use an off-screen image buffer, copies images between objects, and (in the advanced features) even shows how to load and save image files at run time. Two powerful intrinsic functions are used here. One is `LoadPicture`, which loads an image file at run time:

```
pctBuffer.Picture = LoadPicture("SCRIB.BMP")
```

Another is `SavePicture`, which saves an image to disk:

```
SavePicture pctBuffer.Image, "SCRIB.BMP"
```

So let's get started. Here's what this version of Scribble will do: It will enable the user to draw lines by holding the left mouse button down and moving the mouse. No drawing takes place when the mouse button is up; this allows the user to "pick up the pencil," so to speak, rather than having to draw one continuous line.

A refined version of Scribble must be very responsive and fast, but it must also draw a persistent image. This requires an off-screen buffer, which is used to restore the image whenever the Paint event happens. (Note that you can get the same functionality from the AutoRedraw property, but the resulting application would be too slow in this case.)

Figure 4-11 shows what the application looks like.

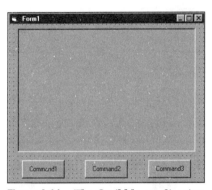

Figure 4-11   *The Scribble application*

Creating Scribble

To begin making this application, create a form and draw the controls shown. The rectangular area in the middle is a picture box.

In addition, create another picture box. The position and size of this second picture box are irrelevant, because it will be invisible at run time and will be resized in Form_Load.

Give the objects the property settings shown in the following table:

Object	Property	Give It This Setting
picture box 1	Name	**pctCanvas**
picture box 2	Name	**pctBuffer**
picture box 2	Visible	**False**
form	Caption	**Scribble**

It's important that `AutoRedraw` be set to `False` for the first picture box and `True` for the second. `AutoRedraw` is off by default.

The Strategy of Scribble: Basic Functionality

It helps to understand the design strategy of this application before actually getting into the code, so let's examine it now. Scribble, despite its relatively simple code, is a good example of an application that requires you to think like a Windows programmer. You have to understand what event Scribble is responding to at each point in the code, and why.

The following table lists each event Scribble responds to and describes the appropriate response.

For This Event	Application Should Respond This Way
pctCanvas_MouseDown	Turn `drawFlag` on and set old mouse coordinates.
pctCanvas_MouseUp	Turn `drawFlag` off.
pctCanvas_MouseMove	If `drawFlag` is on, draw a line segment from the old coordinates to the current mouse position. Draw an identical line segment in the buffer. Finally, save the old coordinates to set up the next drawing operation.
Form_Load	Resize pctBuffer to be equal to pctCanvas.
Form_Paint	Restore pctCanvas from the buffer.

The basic strategy is that the off-screen buffer maintains a copy of everything that happens in the visible picture box, pctCanvas. (When you later add other commands that update pctCanvas, you'll have to update the buffer as well.)

When things need to be redrawn, Windows calls the Form_Paint procedure. Because the AutoRedraw was left off, all the graphics output on screen is lost. But here's where the buffer comes in. No matter what happens on screen, the off-screen buffer retains all the graphics drawn to it. Copying the value of the buffer's Image property updates the picture box:

```
pctCanvas.Picture = pctBuffer.Image
```

You may wonder why one property, `Picture`, is assigned a different property, `Image`. You *could* assign from `pctBuffer.Picture`, but it wouldn't be sufficient in this case. The `Picture` property is empty until it's set. It then stores a handle to a persistent image. Assigning from a `Picture` property won't pick up the latest `Line` output; you simply get the last image assigned to `Picture`.

The `Image` property comes to the rescue. This is a read-only property that returns a handle to the object's current image. So, for example, when you assign from `pctBuffer.Image`, you get a snapshot of everything that's currently in the buffer, which is exactly what you want.

The actual process of tracing mouse movement is straightforward. The application just draws from the previous mouse coordinates — which have been saved — to the current mouse coordinates. These coordinates are passed in as arguments for `Mouse_Up`, `Mouse_Down`, and `Mouse_Move`.

The Code for Scribble

Without further ado, here's the basic code for the Scribble application. Once you get this part to work, it's relatively easy to add the advanced features.

```
Dim drawFlag As Boolean
Dim oldX As Single, oldY As Single


' Form_Load: initialize variables
' This procedure resizes the buffer to have same
'   dimensions as the picture box, pctCanvas.
'
Private Sub Form_Load()
   pctBuffer.Height = pctCanvas.Height
   pctBuffer.Width = pctCanvas.Width
End Sub


' MouseDown: turn on drawing, and set last position.
'
Private Sub pctCanvas_MouseDown(Button As Integer, _
   Shift As Integer, X As Single, Y As Single)
```

```vb
      drawFlag = True
      oldX = X
      oldY = Y
End Sub


' MouseUp: turn off drawing.
'
Private Sub pctCanvas_MouseUp(Button As Integer, _
  Shift As Integer, X As Single, Y As Single)
      drawFlag = False
End Sub


' MouseMove: Draw a line segment from last position,
'   then reset old position to set up next drawing.
'
Private Sub pctCanvas_MouseMove(Button As Integer, _
  Shift As Integer, X As Single, Y As Single)
      If drawFlag Then
         pctCanvas.Line (oldX, oldY)-(X, Y)
         pctBuffer.Line (oldX, oldY)-(X, Y)
         oldX = X
         oldY = Y
      End If
End Sub


' Form_Paint: repaint the image.
' Because AutoRedraw is off, image must be restored
'   from the off-screen buffer.
'
Private Sub Form_Paint()
      pctCanvas.Picture = pctBuffer.Image
End Sub
```

Understanding the Code

Three form variables are used in this application: drawFlag is a
simple Boolean that is True whenever drawing should occur, and
oldX and oldY record the previous mouse position. Having this
information makes it possible to trace the movement of the
mouse.

```
Dim drawFlag As Boolean
Dim oldX As Single, oldY As Single
```

The oldX and oldY variables are declared Single, because the
mouse-event arguments X and Y also have type Single.

Instead of using the variables oldX and oldY, you could instead
take advantage of the CurrentX and CurrentY properties. (See Line
statement syntax in Table 4-2.) Rewriting the application so that it
uses these properties is left as an exercise for the reader. The
Form_Load procedure is called just once, when the form is loaded
into memory. This is the logical place to perform initialization. It's
convenient to resize the buffer here, although that could have been
done (with more fuss) at design time. The buffer must be at least as
tall and wide as the picture box, pctCanvas, to store as many pixels.

```
' Form_Load: initialize variables
' This procedure resizes the buffer to have same
'   dimensions as the picture box, pctCanvas.
'
Private Sub Form_Load()
    pctBuffer.Height = pctCanvas.Height
    pctBuffer.Width = pctCanvas.Width
End Sub
```

The role of the MouseDown and MouseUp events here is relatively simple: turn drawing on or off as appropriate. MouseDown has an
additional task: It records the current mouse position as oldX,
oldY. This sets up "old" coordinates for the next drawing operation, whenever that occurs.

```
' MouseDown: turn on drawing, and set last position.
'
Private Sub pctCanvas_MouseDown(Button As Integer, _
    Shift As Integer, X As Single, Y As Single)
```

```
      drawFlag = True
      oldX = X
      oldY = Y
End Sub


' MouseUp: turn off drawing.
'
Private Sub pctCanvas_MouseUp(Button As Integer, _
  Shift As Integer, X As Single, Y As Single)
     drawFlag = False
End Sub
```

As the mouse pointer traces a path over the pctCanvas control, a MouseMove event is generated at regular intervals. In theory, any movement in space should generate infinite move events, but of course this is absurd. When the user moves the mouse, what Windows actually does is generate a certain number of MouseMove events per second, each event giving a new position.

If drawing is off, MouseMove does nothing. But if drawing is on, this implies that a MouseDown event was received. MouseDown will have recorded a mouse position as oldX, oldY at that time. Meanwhile, the new position is passed in as X, Y. The following statement therefore draws a line from the previous mouse position to the current position:

```
pctCanvas.Line (oldX, oldY)-(X, Y)
```

Now, remember the basic strategy of the application: If anything gets drawn to pctCanvas, it must get drawn to the buffer as well. The code must therefore draw the identical line segment in the buffer:

```
pctBuffer.Line (oldX, oldY)-(X, Y)
```

Finally, MouseMove resets the "old" mouse position so that the next drawing operation will work correctly. Remember that the next time MouseMove is called, new values of X and Y will be passed in.

```
oldX = X
oldY = Y
```

The last part of the puzzle is the Form_Paint event. If the AutoRedraw property of the picture box were set to True, writing this procedure would not be necessary. As I pointed out earlier, however, turning AutoRedraw on would hurt performance too much in this case. Turning AutoRedraw on has this effect: After each and every call to a procedure that calls any graphics methods, Visual Basic repaints the object. The problem is that in this application, procedure calls are being made many times a second.

In any case, you can replace the contents of a picture box by assigning a value to its Picture property. Assigning from the buffer's Image property supplies the complete image of everything that has been drawn there.

```
' Form_Paint: repaint the image.
' Because AutoRedraw is off, image must be restored
'   from the off-screen buffer.
'
Private Sub Form_Paint()
    pctCanvas.Picture = pctBuffer.Image
End Sub
```

Adding Functionality to Scribble

There still remain several things to be done to give Scribble the full functionality I described at the outset.

- Empower the Clear button to clear the picture box.
- Empower the Load button to load a bitmapped image from a file.
- Empower the Save button to save the image to a file.

Note that the first two of these items change the image in the visible picture box (pctCanvas). In line with the basic strategy of the application, the buffer (pctBuffer) must be updated at the same time as pctCanvas is.

If you're creating this application and want to add these features, the first thing you need to do is initialize property settings for the three buttons:

Object	Property	Give It This Setting
command button 1	Name	**cmdClear**
command button 2	Name	**cmdLoad**
command button 3	Name	**cmdSave**
command button 1	Caption	**Clear**
command button 2	Caption	**Load**
command button 3	Caption	**Save**

4

One other addition has to be made in design mode. To effectively clear the image in the picture box (pctCanvas), you need another off-screen buffer. This is because the Cls method clears output from graphics methods such as Line and Circle, but it does not remove any graphics that are part of the Picture setting. The only way to clear a Picture setting is to assign a blank image to it, and that requires another buffer.

To make this possible, add another picture box to the application. While in design mode, you can place the new picture box anywhere and give it any size; it doesn't matter. It will be invisible, just as pctBuffer is. Give it the following settings:

Object	Property	Give It This Setting
picture box 3	Name	**pctBuffer2**
picture box 3	Visible	**False**

One of the existing procedures, Form_Load, needs two new lines of code added:

```
pctBuffer2.Height = pctCanvas.Height
pctBuffer2.Width = pctCanvas.Width
```

The rest of the code to be added empowers the three command buttons. During execution of the Clear command, assigning from pctBuffer2.Image copies the image in pctBuffer2 (which is blank) to the other two picture boxes.

```
pctCanvas.Picture = pctBuffer2.Image
pctBuffer.Picture = pctBuffer2.Image
```

During the Load command, assigning to the buffer's Picture property causes a repaint of the display area, erasing any recent Line-method output in the process.

```
pctBuffer.Picture = LoadPicture("SCRIB.BMP")
```

After loading the buffer, the code uses an assignment to copy buffer contents to the main picture box, pctCanvas. It's much more efficient to do this rather than make another call to the LoadPicture function, because each call to LoadPicture accesses the disk.

```
pctCanvas.Picture = pctBuffer.Image
```

Remember that the Image property is read-only, so you can only assign from it, never to it.

During the Save command, the source argument is the buffer's Image property, not Picture. Use of the Image property takes a snapshot of everything currently displayed in the object, including any recent output from the Line method.

```
SavePicture pctBuffer.Image, "SCRIB.BMP"
```

Here's the complete code that performs the three commands:

```
' cmdClear_Click: clear the picture box
' The image must be loaded from another buffer,
'   because Cls will not remove the "background"
'   picture stored in the Picture property.
'

Private Sub cmdClear_Click()
    pctCanvas.Picture = pctBuffer2.Image
    pctBuffer.Picture = pctBuffer2.Image
End Sub


' cmdLoad_Click: load from a file
' Assigning to Picture causes a repaint, which in
'   turn erases any graphics-method output not saved.
'

Private Sub cmdLoad_Click()
    pctBuffer.Picture = LoadPicture("SCRIB.BMP")
    pctCanvas.Picture = pctBuffer.Image
```

```
End Sub


' cmdSave_Click: save to file
' Assigning from the Image property takes a snapshot.
'

Private Sub cmdSave_Click()
    SavePicture pctBuffer.Image, "SCRIB.BMP"
End Sub
```

Other Assignments to the Picture Property

The number stored in `Picture` is a handle, which means it has special meaning to the system and cannot be used normally. The number itself is meaningless, except to Windows. What you *can* do with the `Picture` property, however, is assign to it and from it.

For example, you can assign from one object's `Picture` property to another. This causes the persistent image already associated with `Picture` to be copied, rather than a snapshot of the display area. (In fact, the Scribble example contains a couple of lines of code where assigning from one `Picture` property to another would have worked fine, but I didn't want to make things seem more complicated.)

You can also assign to `Picture` from any object's `Icon`, `DragIcon`, or `Cursor` property. All these properties contain handles to graphical images, and all of them can be copied to the `Picture` property of a form or picture box.

Array's the Thing

"All the world's an array; and all the men and women merely elements."

— *Will Shakes, computer science professor*

Arrays are among the most flexible data structures in computer programming. An array lets you take a data type and repeat it any number of times; in other words, you can have *n* of something, where *n* is any number you like.

Because arrays are so useful, they are a fundamental part of almost every programming language. Many of the array features discussed in this chapter have been around since Visual Basic 1.0, but not all.

Visual Basic's unique contribution to the use of arrays is to provide something called *control arrays*, which enable you to create controls at run time, as well as reuse code efficiently with similar controls. In addition, the Basic language has long supported dynamic arrays, which provide great convenience as well as flexibility.

What's New in VB 6.0

First of all, you can use the standard assignment operator (=) to copy an entire array to another, as long as the array on the left side of the assignment is a variable-length (dynamic) array. Second, you can return arrays directly from functions. Finally, you can create array properties, because `Property Let` procedures (discussed in Chapter 8) can now return arrays. This chapter discusses the first two of these new features.

If you haven't updated Visual Basic in awhile, you may find some other new features. Both the `ParamArray` keyword and the `Array` function were added after Version 1.0.

The Basic Course: Arrays 101

If you've used any version of Basic at all, you've probably at least seen one-dimensional arrays. The important thing to remember is that the *zeroth* element is always usable by default, so that you actually create one more element than you may think you're creating.

For example, you might declare an array as follows:

```
Dim a(3) As Integer
```

This declaration creates an array of four elements: a(0), a(1), a(2), a(3), as shown in Figure 5-1. Each of these stores an integer value, just as an integer variable would. The lowest index number is 0. The highest index is *n* (in this case, 3).

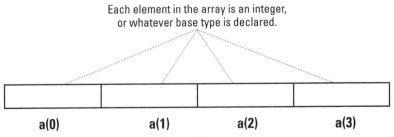

Each element in the array is an integer, or whatever base type is declared.

a(0)   a(1)   a(2)   a(3)

Figure 5-1   *Array starting with index 0*

What's useful and interesting about arrays is that once you create one, you can refer to each element by using its position in the array. So, for example, to get 26 elements, you simply declare an array of size 26, rather than declaring a separate variable for each letter of the alphabet: A, B, C, D, E, and so on.

```
Dim arr(25) As Integer    ' Array with 26 elements
```

Now you can refer to individual elements as arr(0) through arr(25), all as a result of one simple declaration.

But perhaps even more important is that different elements are accessed through a number called the *index*. This turns out to be much more useful than a set of variables named a0, a1, and so on, because you can do calculations on an index number or base it on a loop variable.

So, for example, you can use an array in the following program, which prompts the end user for three variables and prints them all out along with their sum:

```
Private Sub Form_Click
    Dim myarray(3) As Integer
    Dim sum As Integer, i As Integer
    Dim v As Variant

    For i = 1 To 3
        v = InputBox$("Enter a number: ")
        myarray(i) = v
    Next
    For i = 1 To 3
        Print myarray(i) & ", ";
        sum = sum + myarray(i)
    Next
    Print " the sum is: " & sum
End Sub
```

If you're a speed freak or a space monger, you'll notice some weaknesses in this particular example. Basic sometimes seems designed for lazy people; it's natural to write less-than-optimal code that works but won't win any awards. But improvements introduced throughout Basic's history make it possible to do better.

By declaring my array as myarray(3), I actually created four elements, running from myarray(0) to myarray(3). This is wasted space. One of the elements was never used in this example. The most obvious way to optimize the code here is to make 1 the lowest index number rather than 0. You can do this by placing an Option Base statement in the Declarations section:

Option Base 1

This statement tells Visual Basic to make 1 the lowest index number. With this in place, an array declared as a(3) has exactly three elements (see Figure 5-2).

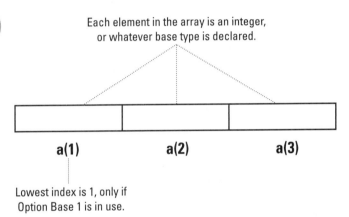

Each element in the array is an integer, or whatever base type is declared.

a(1)   a(2)   a(3)

Lowest index is 1, only if
Option Base 1 is in use.

Figure 5-2   *Array starting with index 1*

When used, the Option Base statement must be placed in the Declarations section of a module or form. You can use the Code Window controls to navigate to this section. Select (General) from the left list box (the Object list box) and (Declarations) from the right list box (the Procedure list box).

Another lazy coding technique I used was to introduce a variant type to get input in string form and translate it into the numeric value I need:

```
For i = 1 To 3
    v = InputBox$("Enter a number: ")
    myarray(I) = v
Next
```

Here's the slightly more efficient version, with the data conversion made explicit:

```
For i = 1 To 3
    myarray(i) = Val(InputBox$("Enter a number: "))
Next
```

Upper and Lower Bounds

Earlier, I mentioned that you can reset array lower bounds to 1 (rather than 0) by using the Option Base statement. Another technique for assigning a lower bound is to selectively assign it by using the To keyword. For example:

```
Dim daysOfWeek(1 To 7) As Integer
Dim teenagers(13 To 19) As String
```

If you need to determine lower and upper bounds of an array, use the intrinsic LBound and UBound functions. These functions do exactly what you think they'd do. An obvious application is to determine length. For any given array theArray, you can determine its length as follows:

```
array_length = UBound(theArray) - LBound(theArray) + 1
```

If you know the lower bound, you can determine the array length even more easily. For example, if all the arrays in your program use the default lower bound of 0, the following formula determines length:

```
array_length = UBound(theArray) + 1
```

Determining length this way is particularly useful inside procedures that are passed arrays as arguments. (I continue this discussion of length-determination techniques in the upcoming section, "Passing and Returning Arrays.")

Initializing Arrays

One area in which Visual Basic is weaker than some other languages is array initialization. VB provides no direct way of initializing an entire array in a single statement. Array elements have to be initialized one at a time. For example:

```
Dim zoo(3) As String
zoo(0) = "monkey"
zoo(1) = "lion"
zoo(2) = "tiger"
zoo(3) = "bear"
```

Fortunately, the Array function comes to the rescue. This is an intrinsic function that takes any number of arguments and returns a variant containing an array. That array, in turn, consists of a series of variant elements. This may sound confusing, but the bottom line is that you can initialize such an array with any kind of data. Here it is used to initialize a series of string values:

```
initArray = Array("monkey", "lion", "tiger", "bear")
```

The limitation here is that although the data is initialized with strings, it is stored in an array of type Variant. Suppose you want to store this data in a true String array, which is more efficient than Variant. You can do this by using a For loop to copy the elements:

```
Dim zoo(3) As String
For i = 0 To UBound(initArray)
    zoo(i) = initArray(i)
Next
```

If you had to initialize a large number of array elements, this technique — using the Array function and then writing a loop to copy the array — could provide the best way to initialize the array.

●—**NOTE**—————————————————————————————

The Array function returns an array of base type Variant in which the lower bound is always 0. This is true even if the Option Base statement is in effect.

For Loops and For Each Loops

So far the examples in this chapter have employed For loops, which use the following syntax to cycle through a loop:

```
For counter = begin To end
    statements
Next
```

Chapter 17 provides more complete syntax, along with descriptions. In this context, *counter* is usually a loop counter that serves as an index for the array, and *begin* and *end* are upper and lower bounds, respectively.

A variation on this syntax is the For Each loop, which cycles through an array or Collection object. Notice that this syntax contains no loop counter, because the counter is implicit.

```
For Each item In group
    statements
Next
```

You need to show a little care with this syntax, because the item is repeatedly set equal to each and every member of the group. This means that even element 0 is included in the loop even if you've been ignoring it.

As an example, here is a For loop used to print out each element of an array. The loop counter, i, is used to index the array.

```
For i = 0 To UBound(arr)
    Debug.Print arr(i)
Next
```

Here is the version using a For Each loop:

```
For Each item In arr
    Debug.Print item
Next
```

Notice how, in this version, neither bounds nor loop counter are used. This version is slightly shorter.

Dynamic Arrays

The support for dynamic arrays is a unique feature of the Basic language that makes it easy to resize arrays. You can use it to allocate additional program memory without ever having to deal with pointers, addresses, or memory-allocation functions. And the Preserve keyword enables you to resize arrays while preserving data.

Dynamic arrays are also called *variable-length arrays*, for obvious reasons.

To create a dynamic array, first declare it with variable length by omitting any bounds inside parentheses. For example:

```
Dim sizableArr() As Integer
```

This declaration can occur at any level, and you can give it any scope. For example, you can place it in a procedure or in the Declarations section, and you can declare with Dim, Static, Public, or Private. This declaration determines the array's scope.

But such a declaration only partially creates an array. The array needs to be given an actual size, which is what the ReDim statement does. This is an executable statement and therefore must be placed inside some procedure. Form_Load will do fine, although you can use any other procedure. For example, the following code allocates an array whose upper bound is 50.

```
Private Sub Form_Load()
    ReDim sizableArr(50)
End Sub
```

There are several unique advantages to dynamic arrays:

- You can use ReDim on the array at any time, to grow more space or to shrink it.
- You can use variables and expressions as well as a constants to assign the new bounds. This enables the new array length to be determined dynamically, possibly in response to a user action.
  ```
  ReDim sizableArr(n)
  ```
- A dynamic array can be the target of assignment (=) from another array.

The last item is a new feature in Visual Basic 6.0. The array on the left of an assignment must be a dynamic (variable-length) array, but the array on the right can be either fixed or variable length. The other requirement is that the base types must match precisely.

```
sizableArr = arr2
```

After such as an assignment, the array on the left side (sizableArr) takes on the same size and bounds as the array on the right side (arr2).

By default, when you resize an array with ReDim, all the data in the array is lost. Figure 5-3 illustrates this point.

before : | 1 | 2 | 3 | 4 |

after : | 0 | 0 | 0 | 0 | 0 | 0 |

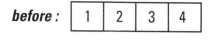
ReDim numArr(1 To 6)

Figure 5-3 *Resizing an array*

5

There was a time when, to preserve the old data, you would have to copy data to a temporary array and then copy it to the newly redimensioned array. Fortunately, the Preserve keyword makes all of this unnecessary. For example:

```
ReDim Preserve numArr(1 To 6)
```

Figure 5-4 shows the results. Notice that if the array expands in size, elements containing zero values (or empty strings, in the case of string arrays) are added to the end of the array.

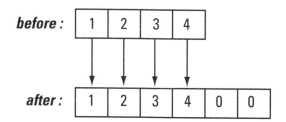

before : | 1 | 2 | 3 | 4 |

after : | 1 | 2 | 3 | 4 | 0 | 0 |

ReDim Preserve numArr(1 To 6)

Figure 5-4 *Resizing an array with ReDim Preserve*

You can also use ReDim Preserve to preserve some of the data when you shrink the size of an array. In this case, some data is lost at the end. Figure 5-5 illustrates how this works.

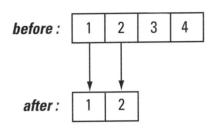

ReDim Preserve numArr(1 To 2)

Figure 5-5 *Shrinking an array with ReDim Preserve*

Note that you are not required to specify lower bounds with arrays allocated by ReDim. I specified lower bounds in the last several examples just to help make those examples clear.

Two Dimensions and Beyond

As with most other programming languages, you can easily go from one-dimensional arrays to two-dimensional arrays and beyond. A two-dimensional array creates a matrix, which is a table with rows and columns. For example, consider the following declaration:

```
Option Base 1
Dim mat(2, 3) As Integer
```

Note that the Option Base statement must appear in the Declarations section, but the Dim statement is a declaration that can appear either in a procedure or in Declarations.

Declaring the matrix as mat(2, 3) produces the data structure shown in Figure 5-6.

mat(1,1)	mat(1,2)	mat(1,3)
mat(2,1)	mat(2,2)	mat(2,3)

Figure 5-6 *Two-dimensional array*

Without the Option Base statement, the index in each dimension begins at 0. Figure 5-7 illustrates the results.

mat(0,0)	mat(0,1)	mat(0,2)	mat(0,3)
mat(1,0)	mat(1,1)	mat(1,2)	mat(1,3)
mat(2,0)	mat(2,1)	mat(2,2)	mat(2,3)

Figure 5-7   *Two-dimensional array with indexes beginning at 0*

Not surprisingly, you access elements in the same way you declare arrays. So, for a given array M, you refer to the element at any given row r and column c as shown here:

```
M(r, c)
```

For example, the following code initializes all elements of an array to 0:

```
Dim mat(10, 20) As Integer
Dim i As Integer, j As Integer

For i = 0 To 10
   For j = 0 To 20
      mat(i, j) = 0
   Next j
Next i
```

Note that because the Option Base statement was not used in this example, indexes start at 0 in both dimensions. You can use code very similar to this example to initialize a two-dimensional array of your choice, changing the array name and the bounds (in this case, 10 and 20) as needed.

The following example does something at least a little more interesting. It prints out a table of matrix coordinates and the product of the numbers involved. Figure 5-8 shows the results when the program is run.

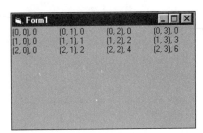

Figure 5-8   *Form that prints out 2-D array elements*

Start with a blank form, and then declare the array in the Declarations section of the Code window. This causes the array to be shared by all the code associated with the form.

```
Dim arr(2, 3) As Integer
```

Now let's review how Visual Basic events work. Because initialization only needs to be done once, the logical place to do that work is in Form_Load, which is executed only when the form is loaded into memory.

Displaying a form is another matter. Every time the on-screen representation of the form needs to be updated for any reason, Visual Basic executes Form_Paint. This is the logical place to display the array contents.

In line with these considerations, the following code initializes the array with the products of the indexes in Form_Load and displays the coordinates with the values in Form_Paint:

```
Private Sub Form_Load()
    For i = 0 To 2
        For j = 0 To 3
            arr(i, j) = i * j
        Next j
    Next i
End Sub


Private Sub Form_Paint()
    Cls
    For i = 0 To 2
        For j = 0 To 3
            s = "(" & i & ", " & j & "), " & arr(i, j)
```

```
        Print s,
      Next j
      Print
    Next i
End Sub
```

Why use two-dimensional arrays? It's possible you may go your entire career without making much use of arrays beyond one-dimensional ones, so I will give no more program examples of them here. Generally, the place I have found them most useful is game programming. The mathematical game/simulation called the Game of Life, for example, requires at least one two-dimensional array, and some algorithms for implementing this game can use several.

Going to any number of dimensions beyond two is certainly possible. Almost certainly, you'd run into limitations due to sheer size considerations long before you'd run into limits imposed by the Visual Basic compiler. Just remember that as you add dimensions, the memory space taken up by the array increases exponentially. The following 5-D array named biggie, for example, is pretty big, hogging over 200K of memory:

```
Dim biggie(10, 10, 10, 10, 10) As Single
```

Remember that all data structures take up memory. This array represents more than 200K of memory not available to other data structures. Incidentally, Visual Basic can handle arrays well in excess of 64K.

● **NOTE**

Generally speaking, you don't need to get into details of element storage as a Visual Basic programmer. Nonetheless, if you share data between languages, you may need to know that Basic uses *column-major* ordering rather than row-major ordering. This means that the leftmost dimension changes most quickly; if you were to note the indexes of elements laid out sequentially in memory, you'd see that the first coordinate (the "row" if you will) changes faster than the second (the "column").

This column-major ordering is the reverse of how most other languages, notably C and C++, handle arrays. For example, suppose an element is accessed in C as a[2][3][4]. This same element would be accessed in Basic as a(4, 3, 2). And if the Option Base 1 directive was on, then indexes would have to be bumped up by 1, resulting in a(5, 4, 3).

Passing and Returning Arrays

How do you pass an array within a program? The question is highly practical. Often, the need arises for passing an arbitrary array to a program that can perform some general operation, such as initializing all the elements to 0.

The rules for passing an array as an argument are simple:

1. In the declaration of the procedure, declare the array as you would any other argument, but follow the array name by parentheses:

```
Sub initArray(a() As Single, n As Integer)
```

2. When you call the procedure, pass the array just by using its name:

```
Dim mine(10) As Single
initArray mine, 10
```

Passing an *array element* is trivial. You can always pass an array element the same way you'd pass an ordinary variable. For example, assuming that you've written a factorial function, the following two sections of code produce similar results to each other:

```
Dim i As Integer, j As Integer
j = 5
i = factorial(j)
```

```
Dim i As Integer, arr(10) As Integer
arr(1) = 5
i = factorial(arr(1))
```

Passing an entire array is a different matter; it lets the Function or Sub procedure operate on all or any part of the array. Here is a version of the initArray procedure mentioned earlier. All it does is set each element of the array to 0. The parameter n tells the procedure how many elements to operate on:

```
Private Sub initArray(Dim a() As Integer, n As Integer)
   Dim i As Integer
   For i = 0 To n
      a(i) = 0
   Next
End Sub
```

Simple, isn't it? However, there is a limitation here. Since the base type of the array (in this case, `Integer`) must be declared, it only works with that type. To cover every kind of array, you'd need to write a separate procedure for each of the major kinds of data — integer, floating-point, string, and `Variant`.

You can use the `UBound` function to determine upper bounds. Therefore, if you want this function to always initialize the entire array, you can rewrite it as follows:

```
Private Sub initArray(Dim a() As Integer)
    Dim i As Integer
    For i = 0 To UBound(a)
        a(i) = 0
    Next
End Sub
```

Unlike passing an array, returning an array is a new feature of Visual Basic 6.0. One of the barriers to returning an array is that you must use direct assignment to transfer the value. As I pointed out earlier in the chapter, Visual Basic now supports this operation, but only if the array on the left side of the assignment is a variable-length (dynamic) array and only if the base types match precisely.

```
sizableArr = arr2
```

To return an array, therefore, you need to create a dynamic array to receive the value. The following example creates a dynamic array, a, and uses it to receive a value returned by the genArray function.

```
Private Sub Form_Load()
    Dim a() As Integer
    a = genArray(10)
    Debug.Print "upper bound is " & UBound(a)
    Debug.Print "a(5) = " & a(5)
End Sub


Function genArray(n) As Integer()
    Dim theArray() As Integer
    ReDim theArray(n)
```

```
      For i = 1 To n
          theArray(i) = i
      Next
      genArray = theArray
End Function
```

The function in this example, genArray, takes a positive integer n and creates an array that has n as its upper bound. Elements 1 to n are then each assigned the same value as their index. For example, genArray(5) would return an array with elements set equal to 0, 1, 2, 3, 4, and 5.

5 Parameter Arrays

The ParamArray capability lets you create variable argument lists so that you can call the procedure with a different number of arguments each time. As I mentioned at the beginning of the chapter, a parameter array should not be confused with passing an array as a parameter. Admittedly, the terminology is potentially confusing here. Instead of using "parameter array," it may be clearer to just talk about the ParamArray keyword.

In any procedure declaration, the last parameter in the list may be declared with the ParamArray keyword. This "end of list" parameter then becomes a stand-in for any number of arguments, starting in that position. For example, suppose you have the following procedure declaration:

```
Function sumargs(n As Integer, _
    ParamArray theRest() As Variant) _
    As Integer
```

Here, the ParamArray parameter, theRest, is in the second position. This means theRest represents all the arguments from the second position onward. These elements are accessed as theRest(0), theRest(1), theRest(2), and so on. The first index is always 0 and is not affected by Option Base.

For example, assume the following call to the sumargs function:

```
sum = sumargs(3, 15, 20, 25)
```

Figure 5-9 shows how each of these arguments is accessed within the procedure declaration.

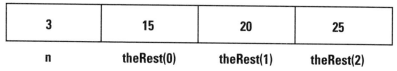

3	15	20	25
n	theRest(0)	theRest(1)	theRest(2)

Figure 5-9 *Using a ParamArray parameter*

As with ordinary arrays, the elements of theRest are accessed through an index. This index can be fixed, calculated, or (more typically) controlled by a loop variable. For example, the following procedure declaration sums all arguments beginning with the second.

```
Function sumargs(n, ParamArray theRest() As Variant)
    Dim i As Integer
    For i = 0 To n - 1
        sumargs = sumargs + theRest(i)
    Next
End Function
```

Whenever you use a ParamArray argument, keep in mind the following:

- The ParamArray argument must be declared as an array of type Variant. This can either be done explicitly, as done here, or implicitly.

- The size of the resulting array depends exactly on the number of arguments passed. In the earlier example of a call to sumargs, three arguments corresponded to theRest (because the first argument was passed to n). Therefore, index numbers run from 0 to 2. There is no theRest(3) unless another argument is passed.

Do not let the index numbers run too high. For any given number of arguments *n*, the index numbers run from 0 to *n*-1.

Note that by using the UBound function on the parameter array, you can make the function even easier to use. The n argument can be eliminated.

```
Function sumargs(ParamArray theRest() As Variant)
    Dim i As Integer
```

```
     For i = 0 To UBound(theRest)
        sumargs = sumargs + theRest(i)
     Next
  End Function
```

Control Arrays

Possibly the most interesting contribution Visual Basic makes to
the world of arrays is the concept of control arrays. They are similar to ordinary arrays but have some restrictions. For one thing,
they must be one-dimensional.

There are at least two reasons for using control arrays. First, a
control array enables you to write code for a whole series of controls that have similar function and appearance. One of the classic
examples of this use is a set of number keys for the digits 0
through 9. Each of the ten keys is implemented as an individual
control — specifically, a command button with Caption set to 0, 1,
2, or other digit. All of these keys respond in essentially the same
way. If you implement them as a control array, you can write one
event procedure for the entire group.

Second, control arrays confer a special flexibility. A control
array has no predefined size, so you can load entirely new controls into memory at run time. This is because at any given time,
a control array can have one, two, or more members. (You have to
have at least one control, but that one can be invisible.)

Control Arrays 1: Keyboard Example

One of the classic exercises in Visual Basic is to write a calculator
application. In fact, it was the first really useful Visual Basic program I wrote, and possibly even the first that anyone ever wrote.
It was included on the disks as one of the sample programs for
Visual Basic 1.0.

The reason I bring it up here is because it illustrates perfectly
the use of control arrays. One of the things you need for this
example is a set of digit keys. There are other keys as well, but
let's look at the digits first (Figure 5-10).

Figure 5-10 *Digit keys with readout*

The text box in this example has the following property settings:

Property	Setting
Name	**Readout**
Text	(blank)

The digit keys are command buttons that are all part of the same control array. You can use any of the following methods for creating a control array:

- Create the first control and set the Index property. It usually works best to set this value to 0.

- Create other members of the control array by using the copy-and-paste technique. Select the first control, choose Copy from the Edit menu, and then choose Paste from the Edit menu.

- Create a new control of the same type as the first (in this case, command button) and then give it the same name as the first.

In any case, after there is a control array with at least one element, you can add additional controls to the array by simply giving them the same name as the first. Each element is automatically assigned the next available Index setting.

If you want to follow along with the example, start by creating a single command button and give it the following settings:

Property	Setting
Name	**Keys**
Caption	**0**
Index	**0**

Now add command buttons to the control array as described earlier. Copy-and-paste is the fastest way to create the other elements. The name of each command button is always Keys, but the Index property will automatically be set to 1, 2, 3, and so on, up to 9. Set the caption of each of these controls to 1, 2, 3, and so on. In this case, it doesn't matter if the captions and index numbers match.

The first step in writing this application is to simply display numbers in the readout. A single event procedure provides this function for all the command buttons.

```
Private Sub Keys_Click(Index As Integer)
    Readout.Text = Readout.Text & Keys(Index).Caption
End Sub
```

As simple as this event procedure is, it provides the keys (no pun intended) to understanding how control arrays work.

For any event procedure of a control array, Visual Basic adds one new parameter: Index. This parameter is inserted at the beginning of the parameter list; the rest of the parameter list is the same as it would be for a normal control. In the case of *commandbutton*_Click, there are usually no parameters at all, so here there is exactly one, Index.

Now, whenever a click occurs for any of these command buttons, Visual Basic calls the Click event procedure and passes the index number to identify the control. Within the event procedure, the following item identifies the current control — that is, the element of Keys that actually got the click:

```
Keys(Index)
```

Therefore, the following statement gets the Caption setting of the button that got the click, and adds it onto the end of the readout:

```
Readout.Text = Readout.Text & Keys(Index).Caption
```

With only one line of code, you've already started creating the awesome Calculator application!

Control Arrays 2: Extending the Calculator

The next step is to add a series of operation keys, for addition, subtraction, division, and so on. These can be added to the same control array, Keys.

Again, it is not really important in what order the command buttons are added or what the index numbers are. In this particular application, the code uses the captions to determine what to do. (Note, however, that the Index property is still important, because the code uses Index to determine which button actually got an event.)

The more complete user interface is shown in Figure 5-11.

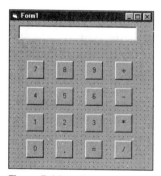

Figure 5-11   *The Calculator application with op keys*

Here's where you'll add some basic functionality of the operation keys (+, -, *, /, and =): They should clear the readout, allowing a new number to be entered. Now you need to call upon a control-flow structure, because digits and operation keys need to be handled differently. The Select Case structure is most helpful here. It works in a way similar to C's select statement.

```
Private Sub Keys_Click(Index As Integer)
    Select Case Keys(Index).Caption
        Case "+", "-", "*", "/", "="
            Readout.Text = ""
        Case "0" To "9"
            Readout.Text = _
                Readout.Text & Keys(Index).Caption
    End Select
End Sub
```

If you come from the C/C++ world, one thing you may notice is that Visual Basic's version of Select Case is somewhat more programmer-friendly: You can test strings as well as numeric expressions. For more information on this control-flow structure, see Chapter 17.

You're still some way from having a working calculator, but at least now all the basic elements are in place. The calculator can become as sophisticated as you like: The basic technique for expanding the application is to add another command button to the array, and write some new functionality for it in the Keys_Click procedure.

The next steps in the development of the Calculator application are left as exercises.

The first exercise is to add a decimal-point key ("."). The logic here is fairly straightforward. A flag variable is needed to indicate whether or not the decimal key has been pressed already. If it hasn't, then set the flag to True and add a decimal point to the readout. If it has, then do nothing. Whenever the readout is cleared, the flag must be set to False. This logic can be summarized as shown in Listing 5-1:

Listing 5-1   *Logic for Response to Decimal Key*

```
If Not decimalPresent Then
   decimalPresent = True
   Append "." to Readout
```

The second, and more interesting, exercise is to add full functionality to the operation keys. This is the critical step in writing the application's logic. When an operation key is pressed, it should first check to see if an operand has already been entered. If not, the application should store the contents of Readout in op1, a form variable.

If an operand *has* been entered, the application should store the contents of Readout in op2. It should then execute the pending operation on op1 and op2, placing the results in both op1 and the Readout display. (The reason for this logic is that any old operation must be processed before a new operation can be executed.)

In either case, the application should finish processing the operator by setting the pending operation (pendingOp) equal to the current caption. It should also set the newEntryFlag to True, so that the next digit key to be pressed starts a new entry.

That's quite a bit to remember, so here's the logic, summarized in Listing 5-2.

Listing 5-2 *Logic for Response to Operation Keys*

```
If Not opPendingFlag Then
    Store Readout value in op1
    opPendingFlag = True
Else
    Store Readout value in op2
    Execute pendingOp on op1 and op2
    Store results in op1
    Place results in Readout

newEntryFlag = True
pendingOp = current Caption setting
```

When the newEntryFlag is set, this means the *next* digit key to be pressed starts a new entry. Digit and decimal-point (.) keys must use the revised logic summarized in Listing 5-3.

Listing 5-3 *Revised Logic for Digit and Decimal Keys*

```
DIGIT KEYS:

If newEntryFlag
    decimalPresent = False
    newEntryFlag = False
    Readout gets current Caption setting
Else
    Append current Caption setting to Readout


DECIMAL POINT:

If newEntryFlag
    decimalPresent = True
    newEntryFlag = False
```

Continued

Listing 5-3 *Continued*

```
Readout gets "."
ElseIf Not decimalPresent Then
  decimalPresent = True
  Append "." to Readout
```

To follow this approach, you'll need to declare form variables op1 and op2, which should be type Double; and pendingOp, which is type String and holds a one-character operator, such as + or -. You'll also need Boolean form variables opPendingFlag, newEntryFlag, and decimalPresent.

Remember that the "current Caption setting", which is referred to a lot, is coded as follows:

```
Keys(Index).Caption
```

In writing the code for this application, you may find it helpful to write helper routines (general procedures), to which you pass the current Caption setting as an argument.

●—NOTE

Although the Calculator application is left as an exercise, I give the answer away in Appendix A, "The Calculator Application." No cheating, unless you're desperate.

Loading New Elements

As I mentioned earlier, the ability to create new controls at run time is one of the capabilities conferred by control arrays. For instance, in the Calculator example of the previous section, you could add any number of new keys at run time by simply loading new elements of the array.

The Load statement performs this operation. Each use of Load adds one new control. For example:

```
Load ctlArray(10)
```

Note that for the statement to be successfully executed, the control must not already exist. Therefore, in this example, ctlArray must be a control array of some kind in which index number 10 is not already in use. If you are going to create new controls this way, you'll need to keep track of what the next available index number is.

Although this capability is intriguing, the cases in which you really need to use it are not that common. You should assume, as a general rule, that loading new controls into memory is taxing, not only on space but on processor time. In most cases, you have a good idea of what controls may or may not appear. If you need to, you can make some controls invisible until needed (setting their `Visible` property to `False`), or place the controls outside the visible area of the form, accomplishing the same result.

In VB 6.0, it is now possible to load a control without using a control array. See the online Help subject "dynamic control addition."

Summary of Keywords in This Chapter

Whew! This has been a long journey. Visual Basic's array-handling capabilities are clearly extensive, and it's easy to lose track of them all. Here is a rundown of the principal keywords and intrinsic functions introduced in this chapter.

In each row, brackets are used to indicate optional items.

Syntax	Description
`Array(`*arguments*`)`	Returns an array of base type `Variant`. The *arguments* can be any type of data that can be assigned to a variant type. (This includes all data except user-defined types.)
`Dim` *array*`([`*bounds*`])` `[As` *type*`]`	Declares an array. If bounds are omitted, the array is a variable-length array, and you must allocate space with ReDim before using it. Multiple-dimensional arrays can be declared by including more than one *bounds*, separated by commas. For example: `Dim mat(5, 5) As Long`
`LBound(`*array* `[,`*dim*`])`	Returns lower bound of specified *array*. If the optional *dim* argument is included, this specifies a dimension number (starting with 1).

Syntax	Description
UBound(*array* [,*dim*])	Returns upper bound of specified *array*. If the optional *dim* argument is included, this specifies a dimension number (starting with 1).
Option Base *n*	Sets default lower bounds for most arrays (excluding those returned by the **Array** function). This statement must be placed in the Declarations section if used.
ReDim [**Preserve**] *array*(*bounds*)	Allocates space for a variable length array. *Bounds* are not optional. The optional **Preserve** keyword prevents data from being lost. This is an executable statement and can only be placed in a procedure.
(*lbound* **To** *ubound*)	This provides a way to declare both lower and upper bounds in an array declaration. For example: Dim chickens(1 to 10)

Advanced Controls

*"Do not adjust your scrollbars. We control
the horizontal. We control the vertical."*
— The Control Voice

Like any good carpenter, the Visual Basic programmer
has a Toolbox. The Toolbox is just what its name
implies: a set of tools that allows you to build your application, piece by piece, block by block. Every control in the
Toolbox opens up a new set of possibilities.

This chapter introduces some controls not covered so
far: scrollbars, text boxes, list boxes, combo boxes, and an
advanced component, the rich text box. Although you can
create your own controls (I explain how to do so in Chapter
9), the ones already provided in Visual Basic do a great deal
of work.

Controls Used in This Chapter

Except for the component introduced at the end of the chapter (the rich text box), the controls in this chapter can be found in the standard Toolbox (Figure 6-1). If you forget where these are located, it's easy to find them. Simply place the mouse pointer over any of the icons, and Visual Basic displays the class name of the control.

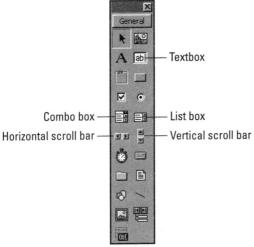

Figure 6-1 *Most controls used in this chapter are in the standard Toolbox.*

Scrollbar Controls

The scrollbar controls (class HScroll and VScroll) could almost be better described as "value controls" or "arrow controls." Contrary to what you might think, scrollbar controls exist independently of any other control or form. You can connect scrollbar controls to other controls by writing the appropriate code, but doing so is neither automatic nor even necessarily easy.

Scrollbar controls should not be confused with the internal scrollbars attached to some controls. For example, text boxes can have their own horizontal and vertical scrollbars, as discussed in the next section. Unlike scrollbar controls, the built-in text-box scrollbars work automatically and don't respond to code.

If scrollbar controls don't work automatically, what good are they? The answer is that they provide a more intuitive way for a user to modify or view a value. They adjust a value, but they do so *visually*.

Figure 6-2 shows how a typical scrollbar works. This is a horizontal control, but a vertical scrollbar works roughly the same way.

Figure 6-2 *How a horizontal scrollbar works*

The most important properties for any scrollbar are generally Min, Max, and Value. For horizontal scrollbars, Min and Max define the relative value associated with the left and right endpoints: This means higher values move you to the right, although you can reverse directions by setting a higher value for Min than Max.

The Value property determines the location of the scrollbar indicator. The meaning of this setting is relative to the Min and Max properties. For example, given Min and Max settings of 0 and 10, a Value setting of 5 sets the indicator at the halfway point. A Value setting of 7, as shown in Figure 6-2, sets the indicator somewhat closer to the Max setting.

At run time, the end user can set the scrollbar indicator directly, unless Enabled is set to False. In your programming code, you can then get the resulting position by getting the Value setting. You can also control the scrollbar programmatically at run time, by setting Value yourself:

```
' This statement moves to halfway point, assuming
'  Min and Max of 0 and 100.

Value = 50
```

Vertical scrollbars work in almost exactly the same way, except that Min and Max represent the top and bottom endpoints, respectively. Figure 6-3 illustrates how this works.

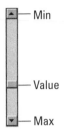

Figure 6-3 *How a vertical scrollbar works*

Again, if you want to reverse directions, set a higher value for Min than for Max. In such a case, higher settings for Value would cause upward movement instead of downward.

The scale for Min and Max is not arbitrary. A larger spread (0 to 1000, for example, instead of 0 to 4) causes the scrollbar indicator to be smaller relative to the size of the bar. Another reason the spread is important is that it affects the meaning of the SmallChange and LargeChange properties. These properties control the distance traveled by the indicator in response to two things: the user clicking the arrows (SmallChange) and the user clicking the bar on either side of the scrollbar indicator (LargeChange).

Putting the Scrollbars to Use

The following sample application shows an obvious use for scrollbar controls. It enables the end user to create colors by setting the values for red, blue, and green. This is a natural use for scrollbars, because it is a more intuitive interface than punching in a lot of numbers. It also responds very quickly.

Figure 6-4 shows the interface, which consists of three labels, three horizontal scrollbars, and one picture box.

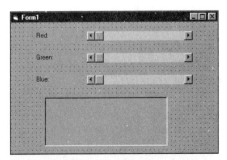

Figure 6-4 *The Set Colors application*

The following table lists the initial property settings for this application.

Object	Property	Give It This Setting
label 1	Caption	**Red:**
label 2	Caption	**Green:**
label 3	Caption	**Blue:**
scrollbar 1	Name	**scrRed**
scrollbar 2	Name	**scrGreen**
scrollbar 3	Name	**scrBlue**

In addition, the Min and Max properties should be set to 0 and 255, respectively, for each of the scrollbar controls.

The following code makes the application run.

```
Private Sub scrRed_Change()
   Picture1.BackColor = RGB(scrRed.Value, _
     scrGreen.Value, scrBlue.Value)
End Sub

Private Sub scrGreen_Change()
   Picture1.BackColor = RGB(scrRed.Value, _
     scrGreen.Value, scrBlue.Value)
End Sub

Private Sub scrBlue_Change()
   Picture1.BackColor = RGB(scrRed.Value, _
     scrGreen.Value, scrBlue.Value)
End Sub
```

There are a couple of ways to optimize this code. One way to make it much more compact is to use a control array (as described in the previous chapter), in which case only one procedure is needed. This is left as an exercise for the reader.

Scrollbar Events: Change and Scroll

You will most likely be interested in two particular scrollbar events when programming scrollbar behavior. One is the Change event, which was used in the example. This event is generated when the user clicks an arrow or the scrollbar itself, or drags the scrollbar indicator to a new position. Notably, in the latter case, the event is only generated once, after the user releases the mouse button.

The Scroll event is similar, except that when the user drags the scrollbar indicator, many Scroll events are generated between any two points. This allows for more instantaneous response on the part of the application.

As an added exercise, try revising the application in the previous section by moving the code for Change event procedures to Scroll event procedures. The resulting application is much more responsive to end-user actions, although it is much more demanding on processor time as well.

Text Boxes

It's likely that the first control you ever encountered when learning Visual Basic was a text box. At first glance, they seem to be the simplest of controls: They don't do anything flashy, they just let the user enter text. But text boxes have some refined features, which I point out in the next few sections.

Working with Text Box Data

When we sat down to write the first tutorials for Visual Basic 1.0, we had to be fairly rigorous about data types — especially about converting data between string and numeric formats. For example, assume you have text boxes named txtFahren and txtCentigrade. Data had to be converted back and forth with functions such as Val and Str:

```
c = Val(txtCentigrade.Text)
f = (c * 1.8) + 32.0
txtFahren.Text = Str(f)
```

Beginning with Visual Basic 2.0, the default type became Variant, which allows you to be much more lax:

```
c = txtCentigrade.Text
f = (c * 1.8) + 32.0
txtFahren.Text = f
```

But even if you don't use the Variant type, Visual Basic automatically converts whenever an unambiguous need for a certain conversion arises. For example, in the following code, string data in txtCentigrade is converted to Double format, and txtFahren gets a string representation of f.

```
Dim c As Double, f As Double


c = txtCentigrade.Text
f = (c * 1.8) + 32.0
txtFahren.Text = f
```

Data types are not irrelevant, however. For example, if c is declared as type Integer in the following code, Visual Basic rounds to the nearest integer as it converts.

```
Dim c As Integer


c = txtCentigrade.Text
```

Another subtlety of conversion is that in some cases, it may be unreliable to depend on string-to-numeric conversion. If the string does not contain a well-formed, valid digit string, the result is a run-time error. The Val function is more forgiving: It stops reading digits as soon as it encounters a non-digit character.

```
c = Val(txtCentigrade.Text)
```

Single-Line Text Boxes and the KeyPress Event

There's more to a single-line text box than meets the eye. One of the common UI conventions in Windows is that pressing Enter should do something. It's convenient for users if they can type some text and then press Enter to cause an action.

The most obvious way to provide a command is to use a command button, which, when clicked, carries out the action associated with the text box. This is fine, but from the user's point of view, it's not nearly as convenient as just pressing Enter; after all, the user's fingers are already on the keyboard.

```
Private Sub Command1_Click()
    Debug.Print "Do the action now."
End Sub
```

Another approach is to use the text box's Change event. The Change event is called in response to *any* change to the text box: This means each individual keystroke. Using this event is okay (even desirable) in some cases, but if you want to wait until the user presses Enter to validate the change, this won't do.

```
Private Sub Text1_Change()
    Debug.Print "Do the action now."
End Sub
```

There's also an annoying side effect: With single-line text boxes, Visual Basic considers pressing Enter to be an invalid action, so it beeps rudely at the user. You probably want to eliminate this, too.

Here's what you want to do, written out as pseudo-code:

```
Test each keystroke:
If keystroke is ENTER
    Eat the keystroke, to suppress the beep
    Take the appropriate action
```

Fortunately, all these steps are quite easy to do with the KeyPress event, which is among the most useful events for a text box. KeyPress is generated whenever the text box has focus and the user presses a key. The key value (in its numeric, ASCII form) is passed as an argument, KeyAscii.

```
Private Sub Text1_KeyPress(KeyAscii As Integer)
    If KeyAscii = 13 Then
        KeyAscii = 0
        Debug.Print "Do the action now."
    End If
End Sub
```

The decimal number 13 is the ASCII code for a carriage return, so testing for 13 detects the Enter key. The third statement is perhaps the most interesting. In a very slick twist, Visual Basic lets you transform the keystroke that's just been intercepted, merely by assigning a new value to KeyAscii! If you assign 0, this has the effect of swallowing the keystroke completely.

```
KeyAscii = 0
```

You can even let the user correct mistakes by pressing the Esc key — just as the Properties window does. The way to do this is to write a procedure for both the GotFocus and KeyPress events. (Both GotFocus and LostFocus are often useful events for text boxes to respond to.) When the text box gets focus, save the current text in a form variable. Then, if the user presses the Esc key, restore the old string.

```
Dim strSaved As String

Private Sub Text1_GotFocus()
    strSaved = Text1.Text
End Sub

Private Sub Text1_KeyPress(KeyAscii As Integer)
    If KeyAscii = vbKeyEscape Then
        Text1.Text = strSaved
    End If
End Sub
```

How did I know to use the key code value, vbKeyEscape? All the special-key values are listed in online Help, under the topic "Key Code Constants." You can also create a variable of type KeyCodeConstants and let Visual Basic prompt you with a pop-up list box when you type this:

```
Dim k As KeyCodeConstants
k =
```

In addition to special keys, you can recognize alphanumeric keys by using the Asc function on a quoted character, as shown in the following example:

```
If KeyAscii = Asc("a") Then
```

```
     MsgBox "You pressed 'a'."
   End If
```

Multiline Text Boxes

The text box control is flexible enough to expand into a text area for reading and writing multiple lines of text — although not surprisingly, you can only make this change at design time.

It's as easy as setting the Multiline property to True. When this is done, you then have another choice to make: What scrollbars, if any, do you want? As I pointed out earlier in this chapter, the built-in scrollbars of a text box have little in common with the scrollbar controls, although they look pretty much the same.

You set scrollbars at design time by setting the ScrollBars property, which has the following possible settings: 0 – None, 1 – Horizontal, 2 – Vertical, and 3 – Both. Of course, I find I most often set multiline text boxes to 2 – Vertical, because I often use them to scroll downward through many lines of text.

Figure 6-5 shows a form containing a multiline text box with both vertical and horizontal scrollbars.

Figure 6-5 *A form with a multiline text box*

Editing functions in a multiline text box are very similar to those for a single-line text box. The main difference is the handling of the Enter key. With a single-line text box, if the user presses Enter, the text box does nothing but beep (as discussed earlier). With a multiline text box, pressing Enter inserts a carriage return, as you would expect, starting a new line. In addition, the up and down arrow keys are operable in a multiline text box, but not in a single-line text box.

List Boxes and Combo Boxes

List boxes and combo boxes can add richly to a UI. A list box offers a set of alternatives; it's far more user-friendly than requiring the user to guess what the valid entries are. Another way of offering a set of choices is with a group of option buttons. Often the choice between list box or option buttons is a matter of taste, although option buttons take up more space and lack the multiple-selection feature.

Combo boxes offer a variation on a theme. Suppose you want to permit the user to enter his or her own text, as well as having alternatives to select from. You can do this with a combo box (as long as its Style property is set to 0 or 1).

Let's start with list boxes. Combo boxes support most of the same methods and properties as list boxes — notably the AddItem method and the Text property, which I discuss first.

List Box: Basic Operation

Unlike most controls, the content of a list box cannot be initialized at design time (see Figure 6-6). At design time, a list box looks quite plain. The text it displays is always the control's internal name. (Changing the setting of the Name property alters the list-box display; this change can occur only at design time.)

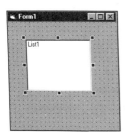

Figure 6-6 *A list box at design time*

To initialize the content of a list box or combo box, use the AddItem method. The appropriate place to do this is usually the Form_Load procedure. For example:

```
Private Sub Form_Load( )
    List1.AddItem "USA"
    List1.AddItem "Canada"
```

```
        List1.AddItem "France"
        List1.AddItem "UK"
        List1.AddItem "Germany"
        List1.AddItem "Italy"
    End Sub
```

Notice I added these out of alphabetical order. You can have these sorted automatically, by going back to design mode and setting the Sorted property to True.

You can also specify a position when you use the AddItem method. This optional argument is a zero-based index; the item is inserted at the indicated index position, bumping up every item from that position onward. The full syntax of the method is shown here. The brackets indicate the second argument is optional.

object.**AddItem** *item* [, *index*]

Figure 6-7 shows what the previous code example would display assuming that the Sorted property is set to True. Because in this case there are more entries than visible space, the list box automatically displays its own vertical scrollbar.

Figure 6-7 *A list box at run time*

At run time, two main events are of interest: Click and DblClick. As the end user clicks items or uses the up and down arrow keys, the control generates Click events. Per Windows convention, this event should not launch a command. It would be annoying if it did, because the user might be using arrow keys to scroll through the list.

If you want the list box to launch a command, you should write code for the DblClick event. The Click event is still useful; you might respond to Click by quickly updating something on the screen. But double-clicking is the preferred way to cause an action.

The Text property specifies the currently selected item in the list box.

```
Private Sub List1_DblClick()
    MsgBox "You selected this item: " & List1.Text
End Sub
```

●—NOTE ────────────────────────────────

If you want to remove an item, use the RemoveItem method, which takes an index number as its argument.

Turning On and Using MultiSelect

At design time, setting the MultiSelect property to 1 or 2 enables multiple selection. These settings are similar, but 2 (Extended) enables the user to use the Shift key for group selection as well as the Ctrl key.

●—NOTE ────────────────────────────────

Only list boxes and file list boxes support the MultiSelect property. Combo boxes, regardless of style, do not support multiple selection.

Multiple selection gives the user far more flexibility, but as you might expect, it complicates the process of getting the selections. The Text property still works, but it only returns one item: the last item clicked — even if it was clicked to remove it from group selection!

```
Debug.Print List1.Text    ' Print last item clicked.
```

To get the full group of items selected, you need to use three properties: List, Selected, and ListCount.

List and Selected are both zero-based arrays. List is a string array containing all the items in the list, as shown in Figure 6-8.

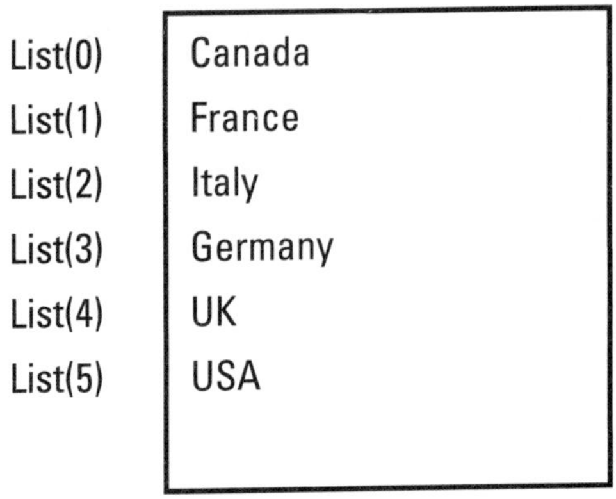

List(0)	Canada
List(1)	France
List(2)	Italy
List(3)	Germany
List(4)	UK
List(5)	USA

Figure 6-8 *How the List property array works*

Selected is a Boolean array in which each element contains True if the corresponding item is in the selection, or False if not. Figure 6-9 illustrates how this works.

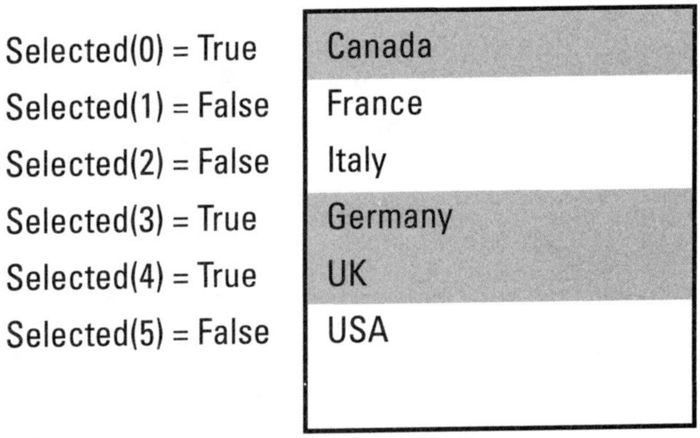

Selected(0) = True	Canada
Selected(1) = False	France
Selected(2) = False	Italy
Selected(3) = True	Germany
Selected(4) = True	UK
Selected(5) = False	USA

Figure 6-9 *How the Selected property array works*

Finally, you need to the use the ListCount property. This is a read-only integer property, equal to the number of items in the list.

One way to use these three properties is to cycle through an array. Remember that ListCount is equal to one more than the highest valid index of the List and Selected arrays, because they are zero-based arrays. The following example assumes that the name of the list box is List1.

```
For i = 0 To List1.ListCount - 1
    If List1.Selected(i) Then
```

```
        Debug.Print List1.List(i)
    End If
Next
```

In addition to printing to the Immediate window, you'll usually want to collect the selected items into some kind of data structure. The most convenient way to do this is to use a `Collection` object.

Introducing the Collection Object

I'm getting a little ahead of the story, because I don't discuss objects much until Chapter 8. But bear with me a little, if you would. It will be fun.

`Collection` is one of Visual Basic's intrinsic classes (in addition to control classes). After you create a `Collection` object, you can add any number of items of almost any type to it; you can then recall those items on demand. When you don't know ahead of time how many items you're going to need space for, use of a `Collection` object is particularly convenient. Unlike arrays, collections grow and contract as needed without any effort on your part.

The following statement creates a `Collection` object. The use of the `New` keyword may be new to you. You can give your object any name you want (here the name is `places`), but type in the other words as shown:

```
Dim places As New Collection
```

You can now add items of any type (except the user-defined type) to the collection by using the `Add` method. You can then retrieve items by using the `Item` and `Count` methods. `Item` uses a one-based index. For example:

```
places.Add "Russia"
places.Add "Norway"
For i = 1 To places.Count
    Debug.Print places.Item(i)   ' Use 1-based index
Next
```

Armed with a `Collection` object, it's easy to collect all the entries from a multiple-selection list box into a data structure. In the following example, I put all the selected entries into a collection and then print out the collection's contents.

```
Private Sub Form_Click()
    Dim places As New Collection

    For i = 0 To List1.ListCount - 1
        If List1.Selected(i) Then
            places.Add List1.List(i)
        End If
    Next

    For i = 1 To places.Count
        s = s & ", " & places.Item(i)
    Next
    MsgBox "The items are" & s

End Sub
```

Given the list selections shown in Figure 6-9, this example displays the message box shown in Figure 6-10.

Figure 6-10   *Printing out contents of a collection*

If you want the collection to be relatively more permanent, you can declare it in the Declarations section.

```
Dim places As New Collection
```

You may also want to clear the collection from time to time, which you can do by calling the RemoveItem method:

```
For i = 1 To places.Count
    places.RemoveItem 1
Next
```

Combo Box: A Wealth of Style

The ComboBox control is really three controls in one. In fact, about the only thing that all three kinds of combo boxes have in common is that they are all variations on the list control.

At design time, you can set the Style property to one of three types: 0 – Dropdown Combo, 1 – Simple Combo, and 2 – Dropdown List. If you're like me, you probably find these names induce a certain amount of dizzying confusion.

Figure 6-11 may help you through the confusion. The first two styles of combo box (0 and 1) give the user latitude: they let him or her type in an entry, as in a text box, *or* use one of the items in the list. Style 2, in contrast, is basically a list box. But like the other styles of combo boxes, it does not support multiple selection.

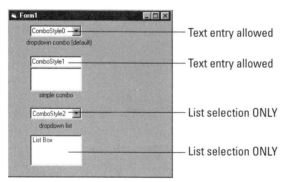

Figure 6-11   *Combo box styles and the list box*

None of the combo boxes generate a DblClick event. Combo boxes with style 2 recognize the Click event but not the other events discussed in this chapter.

With style 0 or 1 in effect, a combo box is both a list box and a text box. If the user makes a selection from the list, the control generates a Click event. If the user types anything into the text-box area, the control generates a Change event. What's tricky here is that the Change event is only generated by a direct-text entry.

Therefore, with styles 0 and 1, if you want to write code that does something in response to changes, you need to place that code in both the Click and Change event procedures.

```
Private Sub myCombo_Click()
    Debug.Print "Alert! New setting! (Click event)"
End Sub
```

```
Private Sub myCombo_Change()
    Debug.Print "Alert! New setting! (Change event)"
End Sub
```

As with text boxes, each and every single keystroke generates a separate Change event.

The approach I recommend is the same as I recommended for text boxes: getting the KeyPress event, and executing an action only if the user presses Enter. This requires just one event procedure.

```
Private Sub myCombo_KeyPress(KeyAscii As Integer)
    If KeyAscii = 13 Then
        KeyAscii = 0
        Debug.Print "Do the action now."
    End If
End Sub
```

The Rich Text Box Control

Building from components is one of the major strengths of Visual Basic. Although other programming environments have joined the component bandwagon, Visual Basic is still distinguished by the ease with which you can add and use components.

One of the most impressive, and immediately useful, of the components provided in the Visual Basic package is the rich text box (class name: RichTextBox). From the user's point of view, the RichTextBox control is similar to the standard text box; it does all the same things. However, with a little code, you'll be able to let the user mix any amount of different fonts inside a single text box.

Adding Components to Your Project

To view the large set of components available to you, press Ctrl + T or else choose the Components command from the Project menu. The dialog box shown in Figure 6-12 appears. The Controls tab should be selected; click that tab if it isn't.

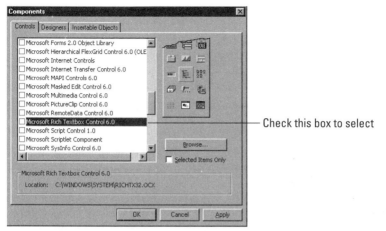

— Check this box to select

Figure 6-12   *The Components dialog box*

There's one drawback you should be aware of in using any of these components: The component's .dll or .ocx file will need to be present on the end user's computer if the component appears anywhere in your application. This is not a problem, of course, if you're just creating something for your own use.

To get started using the RichTextBox control, scroll down through the Components dialog box's Controls tab, if necessary, to Microsoft Rich Textbox Control 6.0 (the names are in alphabetical order) and check the box next to this item. Click the OK button. If you do all this successfully, the RichTextBox icon appears in the Toolbox. Figure 6-13 shows what the icon looks like.

Figure 6-13   *The RichTextBox icon*

Using the Rich Text Box Control

As I mentioned earlier, the RichTextBox control does everything the standard text-box control does. But you can also use it to vary font, font characteristics, font size, color, and many other properties. The most direct control is provided by the "Sel" properties, which govern the currently selected text and (just as importantly) the insertion point. There are many "Sel" properties, but Table 6-1 lists some of the more interesting ones. With each of these properties, you can set or get its value at run time.

Table 6-1   *"Sel" Properties of the RichTextBox Control*

Property	Description
SelBold	If True, selected text is bold.
SelItalic	If True, selected text is italic.
SelFontName	Returns or sets name of font of selected text.
SelFontSize	Returns or sets point size of font in selected text.
SelColor	Returns or sets color value for selected text.

In all these cases, similar principles apply:

- If some text is selected (highlighted) and you set one of these properties, all selected characters are affected. For example, setting `SelBold` to `True` turns the characters to bold.

  ```
  RichTextBox1.SelBold = True   ' Turn on bold.
  ```

- If no text is selected and you set one of these properties, the change still affects the insertion point. For example, if `SelBold` is set to `True`, all new text typed at the insertion point will be bold.

- When you get a property setting, it returns the condition of the selected text or insertion point. However, if multiple characters are selected and their status is mixed, the condition is `Null`. For example, if the user highlights mixed bold and non-bold characters, `SelBold` returns the `Null` value. You can test for `Null` values with the `IsNull` function.

  ```
  If IsNull(RichTextBox1.SelBold) Then
      MsgBox "Bold/non-bold mixed."
  End If
  ```

The following sample application includes a `RichTextBox` control and two check boxes, labeled as shown in Figure 6-14. (Use the `Caption` property.) The names of the check boxes are `chkBold` and `chkItalic`; the rich text box is named `rtfBox`.

Figure 6-14   *Rich Text Box sample application*

Adding Code for the Rich Text Box

The following code uses the SelBold and SelItalic properties to
determine characteristics of selected text and to set those characteristics. Each property is made to reflect the state of the corresponding check box, and vice-versa.

```
' chkBold_Click: user checked or unchecked "Bold"
' Respond by setting the SelBold property,
'  changing current selection to bold or non-bold
'

Private Sub chkBold_Click()
   If chkBold.Value = vbChecked Then
      rtfBox.SelBold = True
   ElseIf chkBold.Value = vbUnchecked Then
      rtfBox.SelBold = False
   End If
End Sub


' chkItalic_Click:user checked or unchecked "Italic"
' Respond by setting the SelItalic property,
'  changing current selection to ital. or non-ital.
'

Private Sub chkItalic_Click()
   If chkItalic.Value = vbChecked Then
      rtfBox.SelItalic = True
   ElseIf chkItalic.Value = vbUnchecked Then
      rtfBox.SelItalic = False
```

```
        End If
End Sub


' rtfBox_SelChange: selection or insertion pnt moved
' Respond by updating check boxes to reflect font
'
Private Sub rtfBox_SelChange()
    If IsNull(rtfBox.SelBold) Then
        chkBold.Value = vbGrayed
    ElseIf rtfBox.SelBold Then
        chkBold.Value = vbChecked
    Else
        chkBold.Value = vbUnchecked
    End If

    If IsNull(rtfBox.SelItalic) Then
        chkItalic.Value = vbGrayed
    ElseIf rtfBox.SelItalic Then
        chkItalic.Value = vbChecked
    Else
        chkItalic.Value = vbUnchecked
    End If
End Sub
```

Understanding the Code

The code in the previous section may seem lengthy, but it's actually short considering what you get for it. With these procedures in place, the user can place or remove bold and italic throughout a rich text box. Everything works smoothly, just as it would in a commercial application such as Microsoft Word.

When a new block of text is highlighted, a SelChange event is generated. The code responds by setting the state of each check box as appropriate, first checking for the Null condition, which would indicate mixed fonts. For example, the following code sets the state of the chkBold check box in response to the new selection:

```
    If IsNull(rtfBox.SelBold) Then
```

```
      chkBold.Value = vbGrayed
ElseIf rtfBox.SelBold Then
      chkBold.Value = vbChecked
Else
      chkBold.Value = vbUnchecked
End If
```

This ensures the check box always reflects reality.

When the user checks or unchecks a check box, a Click event is generated. In response to the chkBold_Click event, the following code is executed. The appropriate response is to turn bold on or off by setting the value of SelBold.

```
If chkBold.Value = vbChecked Then
      rtfBox.SelBold = True
ElseIf chkBold.Value = vbUnchecked Then
      rtfBox.SelBold = False
End If
```

Notice that the state of the Value property may be vbGrayed as a result of a change made earlier by the code. In this case, the Click event procedure takes no action.

Using similar logic, you can create toolbars and menus that enable a wide variety of rich-text features, including underline, strikethrough, color, and font size. No matter what kind of controls you provide for setting fonts, you need a way of indicating the null condition for mixed fonts. For example, the SelFontName property could be controlled by a single-line text box; this text box should be blank when the selection has mixed fonts.

Figure 6-15 shows an example of the application running.

Figure 6-15 *The RTF application in operation*

You can control selection programmatically by the use of the `SelText`, `SelStart`, and `SelLength` properties. These are supported for both text boxes and `RichTextBox` controls. The `SelStart` property, which is a zero-based index, determines the position of the insertion point if no text is selected.

Loading and Saving Rich-Text Files

`RichTextBox` controls can read plain vanilla text files just fine. They also have the ability to deal with files saved in the standard RTF format, supported by many word processors.

One of the main reasons for having a `RichTextBox` control is to view and edit an RTF file or text file. The designers of the control have made this very easy. If you choose, you can have the contents of a file loaded by setting the control's `FileName` property — which you can do at design time. The file is automatically loaded as soon as the control is.

You can also load the filename in application code by calling the `LoadFile` method. This enables you to either hard-code the filename or determine the filename at run time, possibly by prompting the user. The filename can optionally include a path specification.

```
rtfBox.LoadFile "C:\readme.txt"
```

Here is an example that prompts for the name:

```
theFile = InputBox("Enter filename to view:")
rtfBox.Loadfile theFile
```

After changes have been made, you can, if you choose, save the file back to its disk location. The `SaveFile` method carries this out, replacing the old contents of the file, if any.

```
rtfBox.SaveFile "C:\readme.txt"
```

In the next chapter, I show you how easy it is to prompt a user for a filename by using the CommonDialog control (another component you can add to your projects). Using that control with a RichTextBox control is a snap.

```
CommonDialog1.ShowOpen
rtfBox.LoadFile CommonDialog1.FileName
```

6

File Ops Made Easy

7

"We'll keep your résumé on file."

— Noah Way José, Human Resources director

Traditionally, file operations — selecting a file, opening it, and then reading and writing — have occupied a large percentage of a programmer's time. This is especially true under Windows, where applications are expected to provide user-friendly dialog boxes.

Part of the philosophy of Visual Basic is that you should be required to spend as little time coding file operations as possible. Files are just not that exciting. They do, however, bestow the ability to access permanent data residing on the hard disk or a network — an essential part of many applications.

Starting with Visual Basic 1.0, the three file-system controls have provided a lot of flexibility for creating file-oriented dialog boxes, with a minimum of coding. However, the CommonDialog control is even easier to use, so I discuss that first.

What's New in VB 6.0

The file system is one of the main areas in which Visual Basic 6.0 has an important new feature: the FileSystemObject class, which provides advantages over traditional file-system statements.

After you create a FileSystemObject, you can use it to perform many high-level commands, including moving, renaming, and deleting entire directories (also called *folders*). The class FileSystemObject provides access to the entire file system through a hierarchy of File, Folder, and Drive objects. One limitation of the FileSystemObject class is you cannot use it to read and write to binary or random-access data files, although you can use it to read and write text files.

I use the FileSystemObject class in the two featured applications in this chapter. For more detail on this class, see Chapter 18.

> ● **NOTE**
>
> The FileSystemObject class is also available in Active Server pages. See online Help for Active Server for details.

The CommonDialog Control

When you want to display a simple Open File or Save File As dialog box, the fastest approach is to use the CommonDialog control. Although you can write a few lines of code to modify the dialog box, you don't have to create a customized dialog box from scratch, which saves a good deal of work.

The alternative is to design a dialog box yourself, by creating a second form, placing file controls on it (the Drive, DirList, and FileList controls), and displaying it at run time by using the Show method and the Load and UnLoad statements. As shown in the second half of this chapter, there are definitely situations where you need this greater degree of customization. It does require more work, however.

Adding the CommonDialog Control to the Toolbox

The CommonDialog control is not included in the set of standard controls you first see when starting Visual Basic. But it's easy to add this type of control to a project:

1. From the Project menu, choose the Components command. A dialog box appears. (You can also open this dialog box by pressing Ctrl + T.)

2. The Controls tab should be selected. Click the tab if it isn't.

3. Scroll down until you see Microsoft Common Dialog Control 6.0. Select this item (a check mark should appear) and click the OK button.

After following these steps, the common-dialog icon appears at the bottom of the Toolbox, as shown in Figure 7-1.

———— CommonDialog tool

Figure 7-1 *The CommonDialog control in the Toolbox*

The class name, which you can verify by holding the mouse pointer over the icon, is CommonDialog. Following the steps just described adds this class to the current project. You'll have to add this component again in each project that needs it.

Once you've added the CommonDialog control to the Toolbox, it's easy to add an instance of the control to your own application. Just double-click the icon at design time. This adds a CommonDialog control to your form. Where you place this control on the form makes no difference; in this respect, it's like the Timer control. At run time, it won't be displayed until you use the ShowOpen or ShowSave method.

In fact, the dialog control itself is never displayed at run time: It is a hidden control that causes a dialog box to be displayed in response to code. This may sound like an angels-on-the-head-of-a-pin distinction, but remember that the location and size of the dialog control itself are irrelevant.

Setting Properties at Design Time

At design time, you can set almost all the properties for the `CommonDialog` control. Although none of these settings change the general look of the dialog box, they do specify such things as the caption (specified by the `DialogTitle` property), file filter, and initial directory.

You can set a large number of properties efficiently by using the control's property pages. In the Properties window, double-click (Custom) in the list of properties. (If the Alphabetic tab is selected, this item appears near the top; if Categorized is selected, it can be found under the Misc category.)

Figure 7-2 shows the Property Pages dialog box. Some of the properties are self-explanatory. The use of the `Filter` and `FilterIndex` properties is explained in an upcoming section.

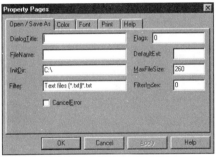

Figure 7-2 *Property Pages for the CommonDialog control*

Using the Control to Display a Dialog Box

Although you can use the Properties Window to set nearly all the properties of a `CommonDialog` control, you do need to write some code. Here is the minimum code needed to display the control at run time as a File Open dialog box and retrieve the user's selection:

```
CommonDialog1.ShowOpen
theFile = CommonDialog1.FileName
```

The `ShowOpen` statement displays the dialog box as a File Open dialog box. The dialog box is modal. The `ShowOpen` method does not return until the user closes the dialog box.

The filename is then available through the `FileName` property. If the user selected a file, `FileName` contains the complete filename, including path specification. If the user did not select a file, this property contains an empty string (`""`).

Setting File Filters for the Dialog Box

One of the more useful ways to customize a `CommonDialog` control is to specify file filters by using the `Filter` and `FilterIndex` properties.

The `Filter` property is a string containing a series of substrings separated by a bar (|). The syntax of these substrings is as follows. The brackets and ellipses (...) indicate you can have any number of display/pattern pairs.

"display | pattern [| display | pattern] ..."

The *display* is a string to be placed in a drop-down list box that the end user sees. The *pattern* is used by the dialog box to actually filter the files.

For example, suppose you want the user to select between text files (`*.txt`), document files (`*.doc`), or all files (`*.*`). The following filter lets the user select these patterns.

```
flt1 = "Text files (*.txt)|*.txt"
flt2 = "Document files (*.doc)|*.doc"
flt3 = "All files (*.*)|*.*"
theFilter = flt1 & "|" & flt2 & "|" & flt3
CommonDialog1.Filter = theFilter
```

The `FilterIndex` property is a zero-based index that selects one of these as default. For example, the following statement makes the first item the default:

```
CommonDialog1.FilterIndex = 0
```

Figure 7-3 shows what a sample use of the `CommonDialog` control looks like, with the filters specified in this section. The filters are displayed when the user clicks the arrow in the drop-down list.

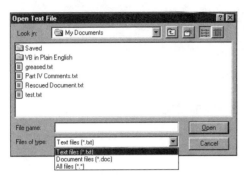

Figure 7-3 *Displaying a dialog box with file filters*

● **NOTE**

If you leave the `Filter` property blank, the dialog box displays all files.

Using the Control to Display a Save File As Dialog Box

The `FileSave` method has almost exactly the same effect as the `FileOpen` method, except that in the upper-left corner, it displays the label "Save in:" rather than "Look in:". Here's an example that incorporates the file filters from the previous section.

```
flt1 = "Text files (*.txt)|*.txt"
flt2 = "Document files (*.doc)|*.doc"
flt3 = "All files (*.*)|*.*"
theFilter = flt1 & "|" & flt2 & "|" & flt3
CommonDialog1.Filter = theFilter

CommonDialog1.ShowSave
theFile = CommonDialog1.FileName
```

The most important difference between File Open and Save File As dialog boxes lies in what you do with the filename once you get it. The appropriate response in one case is to open the file and read in data. The appropriate response in the other case is to open the file and write data. Exactly how you read and write data, of course, depends on the specifics of your application.

Advanced Features of the CommonDialog Control

The `Flags` property of the `CommonDialog` control lets you customize the behavior of the dialog box in a number of ways. You can even specify `dlgOFNAllowMultiselect`, which enables multiple selection. (When this flag is on, the `FileName` property is assigned the names of all the selected files, delimited with a space between each.) See online Help for the `Flags` property.

It's usually easiest to set the `Flags` property in code, because you can use symbolic constants and then use addition to combine flag settings. For example:

```
myflags = dlgOFNExplorer + dlgOFNHideReadOnly
CommonDialog1.Flags = myflags
```

The `dlgOFNHideReadOnly` flag is one you may want to set for File Open dialog boxes; otherwise, the dialog box includes an "Open as read only" check box.

Sample Application: Text File Editor

How many lines of code would you say it takes to create a text editor in Visual Basic, complete with File Open and Save File As commands? A thousand lines? Five hundred? One hundred? Well, guess again, because it takes a lot fewer lines than that. This is possible because the existing control classes do most of the work.

Drawing the Interface

After opening a new project, the first thing you need to do is add the `CommonDialog` icon to the Toolbox. You can do this as described earlier, by first pressing Ctrl + T and then selecting the item Microsoft Common Dialog Control 6.0.

The interface of the text editor sample application has a text box, two command buttons, and a `CommonDialog` control. The size of the control is unimportant, and the command buttons can take the default size. The text box, however, needs to be sized as shown in Figure 7-4.

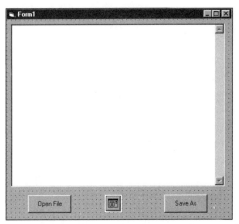

Figure 7-4 *Interface for the sample text editor application*

Setting Initial Property Values

Table 7-1 shows the design-time property settings for this application. The properties of the CommonDialog control can be set just like those for any other control. However, if you're following along with the example, you'll probably find it easiest to set the control's InitDir and Filter properties by using the Property Pages window. (Double-click (Custom) in the Properties window when the CommonDialog control is selected.)

Table 7-1 *Property Settings for the Text Editor Application*

Control	Property	Set Value to
command button 1	Name	**cmdOpen**
command button 2	Name	**cmdSave**
dialog control	Name	**dlgFile**
command button 1	Caption	**Open File**
command button 2	Caption	**Save As**
dialog control	InitDir	**C:**
dialog control	Filter	**Text files (*.txt)|*.txt**
text box	Text	(blank)

Control	Property	Set Value to
text box	Multiline	**True**
text box	Scrollbars	**2 - Vertical**

Writing the Code

The following code — no more than 35 lines — is all that's necessary for a working text editor application. This is remarkably short for the functionality you get. In the sections that follow, I explain how the code works.

```
Dim theFile As String

Private Sub cmdOpen_Click()
    dlgFile.DialogTitle = "Open Text File"
    dlgFile.Flags = dlgOFNHideReadOnly
    dlgFile.ShowOpen
    theFile = dlgFile.FileName
    If theFile <> "" Then readFile(theFile)
End Sub

Private Sub cmdSave_Click()
    dlgFile.DialogTitle = "Save Text File"
    dlgFile.FileName = theFile
    dlgFile.ShowSave
    theFile = dlgFile.FileName
    If theFile <> "" Then saveFile(theFile)
End Sub

Sub readFile(theFile As String)
    Dim f As Object, stream As Object
    Set f = CreateObject("Scripting.FileSystemObject")
    Set stream = f.OpenTextFile(theFile)

    Text1.Text = stream.ReadAll
    stream.Close
```

7

```
End Sub

Sub saveFile(theFile As String)
    Dim f As Object, stream As Object
    Set f = CreateObject("Scripting.FileSystemObject")
    Set stream = f.CreateTextFile(theFile)

    stream.Write Text1.Text
    stream.Close
End Sub
```

Understanding the Code, Part 1: Open File

The Click event procedure for cmdOpen sets some additional properties for the dialog control, dlgFile, and then calls ShowOpen to
display the dialog box.

```
    dlgFile.ShowOpen
```

After this statement returns, dlgFile can be checked for property settings that reflect the user's choices — particularly the setting of the FileName property.

The last two statements in this procedure do the following:
save the selected filename as theFile, a form variable, and call
the readFile function. If the filename is empty (indicating that no
file was selected), readFile is not called.

```
    theFile = dlgFile.FileName
    If theFile <> "" Then readFile(theFile)
```

The readFile function is also defined in the code. This
Function procedure could have been combined with the
cmdOpen_Click procedure, thereby saving a few more lines. Here,
I separated these procedures for clarity.

The readFile function opens the selected file and reads it.
This example uses the new FileSystemObject model to read text.
The first three lines of readFile contain standard code that you
can use, without change, whenever you use FileSystemObject to
read text:

```
    Dim f As Object, stream As Object
    Set f = CreateObject("Scripting.FileSystemObject")
```

```
Set stream = f.OpenTextFile(theFile)
```

After executing these lines, the application now has a text-stream object, stream, that can be used to efficiently read all the text with a single statement.

```
Text1.Text = stream.ReadAll
```

Finally, the procedure closes the stream:

```
stream.Close
```

Understanding the Code, Part 2: Save File

The code for saving a file mirrors that for opening a file, with a few exceptions. In the cmdSave_Click procedure, the code first sets the FileName property. The FileName setting causes the name of the current file to become the default filename to save to, which is what the user would expect.

```
dlgFile.DialogTitle = "Save Text File"
dlgFile.FileName = theFile
```

The procedure then displays the dialog box by calling ShowSave rather than ShowOpen.

```
dlgFile.ShowSave
```

After ShowSave returns, the code gets the user's selected filename by copying the FileName property. This filename is then passed to saveFile, a function defined in the code.

```
theFile = dlgFile.FileName
If theFile <> "" Then saveFile(theFile)
```

This saveFile function uses the same first three lines as readFile for getting a stream object, with one difference. When opening a stream for writing, the function calls the CreateTextFile method, not OpenTextFile.

```
Set stream = f.CreateTextFile(theFile)
```

All that remains is to call the stream's Write method, to write out the contents of the text box, and then close the stream.

```
stream.Write Text1.Text
stream.Close
```

The File-System Controls

The three file-system controls (FileListBox, DirListBox, and DriveListBox) provide a maximum amount of flexibility with minimal programming. You can, for example, create a form with one of each of these controls, resulting in something like the dialog boxes shown earlier in the chapter. You can also create more complex forms that may involve selections from multiple directories.

The file controls are easy to use once you know how to deal with certain quirks. These quirks do not reflect perversity on the part of the designers so much as they reflect the complexity on the part of the file system. Much of the strangeness is due to a single property: FileName.

The icons for the three controls can be found in the standard Toolbox, as shown in Figure 7-5.

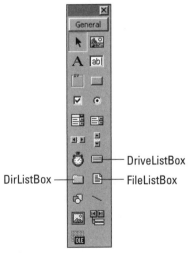

Figure 7-5   *The file-system controls in the Toolbox*

To use these controls, place one of each on a form. (In advanced applications, you may use multiples of each, but the simple case uses just one of each type.) You can then connect them by using properties and events as described in the next few sections. Figure 7-6 shows a conceptual picture of how the Drive and Path properties connect these three controls.

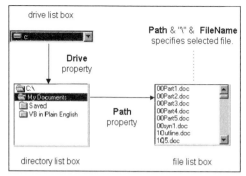

Figure 7-6 *How the file-system controls are connected*

The next few sections examine how to write code for each of these controls.

The Drive List Box

A drive list box is a drop-down list displaying a drive letter (such as c: or a:), along with a small drive icon. Figure 7-7 shows what it looks like.

Figure 7-7 *The drive list box at design time*

The end user can manipulate a drive list box at run time by selecting one of the system drives. To enable the list box to affect other controls, you need to write code.

A drive list box is used in conjunction with a directory list box (and often with a file list box as well). The code for the drive list box has to do one thing: respond to changes by causing the directory list box to change. The following code carries this out for a drive list box named `Drive1` and a directory list box named `Dir1`.

```
Private Sub Drive1_Change()
    Dir1.Path = Drive1.Drive
End Sub
```

The one property of the drive list box accessed here is the `Drive` property. This returns a string such as "a:", "b:", or "c:", which is passed to the `Path` property of the directory list box. `Path` is flexible: It can take a complete path name or a drive letter.

In this case, it gets a drive letter. The effect is similar to a DOS command such as CD C:.

The Drive property is not accessible at design time. If you want to set an initial value, use Form_Load. To set the Drive property, just specify an uppercase or lowercase drive letter. Only the first character of the string you pass is significant.

The Directory List Box

A directory list box is a hierarchical list of directories, with each line containing the folder (directory) icon. A vertical scrollbar appears if needed (see Figure 7-8).

Figure 7-8 *The directory list box at design time*

The end user can manipulate a directory list box by moving up and down through the hierarchy. By double-clicking a directory, the end user chooses it as the current directory. All the directories above this directory are displayed, as well as any child directories one level below it. Although the end user can move anywhere in the hierarchy, he or she is limited to the control's current drive; this drive is set in code or with the help of a drive list box, as shown in the previous section.

Most of the time, a directory list box is used in conjunction with a particular file list box. (There are exceptions: For example, in a file update utility, you might need two directory list boxes but only one file list box.) In most cases, the directory list box need only respond to the Change event. The appropriate response is to update the file list box.

The following code carries this out for a directory list box named Dir1 and a file list box named File1:

```
Private Sub Dir1_Change()
    File1.Path = Dir1.Path
End Sub
```

Both the file and directory list box have a `Path` property. The meaning of this property is roughly the same for both: `Path` specifies what directory gets displayed.

If you get the value of the `Path` property (for either a directory or file list box), it returns a complete path, including drive letter.

The File List Box

A file list box displays a set of files. This makes it recognizably different from a standard list box, which is always blank at design time. A vertical scrollbar appears if needed (see Figure 7-9).

Figure 7-9   *The file list box at design time*

The file list box is controlled by several properties, most notably the `Path`, `Pattern`, and `FileName` properties. The built-in functionality of the control enables the end user to scroll through the list, click, and double-click filenames within the current directory (controlled by the `Path` setting). To enable a file list box to do anything more than that, you need to write code.

`FileName` is the quirkiest property of all. If you *set* this property, you can use a string containing any of the following: drive letter, path name, filename, filename including path, or file pattern. The control responds as appropriate in each case. But if you *get* this property's value, it returns either an empty string (if no file is selected by the user) or a filename without path specification.

To respond to user choices in code, you generally need to get the filename along with the path specification. What complicates this is the `Path` setting's inconsistency. If the current directory is the root directory, the `Path` setting returned includes a backslash (\) at the end:

```
C:\
```

But if the current directory is any other directory, no backslash appears at the end of the string. For example:

```
C:\Novel\Saved
```

Therefore, to get the complete path to the selected file, you need to use code similar to the following. This code uses the `Right` intrinsic string function, which gets the specified number of characters from the end of the string.

```
If Right(File1.Path, 1) <> "\" Then s = "\"
theFile = File1.Path & s & File1.FileName
```

> **NOTE**
>
> The file list box and `CommonDialog` controls work differently in this regard. The `FileName` property of a dialog control contains the complete filename, including path. The `FileName` property of a file list box does not.

Sample Application: File Viewer Utility

The sample application in this section uses all three file controls, plus a text box, to let you view the contents of any file. To keep things simple, I've written this application so that it views the contents in text format. The use of text format also means that some of the code from the first half of the chapter can be reused.

You could make modifications yourself, so that by setting an option the user could view binary contents in hexadecimal format. To write this application, you'd need to use some of the file statements described in Chapter 18. For now, focus on text files, which are easier.

Drawing the Interface

The interface for the file viewer application has one each of the following: drive list box, directory list box, and file list box. It also has a text box. If you want to follow along, place and size the controls as shown in Figure 7-10. The text box is the blank control. Each of the other controls (drive, directory, and file list box) can be recognized by the contents they show at design time.

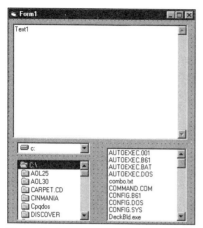

Figure 7-10   *The file viewer application*

Setting Initial Property Values

This is actually a very easy application to create. Only a few properties need to be set at design time. Table 7-2 lists the settings.

Table 7-2   *Property Settings for the File Viewer Application*

Control	Property	Set Value to
text box	Multiline	**True**
text box	Scrollbars	**2 - Vertical**
text box	Text	(blank)
form	Caption	**File Viewer**

Optionally, you could also set the names of the controls to something more suggestive than Text1, Drive1, Dir1, and File1. However, because there is only one of each, the default names can be used without confusion. Bear in mind, however, that all of these controls can be given meaningful names, just as with other controls.

Writing the Code

After the work of placing all the controls is done, the code is surprisingly simple. Only three procedures are used. The first two connect the three controls so that changes to Drive1 are reflected in Dir1, and changes to Dir1 are reflected to File1. (This creates a domino effect, incidentally.)

```
Private Sub Dir1_Change()
    File1.Path = Dir1.Path
End Sub


Private Sub Drive1_Change()
    Dir1.Path = Drive1.Drive
End Sub
```

The only thing that remains is to implement the behavior of the file list box. When the user double-clicks any item in the list box, two things happen. First, the FileName property gets set to the name of the selected file, and second, the DblClick event is generated. The desired response in the DblClick event procedure is to determine the complete filename, including path specification, and then use that filename to read in the file. Here is the complete procedure:

```
Private Sub File1_DblClick()
    Dim s As String, theFile As String
    Dim f As Object, stream As Object

    If Right(File1.Path, 1) <> "\" Then s = "\"
    theFile = File1.Path & s & File1.FileName

    Set f = CreateObject("Scripting.FileSystemObject")
    Set stream = f.OpenTextFile(theFile)
    Text1.Text = stream.ReadAll
    stream.Close
End Sub
```

The first thing the procedure does is declare a series of variables of specific type: strings s and theFile, and object variables f and stream. You can, as usual, omit these declarations (unless Option Explicit is in use). In this case, they get the Variant type, which would work fine. The declarations here are more for clarity than anything else.

The next two statements construct a complete filename, as described earlier in the chapter in the section "The File List Box."

```
If Right(File1.Path, 1) <> "\" Then s = "\"
theFile = File1.Path & s & File1.FileName
```

Finally, the procedure uses the same code used in the text editor application, earlier in this chapter, for reading a file. As always, you can use the traditional file-system keywords, if you choose, for opening and reading a text file. The FileSystemObject class is a new feature of Visual Basic 6.0. The traditional file-system keywords are still supported.

```
Set f = CreateObject("Scripting.FileSystemObject")
Set stream = f.OpenTextFile(theFile)
Text1.Text = stream.ReadAll
stream.Close
```

Enhancing the File Viewer Application

Another useful property of file list boxes, one that the application hasn't taken advantage of yet, is the Pattern property. Unlike some of the other properties, this one can be set at design time. For example, you can set Pattern to *.txt, to display only those files that have a .txt extension.

You can also create a second text box to allow the user to enter a pattern. This text box should be much smaller than the first.

The following procedure causes the file list box to reflect changes to this text box, as the user types a new file pattern.

```
Private Sub Text2_Change()
    File1.Pattern = Text2.Text
End Sub
```

This is just the beginning of what you can do with CommonDialog and file-system controls. If you understand the basic principles, it's not too difficult to write an application that enables the user to select a source directory and a destination directory, and then copies files. (You can even compare dates before deciding what to update, by using the FileDateTime statement described in Chapter 18.) Anything's possible. It's up to you.

7

OOPS, It's Basic!

8

"What's an object, anyway?"

— Countess Lovelace, machine-language
programmer

Object-oriented programming systems (OOPS) — what
a mouthful. Object orientation — what a concept.
OOPS is both fascinating and frustrating. You ask, "What
are these things called objects and what do they do?" Then
you get frustrated when you discover it's not obvious why
any of it's relevant.

But Basic is different from other languages. Never a language for purists, Basic has always had a lot of features that
were put in mainly because they were practical. From the
beginning, Microsoft's Object Basic (which ended up being
Visual Basic for Applications) had a strong utilitarian slant:
to let you get more work done by reaching out and manipulating parts of existing applications — that is to say, by using
objects.

Of course, object orientation is not limited to working
with applications. OOPS has its own rewards; it's a superior
way of packaging code to help give it (and I swallow hard as
I type this) *reusability*. But for most VB programmers, object
orientation is important mainly because it provides the basic
syntax for VBA and custom-control creation. The goal of this
chapter is to clarify this syntax, as well as the broader ideas.

What's New in VB6

In the area of OOPS, Visual Basic 5.0 was the big breakthrough. However, Visual Basic 6.0 makes some small but useful extensions to the object-oriented features of Version 5.0. If you're developing applications for a distributed-computer environment (that is, sharing code between computers on a network), the new ability of the CreateObject function is significant. This function now lets you allocate an object from code at a remote location.

Another new feature of Visual Basic 6.0 in the OOPS area is that you can now use user-defined types as property and method arguments and return values.

The Object Way

If you've come from C + +, you probably don't need a discussion on what objects are about (which is this section). You can skip ahead. If you stick around, I'll try to keep things as interesting as possible.

One of the fundamental concepts in Basic — indeed, in any programming language — is the concept of data type. You use strings for one purpose, integers for another, and floating-point for still another. When you get down to the essentials, what OOPS is all about is letting you extend the concept of data types.

Something like this has been possible for a long time with Basic's user-defined types, which consist of simple data members. User-defined types are passive. They are limited compared to what you can do with objects, as you'll see. By *user-defined type*, by the way, I am referring only to structures created with the Type...End Type syntax.

```
Type point
    Dim x As Single
    Dim y As Single
End Type
```

●—NOTE————————————————————————

Despite what I just said, the syntax for user-defined types has nothing in common with that for objects in Visual Basic. When VB added object-oriented features in Version 2.0 and later in 5.0, there was never any attempt to build on the existing syntax for user-defined types. That path was avoided in favor of taking a completely new approach. This is different from the approach of C++, for example, in which classes and objects are smooth, logical extensions of the old C struct type.

Object orientation goes beyond the passive user-defined type by making a single, daring leap. OOPS asks these questions: What if you could make data more active? What if you could give your data *behavior*? What if the data could respond to communication and/or events? The data structures that can perform this magic are called *objects*. An object is a data type with intelligence. It has built-in function code. It's very nearly a data structure that can think, feel, and act for itself.

(Do you begin to see the connection between objects and VBA? A spreadsheet, for example, is far more than passive data — it *does* things. It automatically updates columns, for example, in response to certain events. A spreadsheet is a classic object.)

This is easier to understand with an example. One of the most useful object types is the Collection class. A single Collection object can contain many other objects. It can also contain numbers, dates, and strings. A Collection object automatically grows and shrinks as it needs to, grabbing the space it needs for any amount of data. (This is not true of objects generally, by the way; the Collection object is specially designed with this behavior.)

Figure 8-1 shows a Collection object at work. You communicate with this object by using properties and methods, just as you do with controls.

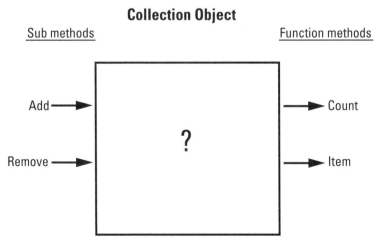

Collection Object

Sub methods   Function methods

Add ⟶   ⟶ Count

?

Remove ⟶   ⟶ Item

Figure 8-1 *Bird's-eye view of a Collection object*

One of the important points of Figure 8-1 is that the internal structure of a `Collection` object is completely unknown. This is characteristic of all object types, not just `Collection`. Furthermore, this is an essential difference between objects and user-defined types. A basic principle of OOPS is that you communicate with an object; you never look inside it. To use a crude analogy, you communicate with another human by using channels of communication, such as language and facial expression; you don't look inside his or her brain!

The hiding of an object's internal structure is called *encapsulation,* and it's one of the three basic pillars of object orientation. Don't worry about memorizing it; it's not important right now (unless you want to impress your programmer friends at cocktail parties).

Now, how do you communicate with an object? One way is through methods. The methods for a `Collection` object are `Add`, `Remove`, `Count`, and `Item`. The other way is by referring to a property. A property reference looks a lot like a data member of a user-defined type, but it can potentially be much more sophisticated. For example, the `Count` and `Item` methods could have been implemented as properties instead of methods. In the `Stack` class example later in this chapter, I in fact rewrite them as properties.

Properties, after all, are a very special feature of Visual Basic, used both with controls and with other kinds of objects. To promote ease of use, properties *look* like data members. But in reality, properties are more like methods. Property procedures (`Property Get` and `Property Let`) are very much in the spirit of object orientation. The user of an object can get and set values as much as they want, unconcerned with what goes on internally. With each access, however, the object has a chance to respond in an active way to the data transfer, doing whatever validation or housekeeping is needed.

I first introduced the `Collection` object type in Chapter 6. Here are some more examples. Don't worry about object creation with `Dim` and `New`; I explain that later.

```
Dim theBlob As New Collection

theBlob.Add Date + Time
theBlob.Add 54
Print theBlob.Count   ' Print number of items (=2)
```

For a Visual Basic programmer of any experience, one of the best ways to understand objects is to keep in mind that controls are a subset of objects. The only thing really new in this chapter so far is the idea that some objects exist in code only. These objects have properties and methods, but lack some of the other features of controls, such as displaying themselves on the screen.

To put things another way, a control is just a specialized object with the added feature of graphical display. (There's a little more to it, but that's the basic idea.) For example, a list box is similar to a `Collection` object, except that you can only add items of type `String`. A list box also has graphical representation and can respond to events.

The complete set of methods and properties of the `ListBox` class is large; for the sake of illustration, Figure 8-2 shows just a few.

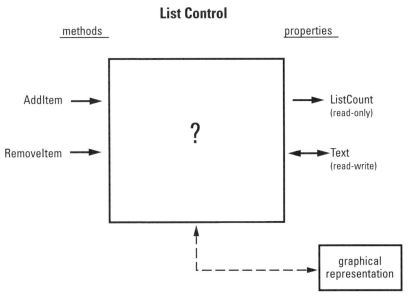

Figure 8-2 *Bird's-eye view of a list box*

Objects Versus Classes

It's impossible to deal with objects without, sooner or later, bumping into something called a *class*. This is a concept worth knowing.

Simply stated, a class is an object type. The phrases *class* and *object type* are almost interchangeable. *Class* is a better term, though, because it's less likely to be confused with *object*.

Is the distinction between class and object important? Yes! Here's why: Most of the characteristics of a data structure are fixed by its type. Two Integer variables, for example, may have different values, but they share a great deal in common: size, range, and data format, for example. In the same way, two Collection objects may have different contents, but they share a great deal in common as members of the same class (Collection).

To use objects, you first need a general type — this is the class. Once you have a class, you can create any number of objects of that type. The class is like the blueprint for a car, truck, or pre-fabricated house. You need only come up with the blueprint once. You can then create all the objects you need.

Of course, objects of the same type can have differences: They can have different property settings or different internal data. For example, the TextBox class enables you to create any number of text boxes. All text boxes have similar behavior and support the exact same list of properties and methods, but each can contain different data.

To summarize:

- You start with a class, which defines an object type. The class definition includes the list of properties and the code for all the methods.

- You declare one or more objects of that class. These objects automatically share many things in common, including behavior.

- After creating multiple objects of the same class, you can give them different settings. Objects of the same class share behavior and format, but they can have different states (that is, data).

If you're new to all this, the class/object distinction may take some getting used to. It's simple, though, if you keep reminding yourself that a class is just an object type.

If you're coming from the C++ world, Visual Basic does some things with classes that may surprise you. If you want to define a new class, you can't do it by using a statement like `Type...End Type`. There is no "Class" statement. Instead, as you'll see later, you must open a new module: a class module. A C++ programmer might find this strange, because VB classes don't depend on keywords to begin and end the class definition. Instead, a class is a unit within a project. You manage classes in the Project window, not in the language.

● NOTE

The Visual Basic online documentation sometimes uses the word *object* where strictly speaking, it would be more accurate to use *class*. For example, the topic on the `FileSystemObject` class is named "FileSystemObject Object."

Now Let's Make Some Objects

Enough preliminaries. You want to start creating objects. First, though, you have to choose an approach:

- The fast track: Use `Dim` and `New` together
- The long track: Allocate an object separately with `New`
- The longer track: Allocate an object from outside of Visual Basic by using `CreateObject`

Now let's get started. I'll take you on the fast track first.

The Fast Track: Dim and New Together

If a class is intrinsic (for example, `Collection`) or if it's one you've defined in your own project, you can take the fast track. Just declare an object this way:

```
Dim object As New class
```

The `New` keyword is what's new here. Notably, this is already a departure from ordinary data types such as `String`, `Integer`, or `Variant`, which never require you to use this additional `New` keyword (and in fact, do not support it). The reason for `New` will be clear after you read the next section.

You can combine object declarations with any number of other declarations on the same line. Remember that instead of using As *type*, you must use As New *class*. For example:

```
Dim myColl As New Collection

Dim myObj As New myClass   ' myClass defined in project

Dim Form2 As New Form1     ' Allocate a new form, based
                           '  on Form1.


Form2.Show   ' Load and show the form.


Dim co1 As New Collection, co2 As New Collection
Dim i As Integer, var1, myObj As New myClass
```

You can also you use the As New class syntax in similar kinds of declarations, such as Static, Public, and Private.

```
Public myColl As New Collection
Static v1, v2, myObj As New myClass
```

The use of New Form1 earlier merits some explanation. Whenever you design a form, you in effect create a new class that can be used to create objects. For example, you can create a simplistic form whose purpose is to reproduce itself. The form needs one control: a command button to let the user control the reproduction. Here is the code for the command button, Command1:

```
Private Sub Command1_Click()
    Dim localFormVar As New Form1
    localFormVar.Show
End Sub
```

What happens here is that no matter how many copies of the form are created, there is always a Form1 class — based on the form created at design time. The Form1 class is available even if the original copy is closed. The variable, localFormVar, is local to Command1_Click. Each form has its own copy of this variable, which acts as a pointer to the next form in the series. Try adding this code to a simple application. You'll see that during run time, you can create and close any number of forms!

One of the convenient things about using `Dim` and `New` together is that you can use them to efficiently create an array of objects. For example:

```
Dim objs(10) As New Collection
objs(1).Add "dog"
objs(1).Add "cat"
Debug.Print "objs(1) count is " & objs(1).Count
Objs(2).Add "house"
Debug.Print "objs(2) count is " & objs(2).Count
```

The Long Track, Using New

Starting with Visual Basic 2.0, the designers of VB did a strange thing. I don't know if I could have stopped them, but I had gone onto Visual C + + by then. There are some technical reasons for what they did; it has to do with the fact that Visual Basic objects were destined to break free of the language itself, to have the potential to become OLE and COM objects.

The strange thing is this: Declaring an object variable does not, by itself, allocate an object in memory! This is peculiar if you're used to C + + or most OOPS languages. Requiring a separate allocation step also makes objects out of step with primitive types. For example, you do create an integer merely by declaring an `Integer` variable, which can then be used right away. For example:

```
Dim i As Integer
Print "The value of i " & i
```

But that's not how object variables work. (In C + +, yes; in Visual Basic, no.) The general process in Visual Basic is this:

1. Create an object variable. (`Dim`.)

2. Allocate an object in memory with `New` or `CreateObject` (depending on the type of object), and then assign it to the object variable.

The previous section combined these steps into one, by using `Dim` and `New` together.

Okay, this may seem weird. What's the difference between an object and an object variable, for heaven's sake?! Well, an object variable only *refers* to an object, and then only after the object is assigned. The truth is that you never really see an object in code — not exactly, anyway. You get a reference to an object, assign that reference to an object variable, and then use the variable to communicate with the object. It's possible to have many different variables referring to the same object at the same time.

An object variable is really just a handle or a pointer to an object. For reasons difficult to explain here, this approach makes objects independent of the language itself. In theory, an object can be allocated anywhere: another process, another application, even another computer on a network. It doesn't matter. All your object variable does, as far as Visual Basic is concerned, is serve as a handle to some object created somewhere. The object itself is not tied to Visual Basic or even to your computer. Now, in the simplest case, you are going to create and use objects only within your own application. You don't care about distributed COM, and all that other neuron-roasting-brain-grinding stuff. But the object syntax is not made to accommodate the simple case here. It's made to accommodate the bigger vision. The attitude is that if you want to be object-oriented, you've got to do a little extra work.

All you can do, then, is understand that an extra step is required and then get used to it. A couple of examples should help. Consider the following lines of code:

```
Dim objVar1 As Object, objVar2 As Object
Set objVar1 = New myClass
Set objVar2 = objVar1
```

Another bit of object strangeness seen here is that you can never assign directly to an object variable. You must use the Set keyword at the beginning of the assignment. There's a good reason for this rule: It eliminates all confusion with default property assignments, which look like direct assignments to an object (see Chapter 3).

In any case, Figure 8-3 shows what happens. The first line declares two object variables but does not use New. Consequently, the object variables are, at first, not initialized to anything and are not yet usable. The Set keyword then comes to the rescue. But note that only one object is created. It is one object with two names. In this scenario, objVar2 becomes an alias for objVar1 (see Figure 8-3).

An analogy would be a man with two titles, such as The President and Mr. Roosevelt. You can't do something to Mr. Roosevelt without it affecting The President, and vice versa. They are not separate entities.

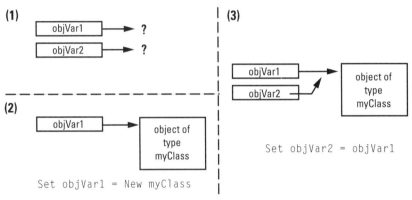

Figure 8-3 *One object, two object variables*

Let's move on to a better example. Here, New is used twice. Now, instead of objVar2 getting assigned to objVar1, it gets a reference to a new object of its own.

```
Dim objVar1 As Object, objVar2 As Object
Set objVar1 = New myClass
Set objVar2 = New myClass
```

Figure 8-4 tells the story. Each use of New creates a separate object. The Set keyword associates each of these objects with an object variable (the first with objVar1, the second with objVar2). These two objects are distinct. Although they might be initialized to the same property settings, they retain their independence. Changes made through objVar1 won't affect changes made through objVar2, and vice versa. They are separate, whether or not they are equal.

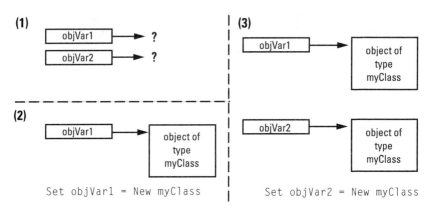

Figure 8-4 *Two objects*

In essence, an object variable does not *contain* an object; it can *refer* to an object but first must be explicitly associated with that object. An object variable is what, in C + + terms, would be called a *reference variable*. (It has much in common with a pointer.) There are two main ideas to keep in mind about object variables:

- An object variable cannot be used until it's associated with an object, which must be explicitly allocated in memory. If the class is an intrinsic type or defined in the project, the allocation is performed by New.

- It is possible for more than one object variable to refer to the same object in memory.

●─NOTE ─────────────────────────────────────

Like other types of data, object variables do not need to be explicitly declared. You can implicitly declare them, because Variant supports the Object type as one of its data formats. So you can skip the step of using Dim to declare the object variable. However, you can't skip the step of allocating the object and assigning it to the variable. This means you'll have to use either a Dim statement or a Set statement, or both.

The Longer Track, Using CreateObject

If a class is not defined either in the current project or in the Visual Basic environment, you cannot use New to allocate an object of that class. You must instead use the CreateObject function.

Here's a quick example of how it works. I've used this in previous chapters, by the way.

```
Dim fso As Object
Set fso = CreateObject("Scripting.FileSystemObject")
```

Now, there's a new bit of strangeness here. The
FileSystemObject class is provided as part of the Visual Basic
package. Why isn't it considered an intrinsic class?

You'll just have to get used to the fact that certain classes
require the use of CreateObject. This includes the latest code-
only classes provided with Visual Basic 6.0, including
FileSystemObject and Dictionary. These are considered extended, rather than intrinsic, classes. (In theory, at least, they are provided by a "Scripting" server.)

● — **NOTE** ———————————————————————————————

If you add class references to a project by choosing the References
command or Components command from the Project menu, objects of
downloaded classes can be allocated directly with New.

One drawback of CreateObject is that you cannot combine it
with a Dim statement. A separate allocation step is always
required, as shown in the previous example. (But note that object
variables can be implicitly declared just like other variables, effectively skipping the Dim step.)

The CreateObject function opens up a new world of possibilities. The class can come from outside of the Visual Basic environment and your own project code. This means it can come from
anywhere: an application, a DLL file, even another computer on
the network.

The syntax of CreateObject recognizes the existence of an
OLE server — that is to say, the application or DLL providing the
object's class definition.

```
Set myObjVar = CreateObject("appname.class")
```

Here are some more examples, using object variables file,
dict, and xlss.

```
Set file = CreateObject("Scripting.FileSystemObject")
Set dict = CreateObject("Scripting.Dictionary")
Set xlss = CreateObject("Excel.Sheet")
```

In Visual Basic 6.0, CreateObject has been enhanced to recognize a second, optional argument. This argument is a string specifying the location of a remote computer (that is, another computer on the network). For a network share called "\\theServer\public", you'd use this code:

```
Set obj = CreateObject("appname.class", "theServer")
```

●—NOTE

There is yet another way of getting a reference to an object: the GetObject function. This does not allocate a new object, but loads or gets a reference to an existing object. See Chapter 18 for more details.

Defining a New Class Within a Project

The easiest way to define a new class is to add a class module to your project. There are other ways to define classes, but use of a class module is the simplest way to get started. Once you understand the basic principles, it's easy to progress to more sophisticated kinds of class definitions.

Remember that Visual Basic has no "Class" statement. Nor do you have to worry about problems such as forward references, type information, linking, or all those other messy problems that give C++ people headaches. All these things are taken care of automatically, through VB project organization. The only drawback to this approach is that each class definition is saved in its own file. If you want to define many classes, you have to add many files. This won't be an issue in simple cases, however.

Overview of Class Modules

Defining a new class within Visual Basic is pretty simple. Except in the case of property procedures (more about that in a moment), you don't even have to learn any new syntax. Basically, this is the process:

1. Open a new class module by choosing Add Module from the View menu. Once the module is open, assign it the class name.

2. For each method you want to define, write a Sub or Function procedure. All procedures in a class module

become method definitions, unless you explicitly declare them `Private` or `Friend`.

3. For each property you want to define, you can either declare a `Public` form variable or create a pair of `Property Get` and `Property Let` procedures.

This is an incredibly simple procedure, considering how much flexibility it provides.

Keep in mind that class modules are not like standard code modules, despite their similarity. You define a class once and then use it to create any number of objects. (This is why I've emphasized the class/object distinction.) When you write a class module, you are drawing up the blueprint for an object. Once completed, you can use that blueprint any number of times. The data members of a class are object data fields, and the procedures are methods that can manipulate those fields.

Class Example: A Stack Class

I'll use a `Stack` class as an example because it is both easy to implement — building on an existing class (`Collection`) — and useful.

A stack is similar to a collection except that it has a last-in-first-out (LIFO) mechanism. You add an item by pushing it onto the top of the stack; you can also, at any time, pop an item off the top. The catch is that whenever you pop off an item, you get the last item that was pushed. A good analogy is a stack of dishes: you put and take items only off the top.

The first step in designing is to decide what properties and methods to support. Figure 8-5 shows a simple design for the `Stack` class. There are just two methods and two properties, although you can certainly add more later on.

As with all classes, the internal structure is unknown and inaccessible to the user of the class. This is a great benefit, because once the class is tested, debugged, and works properly, you can give it to anyone and it will be trouble free. Because the internals are inaccessible, no one can make faulty assumptions about how the code works (assumptions that might be violated by the next update of the component).

In Figure 8-5, arrows show the direction of control and data flow. The Push method, which puts a value on top of the stack, does not return a value. The Pop method gets the top item on the stack and therefore does return a value.

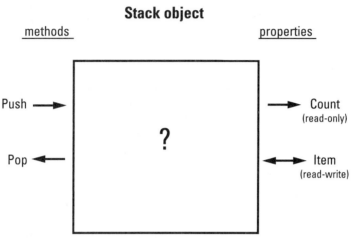

Figure 8-5 *A design for a Stack class*

Creating the Class Module for Stack

This step couldn't be simpler. Just open a class module by doing the following:

1. Open the View menu.
2. Choose Add Class Module.

Only one thing remains to do in creating the class: You must name it. When the class module is opened, you'll see that the Properties window displays three properties. One of these is the Name property. Set this to the name of the class — in this case, Stack. Ignore the other items in the Properties window for now. These are not the same as the properties you'll define in the code.

Another thing you should do is open the File menu and save the class under a meaningful filename such as Stack.cls. (By convention, .cls is the filename extension for class modules.)

Adding the Push and Pop Methods

Within a class module, any procedure declared as Public defines
a method. (All procedures are Public by default.) Methods apply
to individual objects. When a method is called, it will be used to
manipulate or communicate with a Stack object.

The following code declares an internal, private data member
and also defines the two methods, Push and Pop.

```
Private theColl As New Collection

Sub Push (item As Variant)
    theColl.Add item
End Sub

Function Pop() As Variant
    Dim i As Integer
    i = theColl.Count
    If i > 0 Then
        Pop = theColl.item(i)
        theColl.Remove i
    Else
        Pop = Null
    End If
End Function
```

The effect of this code is that at run time, each and every
Stack object will get its own private copy of the data member
(theColl) and will also support the Push and Pop methods. (For
clarity, you could define the procedures as Public, but they are
public by default.)

The Pop method has a modest amount of error checking. It
doesn't pop items off the stack if there are none left. It is possible
to add more comprehensive error handling here: displaying an
error message with MsgBox, for example. This is left as an exercise.

Adding the Count Property

As I mentioned earlier, there are two ways to create a property. The simplest way is to declare a public data item:

```
Public Count As Integer
```

This approach gives the user of a Stack object direct access to a data member. That creates problems in this case. One problem is that Count ought to be read-only. The other problem is that Count should reflect the up-to-the-moment condition of the stack rather than just be a passive piece of data.

The way to solve these problems is by writing Property Get and/or Property Let procedures. You can write one or the other or both, depending on whether a property is read-only, write-only, or read-write. Here's what these procedures do:

- Property Get *propertyname* is called when the user of the object attempts to get the value. The procedure must return the current value to the object user.

- Property Let *propertyname* is called when the user of the object sets a new value.

(The name Let comes from the ancient Let keyword, still supported in Basic, that can be used in assignments. It has long since become unnecessary, of course.)

Remember that Count is read-only. Therefore, you write a Property Get procedure for Count but not a Property Let procedure. Here is what the skeleton looks like:

```
Property Get Count() As Integer

End Property
```

The Integer keyword determines the property's type, and Count is the name. As before, you can insert the Public keyword at the beginning of the first line, but this is optional and largely unnecessary (because Public is the default).

Just as with a function procedure, a Property Get procedure must return a value, and it does this by assigning to the name. Here's the complete version of the procedure. It gets the Count return value from the collection (theColl) and passes that along.

```
Property Get Count() As Integer
```

```
      Count = theColl.Count
End Property
```

Wow, that was easy! It hardly seems to have needed all the build-up, did it?

How to Add Other Properties

Every property will have different specifics, but here's the general process for adding a property. I assume that you've already decided on the property name and type.

First, from within the class module, create `Property Get` and `Property Let` procedures. If you don't remember the syntax, the easiest thing to do is to open the Tools menu and choose the Add Procedure command. The dialog shown in Figure 8-6 appears.

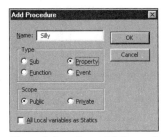

Figure 8-6   *The Add Procedure dialog*

Type the property name as the procedure name. In the first option-button group, select `Property`. Leave the second option-button group set to `Public`, and then press OK.

As an example, if you enter the name `Silly`, the command generates the following code:

```
Public Property Get Silly() As Variant

End Property



Public Property Let Silly(ByVal vNewValue As Variant)

End Property
```

Instead of using `Silly`, of course, use whatever name you want for your property.

The code that's generated serves as your basic skeleton. Several things still remain to do to fix up the code, however:

1. If you want a type other than `Variant`, replace the `Variant` keyword in each procedure definition. The type used in the two procedures must match exactly. While you're at it, you can also replace the `vNewValue` argument name by something you like better.

2. The `Property Get` procedure must return a value at some point, using the property name. You will need a statement like the following:

   ```
   Silly = value_of_silly
   ```

3. Typically, the actual property data is stored in some private data member. If you use this approach, you must choose a name that does not conflict with the property name itself. In this case, you might choose `m_Silly`. Declare this in the Declarations section as `Dim` or `Private`.

4. Add any other code that's appropriate to the property.

For example, after following all these steps, you might end up with code similar to the following. This is admittedly a simple example; in your own code, you can choose to carry out a lot more actions in response to either getting or setting the property. But this is the minimum you'd normally use.

```
Private m_Silly As Long

Public Property Get Silly() As Long
    Silly = m_Silly
End Property

Public Property Let Silly(ByVal newval As Long)
    m_Silly = newval
End Property
```

This code creates a read-write property named `Silly`, of type `Long`. The actual data gets stored in a private data member named m_Silly. The users of the class never see m_Silly. All they know is that they assign or get the value of a property named Silly. For example:

```
Dim stk As New Stack
stk.Silly = 1          ' Set Silly to 1.
Debug.Print stk.Silly  ' Print out this value.
```

The code used here to implement Silly is pretty typical. Right now, it's limited; Silly functions merely as a data field. But if you choose, you could add additional code to Property Get and Property Let to take other actions, such as checking for valid range, allocating memory, updating a list — whatever would make sense for the particular property.

One final tip: If you want to make a property read-only, delete the Property Let procedure. If you want to make it write-only, delete Property Get.

Testing and Using the Stack Class

Once the completed class module is part of your project, any other form or module in the project can create any number of objects of that class. In this case, you'll be able to create any number of Stack objects.

To test this out, return to Form1 in your project (or whatever the name of the form is), and then add this code:

```
Private Sub Form_Load()
    Dim myStack As New Stack
    Dim anotherStack As New Stack

    myStack.Push 3.141592
    myStack.Push "Isn't this great?"
    myStack.Push Date + Time
    MsgBox "The last item pushed was " & myStack.Pop
    MsgBox "Next-to-last pushed was " & myStack.Pop

    anotherStack.Push 27
    MsgBox "The size of anotherStack is " & _
        anotherStack.Count
End Sub
```

Because the Stack class is defined within a project, you can use it in a Dim statement with As New. You can also use the longer technique described earlier:

```
Dim anotherStack As Object
Set anotherStack = New Stack
```

In addition to taking longer to type in, this version of the code is slightly less efficient. Because the class of anotherStack is not set during its declaration, references using anotherStack must be late-bound. (If you don't understand that concept right now, don't worry. I explain it in much more detail in the section "Early Binding, Late Binding, and Polymorphism.")

Property Declaration for Experts

Visual Basic supports many variations in property declarations. Starting with Version 6.0, you can create properties of a user-defined type or array type.

But perhaps the most innovative aspect of properties is the ability to use arguments. At first glance, this may strike you as odd: How can properties have arguments? An argument to a property looks very much like an array reference, and this is generally how they are used.

For example, you can use an argument as an index into a collection. Although Item is implemented as a method in the Collection class, it would be nice to implement it as a property in the Stack class. Users of the class could then assign a new value directly to an item.

```
aStack.Item(2) = n    ' Assign n to the second item.
```

Here the number 2 is an argument to the Item property. To enable the new Item property to receive this argument, you need to utilize the full syntax for property declarations. This syntax is shown here:

```
Property Get propertyname (args) As type
End Property


Property Let propertyname (args, ByVal newval As type)
End Property
```

The optional *args* item includes any number of arguments, separated by commas if there is more than one. Note that the new-value argument (*newval*) appears in the argument list as usual, but it appears after the other arguments, if any.

Here is example code that implements the Item property for the Stack class:

```
Public Property Get Item(ByVal index As Long) _
 As Variant
    Item = theColl.Item(index)
End Property

Public Property Let Item(ByVal index As Long, _
 ByVal newval As Variant)
    theColl.Add newval, , index
    theColl.Remove index + 1
End Property
```

Remember that in the Collection class, Item is a method, not a property, so you can't assign to it. The Property Let procedure must employ some sleight of hand: It inserts the new value at the requested position and deletes the old. This simulates a direct change to an element. The user of the object has no idea that this juggling is going on and doesn't need to know.

The only problem with this solution is that it is not the most efficient. If instead the Stack class were based on the new Dictionary class described in Chapter 16, you could provide a more efficient solution. This is left as an exercise. (Tip: A Dictionary object would need to be declared as a module-level variable and then allocated in Class_Initialize by calling the CreateObject function.)

Supporting the For Each Statement

The Stack class is designed to act as a collection class, and for the most part, it does. However, for a class to be a fully functional collection class in VB, it should work with the For Each statement. This requires that the class have an *enumerator*: a special object that the For Each statement uses to cycle through a group. Unfortunately, Visual Basic does not offer support for writing your own enumerator from scratch. You can, however, supply the enumerator of an embedded object such as theColl in the Stack class.

To supply an enumerator for any class, carry out the following steps. Except where otherwise noted, you must carry out these steps exactly.

1. Add the following procedure to your class module. In place of theColl, you can give the name of a collection-class object contained in your own class. Otherwise, the code should be exactly as shown.

```
Public Function NewEnum() As Iunknown
    Set NewEnum = theColl.[_NewEnum]
End Function
```

2. From the Tools menu, choose the Procedure Attributes command. When a dialog box appears, enter **NewEnum** as the procedure name, and click Advanced.

3. In the Procedure ID text box, enter −4.

4. Check the box labeled "Hide this member" and then click OK.

After all these steps are completed, you'll be able to write code that uses For Each to cycle through the group (as well as the standard For statement, which is always usable). For example:

```
For Each thing In mystack
    Debug.Print thing
Next
```

Advanced Features of Visual Basic OOPS

Object-oriented purists will object that even in Versions 5 and 6, Visual Basic still lacks some important features. The truth is that although Visual Basic isn't a complete object-oriented language, it's getting closer.

Inheritance and Derived Classes

The major feature that Visual Basic still lacks is something called *inheritance* or *derived classes*. This is a nice feature, although in some quarters it's still debated whether or not it's essential to a truly object-oriented universe.

Inheritance enables you to take an existing class (written by you or someone else, it doesn't matter), add some new features, and then use it yourself or pass it along to others. The theory is that as you derive a class and add features to it, you're making a more specialized version of the old class. An example would be the Stack class developed earlier in this chapter, which can be considered a more specialized version of a Collection class.

If you want to wax poetic, you can compare inheritance to evolution, in which a single-celled organism evolves into a great variety of more specialized creatures. The benefit of this system is that once a major problem is solved, you don't have to solve it again. In the case of the simple organism, for example, the basic problem of how to build and decode a DNA molecule has been solved once and for all. The more specialized creatures don't have to evolve that ability again; they focus on developing advanced skills. There's a hierarchy, but it's a friendly one (see Figure 8-7).

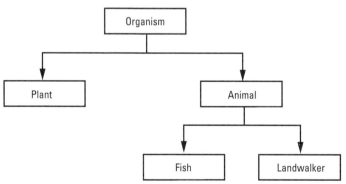

Figure 8-7   *An inheritance hierarchy*

The idea of inheritance in programming code is similar: The base type provides common functionality. When you write a derived class you can focus, in theory, on the specialized features that build upon the original functionality. You inherit all the old capabilities.

Inheritance sounds great. But the truth is that you can get most of the same benefits other ways. If you've been following this chapter, you've already seen how I've simulated inheritance by containing a `Collection` object inside the `Stack` class. Property and method calls can be passed along to the embedded `Collection` object, giving the same benefits you'd get if you derived the `Stack` class from `Collection`.

So inheritance is not as unique a feature as it seems at first. All that matters is that an existing class is being reused; ultimately it doesn't matter if you derive a new class from the old class, or just contain an object of that class. There's a drawback to object containment, however: Unlike inheritance, this approach requires you to explicitly pass along each and every method and property call you want to support (see Figure 8-8). This is extra work. With true inheritance, you'd get it for free: For example, a `Stack` object would automatically get all the same properties and methods as a `Collection` object. You'd only have to write code for the new methods, `Push` and `Pop`. What this all comes down to is a matter of convenience.

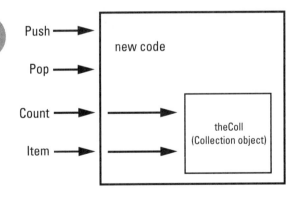

Stack object

Figure 8-8 *Object embedding with a class module*

If the Visual Basic team has plans to support inheritance in the future, I don't think they've announced any promises to that effect (at least not at the time of this writing). It's a nice, convenient feature, so users may keep asking for it. On the other hand, inheritance is not supported in the COM world, so there may be no rush to include it in VB. The development priorities in VB have always been to support the emerging systems architecture for Windows.

In C + +, the most important aspect of inheritance is that it lays a foundation for *polymorphism*. Visual Basic, however, supports polymorphism in a way that does not depend on inheritance. I discuss polymorphism next.

Early Binding, Late Binding, and Polymorphism

The third major aspect of object orientation (after encapsulation and inheritance) is *polymorphism* — the capability of communicating with an object without knowing its type. Visual Basic fully supports polymorphism. To get a grasp on what this multi-syllabic monster of a word means, you need to understand early and late binding.

Binding is the process of hooking up a reference to a procedure (such as obj.Add) to the procedure's actual address. In the simple case, *early binding,* the address of a method call is known at design time, well before the code is ever run. For example:

```
Dim obj As New Collection

obj.Add "Big bad tiger."
```

In this case, the object variable obj can only refer to an object of the Collection class. So when the Add method is called, the code uses the address of the Add method defined for Collection. This is simple. The same considerations apply to the following code:

```
Dim obj As Collection
Set obj = New Collection

obj.Add "Big bad tiger."
```

Once again, the variable obj is limited to use with Collection objects, so calls to methods are early bound. But consider this code, which declares obj to have type Object:

```
Dim obj As Object
Set obj = New Collection
```

```
obj.Add "Big bad tiger."
```

Declaring `obj` with type `Object` changes everything. Because `obj` is declared with type `Object`, it can refer to different types of objects at different times. You might point out that the type is obvious in this example, because it's plain to see that `obj` is assigned a `Collection` object. But Visual Basic cannot rely on this fact: There is no guarantee that the actual type of `obj` will always be so unambiguous. For example, at run time, `obj` might be assigned a different class of object at random:

```
Dim obj As Object
n = Int(Rnd(0) * 2)
If n = 0 Then
    Set obj = New Collection
Else
    Set obj = New myCollectionClass
End If
```

```
obj.Add "Big bad tiger."
```

With this code, the question of how to execute the call `obj.Add` is troublesome. Does Visual Basic call the version of `Add` defined in the `Collection` class or the version defined in `myCollectionClass`? Moreover, what happens if the latter doesn't exist — what if `myCollectionClass` doesn't define an `Add` method at all, at least not one that takes a single string argument?

The answer is that in this situation, Visual Basic uses *late binding*. The address of the call to `obj.Add` is not determined until run time. At that point, the actual type of `obj` will be known. The method name, `Add`, is then compared to the list of methods and properties actually supported in the class (`Collection` or `myCollectionClass`, as the case may be). If, at that point, `Add` is not supported or the numbers or types of the arguments do not match, a run-time error is generated.

Late binding has some clear drawbacks:

- It is less efficient. Rather than simply calling a method whose address is known, a list of methods must be sequentially searched to find the method name (`Add`). Although, at

run time, an index to a symbol table is used rather than the
actual character string, having to search a table is still far
less efficient than calling a procedure directly.

• It is less reliable. You could get the following error at run
  time: "Object doesn't support this property or method."
  This results in abrupt termination of the program (although
  On Error GoTo can be used to mitigate the problem).

Clearly, then, you want to avoid using late binding where possible. When given a choice, declare an object variable by using an
intrinsic class rather than the more general Object type.

```
Dim obj As Collection
Set obj = New Collection
```

Sometimes late binding is desirable, however. This is where
polymorphism comes in. Suppose you have a group of controls,
and you want to write code that hides each control. Here is a version that uses early binding:

```
Dim ctrl1 As New ListBox
Dim ctrl2 As New CommandButton
Dim ctrl3 As New Picture

ctrl1.Visible = False
ctrl2.Visible = False
ctrl3.Visible = False
```

Here, the address of each call to the Property Let Visible
procedure is well known, because the types of ctrl1, ctrl2,
ctrl3 are all known. Each call to this procedure is bound to a different class: ListBox, CommandButton, or Picture.

But suppose that instead of using this approach, you create
and initialize an array of object variables:

```
Dim ctrls(3) As Object
```

Each element of ctrls, it is assumed, is somehow initialized
by being assigned some object. Now you can set Visible for every
object in the array by using this code:

```
For Each item In ctrls
    item.Visible = False
Next
```

The beauty of this approach is that in these three lines, the type of each item in the array, `ctrls`, does not have to be known. You can even add new objects in the future — objects whose class does not yet exist — and this code will continue to run perfectly well. For this code to work, the new classes don't even have to consist of controls; they can be any objects whose class supports `Visible` as a `Boolean` property.

The difference in the two approaches can be shown visually. Figure 8-9 illustrates early binding. Each call to `Property Let Visible` is fixed for all time as soon as the program is compiled. Each call is "hard coded," fixed with regard to memory address.

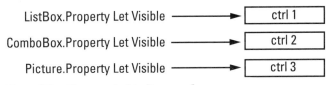

Figure 8-9   *How early binding works*

Figure 8-10 illustrates late binding and polymorphism. With this approach, there is no limit to the different classes that can be used, either now or in the future.

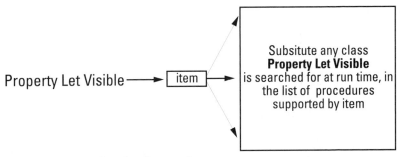

Figure 8-10   *How late binding works*

This use of late binding is an example of polymorphism. The word means "many shaped," although this definition may not clarify much. What's important about polymorphism is that it adds a capability not possible in traditional programming. Polymorphism really means that although a method or a property has a general meaning, the decision about how to implement it is infinitely flexible. This capability is significant because it permits program decentralization. New types of objects can be developed in the future and then plugged into an existing structure.

● **NOTE**

Many people feel that true polymorphism requires interfaces, as described in the next chapter.

Windows, for example, is itself highly polymorphic. If it were not, the developers of Windows would have had to enumerate ahead of time all the different applications that could run under Windows. It would then be impossible to develop new applications in the future, because each new application provides its own window class for Windows to call. Polymorphism in Windows means that new classes can be added at any time.

Interfaces

If you've come from the C++ or Object Pascal world, you may have noted that Visual Basic's use of late binding is rather free-wheeling and chaotic. It is all too easy to make calls that can result in a run-time error. To write high-quality code, it then becomes necessary to make heavy use of error handling (On Error GoTo) or else test your applications much more thoroughly. In addition, requiring a search of the symbol table is less efficient than C++'s approach, which uses an indirect call but doesn't require a search of names in a table.

What would be nice is an approach that permitted late binding (and therefore polymorphism) under controlled circumstances. Specifically, how can you call a certain method or access a property, knowing ahead of time that this item is supported and that the type information is correct?

Visual Basic provides a way of doing this through the use of *interfaces*. Simply put, an interface is a list of services — methods and/or properties — that a class agrees to support. When you get any object of any class that supports an interface, you know that you can use any of these same methods and properties. The interface itself does not provide executable code; it just declares a list of methods and properties, including type information (what type of arguments each method accepts).

NOTE

There are some terminology issues here. Many, or even most, definitions of polymorphism require that an interface or something like it is used. True polymorphism, to an OOPS devotee, is only possible when the meaning and type of a method are well defined.

Also note that *implementing* an interface means that a class provides definitions for all the methods and property procedures declared in that interface.

Interfaces have a significance beyond the Visual Basic environment. The interface mechanism supported by Visual Basic is fully compatible with interfaces used in the Component Object Model (COM), a binary standard for objects that communicate with each other throughout a system. This means that objects created with different programming tools — Visual Basic, Visual C++, or the Windows SDK — can all use the COM specification for communicating with each other. The objects can reside in separate processes. With Distributed COM, they can even reside on separate computers. Unlike DDE, COM interfaces are structured, well behaved, and utilize a great deal of type information.

You can use Visual Basic to do it all: define interfaces, implement interfaces in your classes, and write code that calls interface methods and properties. At each stage, the support for interfaces is compatible with COM.

To take an example, suppose that someone has defined an interface called IStat. (By convention, an interface has an initial capital "I" in its name.) Suppose also that IStat defines the following three methods:

- getClassName, which returns a string
- getStringSummary, which returns a string
- getStatusNum, which returns an integer

Given this interface, you could write the following procedure, knowing that any object of type IStat will support these methods.

```
Sub reportStatus(objstat As IStat)
    Dim s As String
    s = "Class: " & objstat.getClassName & Chr(13)
    s = s & "Value: " & objstat.getStringSummary
```

```
    Debug.Print objstat.getStatusNum
    MsgBox s
End Sub
```

In this example, IStat looks like a class, but actually, the obj-
stat argument will accept any object of any class that implements
IStat. Because the procedure can only get such an object, you are
guaranteed that the object supports all the IStat methods. Each
class can implement the IStat methods with different code, but
support for all the methods is ensured.

For information on defining and implementing interfaces, see
Chapter 16.

Other Kinds of Classes

Once you understand how to create code modules, it is not very
difficult to define other kinds of classes. You can take several
routes:

- A class module is a unit within a project. You can reuse it
  by adding it to each project that needs it. One slight drawback of class modules is that if they are reused, the same
  code is copied into each EXE that uses it, potentially taking
  up more space on the hard disk and also in memory.

- ActiveX components, of which there are several types, are
  all independent projects that provide class information to
  other applications at run time. In all cases, the links to
  ActiveX components are added through the References or
  Components command on the Project menu.

- An ActiveX DLL is a library providing class and type information to applications at run time.

- An ActiveX EXE is primarily an independent application,
  but it has the added feature of being able to expose some
  of its application objects to other applications. Word, Excel,
  and Access are all examples of this kind of component.
  (Note that Microsoft does not discourage other software
  vendors from developing ActiveX components; quite the
  opposite. Look how easy it is to develop components in
  Visual Basic.)

- An ActiveX document is an application that is packaged so it can be run in a Web page. The output of the project is a file with a .vbd extension that can be run, locally or remote, by Internet Explorer.

- For most VB programmers, the most interesting ActiveX component of all is the ActiveX Control. This is the custom-control format that replaces the old OLE and VBX formats. An ActiveX Control project contains one or more control classes in a format similar to DLL (the file must be present at run time). But control classes have the additional features of recognizing events and displaying themselves. The next chapter introduces this amazing technology.

8

Writing Controls 101

9

*"Stand back. The learner is about to become
the master."*

— Bruce Wee to Master Fu Tile

For many people, the most exciting thing about Visual
Basic 5.0 was creating custom (ActiveX) controls
without leaving VB. Certainly this feature has great appeal.
You create a blueprint for a new control that can be drawn,
resized, and manipulated in the Visual Basic environment as
often as a programmer wants.

Some of these people got into the control-writing experience only to find out that it was a little daunting. Although the
custom-control (ActiveX) interface is designed to be easy in
some respects, certain things make the process more complex:

- There are some pitfalls in getting started, which I
  steer you around in this chapter.

- Although a completely generic control — a control that
  does nothing — is trivial to create, additional complex-
  ities creep in once you start to add properties.

This chapter deals with two of the easier tasks in creating a control: painting the control and adding events. The next chapter moves on to the more complex subject of properties, along with other matters such as creating the control's icon.

What's New in VB6

The ability to create ActiveX controls was introduced in Visual Basic 5.0, and most of this chapter concerns features found in that version. However, Version 6.0 adds the option of creating windowless controls, also called *lightweight controls*.

This is a useful option to have. As explained in Chapter 3, not all lightweight controls are alike. They can block out other background graphics and can respond to Click events, as does the Image control. Or they can be transparent, melding in with the rest of their container's background.

Lightweight controls are relatively less solid than standard controls. Standard controls that overlap a lightweight control automatically appear on top of the lightweight control. Lightweight controls act as part of the background graphics of their container. However, lightweight controls also use up less system resources and therefore contribute to faster loading of an application.

9 Getting Starting with ActiveX Controls

To begin with, you probably want to jump in by opening a new project and selecting the option ActiveX Control. This seems logical, but do not — I repeat, *do not* — do this.

Instead, start with a Standard EXE project. You can even use one you're working on now. It's usually best, though, to start a new Standard EXE project and use this exclusively for writing, developing, and testing the control. After the control is finished and you are ready to release Version 1.0, you can place it in an ActiveX Control project.

Figure 9-1 illustrates the relationship between modules and projects. Two sample projects appear in this example. The Standard EXE project has several modules — a form, a class module, and a custom control. The ActiveX Control project has two modules of its own, both of which are control classes. Each project can have any number of modules. After a module is developed and tested in a Standard EXE project, you can then share it with an ActiveX Control project. In this case, one module is shared: a control class.

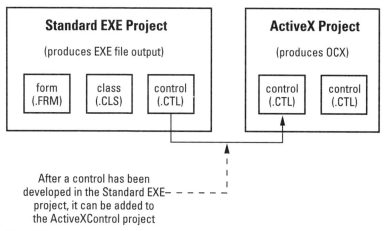

Figure 9-1   *Project organization and custom controls*

By far the best approach is to develop a control inside a Standard EXE project. This enables you to easily test and revise the control, because you are able to quickly switch between the control module (.ctl file) and a sample form that uses it. Later, use the finished source code in an ActiveX Control project. This type of project produces an OCX file, similar to a DLL, which can be used by any number of projects.

Here is a general summary of the process:

1. Open a Standard EXE project.

2. Once the new project is opened, open the Project menu and choose Add User Control. You're given several module types to select from; again, choose User Control.

3. When you're ready to test the control, switch back to the form (Form1) and draw a sample control on the form.

Only after the control is finished and tested should you create an ActiveX Control project. You then simply add the .ctl file you already created for the EXE project.

A First Control: the BigX

If you've read the previous section, you know you should start by opening a Standard EXE project and then choosing Add User Control from the Project menu. Once the control module is opened, use the Properties window to assign the name: in this case, BigX. Done? Great, you're ready to design the control.

There's one other point to keep in mind: You're going to have to close the control's designer window fairly often. Therefore, don't maximize the designer window. Keep windows overlapping so they can be easily closed. If the window is already maximized, get back access to all the windows by choosing Cascade from the Window menu. You have to close the control's designer window before you can add the control to a form.

(By the way, "designer window" is not a storefront on Rodeo Drive or Park Avenue, despite the sound of the phrase.)

In the designer window, you see a blank grid (Figure 9-2). The dimensions of this grid determine the control's default size. (Remember that when an application programmer double-clicks a Toolbox icon, the new control assumes this default size.)

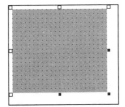

Figure 9-2 *Control designer window*

Change the size to whatever default size you like. When you're done, the control will draw a big "X" in whatever space it gets. So in this case, at least, size doesn't matter.

To create the look of the control, you can use all the graphics techniques open to a regular Visual Basic programmer:

- Lightweight graphics controls (Line, Shape, Image).
- Standard controls. Using these will make the new control into a kind of composite of other controls, but this is perfectly valid.
- The graphics drawing methods.

In this case, you'll use the last technique — graphics methods. The Line method is all you need. Remember that graphics methods are used in the Form_Paint event, as discussed in Chapter 3. The equivalent event here is UserControl_Paint. Only two lines of code need to be added here, and you're done!

```
Private Sub UserControl_Paint()
    Line (0, 0)-(ScaleWidth, ScaleHeight)
    Line (0, ScaleHeight)-(ScaleWidth, 0)
End Sub
```

As with a form or picture box, ScaleWidth and ScaleHeight give the current extent of the control's internal display area.

It's time to test the control. This is easy to do because you're in a Standard EXE project. (You did listen to me before, didn't you?) You must first close the control designer window before you can draw the control elsewhere. This is impossible to do if the designer is maximized, so you may have to first open the Window menu and choose the Cascade command.

Open the form designer for your blank form (Form1). Already, the new control's icon appears in the Toolbox. Unfortunately, it's the default icon for custom controls, illustrated in Figure 9-3. In the next chapter, I show you how to replace the icon.

Figure 9-3 *The default control icon*

Now the fun begins. By double-clicking or using the drag-and-draw approach, you can create any number of BigX controls (Figure 9-4).

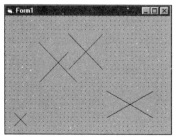

Figure 9-4 *Examples of the BigX control*

Lightweight Controls and Transparency

As demonstrated in Figure 9-4, the `BigX` control is solid and has its own sphere of influence. Each instance of `BigX` is territorial, as it were.

This is perfectly fine for many situations. It is possible, however, that you might want to create a `BigX` control that is principally a drawing tool, as are the standard `Line` and `Shape` controls. If this is what you want to do, follow these steps:

1. Locate the `Windowless` property in the Properties window and set it to `True`. (A windowless control is actually the same thing as a lightweight control.)

2. If you want a windowless control to blend in with other background graphics (as `Line` and `Shape` controls do), set the `BackStyle` property to Transparent and set the `ClipBehavior` property to None.

The default setting of `BackStyle` is Opaque, which causes the control to block out any background graphics it overlaps, even though it is a lightweight control. If the `BackStyle` setting is Transparent, the two lines of the "X" are drawn as usual, but anything between the lines shows through.

●─NOTE

When you set `BackStyle` to Transparent, you must make sure `ClipBehavior` is set to None, or the control will be invisible. Other properties that influence the behavior of transparent controls include `MaskPicture`, `MaskColor`, and `HitBehavior`.

Figure 9-5 shows an example of lightweight, transparent `BigX` controls drawn onto a form. Notice how each "X" overlaps the other's areas.

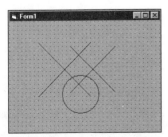

Figure 9-5 *The lightweight (windowless) BigX control*

Conversely, if you want to make the control more solid-looking, you can set the BorderStyle property to Fixed Single rather than None. Not surprisingly, this setting is incompatible with setting Windowless to True. Visual Basic will not allow you to have a border for a windowless (lightweight) control.

Finally, for a windowless control, you probably want to set CanGetFocus to False, or else come up with a way for the control to indicate it has the focus. Otherwise, the resulting behavior is likely to confuse the end user.

> ●─NOTE
>
> The properties mentioned in this section—Windowless, BackStyle, and ClipBehavior—are all properties of the UserControl object, rather than properties made public by the BigX control class. The properties you see as a designer of the control are, for the most part, different from the properties that the user of your control sees.

Adding a Click Event

After you create a control, the first thing you probably want to do is add your own properties and events. Of these, events are easier to add.

If you switch to Form1 and draw a BigX control, you can then use the Code window to view the list of events supported. There are only five standard events: DragDrop, DragOver, GotFocus, LostFocus, and Validate. You get these events for free. But this is a minimal list. Even such a basic event as Click has to be added if you want the control to support it.

To add an event to a control, you need to do two things: Declare the event and then generate it (or *raise* it) in response to some situation. For example, in the case of a simplistic Click event, do the following after switching back to the control class's Code window:

1. In the Declarations section of the control class, add the following statement. (Tip: first select (General) in the list box in the top-left corner.)

```
Event Click( )
```

2. Raise the event from within UserControl_Click.

```
Private Sub UserControl_Click( )
    RaiseEvent Click
End Sub
```

This implements one of the simplest possible cases: a `Click` event that gets passed along directly to the control's user. In the next section, I show a more sophisticated variation on this event.

If you make these additions to the control's code, you now see the `Click` event appearing at the top of the list. Figure 9-6 shows this list of events for an instance of the `BigX` control.

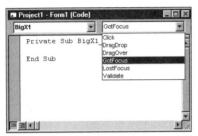

Figure 9-6   *The event list for a BigX control, with Click*

Remember that you can view this list by switching to `Form1`, drawing a `BigX` control if there isn't one already, and then opening the Code window.

At this point, it's possible to get a little confused about the different modes and kinds of events. In designing and testing a custom control class, you have to deal with the fact that there are now three stages of interaction rather than the standard two (design mode and run mode).

1. While designing the control, you use the special `UserControl` object. This object has a fixed set of events and properties. The list of events is fairly long, enabling you to detect and respond to a wide variety of situations. For example, there is a `Click` event, although exposing this event as part of your control's design is always optional.

2. The next stage is application design mode (run mode for the control). Here the user of the control does not see `UserControl` events, at least not directly. The user sees only a few standard events, plus whatever other events you, the control designer, declared in Step 1. In this stage, the programmer draws controls on a form and writes application code in the form's Code window.

3. The final stage involves the end user (run mode for both the control and the application.) The end user doesn't have

to know anything about control classes or events *per se*, although they generally understand what a command does: Click this to do that.

Figure 9-7 shows another view of this process. When the user clicks the mouse button in a `BigX` control, the control receives this event as a `UserControl_Click` event and decides what to do. By executing the statement `RaiseEvent Click`, the control (in effect) passes the event along to the application's form code. The form code, in turn, can respond to the action in a standard event procedure such as `BigX1_Click`.

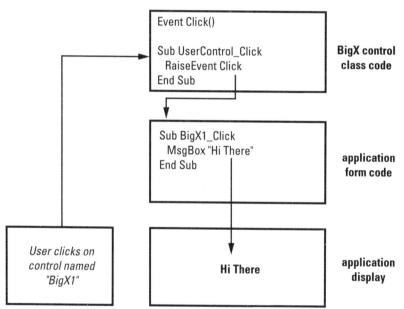

Figure 9-7   *Events in control-class and form code*

Adding Custom Events

Rather than just passing an event along to the user of the control, it's possible to generate entirely new kinds of events. To illustrate, let's design a variation of the `Click` event that passes a different value depending on which of four regions the user clicks. Among other things, this demonstrates how to generate an event that has an argument.

As Figure 9-8 illustrates, the region argument may be set to 1, 2, 3, or 4. The user of the control can test the region argument to determine where the click happened.

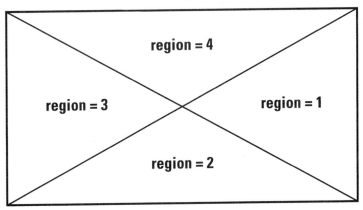

region = 4

region = 3   region = 1

region = 2

Figure 9-8 *The ClickArea event*

To create this event, the BigX control class needs a declaration and at least one call to RaiseEvent. First, the following statement is added to its Declarations section:

```
Event ClickArea(region As Integer)
```

Second, statements are added to UserControl_MouseDown to produce the following procedure:

```
Private Sub UserControl_MouseDown(Button As Integer, _
   Shift As Integer, X As Single, Y As Single)

   Dim region As Integer

   If X > Y Then
      If X + Y > 0 Then region = 1 Else region = 2
   Else
      If X + Y > 0 Then region = 4 Else region = 3
   End If
   RaiseEvent ClickArea(region)
End Sub
```

The control must use hit testing to determine which of its four subregions was clicked. This requires testing mouse coordinates X and Y, which are provided by mouse events such as MouseDown and MouseUp. Here I decided to use the MouseDown event.

After switching to Form1 and drawing a BigX control, you can use the following statement to verify that the ClickArea event works as designed.

```
Private Sub BigX1_ClickArea(region As Integer)
   MsgBox("You clicked region " & region)
End Sub
```

In general, the syntax for creating an event follows this pattern. First, in the control class's Declarations section, you need an Event declaration. The brackets indicate that argument_list is optional.

Event event_name([argument_list])

Adding this declaration ensures event_name appears in a form's Code window, for any instance of the control. The types and names in the argument_list determine the argument list that gets displayed in this same window, including default argument names.

Of course, an event is useless if it is never invoked. From within the control class code, you must raise the event somewhere, using the following syntax:

RaiseEvent event_name [(actual_args)]

As in an ordinary function call, the actual_args do not have to correspond to the previously declared argument_list, except in number and type. They can have any value.

Arguments passed this way reflect standard Visual Basic syntax. Unless declared as ByVal, arguments are passed by reference — which means the called procedure can make permanent changes to the arguments. Consequently, the code in the control class can check to see if an argument has been changed and then respond as appropriate. This is what the KeyPress event does with the KeyAscii argument, for example, enabling the user of the control to communicate information back to the code in the control class.

Another Example: Smiley Smile

Let's move on to a more complex example. The control class in this section, Smiley, is intended to demonstrate a couple of important points. First, a Visual Basic custom control can incorporate existing controls. Second, the most code-intensive part of creating a control class is often painting the control.

Unlike standard VB programming, your control class will need to support instances of any size. This is one of the features that gives controls versatility. (Some controls refuse to be resized, such as the Timer control, but these are exceptions.)

Consequently, you'll need to respond to the UserControl_ Resize event, UserControl_Paint event, or both. You'll also need to get the size of the control's display area (ScaleWidth, ScaleHeight) and repaint the control accordingly.

The Smiley sample control inscribes a circle inside its rectangular region. It then draws eyes and a mouth appropriate to the circle's size, but always in the same proportions. Figure 9-9 shows an example of the Smiley control when drawn on a form.

Figure 9-9 *The Smiley control*

One event is also included: Click. This control adds a twist: The event is generated only if the end user clicks inside the circle, not outside.

To create this control, first open a new control class (Add User Control from the Project menu). Name the class Smiley by using the Properties window, and then add three Shape controls and give them the following settings:

Control	Property	New Setting
shape control 1	Name	shpHead
shape control 2	Name	shpLeft
shape control 3	Name	shpRight

Control	Property	New Setting
shape control 1	Shape	Circle
shape control 2	Shape	Oval
shape control 3	Shape	Oval

In addition, give both the shpLeft and shpRight controls the following settings to fill them in with solid black color:

- Set FillStyle to **0 – Solid**.
- Set FillColor to pure black (**&H00&**).

When you're done adding and setting these Shape controls, the designer window should look roughly as shown in Figure 9-10. Don't worry if the exact size and dimensions don't match precisely, because the code for Smiley will move, resize, and adjust the X and Y values as soon as the control is used in an application.

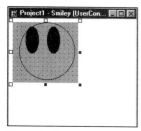

Figure 9-10   *Shapes used in the Smiley control*

Adding the Code to the Control Class

The following code draws the Smiley control in a region of any size. It also declares a Click event. If the mouse button is pressed down and the coordinates fall inside the limits of the circle, the code raises the Click event so the user of the control can respond.

```
Event Click()

Private Sub UserControl_MouseDown(Button As Integer, _
  Shift As Integer, X As Single, Y As Single)
    w = ScaleWidth / 2
    h = ScaleHeight / 2
    radius = w
```

```
    If radius > h Then radius = h

    dX = X - ScaleWidth / 2
    dY = Y - ScaleHeight / 2

    If Sqr(dX * dX + dY * dY) <= radius Then
        RaiseEvent Click
    End If
End Sub

Private Sub UserControl_Paint()
    pi = Atn(1) * 4
    x = ScaleWidth / 2
    y = ScaleHeight / 2
    radius = x
    If radius > y Then radius = y

    Circle (x, y + radius * 0.05), radius * 0.65, , _
        pi + 0.4, 2 * pi - 0.4

End Sub

Private Sub UserControl_Resize()
    shpHead.Width = ScaleWidth
    shpHead.Height = ScaleHeight

    x = ScaleWidth / 2
    y = ScaleHeight / 2
    radius = x
    If radius > y Then radius = y
    ratLeft = 0.5
    ratTop = 0.5
    ratWidth = 0.15
    ratHeight = 0.35

    shpLeft.Left = x - ratLeft * radius
```

```
shpLeft.Top = y - ratTop * radius
shpLeft.Width = ratWidth * radius
shpLeft.Height = ratHeight * radius

shpRight.Left = x + (ratLeft - ratWidth) * radius
shpRight.Top = y - ratTop * radius
shpRight.Width = ratWidth * radius
shpRight.Height = ratHeight * radius
```

```
End Sub
```

Most of the work in this control class involves determining how big all the elements of the face should be and then drawing them.

Understanding the Code

If you're not interested in the mathematics involved, you might want to skip this section. It does get a bit complicated, because there's no way to use this much graphics without doing some math. But not all controls are so graphics oriented.

In the code for the Smiley control class, the first thing that happens is an event is declared:

```
Event Click()
```

This is a simple event, of course, but some work is required to determine when it should be raised. The MouseDown event accomplishes this by doing several things: determining the radius of the circle, determining the distance of X and Y from the center, and then comparing the distances to the radius. The X and Y distances are assigned to dX and dY respectively.

```
dX = X - ScaleWidth / 2
dY = Y - ScaleHeight / 2
```

If the distance from the center to (X, Y) is less than or equal to the radius, the event is raised. This test applies the Pythagorean theorem to determine distance from center, and then compares the result to the circle's radius.

```
If Sqr(dX * dX + dY * dY) <= radius Then
    RaiseEvent Click
End If
```

Drawing the Mouth

You cannot use a lightweight graphics control to draw the mouth, because there is no arc control (although you certainly could develop such a control). The mouth must be drawn directly by using the `Circle` method. This method is called in `UserControl_Paint` to ensure the mouth is drawn often enough.

The `UserControl_Paint` procedure first calculates pi (π) as an aid in determining arc angles. (See Chapter 4 for more discussion of arc angles and π.)

```
pi = Atn(1) * 4
```

The current center point (`x`, `y`) is then calculated as well as the current radius of the circle. (These may be different every time `UserControl_Paint` is called.) After that's done, the `Circle` method draws the mouth. Making measurements relative to the current center and radius ensures the mouth is always proportional to the circle.

```
Circle (x, y + radius * 0.05), radius * 0.65, , _
    pi + 0.4, 2 * pi - 0.4
```

Drawing the Head and Eyes

Unlike the mouth, the head and eyes are lightweight graphic controls. You don't repaint them yourself. However, the code needs to move and resize them whenever the size of the control changes. The place to respond to this event is `UserControl_Resize`.

The first thing the code for the `UserControl_Resize` procedure does is resize the circle (`shpHead`), inscribing it in the limits of the display area.

```
shpHead.Width = ScaleWidth
shpHead.Height = ScaleHeight
```

My strategy for the rest of the code is to assign a series of ratios. These ratios ("rat" variables) specify relative distance from the left edge, distance from the top, width of the eyes, and height of the eyes — all in proportion to the radius of the circle.

```
ratLeft = 0.5
ratTop = 0.5
ratWidth = 0.15
ratHeight = 0.35
```

You can experiment by adjusting these ratios. The rest of the code uses these ratios to size and position the two eyes, relative to the current center point and current radius. This approach guarantees that the proportions will be constant for all instances of Smiley, big or small.

Note that ratLeft refers to the distance from left edge to the left eye. There is no separate ratio for the right eye. The right eye is just drawn as a reflection of the left eye.

Using the Control on a Form

This is the fun part. Switch to Form1 and draw as many Smiley controls as you like. You can quickly draw smiley faces until you are sick of them (Figure 9-11).

Figure 9-11   *The invasion of Smiley*

For even more fun, you can insert the following code in one of the controls, to verify that the hit testing for the Click event works as I've described.

```
Private Sub Smiley1_Click()
    MsgBox "Hey, you clicked inside my face!"
End Sub
```

Smiley may not seem that useful yet, but the basic principles (hit testing, using ScaleWidth and ScaleHeight to get the size, and drawing everything proportional to that size) are relevant to a large number of controls you might create. Also, in the next chapter, you add some properties to Smiley that will help make it more practical.

Controls 102: Properties

"Time for you to leave. No hurry back now."
— Master Fu Tile

When you write a custom control, there is a real
sense in which you have progressed from learner
to master. Instead of creating a specific application (which
can sometimes be work enough), you're designing something to be universally useful to other Visual Basic programmers. Moreover, it has to work closely with the Visual Basic
environment.

There's a little more to creating a property than meets
the eye. A couple of extra steps are required that might not
seem obvious at first. This is because properties are such an
essential part of Visual Basic and are involved in transitions
between modes.

In this chapter, I attempt to make the steps for adding
properties as simple and clear as possible. I then discuss
special properties (for example, colors and enumerated properties) and painting an icon.

Adding a Simple Property

In this section, I take a three-pronged approach to showing you how to add a property. First, I summarize the steps and show a simple example. Then, in the next section, I give the theory — the reasons you need to do the extra work.

When you create a control, by the way, you automatically get a set of standard properties with it. These include the familiar Left, Top, Height, and Width. Index is also provided, guaranteeing the ability to support control arrays; so is TabIndex, which is an aid to working with other controls on a form. Few other properties are supported, however. Even with a simple control such as BigX (introduced in the previous chapter), it would be nice to have ForeColor and DrawWidth properties, but even these are lacking.

You'll start by adding DrawWidth, a simple integer property. First, however, here is a summary of the steps:

1. Create Property Get and Property Let procedures, as explained in Chapter 8. Because you're dealing with a graphical control, you may need to add a Refresh statement to force repainting.

2. From within Property Let *propname*, call the PropertyChanged statement:

   PropertyChanged "*propname*"

3. From within UserControl_ReadProperties, add a statement to read the property's value:

   data = PropBag.ReadProperty("*propname*", *def*)

4. From within UserControl_WriteProperties, add a statement writing the property's value:

   PropBag.WriteProperty "*propname*", *data*, *def*

In Steps 3 and 4, *data* is the location in which you store the property data (this is flexible) and *def* is the default value.

These steps outline the minimum you need to do. You could skip Steps 2 through 4, but in that case, the property will not be fully operable from the standpoint of the control's user. An application must load and save its property values at certain times, and it depends on each control to do its part. More on that in the next section.

Here are some tips on adding the code for supporting properties:

- As explained in the Chapter 8, you can automate creation of Property Get and Property Let procedures by opening the Tools menu and choosing Add Procedure.

- You can get to the UserControl procedures quickly by using the two list boxes in the Code window for the control class.

- You can automate *all* the steps for writing the property code by using the ActiveX Control Interface Wizard as described near the end of this chapter.

It's a little easier to add properties that do not share the same name as a UserControl property, because then there is no name conflict. Let's start with this simple case: LineWidth, which provides access to the UserControl DrawWidth property.

```
Public Property Get LineWidth() As Integer
    LineWidth = DrawWidth
End Property


Public Property Let LineWidth(ByVal newval As Integer)
    DrawWidth = newval
    Refresh
    PropertyChanged "LineWidth"
End Property


Private Sub UserControl_ReadProperties( _
 PropBag As PropertyBag)
    DrawWidth = PropBag.ReadProperty("LineWidth", 1)
End Sub


Private Sub UserControl_WriteProperties( _
 PropBag As PropertyBag)
    PropBag.WriteProperty "LineWidth", DrawWidth, 1
End Sub
```

10

What's going on here is that the code responds to changes in LineWidth by reading and writing to its own DrawWidth property. From the point of view of the control class, LineWidth is only a property name. The actual data is stored and retrieved in DrawWidth, which is an internal (UserControl) property.

When the property value needs to be read, the code gets the new LineWidth value from the temporary storage location (the Property Bag) by using the ReadProperty method. The value gets placed in the control class's internal, private DrawWidth property.

```
DrawWidth = PropBag.ReadProperty("LineWidth", 1)
```

Similarly, values are written out by using the Property Bag's WriteProperty method. The second argument specifies the data to be written. The data is provided by the internal DrawWidth property and is written to the public property, LineWidth.

```
PropBag.WriteProperty "LineWidth", DrawWidth, 1
```

When all this code is added to a control and the control is then drawn on a form, the LineWidth property will appear in the Properties window. Any change made to the property setting is preserved when the application switches to run mode or is saved to disk.

You can add this code to the BigX control from the last chapter. You can then switch to Form1, draw instances of the control, and select different line widths for each. Figure 10-1 shows some possible results.

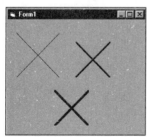

Figure 10-1 *BigX control with LineWidth property*

There's one problem with this example. Although LineWidth is convenient in terms of the control class code, it is less than ideal from the standpoint of the user of the control. Most VB programmers would prefer to use standard property names such as DrawWidth, as these standard names are more familiar.

Coming up with a new name is liable to confuse someone. But using the same name for both an internal and external property creates a naming conflict. Fortunately, you can get around the conflict by using this expression:

```
UserControl.DrawWidth
```

This unambiguously refers to the control class's own private DrawWidth property, even if a public property has the same name. Armed with this coding tool, it's now possible to expose DrawWidth as a public property. The following code is a revision of the last example, substituting DrawWidth for LineWidth, and using UserControl to qualify references to the internal DrawWidth property. I've added comments to clarify what each procedure does.

```
' Property Get DrawWidth: Get data from internal
'   DrawWidth property and return it.
'
Public Property Get DrawWidth() As Integer
    DrawWidth = UserControl.DrawWidth
End Property


' Property Let DrawWidth: Place new setting into
'   internal DrawWidth property. Then force repaint and
'   flag the change.
'
Public Property Let DrawWidth(ByVal newval As Integer)
    UserControl.DrawWidth = newval
    Refresh
    PropertyChanged "DrawWidth"
End Property


' UserControl_ReadProperties: Read new DrawWidth
'   setting into internal DrawWidth property.
'
Private Sub UserControl_ReadProperties( _
  PropBag As PropertyBag)
    UserControl.DrawWidth = _
      PropBag.ReadProperty("DrawWidth", 1)
```

```
End Sub

' UserControl_WriteProperties: Use internal DrawWidth
'   setting to write out value of DrawWidth.
'
Private Sub UserControl_WriteProperties( _
  PropBag As PropertyBag)
      PropBag.WriteProperty "DrawWidth", _
        UserControl.DrawWidth, 1
End Sub
```

In examining the code for this example, the important thing to keep in mind is that any reference to data involves the internal property, UserControl.DrawWidth. For example, the Property Get procedure uses this internal setting to return a value to the user of the control:

```
DrawWidth = UserControl.DrawWidth
```

The unqualified use of DrawWidth refers to the public property name, which is what the user of the control sees. In this case they happen to be the same, which is why there is a potential naming conflict.

Theory of Controls and Properties

10

As the previous section demonstrated, even the simplest property takes a number of lines of code to implement — in several different procedures. This isn't due to perversity on Visual Basic's part. The extra steps are necessary to provide maximum flexibility to the controls (letting you store property data wherever you want) while also providing good performance for Visual Basic itself.

When you've been using Visual Basic, did you ever wonder how property values get loaded and saved at the right time? This is where UserControl_ReadProperties and UserControl_WriteProperties come in. You use a control by drawing it onto a form. But a form can't know about all the properties of all its controls. Even if there were some way of registering this information with the form, the form couldn't load and save the property data without knowing how property data is stored in each control. Such a set-up would violate the basic principles of object orientation. (See Chapter 8.)

Consequently, every control must do its part when it comes to reading and writing property settings. The most obvious case is loading and saving to disk, but reading and writing occurs at other times. Here's what happens to a control when its application moves from design mode to run mode:

1. Just before Visual Basic is about to leave design mode, it checks a flag for each property in a control. If any property has been flagged as changed, `UserControl_WriteProperties` is called to write out current settings. If no change has been made since the last write, then calling `UserControl_WriteProperties` is unnecessary. Updated values are written out to an object named the Property Bag (`PropBag`), which holds values needed to restore the design-time settings later.

2. When the application moves into run mode, the control is destroyed and re-created, starting off as a blank slate. Values are read from the Property Bag by calling `UserControl_ReadProperties`. This causes the run-mode state of the control to reflect any property values that were set in design mode. If this step were skipped, it would be pointless to set any properties at design time.

3. When the application returns from run mode, the last design-mode values must be restored. Visual Basic must "remember" what property values were set to just before going to run mode. (Any changes made during run time are now ignored.) These values are stored in the Property Bag. To reload these values, Visual Basic again calls `UserControl_ReadProperties`.

Figure 10-2 illustrates this process for a typical control.

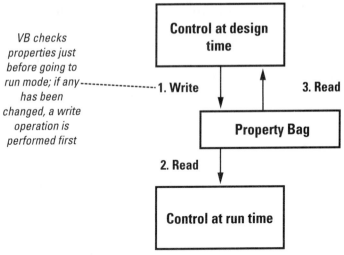

VB checks
properties just
before going to
run mode; if any
has been
changed, a write
operation is
performed first

Figure 10-2 *Reading and writing to the Property Bag*

Looking at this process should help clarify why you need to read and write the value of each property you create, placing code in `UserControl_ReadProperties` and `UserControl_WriteProperties`. Otherwise, the user of the control would set properties at design time only to find that the settings had been ignored. This would be very rude to do to your users.

These procedures are also called when the form is saved or loaded from disk. Again, the form requires each control to save or load its own property values.

Colors, Pictures, and Other Special Properties

The `DrawWidth` property is a simple integer property. Once it's added to the control, the control's user can enter any number he or she likes. This is fine in this case, but what about cases in which you want to provide a more sophisticated way to enter the value?

A case in point is any kind of color value. If you declare a property as a `Long`, then the control's user has to enter numbers directly. This is workable if the user is content with figuring out the hexadecimal representation of a color (&HFF& for red, for instance) and entering that value. But most users would prefer to at least have the option of using the color palette, which standard controls provide for all color values.

Fortunately, there is a very simple way to do this when writing a custom control: Declare the property as type OLE_COLOR.

For example, you can expose the ForeColor property with code similar to that used to expose DrawWidth. To review, the steps for adding a property are as follows: First, create new Property Get and Property Let procedures, and then add one statement each to the procedures UserControl_ReadProperties and UserControl_WriteProperties.

Here are the property procedures for ForeColor. Notice that the return type and argument type are both OLE_COLOR.

```
Public Property Get ForeColor() As OLE_COLOR
    ForeColor = UserControl.ForeColor
End Property


Public Property Let ForeColor(ByVal clr As OLE_COLOR)
    UserControl.ForeColor = clr
    Refresh
    PropertyChanged "ForeColor"
End Property
```

As before, references to the property qualified by UserControl refer to the control class's internal property. Unqualified references refer to the public property exposed to the user of the control.

To complete the property code, add one statement each to the ReadProperties and WriteProperties event procedures, resulting in the following code:

```
Private Sub UserControl_ReadProperties(PropBag As _
  PropertyBag)
    UserControl.ForeColor = _
    PropBag.ReadProperty("ForeColor", &H0&)
    UserControl.DrawWidth = _
    PropBag.ReadProperty("DrawWidth", 1)
End Sub
```

```
Private Sub UserControl_WriteProperties(PropBag As _
  PropertyBag)
    PropBag.WriteProperty "ForeColor", _
    UserControl.ForeColor, &H0&
    PropBag.WriteProperty "DrawWidth", _
    UserControl.DrawWidth, 1
End Sub
```

In this case, I'm assuming that the DrawWidth property has already been added. If so, the code for reading and writing ForeColor exists right alongside that for reading and writing DrawWidth. If you're not supporting DrawWidth, then omit the statements referring to that property.

After the code for supporting ForeColor is added, your control gets a great deal of extra functionality. The user of the control gets the use of Visual Basic's built-in palettes for setting color values (Figure 10-3).

10

Figure 10-3 *Support for the OLE_COLOR property, ForeColor*

Table 10-1 summarizes some of the more interesting property types. Remember, also, that you can specify any of the standard data types, such as Integer, String, or Variant. The Properties window reformats entries as appropriate. For example, settings for a Date property are reformatted in the standard short format for dates (changing July 12, for example, to an entry such as 7/12/98).

Table 10-1   *Special Property Types*

Type	Action in the Properties Window
Boolean	The Properties window provides a drop-down list with values True and False.
Font	Clicking the Edit button (...) displays a dialog box for choosing complete font characteristics, including name, size, and attributes.
OLE_COLOR	Clicking the Edit button (...) displays a pop-up window with System and Palette color selection tabs.
OLE_TRISTATE	The Properties window provides a drop-down list with the values 0 – Unchecked, 1 – Checked, and 2 – Gray. This is useful for providing check-box functionality, especially if a check box is a child control.
Picture	Clicking the Edit button (...) displays a dialog box for choosing a graphics image file. Because Picture is a handle to an object, you must use the Set keyword to assign it, as explained in the text.

Most property values can be written and read as ordinary variables. Picture values are different, however. In this context, Picture is a special object type, not just the name of a property. You therefore need to use the Set statement, as is done in the following example code:

```
Public Property Get Picture() As Picture
    Set Picture = UserControl.Picture
End Property

Public Property Set Picture(ByVal new_pict As Picture)
    Set UserControl.Picture = new_pict
    Refresh
    PropertyChanged "Picture"
End Property
```

When updating the property in the UserControl_ReadProperties event, you again need to use Set:

```
Set Picture = PropBag.ReadProperty("Picture", Nothing)
```

An even more interesting case arises when you want to provide your own list of choices for a property value. Such a property is *enumerated,* because it can be set to one of several values in a list. (*Enumeration* is another name for a list.) An example of such a property is ScaleMode, which can be set to one of eight distinct values, from 0 (User) to 7 (Centimeter). There are many examples of such properties. In the Properties window, all such properties provide a drop-down list of valid settings.

Let's assume that you want to develop a completely new property and give it its own unique list of settings. The first thing you have to do is define an enumeration, which is a set of constants. An enumeration has the following syntax, which should be placed in the Declarations section of a module. Brackets indicate optional items.

```
Enum enum_name
    name1
    [name2]
    .
    .
    .
    [nameN]
End Enum
```

In addition, each name can optionally be followed by a constant:

```
name [= constant]
```

For example, the following Enum declaration assigns the numbers you'd expect for symbolic constants named One, Two, and Three:

```
Enum SmallRange
    One = 1
    Two
    Three
End Enum
```

The name One gets assigned the number 1 explicitly. Each other name is, by default, set to one more than the name before it: 2 is assigned to Two and 3 is assigned to Three. If no number is assigned a value explicitly, the enumeration begins at 0.

Consider the Smiley example at the end of the previous chapter. It would be nice to have a custom property named Face that would select one of three styles: Happy, Neutral, and Sad. This can be done by first placing an Enum declaration in the Declarations section of the class code:

```
Enum FaceType
    Happy
    Neutral
    Sad
End Enum
```

This declares a new type, FaceType, which supplies the type for the Face property:

```
Private m_Face As FaceType

Public Property Get Face() As FaceType
    Face = m_Face
End Property

Public Property Let Face(ByVal newval As FaceType)
    m_Face = newval
    Refresh
    PropertyChanged "Face"
End Property
```

10

Notice that the property data is stored in a private data member, m_Face. You'll see how this variable is used shortly. Note that the Property Let procedure calls the Refresh method, because changing the FaceStyle property requires an update of the display.

Figure 10-4 illustrates what happens as a result of the enumeration type. When the control is drawn onto a form and the user of the control looks at the Properties window setting for the control, the Face property provides a drop-down list of choices. Notably, the user of the control can select only from these choices.

Figure 10-4 *Support for an enumeration property, Face*

Right now this property does nothing. The main task remaining is to rewrite the UserControl_Paint procedure so it draws a different kind of mouth depending on what the value of m_Face is. First, however, let's take care of the ReadProperties and WriteProperties events.

The following statement is added to UserControl_ReadProperties:

```
m_Face = PropBag.ReadProperty("Face", 1)
```

And this statement is added to UserControl_WriteProperties:

```
PropBag.WriteProperty "Face", m_Face, 1
```

Finally, the new version of UserControl_Paint tests the private data variable (m_Face) to determine what kind of mouth to draw. This is what enables the property to have a real effect.

```
Private Sub UserControl_Paint()
    pi = Atn(1) * 4
    x = ScaleWidth / 2
    y = ScaleHeight / 2
    radius = x
    If radius > y Then radius = y

    If m_Face = Happy Then
        Circle (x, y + radius * 0.05), radius * 0.65, _
            , pi + 0.4, 2 * pi - 0.4
```

```
    ElseIf m_Face = Neutral Then
        x1 = x - radius * 0.6
        x2 = x + radius * 0.6
        y1 = y + radius * 0.5
        Line (x1, y1)-(x2, y1)
    Else
        Circle (x, y + radius * 0.95), radius * 0.65, _
            , 0.5, pi - 0.5
    End If
End Sub
```

Note that instead of using an If...Else statement, you could substitute a Select Case statement, which would work as well or better.

Most properties added to a control class usually follow this general pattern: Declare a private data member (such as m_Face in this example), read and write property settings to the data member, and then use the data member to determine how something is drawn on the screen or calculated.

With all of this code added, the Face property is now fully functional. At design time, it can be used to draw any of three expressions (see Figure 10-5).

Figure 10-5   *The Three Faces of Steve*

The following is a complete code listing for the Smiley control, with support for three properties: DrawWidth, ForeColor, and Face. Here I've arranged the code in the following order: declarations for the class, Property Get and Let procedures, code that raises the Click event, code that paints the control, and finally the ReadProperties and WriteProperties procedures.

```vb
' Declarations for the control class.
'
Event Click()
Enum FaceType
   Happy
   Neutral
   Sad
End Enum
Private m_Face As FaceType


' Property procedures: Face, DrawWidth, ForeColor
'
Public Property Get Face() As FaceType
   Face = m_Face
End Property

Public Property Let Face(ByVal newval As FaceType)
   m_Face = newval
   Refresh
   PropertyChanged "Face"
End Property

Public Property Get DrawWidth() As Integer
   DrawWidth = UserControl.DrawWidth
End Property

Public Property Let DrawWidth(ByVal newval As Integer)
   UserControl.DrawWidth = newval
   Refresh
   PropertyChanged "DrawWidth"
End Property

Public Property Get ForeColor() As OLE_COLOR
   ForeColor = UserControl.ForeColor
End Property
```

10

```
Public Property Let ForeColor(ByVal clr As OLE_COLOR)
   UserControl.ForeColor = clr
   Refresh
   PropertyChanged "ForeColor"
End Property



' Code that fires the Click event: MouseDown
'
Private Sub UserControl_MouseDown(Button As Integer, _
 Shift As Integer, X As Single, Y As Single)
   w = ScaleWidth / 2
   h = ScaleHeight / 2
   radius = w
   If radius > h Then radius = h

   dX = X - ScaleWidth / 2
   dY = Y - ScaleHeight / 2

   If Sqr(dX * dX + dY * dY) <= radius Then
      RaiseEvent Click
   End If
End Sub



' Code that paints the interface: Paint, Resize
'
Private Sub UserControl_Paint()
   pi = Atn(1) * 4
   X = ScaleWidth / 2
   Y = ScaleHeight / 2
   radius = X
   If radius > Y Then radius = Y

   If m_Face = Happy Then
```

10

```
            Circle (X, Y + radius * 0.05), radius * 0.65, _
               , pi + 0.4, 2 * pi - 0.4
         ElseIf m_Face = Neutral Then
            X1 = X - radius * 0.6
            X2 = X + radius * 0.6
            Y1 = Y + radius * 0.5
            Line (X1, Y1)-(X2, Y1)
         Else
            Circle (X, Y + radius * 0.95), radius * 0.65, _
               , 0.5, pi - 0.5
         End If

End Sub

Private Sub UserControl_Resize()
      shpHead.Width = ScaleWidth
      shpHead.Height = ScaleHeight

      X = ScaleWidth / 2
      Y = ScaleHeight / 2
      radius = X
      If radius > Y Then radius = Y
      ratLeft = 0.5
      ratTop = 0.5
      ratWidth = 0.15
      ratHeight = 0.35

      shpLeft.Left = X - ratLeft * radius
      shpLeft.Top = Y - ratTop * radius
      shpLeft.Width = ratWidth * radius
      shpLeft.Height = ratHeight * radius

      shpRight.Left = X + (ratLeft - ratWidth) * radius
      shpRight.Top = Y - ratTop * radius
      shpRight.Width = ratWidth * radius
      shpRight.Height = ratHeight * radius
```

10

```
End Sub


' Code that reads and writes property values.
'
Private Sub UserControl_ReadProperties(PropBag _
 As PropertyBag)
    m_Face = PropBag.ReadProperty("Face", 1)
    UserControl.DrawWidth = PropBag.ReadProperty _
     ("DrawWidth", 1)
    UserControl.ForeColor = PropBag.ReadProperty _
     ("ForeColor", &H0&)
End Sub

Private Sub UserControl_WriteProperties(PropBag _
 As PropertyBag)
    PropBag.WriteProperty "Face", m_Face, 1
    PropBag.WriteProperty "DrawWidth", _
     UserControl.DrawWidth, 1
    PropBag.WriteProperty "ForeColor", _
     UserControl.ForeColor, &H0&
End Sub
```

Other Useful UserControl Events

The UserControl object offers a number of events that you might
want to respond to in your class code. One of the most useful is
InitProperties. Before the user of a control ever assigns a property setting, the property will assume a default value. If you want
a default other than zero, you need to assign the default in
UserControl_InitProperties. For example:

```
Private Sub UserControl_InitProperties()
    m_Face = Happy    ' Start with a happy face.
End Sub
```

Note that if a property is exposing some internal property (such as DrawWidth), you'll inherit the internal property's default if you don't initialize it here. That default is probably satisfactory in most cases.

The UserControl object provides a number of other useful events. Some of the important events in the lifetime of the control are summarized in Table 10-2.

Table 10-2 *Events in the Lifetime of the Control*

Event Procedure	Description
UserControl_Init	Called just after the new control has been loaded into memory. This is the appropriate place to initialize variables, other than those tied to properties.
UserControl_ InitProperties	Called during property initialization. Initialize properties by initializing the memory location where the data is actually stored (such as m_Face in the case of the Face property).
UserControl_ Terminate	Called just before the control is removed from memory. This is the appropriate place to perform any relevant clean-up, such as closing files.

Painting the Icon

Once you start to develop several controls, you'll probably find the use of the default control icon annoying (see Figure 9-3). Although this is a reasonably nice looking icon, it provides no way of distinguishing between multiple custom controls in the Toolbox.

Fortunately, it's not too difficult to develop a Toolbox icon, although there are some things to keep in mind. In general, to create a Toolbox icon, you need to create a bitmap file (.bmp) with the following characteristics:

- The bitmap should be exactly 16 pixels tall and 15 pixels wide. This applies to the total extent of the bitmap. There can be no leftover space.

- The background should be medium gray. This is important so that when the icon is placed in the Toolbox, it blends right in.

Once you've created the bitmap, save it in a file in the same directory as the project, open the control's designer window for editing, and then click the control's ToolboxBitmap property. A button with ellipses (...) appears. Click this button to edit the property's setting and choose the bitmap file you created.

You can use any Paint program you like to create the bitmap. For this kind of work, I find that using the basic Microsoft Paint application works just fine. (This is one of the accessories that comes with Windows.) If you use Microsoft Paint, you will want to set up the environment as follows:

- Open the View menu, choose the Zoom submenu, and then choose Custom. When the Custom dialog box appears, I recommend choosing 800% magnification.

- Choose the Show Grid command, also found on the Zoom submenu. (See previous item.)

- Open the Image menu, choose Attributes, and then specify 15 times 16 pixels.

Figure 10-6 shows a sample session in Microsoft Paint, in which a bitmap is being created for the Smiley control.

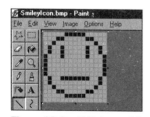

Figure 10-6   *Editing a bitmap for Smiley*

The 800% magnification, mentioned earlier, is very useful here because it lets you manipulate individual pixels easily. A Toolbox icon has a limited number of pixels, so every pixel counts.

Once this same icon is assigned to the ToolboxBitmap property, the Toolbox appears as shown in Figure 10-7. This figure shows a partial view of the Toolbox. Remember that icons for new controls are always added at the bottom.

Figure 10-7 *Smiley in the Toolbox*

You're Off to Use the Wizard

A good deal of the work of writing a control class can be automated by using the ActiveX Control Interface Wizard. Like other Wizards in Microsoft products, this is a kind of subprogram that takes you through the steps of specifying what you want to create and then writes your code for you.

To use this Wizard, you must first have created a control class. You should also have named it. Only then should you use the Wizard. The Wizard is useful any time you want add a property, event, or method. You can use it over and over with the same class.

Assuming you already have an existing control class, you can start the Wizard as follows (see Figure 10-8).

1. Open the Project menu.
2. Choose Add User Control. A dialog box is displayed presenting a series of choices, each shown as an icon and a title.
3. Choose the icon labeled "VB ActiveX Control...".

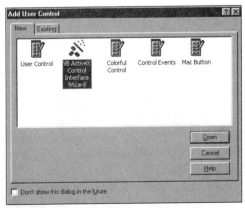

Figure 10-8 *Choosing the Wizard*

If your project has only one control class, the Wizard proceeds to let you create new features for that class. If there is more than one control class, the Wizard first asks you to select one of these classes.

The Wizard is so useful that you may wonder why I didn't start by mentioning it at the beginning of Chapter 9. I didn't mention it sooner because even though the Wizard writes your code, you still need to understand what the statements do. Once you have a grasp of the syntax, you're in a much better position to take advantage of the Wizard's timesaving features, because you then understand what needs to be changed and what doesn't.

The Wizard cannot do everything for you. Most obviously, it has no idea how to display your control. You will need to write all the code for UserControl_Resize and UserControl_Paint yourself. And although the Wizard can declare events for you (this is only a small time saving), you have to decide where and when to raise the events yourself. In general, the Wizard is most useful in generating all the code that has to be written to support properties, including the Property Get and Property Let procedures. It also adds the needed statements for the ReadProperties and WriteProperties events.

Another really useful thing that the Wizard can do is let you enter a description of each new property you create. This description, in turn, is displayed in the Properties window when the control is drawn onto a form and the property in question is selected. However, you can enter property descriptions yourself by starting the Object Browser (press F2), finding the property on the right-hand side of the screen, and right-clicking the property name. When the pop-up dialog box appears, choose the Properties... command. See Chapter 16 for more information on the Object Browser.

Although ultimately there's nothing the Wizard can do that you can't, you'll quickly come to appreciate it as a timesaving device, especially when you want to add another property.

Some Final Thoughts on Custom Controls

As I mentioned in Chapter 1, my involvement with custom controls began in Visual Basic 1.0, where I had put together the first draft of the documentation rather quickly. The example program

(Circle) was minimal, but it was easy to follow and it did a bit of everything.

Back then, of course, you had to learn C and (what was worse) Windows programming. Sometimes I feel a bit like a grizzled veteran, wanting to admonish the troops, "Back in my day, we had to do things the hard way. We had to learn C. We had to make API calls. We were tough, and we liked things that way."

People who start writing custom controls today have it easier. There's almost no really new syntax to learn. The most important thing to understand is the role of the UserControl object, and its key events and properties.

And yet, compared to writing a simple Visual Basic application, writing a custom control is harder. Unless you want a rather limited control, you have to be ready to draw yourself into any possible size. You have to work closely with the Visual Basic environment. Let's face it. It really is more work. And most of that work — the program logic that determines how to display complex graphics — can be as difficult as it would be in C.

But look what you get. You've packaged functionality in a universally accessible form. There are lots of reasons why another VB programmer would prefer to use a custom control rather than any other kind of object:

- You have a user interface that instantly fits into any size and shape the programmer wants.
- Your users manipulate the control through object-property syntax, which they already understand.
- Your users can respond to events by using event procedures, a syntax they've probably used many times before.

Perhaps it was because of the custom control technology that Visual Basic took the world by storm. Perhaps not. But one thing is clear: Writing ActiveX controls puts you in the big game, designing properties and events right alongside Visual Basic's designers. There are few, if any, limits. And with the support for lightweight controls in Visual Basic 6.0, your possibilities are greater than ever. Brace yourself to write more code, but look to the future, fire up your imagination, and have fun.

11

Interface to Database

> *"Danger, Captain. The entity will learn what
> a juvenile and paranoid culture we are if it
> manages to access our data banks."*
>
> — Commander Schlock

When I starting working on Visual Basic, I joined the
Data Access Business Unit (DABU), which has long
since been reorg-ed out of existence. This unit had the mission of creating the first Microsoft database product (what
later became Microsoft Access), and it acquired the Basic
development staff to create its macro language. When Visual
Basic became a project, it was at first a kind of stepchild of
DABU.

So the connections between Visual Basic and database
systems are historically strong. Visual Basic has always
addressed the needs of the business-oriented programmer.
It's no surprise, then, that it has so many add-ons dealing
with managing and viewing data.

This isn't primarily a book on database programming. That's a big subject — encompassing things like the SQL language and relational-database theory — and it merits its own book. What this chapter provides is a general introduction.

What's New in VB 6.0

When Visual Basic introduced the standard Data control, it was a marvel. It let you write database applications with little or no programming. But we're living in a changing world. In the computing environment of the future databases will be *distributed*. Data can reside anywhere on a network. Applications should be able to work with data equally well no matter where it's stored.

Because of the importance of network computing, Microsoft followed up the standard Data control with the remote data control (RDO Data control). But even this approach, which still required different data controls for different situations, was not ideal.

Visual Basic 6.0 introduces the ADO Data control. ADO stands for ActiveX Data Objects, and the control is part of the new ADO family of classes in Version 6.0.

The ADO control offers a number of advantages, not least of which is that it works with both local and remote databases equally well. ADO works smoothly with many different kinds of data collections, regardless of whether they are local or remote, text or graphics, relational or non-relational. Some of the data sources that can be supported include databases, text files, and e-mail systems. All this is part of Microsoft's vision of the future, in which everything running on a network can communicate and share resources.

In this chapter, I'm going to focus most of the attention on developing a simple application using the ADO Data control. If you don't have a version of Visual Basic as recent as 6.0, you can use the standard Data control to do some of the things described here — but I emphasize that you can only do *some* of those things. There are limitations to the standard Data control, as I point out where relevant.

Adding the ADO Data Control to a Project

11

To start using the ADO Data control, you have to first add it to a project, just as you would any other add-on component. I've stepped through this in a couple of other chapters, but in case you need a review, here's what you do:

1. Bring up the Components dialog box by opening the Project menu and choosing Components. You can also bring up this dialog box by pressing Ctrl + T.

2. Make sure the Controls tab is selected, if it's not already.

3. Scroll down until you see Microsoft ADO Data Control 6.0 (OLEDB), and then check the box next to it.

4. Click OK.

Figure 11-1 shows a picture of the Components dialog box with the ADO Data Control selected.

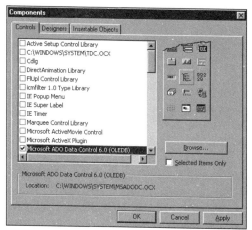

Figure 11-1 *Selecting the ADO Data Control*

As with other add-in controls, the use of the control requires that a particular .ocx file be available at run time: In this case, the file is msadoc.ocx. If you create an application that uses the control and you want to distribute it widely, you need to make sure this .ocx file is installed in the c:\windows\system directory of each user's computer.

Once you have added the ADO Data Control to your project, its icon is added to the bottom of the Toolbox. Figure 11-2 shows a picture of this icon.

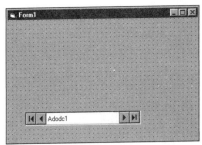

Figure 11-2 *The ADO Data control icon*

With this icon in place, you're ready to go.

Creating a Simple Interface to a Database

Once the ADO Data control is added to your project, you can add the control to a form by double-clicking or using the drag-and-draw approach. In either case, the control, when drawn onto a form, looks a good deal like a scrollbar (see Figure 11-3). If you've used the standard Data control, the ADO Data control will look quite familiar, because the look of the control is essentially identical. The only thing noticeably different is the class name: Adodc.

Figure 11-3 *The ADO Data control, drawn onto a form*

After the ADO Data control is linked to a database and a table (or more generally, to a *record source*), the end user can use the control to step forward and backward through the records. By itself, of course, this isn't useful; the user needs to *see* the data that he or she is stepping through. This is why, in the next section, text boxes and other controls will be bound to the ADO Data control. The process of binding associates these other controls with individual columns (or fields) so that they can show the contents of a record.

In this section I introduce a simple application that steps
through one of the tables in a Microsoft Access database. The
same general procedures will work with many other kinds of data
collections.

When you install Access, it comes with a sample database,
Nwind.mdb, which maintains all the data for that world-famous
company, the Northwind Traders. This database consists of a
number of tables and reports. One of the tables is named
Products. Table 11-1 describes its structure.

Table 11-1   *Structure of the Products Table in Nwind.mdb*

Column (Field)	Type
ProductID	Number
ProductName	Text
SupplierID	Number
CategoryID	Number
QuantityPerUnit	Text
UnitPrice	Currency
UnitsInStock	Number
UnitsOnOrder	Number
ReorderLevel	Number
Discontinued	Boolean

To keep things simple, the example in this chapter will show a
subset of this information for each record. But after you understand the example, it's quite easy to expand it to include as many
fields as you want. In addition, although this example won't use
every field, it will use the Currency and Boolean fields, to show
off how convenient the DataFormat property is when you use the
ADO Data control.

The sample application has the interface shown in Figure
11-4. If you want to follow along, set the labels accordingly. The
content of the text boxes does not matter, by the way, because at
run time, all the text will be replaced anyway.

11

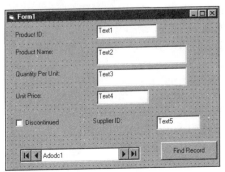

Figure 11-4   *The ProductsTable sample application*

To create and run this particular example, first make sure you have a copy of Nwind.mdb available. In any case, you can apply the same general principles to working with other data collections.

Connecting the Controls with Property Settings

All the data controls (Data, RDO Data, and ADO Data) involve the same general process for creating a database application. The steps must be completed in the following order.

1. Associate the data with a set of records. In the case of the ADO Data control, this involves setting the ConnectionString and RecordSource properties. (The standard Data control uses the DatabaseName property rather than the ConnectionString property.)

2. After the first step is completed, bind other controls to the data control by setting each control's DataSource property.

3. Associate each of these other controls to an individual field by setting the DataField property. (A field is typically a column in a table.)

Completing this process establishes the set of relationships illustrated in Figure 11-5.

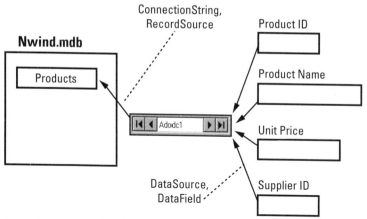

Figure 11-5 *Relationships of the ADO Data control*

For fields that have a special type such as Boolean or Currency, you'll also want to set the corresponding control's DataFormat property so that it displays the value in the exact format you want. (But note that the DataFormat property is not available with the standard Data control.)

To begin, click the ADO Data control, Adodc1, and then double-click the ConnectionString property. This property must be set before any of the others are. Visual Basic responds by displaying a dialog box. Here you can see a difference between the ADO Data control and the standard Data control. The property-setting interface for ConnectionString is more flexible and supports a number of different connection types. The standard Data control uses the DatabaseName property instead, which is more limited.

If you're following the example, set the ConnectionString property to the OLE Data Name Source, Nwind.mdb, as shown in Figure 11-6. You can also select Use Connection String, click the Build button, and follow the steps for building a connection string. Visual Basic leads you through the process.

The next step is to set the ADO Data control's RecordSource property: This selects a table within the database file, Nwind.mdb. To set the property, double-click RecordSource in the Properties window. Visual Basic displays a dialog box. The two fields have to be set in this order:

11

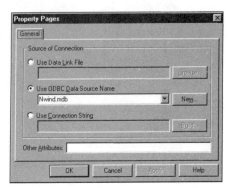

Figure 11-6 *Setting the ConnectionString property*

1. Command Type: **2 – adCmdTable**
2. Table or Stored Procedure Name: **Products**

Again, the interface used here shows the greater flexibility of the ADO Data control compared to the standard Data control. Tables are only one type of record source that ADO supports.

Figure 11-7 shows the dialog box and the correct settings for this example.

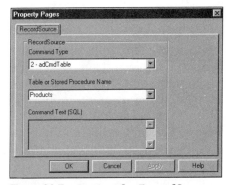

Figure 11-7 *Setting the RecordSource property*

If you are using a standard Data control, you can follow along by selecting the **Products** table from the drop-down list provided for the RecordSource property.

At this point, the ADO Data control (Adodc1) is connected to the Products table within the database file, Nwind.mdb. All that remains is to bind the check box and each of the text boxes by associating them with Adodc1 and also by binding each to a different column (field). This is done by setting their DataSource and DataField properties. The settings are shown in Table 11-2.

11

Table 11-2   *Settings for the ProductsTable Application*

Control	Property	Setting
text box 1	DataSource	**Adodc1**
text box 2	DataSource	**Adodc1**
text box 3	DataSource	**Adodc1**
text box 4	DataSource	**Adodc1**
text box 5	DataSource	**Adodc1**
check box	DataSource	**Adodc1**
text box 1	DataField	**ProductID**
text box 2	DataField	**ProductName**
text box 3	DataField	**QuantityPerUnit**
text box 4	DataField	**UnitPrice**
text box 5	DataField	**SupplierID**
check box	DataField	**Discontinued**

After you get the general idea of how this works, you don't need to consult this table too closely. The basic ideas are simple. The DataSource property of every control (other than the labels) is set to **Adodc1**. The DataField setting of each text box is similar to its label. For example, the DataField setting of the text box labeled "Product ID:" should be **ProductID**.

The final touch is to use the DataFormat property to set formats for the UnitPrice and Discontinued fields. For the other controls, the default format works just fine. The UnitPrice field should use Currency. The check box labeled Discontinued requires a little extra work.

●─**NOTE**───────────────────────────────

The DataFormat property is only enabled if you are working with the ADO Data control. It will not work for controls bound to a standard Data control.

11

Although check box operation corresponds roughly to a Boolean field, it can assume three states, not two. This tri-state operation changes some of the numbers. The values 1, 0, and 2 must be assigned to True, False, and Null to reflect how the check box actually works. Figure 11-8 shows how to assign correct format settings for the check box. After this is done, the check box will map correctly to the Boolean field.

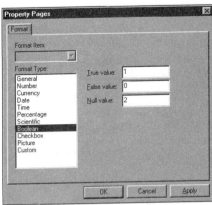

Figure 11-8   *Mapping a Boolean field to a check box*

The ADO Data Control in Operation

With all the properties set as described in the previous section, the sample application is ready to roll. You need only press F5 to start using the application to step through the Products table.

Figure 11-9 shows an example of the application at run time.

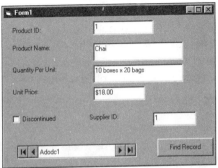

Figure 11-9   *The ProductsTable application while running*

At run time, the operation of the ADO Data control, the remote data control, and the standard Data control is identical. In fact, if a user has previously worked with the standard Data control, he or she will have no idea that you've updated to a different control. This uniformity of operation is nice, because it means that you can update the control in an existing application without having to re-educate your end users. At the same time, the move from using the standard Data control to the ADO Data control means that your application will potentially be able to connect with a wider range of data sources.

The operation of the data controls at run time is as follows:

- The two inner buttons display left and right arrows. These buttons cause the application to move back one record (left arrow) or forward one record (right arrow).

- The two outer buttons also display left and right arrows, along with a vertical line. These buttons cause the application to move to the first record in the set (left arrow) or the last record in the set (right arrow).

The amazing thing is that all these commands work, and you still haven't written a single line of code. The next section shows how you can introduce code into the application to aid user navigation.

Searching the Recordset with the Find Method

If you look back at Figure 11-4, you'll see that I put in a Find Record command button without (so far) enabling it to do anything. Find Record is a very useful command to add to the application, but it does require some code: in particular, the use of the `Recordset.Find` method. The `Recordset` object, in turn, is a property of the ADO Data control, `Adodc1`.

Okay, if your head's spinning a little right now, that's understandable. Let me clarify. The data control, `Adodc1`, does not have a lot of interesting methods of its own. Most of the things you'd want to do involve its `Recordset` property. So, if you wanted to use the `Find` method, for example, you'd use the following syntax:

```
Adodc1.Recordset.Find arguments
```

11

Other useful `Recordset` methods include `MoveFirst`, `MoveLast`, `MoveNext`, and `MovePrevious`. These methods perform the same actions that the user can perform by clicking the buttons on the `Adodc1` control itself.

```
adodc.Recordset.MoveFirst      ' Move to first record.
adodc.Recordset.MoveLast       ' Move to last record.
adodc.Recordset.MoveNext       ' Move to next record.
adodc.Recordset.MovePrevious   ' Move to prev. record.
```

All of these methods are potentially useful, especially as a way of providing additional control for the end user. You could, for example, use `KeyPress` events to intercept keystrokes for every control on the form. Then, in response to the PgUp or PgDn key, you could move to the next or previous record by calling `MoveNext` or `MovePrevious` in the code.

The `Find` method is one of the most useful of the `Recordset` methods. It can potentially take four arguments, but the easiest way to use it is to specify a single argument: a string containing search criteria. An example is `UnitPrice > 10`, which searches for the next record in which the `UnitPrice` field is greater than $10.00.

```
Adodc1.Recordset.Find "UnitPrice > 10"
```

You can, if you choose, hard-code such criteria into application code. In this example you're going to be unexpectedly nice to the end user, however, and let the user enter any criteria he or she wants.

●─NOTE─────────────────────────────

The Recordset property of the standard Data control does not support a Find method. Instead, it supports a Seek method, the purpose of which is roughly the same. Seek is more difficult to use and much more limited than the Find method. This is one of many reasons why the ADO Data control is a better technology to work with if you have a choice.

Without further ado, here is the code that empowers the Find Record command button. First, here is the simple form of the code:

```
Private Sub Command1_Click()
    pr = "Enter search criteria. For example:" & _
```

```
        Chr(13) & "ProductName = 'Sasquatch Ale'"
   strSearch = InputBox(pr)
   If s <> "" Then Adodc1.Recordset.Find strSearch
End Sub
```

All this code does is grab a string from the user (storing it in
the variable strSearch) and then pass it to
Adodc1.Recordset.Find. If the user clicks Cancel in the InputBox
dialog box, the output string comes back empty, causing the procedure to take no further action.

If you enter this code into the application and try running it,
you'll find that this works like magic — until such a time as an
invalid search string is entered. At that point the application rudely terminates without explanation. The way to make this less
user-unfriendly is to add error-handling code, as follows. It will
print the annoying message shown, but at least it won't terminate.
(For more information on the On Error statement, see Chapter
17.)

```
Private Sub Command1_Click()
   On Error GoTo Err_Handler

   pr = "Enter search criteria. For example:" & _
     Chr(13) & "ProductName = 'Sasquatch Ale'"
   strSearch = InputBox(pr)
   If s <> "" Then Adodc1.Recordset.Find strSearch

   Exit Sub


Err_Handler:
   MsgBox "I beg your pardon, but I " & _
   "haven't a clue what you mean. "
End Sub
```

Either way, the application prompts the end user with an
InputBox dialog box, enabling the user to enter any criteria string
he or she wishes (see Figure 11-10).

11

Figure 11-10 *Prompting for a search criteria string*

When you run the application and activate the Find Record command as an end user, it's helpful to be aware of certain quirks. Remember that whatever string you enter is passed directly to the Find method in this example.

One quirk is that string literals are enclosed in single quotation marks here, not double. To represent a single quote mark (') literally, use two single quote marks in a row. For example, suppose you wanted to find this product name:

```
Jack's New England Clam Chowder
```

The correct search-criteria string to enter in the dialog box is:

```
ProductName = 'Jack''s New England Clam Chowder'
```

Quotation marks, of course, are not used with values of numeric fields such as ProductID.

All the standard arithmetic operators are usable here, but in addition, the LIKE operator is useful when you want to only specify part of a name. You can specify a pattern by using wildcard operators _ and % to specify any one character or any group of characters, respectively. For example, to find the next product name beginning with "J" use the following:

```
ProductName LIKE 'J%'
```

For more information on the LIKE operator and other ins and outs of using search criteria, see the topic "Search criteria" in online Help.

Finally, you should be aware that, by default, the Find method searches forward through the records starting with the current record. If you prefer, you can use Find method syntax to start the search at the first record.

```
Adodc1.Recordset.Find s, , , 1
```

You're Off to Use the Wizard (Again)

11

Would you be angry with me if I told you that a great deal of the work in this chapter could be entirely automated? It can, but remember that it's always good to do things manually at least once, so you know what the underlying code is doing and how to modify it.

You can use the VB Data Form Wizard to generate both the user interface and application code for a data form using the ADO Data control, just like the example presented earlier. The Wizard is remarkably easy to use. There are some things the Wizard cannot do for you, of course. You'll need to write code if you want to use the Recordset.Find method. You'll also need to write code if you want to do any kind of complex database operations. But the Wizard gives you a powerful application to begin with, which you can then modify.

To use the Wizard, start with any Standard EXE project, and then do the following:

1. Open the Project menu.

2. Choose the Add Form command.

3. When a dialog box appears offering different kinds of forms to choose from, choose the item labeled VB Data Form Wizard.

4. From that point on, follow the directions that appear on screen. A couple of the dialog boxes refer to profile settings, but you can ignore those for now if you want.

After you're finished, Visual Basic generates the new form and any application code needed, just like magic. One of the Wizard dialog boxes asks you if you want any command buttons added. You can select any or all of the following: Add, Update, Delete, Refresh, and Close. The Wizard writes the application code needed to empower each of the buttons you select for inclusion on the data form.

After the Wizard generates a form for you, you can of course modify the form by moving and sizing controls. You can also add to the code.

11

There is one important thing you must do to get the data form to work. If this form is not the only form in your application, you must take some action to make sure the form gets displayed. You can display the form at run time by calling its Show method from the startup form. The following statement assumes that you've given the name frmProducts to the data form.

```
frmProducts.Show
```

You can also choose to select the new form as the startup form, which is a more direct approach. Open the Project menu, choose the *projectname* Properties command at the bottom of the menu, and then enter the name of the data form in the Startup Object text box.

Figure 11-11 shows a sample data form that can be produced by using the VB Data Form Wizard.

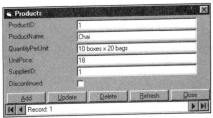

Figure 11-11 *A data form produced by the Wizard*

In Figure 11-11, notice that the Wizard has produced a series of command buttons. Each of these is empowered by a call to the appropriate Recordset method. For example, here is the code that the Wizard generated for the Add button:

```
Private Sub cmdAdd_Click()
    On Error GoTo AddErr
    datPrimaryRS.Recordset.AddNew


    Exit Sub
AddErr:
    MsgBox Err.Description
End Sub
```

The Wizard assigns the name `PrimaryRS` to the ADO Data control. In Wizard-generated code, you will therefore see the data path `PrimaryRS.Recordset` when the code refers to `Recordset` method for the control.

In the previous section, I mentioned that the `Recordset` property supports a number of methods for traversing the table. If you look at the code generated by the Wizard, you'll see that it supports a number of other methods for modifying the database. These include `AddNew` (used in the example just shown), `Delete`, `Refresh`, and `UpdateBatch`.

Other ADO Classes

Believe it or not, this chapter has just begun to scratch the surface of what's possible with ADO technology. The ADO Data control is actually related to a family of classes named ActiveX Data Objects, or just ADO. The ADO family is intended to replace the previous data-interface families, DAO (Data Access Objects) and RDO (Remote Data Objects). Now, you may be starting to feel like you're swimming in alphabet soup here. But fortunately, you don't need to lose any sleep trying to memorize what all these things stand for.

All you really need to know is this: If you're writing brand-new applications dealing with organized data collections, use the ADO family of classes. This family is more powerful and flexible than its predecessors, but at the same time it's conceptually simpler. It's wonderful (and rare) when you get all these benefits at once. Table 11-3 summarizes the ADO family.

All these class names are prefixed by `ADODB` when you use them in code. This distinguishes these classes from DAO and RDO classes that may use the same names. For example:

```
Dim cnn1 As ADODB.Connection
Dim rstProducts As ADODB.Recordset

Set cnn1 = New ADODB.Connection
Set rstProducts = New ADODB.Connection
```

11

Table 11-3 *ADO Classes*

Class	An Object of This Class Does the Following
Connection	Establishes and maintains a connection to a database or other data source. Transactions are managed here. The Open method of this class establishes the actual connection.
Command	Provides a command in binary form. Frequently used commands can be encapsulated in a Command object so that ADO can execute them more efficiently.
Parameter	Enables the code to set or get a parameter used with a Command object. Each Command object maintains a collection of Parameter objects.
Recordset	Provides access to a table or other set of records. A Recordset object views one record at a time and provides methods for traversing the set. The Open method of this class gets access to a record set by specifying a table name, SQL statement, or command and a Connection object. (Note: This is the same class that provides the Recordset property of the ADO Data control; but when you use the control, the Open method is not needed.)
Field	Provides access to a field (column) of a Recordset object, including name, type, and value in current record. Modifying this value modifies the actual data in the data source. Each Recordset object maintains a collection of Field objects.
Error	Contains information on an error generated during an operation or command. Each Connection object maintains a collection of zero or more Error objects.
Property	Provides access to a property of one of the other classes. A unique feature of this class is that it supports dynamic properties, enabling a data source to add properties to an object at run time. Connection, Command, Recordset, and Field objects all maintain their own collection of Property objects.

As I said at the beginning, interfacing with databases and other organized collections of data is one of those Really Big Subjects that merits volumes of material unto itself. Hopefully this chapter has served as a demonstration of how Microsoft has rethought the whole data-collection paradigm and finally produced the kind of more elegant solution they wanted all along. Unfortunately, this means rewriting an awful lot of code if you want to migrate from an earlier system such as DAO. Probably the best approach is to use the new ADO family of classes when you begin writing new applications.

If you do go off exploring the world of database and information management systems, have a good trip. Pack well, watch your step, and don't mistake the map for the territory. Come back safely.

Task Summary: How Do I . . . ?

This chapter summarizes many of the tasks described in earlier chapters, as well as a few other tasks: in particular, multiple form operations. Each task is phrased in the form of a question, which is then answered as directly as possible.

Here's a list of all the questions by number to enable you to find them more easily in the pages that follow:

The Basics

1. How do I draw a control?
2. How do I set initial property values?
3. How do I respond to an event?
4. How do I set a property at run time?
5. How do I declare a variable?
6. How do I work with scope?
7. How do I turn off implicit declaration?

12

Graphics

8. How do I determine available space?

9. How do I draw lines?

10. How do I draw rectangular regions?

11. How do I draw circles?

12. How do I draw ovals?

13. How do I draw arcs?

Arrays

14. How do I declare an array?

15. How do I specify lower bounds?

16. How do I determine length and bounds?

17. How do I use dynamic arrays?

18. How do I return an array from a function?

19. How do I create and use a control array?

File Operations

20. How do I add a common dialog control?

21. How do I use common dialog controls?

22. How do I use the FileSystemObject class?

23. How do I read and write to files?

24. How do I use drive and directory list boxes?

25. How do I use a file list box?

Multiple Forms

26. How do I add a new form to a project?

27. How do I open and close forms?

28. How do I create a modal dialog box?

29. How do I designate the startup form?

30. How do I work with an MDI form?

31. How do I name project files?

Object-Oriented Programming

32. How do I create an object?

33. How do I define a class?

34. How do I add methods?

35. How do I add a property?

36. How do I define an interface?

37. How do I implement an interface?

38. How do I use an interface?

Custom (ActiveX) Controls

39. How do I create a custom control?

40. How do I paint a control's interface?

41. How do I add an event?

42. How do I add a property?

43. How do I add a color or other special property?

44. How do I add a property description?

45. How do I create the control's icon?

The Basics

This section concerns the basics of using Visual Basic to write applications: drawing controls, setting properties, responding to events, and working with variables.

1. How Do I Draw a Control?

There are two ways to draw a control, and both involve clicking the control's icon in the Toolbox. The first technique is to double-click the icon. The second is to click it once and then use the drag-and-draw approach.

To use the double-click technique:

1. Double-click the control's icon. The control appears in the middle of the form in the control's default size.

2. Move and resize the control as you need to.

To use the drag-and-draw technique:

1. Click the control's icon once.

2. Click a corner of the region you want to draw the control in.

3. Drag the mouse pointer to the opposite corner of desired region.

4. Release the mouse button.

12

2. How Do I Set Initial Property Values?

Use the Properties window while in design mode. There are three basic steps to using this window:

1. Click the control of the property you want to set. Or, to set a form property, click a blank portion of the form.

2. In the Properties window, click the property you want to set. (You can scroll through the list if necessary.)

3. Type the new value. Or, if the property is a color, picture, or other special property, click the drop-down arrow or Edit button (...).

3. How Do I Respond to an Event?

Bring up the Code window, select the appropriate event procedure, and enter new statements between Sub and End Sub.

1. Bring up the Code window by double-clicking a control on the form. Or, to respond to a form event, double-click a blank portion of the form.

2. In the list box in the top-right corner (the Procedure box), select the event you want to respond to if it is not selected already.

As a result, the cursor should be placed in an event procedure with the following syntax:

```
Private Sub object_event (args)


End Sub
```

Here, object is either Form or the name of the control. args is the argument list. This will be blank for some events (such as Click).

4. How Do I Set a Property at Run Time?

First write an event procedure or a procedure that is called by an event procedure. Then from within the code, use the following statement syntax:

```
object.property = new_value
```

Here *object* is the name of a control. To set a form property, omit the reference to *object*:

```
property = new_value
```

For example, suppose you have a text box named `txtReadout`. The following statements set various attributes (properties) of that text box.

```
txtReadout.ForeColor = vbRed
txtReadout.Height = 500
txtReadout.Width = 3000
txtReadout.Visible = True
txtReadout.Text = "Hello, world."
```

In these statements, the default units are twips, or one-twentieth of a printer's point when printed. (They are very small units.)

The following example statements adjust some properties of the form:

```
ForeColor = vbBlue
Height = 4000
Width = 6000
```

Note that some properties cannot be set at run time. One such property is the `MultiLine` property of text boxes. Other properties can only be set at run time.

5. How Do I Declare a Variable?

Use a `Dim`, `Public`, `Private`, or `Static` statement. You do not necessarily have to declare variables explicitly, although it is a good idea. If you use a variable without declaring it, it gets the default type, `Variant`. A variant can contain any data except a user-defined type; it can hold numbers, strings, dates, arrays, and even object variables.

To explicitly declare a variable, use a `Dim` statement or similar statement:

```
Dim var1
```

You can optionally declare the variable to have a specific type:

```
Dim var2 As Integer
```

12

You can also combine several declarations in one `Dim` statement. Each variable has its own `As` clause or else it takes the default type. (There is no `Integer` group declaration as in C, for example.)

```
Dim i As Integer, j As Long, v1, v2, s As String
```

In this example, `i` has `Integer` type, `j` has `Long` type, `v1` and `v2` both have the default type (`Variant`), and `s` has `String` type.

Other types include `Single` and `Double` (floating-point types), `Currency` (fixed point), `Date`, and `Object`. See Chapter 13 for a complete summary of types.

6. How Do I Work with Scope?

There are at least four distinct types of scope and lifetime: local, form/module, public, and local static.

- To declare a local variable, place a `Dim` declaration inside a procedure:

  ```
  Dim x
  ```

- To declare a form or module variable, go to the Declarations section of the Code window. You can get to this section by selecting (General) in the left list box and then selecting (Declarations) in the right list box. Then enter a `Dim` or `Private` declaration. The variable is shared by all procedures in the form or module.

  ```
  Dim x
  ```

- To declare a public (global) variable, follow the same directions as for form variables, but enter a `Public` declaration. The variable is visible to all forms and modules in the project.

  ```
  Public x
  ```

- To declare local static, place a `Static` declaration inside a procedure. A static variable has the same visibility as a local variable, but it retains its values between procedure calls.

  ```
  Static x
  ```

7. How Do I Turn Off Implicit Declaration?

Use the Option Explicit statement. This statement must be placed in the Declarations section of each form or module that uses it. To get to this section of code, open the Code window, select (General) in the left list box, and select (Declarations) in the right list box.

The statement is simple, and has no arguments or optional syntax:

```
Option Explicit
```

If you want Option Explicit set all the time, you can select it as an option, and Visual Basic will automatically place Option Explicit in each form and module you create.

1. Open the Tools menu.
2. Choose the Options command.
3. Select the Editor tab, if not selected already.
4. Under Code Settings, check the box labeled Require Variable Declaration.

Turning off implicit declaration has some definite advantages, particularly for long programs. Although not as convenient, it prevents a misspelled variable name from being accepted as another variable. This, in turn, prevents a major source of bugs. On the other hand, if you're working with a short program or only use very short variable names, turning off implicit declaration is less likely to be helpful.

Graphics

This section describes how to use Visual Basic to perform basic graphics operations: determining available space to draw into and drawing various kinds of lines, blocks, and shapes. There is, of course, more to graphics than covered here, so reading Chapter 4 is recommended.

8. How Do I Determine Available Space?

The ScaleHeight and ScaleWidth properties determine the amount of space to draw into and what's available to child controls. Unlike the Height and Width properties, ScaleHeight and ScaleWidth specify the amount of space in the internal display area. (Height and Width are always bigger because they specify the total size including border and title bar.) Furthermore, ScaleHeight and ScaleWidth use the object's own coordinate. Height and Width use the coordinate system of the object's container.

Setting ScaleHeight and/or ScaleWidth has the effect of resetting units in terms of the object's *current display area*. For example, setting ScaleHeight to 100 changes a unit to equal 1/100th of the current height of the display area.

To summarize:

- ScaleWidth returns the number of units available to draw into along the *x* axis of the object's internal display area.

- ScaleHeight returns the number of units available to draw into along the *y* axis.

- Setting ScaleWidth and/or ScaleHeight resets the meaning of units in terms of the current display area.

- Coordinates run from (0,0) at the top-left corner to (ScaleWidth, ScaleHeight) at the bottom-right corner. Coordinates increase as you move down and to the right. However, assigning a negative value to either ScaleWidth or ScaleHeight reverses directions.

- Also, ScaleTop and ScaleLeft return the coordinates of the top-left corner. These can be reset, assigning new coordinates to this corner. The default is (0, 0).

9. How Do I Draw Lines?

There are two ways to draw lines:

- You can use a Line lightweight graphics control. This technique works fine when you have a fixed number of lines. If you need to, you can adjust the line in response to a Resize event.

- You can use the `Line` method of a form or picture box. This method has the following syntax, in which the endpoints are (*x1*, *y1*) and (*x2*, *y2*):

  Line (*x1*, *y1*)-(*x2*, *y2*) [, *color*]

For example, the following `Line` method call draws a line from the top-left corner to the bottom-right corner of the current form.

    Line (0, 0)-(ScaleWidth, ScaleHeight)

The `Line` method also supports the use of the optional `Step` keyword for either or both points, to specify that a point is located relative to the current drawing coordinates (`CurrentX`, `CurrentY`). If `Step` is used before the endpoint (*x2*, *y2*), it indicates that the endpoint coordinates are relative to the starting point (*x1*, *x2*).

  Line [**Step**] [(*x1*, *y1*)]-[**Step**] (*x2*, *y2*) [, *color*]

If the starting point is omitted, the line is drawn from the current drawing coordinates (`CurrentX`, `CurrentY`).

10. How Do I Draw Rectangular Regions?

There are two ways to draw rectangular regions:

- You can use a `Shape` lightweight graphics control and set the value of its `Shape` property to 0 – Rectangle or 1 – Square. You can fill the interior of the shape with color by setting its `FillStyle` and `FillColor` properties. This technique works fine when you have a fixed number of shapes. If you need to, you can resize the shape in response to a `Resize` event.

- You can use the `Line` method of a form or picture box and include the special B argument, for block mode. If you specify B, you can also specify F, for fill mode. This version of `Line` has the following syntax.

  Line (*x1*, *y1*)-(*x2*, *y2*), [*color*], [**B**[**F**]]

For example, the following `Line` method call fills the top half of the current form with the default drawing color (`ForeColor`).

    Line (0, 0)-(ScaleWidth, ScaleHeight / 2), , BF

The following example draws a block without filling it:

```
Line (1000, 1000)-(2000, 2000 / 2), , B
```

If you omit the F argument, you can still fill the rectangle if you choose, by setting the forms FillStyle and FillColor properties.

This version of the Line method can also be used with the optional Step keyword or by omitting the first point, as described in the previous section.

11. How Do I Draw Circles?

There are two ways to draw circles:

- You can use a Shape lightweight graphics control and set the value of its Shape property to 3 - Circle. You can optionally fill the interior of the shape with color by setting its FillStyle and FillColor properties. This technique works fine when you have a fixed number of shapes. If you need to, you can resize the shape in response to a Resize event.

- You can use the Circle method of a form or picture box. This method has the following syntax:

```
Circle (x, y), radius [, color]
```

For example, the following code uses the Circle method to draw a red circle at the center of the current form, with a radius of 500 units.

```
Circle (ScaleWidth / 2, ScaleHeight / 2), 500, vbRed
```

You can optionally fill the circles you draw by setting the value of the container's FillStyle and FillColor properties.

12. How Do I Draw Ovals?

There are two ways to draw ovals (ellipses):

- You can use a Shape lightweight graphics control and set the value of its Shape property to 2 - Oval. You can optionally fill the interior of the shape with color by setting its FillStyle and FillColor properties. This technique works fine when you have a fixed number of shapes. If you need to, you can resize the shape in response to a Resize event.

- You can use the `Circle` method of a form or picture box and use the *aspect* argument. This method has the following syntax:

```
Circle (x, y), radius, [color], , , aspect
```

The *aspect* argument specifies the ratio of the height (*y* dimension) over the width (*x* dimension). The default value is 1. When *aspect* is used and is not 1, the meaning of the radius argument is modified: *radius* specifies the radius of the longer of the two dimensions.

For example, the following example draws an oval (ellipse) that is 2000 units wide and 400 units tall (see also Figure 12-1):

```
Circle (2000, 1000), 1000, , , , 0.2
```

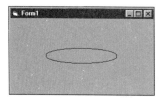

Figure 12-1 *An ellipse with aspect = 0.2*

13. How Do I Draw Arcs?

To draw an arc using the `Circle` method, you need to do several things:

1. Determine the circle or oval that the arc is taken from. This will enable you to get center, radius, and aspect values, as appropriate.

2. Using a separate sheet of paper, if necessary, draw the arc on top of its circle or oval.

3. Moving along the arc, determine which endpoint is the farthest you can go in a clockwise direction. This gives you the *start* value. The other endpoint is your *end* value.

4. Assign *short* and *end* values by using radians, considering angle zero to be the three o'clock position.

Once all the inputs are determined, use the following syntax:

```
Circle (x, y), radius, [color], start, end [, aspect]
```

The *start* and *end* arguments are angle measurements in radians. You can use degrees and convert to radians by multiplying the degrees by pi / 180. For example, the following code draws an arc from angle 135 degrees, counterclockwise, to 45 degrees.

```
pi = Atn(1) * 4
angle1 = 135 * pi / 180
angle2 = 45 * pi / 180
Circle (2000, 2000), 1000, , angle1, angle2
```

Switching the arguments angle1 and angle2 would cause Circle to draw an arc along the other part of the circle. Remember that 0 degrees is in the three o'clock position, and 135 degrees and 45 degrees are positioned, in a counterclockwise direction, from that point on the circle. For a picture of the results, see Figure 4-5 in Chapter 4.

Arrays

This section describes how to accomplish the most common tasks involving arrays, including declaration, determining bounds, and resizing.

14. How Do I Declare an Array?

The simplest way to declare a one-dimensional array is to specify its upper bound:

```
Dim name(upper_bound) [As type]
```

For example:

```
Dim arr1(10)
Dim integerArr(20) As Integer
```

You can, as usual, combine declarations on the same line:

```
Dim arr1(10), integerArr(20) As Integer
```

The syntax for declaring two-dimensional arrays is this:

```
Dim name(ubound_dim1, ubound_dim2) [As type]
```

Or, generalizing to any number of dimensions:

```
Dim _name(ubound_dim1 [, ubound_dim2]...) [As type]
```

For example:

```
Dim matrix1(20, 30) As Double
Dim 3Darray(10, 10, 10) As Long
```

12

By default, arrays have a lower bound of 0 in each dimension. As a result, the length of an array is *upper_bound* + 1. However, you can choose a different lower bound, as described in the next section.

15. How Do I Specify Lower Bounds?

By default, the lower bounds of an array is 0. There are two ways of setting different lower bounds:

- You can use the Option Base statement to change the default lower bounds for all arrays. To use this statement, you must insert it in the Declarations section of a form or module. (In the Code window, select (General) in the left list box and (Declarations) in the right list box.) The Option Base statement takes one argument: the new default lower bound. For example:

```
Option Base 1
```

- You can set lower bounds selectively by using the To keyword in an array declaration. Each dimension can be declared as follows:

```
lower_bound To upper_bound
```

For example, the following declaration declares an array of strings named addresses, whose indexes run from 1 to 100.

```
Dim addresses(1 To 100) As String
```

In the next example, the array matrix2 is declared with two dimensions: The first dimension has indexes running from 1 to 20. The second dimension has indexes running from 5 to 15. It takes the default type, Variant.

```
Option Base 1

Dim scores(20, 5 To 15)
```

16. How Do I Determine Length and Bounds?

Use the LBound and UBound functions to determine the lower and upper bounds of an array. These functions are particularly useful inside a function that is passed an array of unknown size, because you can use them to get the length.

The syntax for the two functions is shown. As always, brackets indicate an optional item.

LBound(*arrayname* [, *dimension*])

UBound(*arrayname* [, *dimension*])

For example, suppose you have a function that is passed a one-dimensional array of Variant, of unknown upper and lower bounds. The following code returns the array's length.

```
Function getLength(arr() As Variant) As Long
    getLength = UBound(arr) — LBound(arr) + 1
End Function
```

Of course, if you know ahead of time that all your arrays have the same lower bound, then using the LBound function isn't necessary. For example, if you're using the default lower bounds of 0, the length is just the upper bound plus 1:

```
length = UBound(my_array) + 1
```

If Option Base 1 is in effect, the length is the same as the upper bound:

```
length = UBound(my_array)
```

17. How Do I Use Dynamic Arrays?

Declaring and using dynamic arrays always involves at least two steps:

1. Declare the array with a Dim, Private, Public, or Static statement, but omit any upper or lower bounds. The statement can be placed inside a procedure or at the module level (in the Declarations section). For example:

```
Dim flex_array()
```

2. Use a `ReDim` statement to set the actual bounds and number of dimensions. `ReDim` is an executable statement, so it can only be placed inside a procedure. Here's a simple example:

```
ReDim flex_array(50)
```

Unlike a regular, fixed-length declaration, the `ReDim` statement can take a constant, variable, or other expression. This flexibility allows you to resize the array in response to changing conditions.

```
new_size = Input("How many items will you need?")
ReDim flex_array(1 To new_size)
```

You can resize a dynamic array as often as you want. Doing so deletes all the existing data, unless you use the `Preserve` keyword. For example, the following statement increases `flex_array` by 10 elements. The new elements are added at the end of the array and initialized to 0, empty strings, or `Empty,` as usual.

```
ReDim Preserve flex_array(UBound(flex_array) + 10)
```

18. How Do I Return an Array from a Function?

To create a function that returns an array, follow these steps:

1. Declare the `Function` procedure with an `As` type clause. Follow the type by an empty set of parentheses. For example:

```
Function retArray(n) As Integer()

End Function
```

2. Within the function, create a dynamic array, and then return a value by assigning the array directly to the function name. For example:

```
Dim theArray() As Integer
ReDim theArray(n)
'...
retArray = theArray
```

To call such a function, create a dynamic array and then assign the function return value directly to the destination array. For example:

```
Dim a() As Integer
a = retArray(10)
```

12

●—**NOTE**————————————————————————————————

The ability of functions to return an array is a new feature of Visual Basic 6.0.

19. How Do I Create and Use a Control Array?

There are at least two ways to create a control array at design time:

- You can copy an existing control (press Ctrl + C) and then use the Paste command (press Ctrl + V). Copy and Paste are both available on the Edit menu. As soon as you use the Paste command, Visual Basic will ask you if you want to create a control array.

- You can set the Index property of an existing control to any number, preferably 0. (Controls that are not part of an array have a blank Index setting.) Setting Index to any number creates a new control array. Thereafter, you can add other controls to the array by giving them the same name as the first control. They must also have the same type.

You can also just give a control the same name as an existing control with the same type.

In all these cases, the name of the existing control (the one used to create the control array) becomes the name of the array. All members of a control array share the same name and are differentiated by their individual Index property settings.

One of the advantages of a control array is that the controls share all their event procedures. In some cases, at least, this can reduce the amount of code you have to write. From within an event procedure, an additional Index argument specifies which control actually got the event. For example:

```
Private Sub btnArray_Click(Index As Integer)
    MsgBox "You clicked " & btnArray(Index).Caption
End Sub
```

Notice how btnArray must be indexed before you can refer to properties; btnArray(Index) refers to the button that actually got the event.

12

File Operations

This section explains the use of the common dialog control, the standard file controls, and reading and writing to text files through the use of the FileSystemObject class.

20. How Do I Add a Common Dialog Control?

Bring up the Components dialog box and then select the component. You have to do this for each project that uses this control.

1. Display the Components dialog box by choosing Components from the Project menu, or press Ctrl + T. Make sure the Controls tab is active.
2. Scroll down until you can see the item labeled Microsoft Common Dialog Control 6.0. Click the check box to place a check there (see Figure 12-2).
3. Press OK.

The common-dialog-control icon is then added to the Toolbox. You can then click or double-click to draw a dialog control on a form, just as you can any other type of control. The position and size of the control are irrelevant, because it does not appear at run time. The dialog control has the ability to display a dialog box at run time (in response to certain method calls), but the control itself will not be visible.

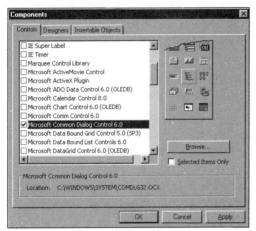

Figure 12-2   *Selecting the CommonDialog component*

21. How Do I Use Common Dialog Controls?

Use of a common dialog control is a three-step process: Set properties, display the dialog box, and then check properties. Here are
the steps outlined for file operations:

1. You can optionally set properties such as the `Filter` and
   `FilterIndex` property. For example:

   ```
   dlg1.Filter = "Text files (*.txt)|*.txt" & _
    "|All files (*.*)|*.*"
   dlg1.FilterIndex = 1   ' Default to 2nd item
   ```

2. Call `ShowOpen` or `ShowSave`, as appropriate. These are modal
   functions. They do not return until the end user closes the
   dialog box.

   ```
   dlg1.ShowOpen
   ```

3. Examine the value placed in the `FileName` property. This
   contains the filename, if any, that the end user selected.

   ```
   theFile = dlg1.FileName
   ```

Note the following:

- When used with `ShowOpen` and `ShowSave`, a dialog box's
  only real function is to get a filename from the end user.
  It's then up to your application code to do something useful with the filename.

- If a file has been selected, the `FileName` property contains a complete filename, including path specification. Otherwise, it's empty.
- Other kinds of dialog boxes can be displayed by using the following methods: `ShowColor`, `ShowFont`, `ShowHelp`, `ShowPrinter`.

22. How Do I Use the FileSystemObject Class?

Use of the `FileSystemObject` class involves the following steps:

1. Allocate an object variable. Call the `CreateObject` function to assign a `FileSystemObject` to that variable. Don't forget to use the `Set` keyword.

```
Dim f As Object
Set f = CreateObject("Scripting.FileSystemObject")
```

2. If you want to create a text stream that you can read from, use the `FileSystemObject` to call `OpenTextFile`.

```
Dim stream
Set stream = f.OpenTextFile(theFile)
```

3. If you want to create a text stream that you can write to, use the `FileSystemObject` to call `CreateTextFile`. It doesn't matter whether the file already exists or not.

```
Set stream = f.CreateTextFile(theFile)
```

See the next section for more information on use of text streams. See Chapter 18 for a description of all the methods you can call through `FileSystemObject`. These include file copy, delete, and move operations. Many of these work on entire directories at a time.

● NOTE

The `FileSystemObject` class is a new feature of Visual Basic 6.0.

23. How Do I Read and Write to Files?

For text files, you can use a stream object allocated through a `FileSystemObject`. To read or write to binary and random access files, you need to use the traditional file commands (these are described in Chapter 18).

12

- To get a text stream, first create an instance of FileSystemObject.

```
Dim f As Object
Set f = CreateObject("Scripting.FileSystemObject")
```

- To open a stream for reading, call the OpenTextFile method. You can then call the stream's Read, ReadLine, and ReadAll methods.

```
Dim stream
Set stream = f.OpenTextFile(theFile)
s = stream.Read(n)    ' Read n characters.
s = stream.ReadLine   ' Read up to newline.
s = stream.ReadAll    ' Read the entire file.
```

- To open a stream for writing, call the CreateTextFile method. You can then call the stream's Write and WriteLine methods.

```
Set stream = f.CreateTextFile(theFile)
stream.Write s        ' Write out string s.
stream WriteLine s    ' Write s and append newline.
```

- In either case, call the stream's Close method when you are done.

```
stream.Close
```

24. How Do I Use Drive and Directory List Boxes?

Usually, you'll need to create at least one each of the drive, directory, and file list boxes. Assuming that these are named Drive1, Dir1, and File1, add the following code to connect the three controls:

```
Private Sub Dir1_Change()
    File1.Path = Dir1.Path
End Sub

Private Sub Drive1_Change()
    Dir1.Path = Drive1.Drive
End Sub
```

If your controls have different names, the code for these events will, of course, reflect those different names. For example, suppose your controls have the names drvSource, dirSource, and filSource.

```
Private Sub dirSource_Change()
    filSource.Path = dirSource.Path
End Sub


Private Sub drvSource_Change()
    dirSource.Path = drvSource.Drive
End Sub
```

These event procedures have the effect of making all changes to the drive list box (drvSource) affect the directory list box (dirSource), and all changes to the directory list box affect the files list box (filSource). If a file list box is not involved, then there's usually no need to respond to the directory list box's Change event.

25. How Do I Use a File List Box?

Typical file-list box operation involves getting the currently selected file — usually in response to a double-click or a command button being clicked — and then executing some operation on that file. The selected file is determined by use of the Path property, which specifies the directory being viewed; and FileName, which specifies filename not including path.

Path is problematic because sometimes the setting ends with a backslash (for example, C:\), and sometimes it does not. The complete filename specification is therefore determined by concatenating the Path and FileName properties, and inserting a backslash if needed.

```
If Right(File1.Path, 1) <> "\" Then s = "\"
theFile = File1.Path & s & File1.FileName
```

The following example uses this code in the context of an event procedure. I'm assuming that do_operation_on is a function defined somewhere in the application code.

```
Private Sub File1_DblClick()
    If Right(File1.Path, 1) <> "\" Then s = "\"
    theFile = File1.Path & s & File1.FileName
    do_operation_on(theFile)
End Sub
```

Multiple Forms

This section explains how to create, add, display, and unload additional forms, including MDI (multiple document interface) forms.

26. How Do I Add a New Form to a Project?

You can add a second, third, or fourth form (or more) to a project by following a few simple steps:

1. Open the Project menu.
2. Choose the Add Form command.
3. When the Add Form dialog box is displayed (see Figure 12-3), choose the default (Form). Or you can also choose one of the other options (example: Web Browser or Dialog) if appropriate. Choose VB Data Form Wizard if you want an easy way to create a form for a database application.
4. Draw, move, and resize controls on the form as needed.

When you add an additional form to a project, keep in mind that the mere presence of a form does not guarantee that the form will ever be displayed. You must add code to the main form to display other forms, as described in the next section.

27. How Do I Open and Close Forms?

This is easy. The Show method does everything you need to load, display, and give focus to a form.

```
Form2.Show
```

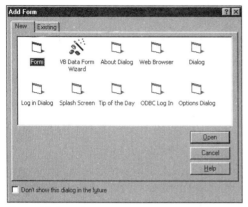

Figure 12-3 *The Add Form dialog box*

This command loads and shows a modeless form. *Modeless* means the current event procedure (presumably attached to Form1 or some other form) continues to run while the new form (Form2) is displayed. You can, if you wish, set some properties before displaying the form:

```
Form2.Left = 1000
Form2.Top = 1000
Form2.Show
```

To display a form as a modal form, call the Show method and pass the constant vbModal as an argument.

```
Form2.Show vbModal
```

This statement loads and shows a modal form. *Modal* means this statement does not return until the new form (Form2) is closed. This also prevents the end user from switching to any other form in the application until Form2 is closed.

To close any form, use the Unload statement. If this closes the only form that is currently loaded, the application terminates. For example, in a single-form application, you might use the following command-button code:

```
Private Sub cmdExit_Click()
    Unload Form1
End Sub
```

28. How Do I Create a Modal Dialog Box?

There are several different ways to create a modal dialog box:

- You can create a second form and display it on the screen by calling its Show method, as described in the previous section. To make the form modal, specify vbModal as an argument to Show.

  ```
  Form2.Show vbModal
  ```

- Choose the Add Form command from the Project menu. When given a choice of what kind of form to add, choose Dialog. When displaying the form with the Show method, you still need to specify vbModal.

  ```
  Dialog1.Show vbModal
  ```

- You can use the InputBox or MsgBox functions. You can also use the common dialog control (as described in Question 21). All of these techniques result in displaying a modal dialog box.

  ```
  pr = "I won't go away until you type something."
  inputString = InputBox(pr)
  ```

29. How Do I Designate the Startup Form?

There are several ways of specifying which form is displayed first:

- By default, the very first form added to the project (Form1) is the startup form. This remains true regardless of what name you give it.

- To select a different form as the startup form, choose the *projectname* Properties command from the bottom of the Project menu. Make sure the General tab is selected. Then, in the Startup Object field, enter the name of the new form to be the startup form.

- Choose the *projectname* Properties command as just described. Instead of selecting the name of a form in the Startup Object field, select Sub Main. Making this selection causes there to be no startup form. Instead, you must write a Sub procedure named Main and place it in some form or module in the project.

  ```
  Sub Main
  ```

```
    ' Enter first statements to be executed.
End Sub
```

In any case, remember that no form is ever loaded unless one of the following conditions is true:

- The form is the startup form, in which case loading is automatic.
- The form is explicitly loaded by using the Load statement or the form's Show method.

30. How Do I Work with an MDI Form?

An MDI form is a form that can contain other forms, in a kind of application-document architecture similar to Microsoft Word or Excel. To create an MDI form, you need to follow at least three steps:

1. Create an MDI form by opening the Project menu and choosing Add MDI Form. Visual Basic will only let you create one such form.
2. To add child forms to the MDI form, create new forms and set the MDIChild property of each of these forms to True.
3. At run time, load the MDI form first, and then have it load the child forms. One way to do this is to select the MDI form as the startup form, as described in the previous section, and then load the other forms by calling their show methods.

Here is an example of an event procedure you might write for an MDI form:

```
Private Sub MDIForm_Load
    child=Form1.Show
End Sub
```

31. How Do I Name Project Files?

To assign filenames to project files, open the File menu and choose the Save Project As command. In response, Visual Basic gives you an opportunity to specify the name of a file to save to, for each form and module in the project. It also gives you an opportunity to specify the name of the project file.

Figure 12-4 shows a typical dialog box that the Visual Basic environment displays during execution of Save Project As.

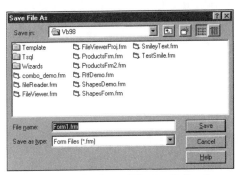

Figure 12-4 *The Save File As dialog box*

You can also assign each form and module an internal name (these are used in code) as well as assign the project an internal name. To name a form, module, or project, follow these steps:

1. Choose the item in the project window by clicking it.

2. Use the Properties window to assign a new value to the Name property. If necessary, use the list box at the top of the Properties window to make sure the form or module itself is selected rather than a control.

Object-Oriented Programming

This section covers the basics of working with objects, class modules, and interfaces in Visual Basic.

32. How Do I Create an Object?

You use a different technique depending on whether the object's class is intrinsic, part of the project, or exported from outside the Visual Basic environment. The FileSystemObject and Dictionary classes fall into this latter category.

- If the class is intrinsic or defined within project code, you can create an object by using As New *class* in a data declaration. For example:

  ```
  Dim myCollection As New Collection
  ```

- Alternatively, you can declare an object variable now and allocate the object in a subsequent statement. For example:

```
Dim myCollection As Collection
Set myCollection = New Collection
```

- If the class is not intrinsic or defined within the project, you must use the CreateObject function, which takes a string of the form *"appname.class"*. For example:

```
Dim f As Object
Set f = CreateObject("Scripting.FileSystemObject")
```

In each case, note that an object is not actually allocated until New or CreateObject is used. An object variable is not usable until it is assigned an actual object.

Also note that all assignments to an object variable require use of the Set keyword except in the case where Dim and New are combined into one statement.

33. How Do I Define a Class?

To create a class, just add a class module to the project:

1. Open the Project menu.
2. Choose Add Class Module.
3. When offered a series of choices, select Class Module.
4. As soon as the module is open, use the Properties window to provide a new setting for the Name property. The name you enter becomes the class name.

●—NOTE ─────────────────────────────────────

Visual Basic maintains classes as project units, similar to forms and code modules. There is no "Class" statement as there is in C++, Java, and most other OOPS languages.

34. How Do I Add Methods?

To add methods to a class module, just write procedures in that module. Any procedure in a class module not declared Private or Friend is automatically a method. Methods can either return a value or not return a value, depending on whether you define them with the Function or Sub keyword.

```
' This is an example of a method not returning a value
'
Sub Push (item As Variant)
'...
End Sub


' This is an example of a method returning a value
'
Function Pop() As Variant
'...
End Function
```

Because they are defined in a class module, these procedures
are methods. They therefore are called through an object variable.
Aside from the object reference (*object.method*), ordinary function
and Sub procedure syntax applies. For example:

```
Dim stck As New Stack
stck.Pop "This is an item"
```

35. How Do I Add a Property?

First use the Add Procedure command from the Tools menu.
Enter the property name and select Property as the procedure
type. This command generates code similar to this (assuming
property name Silly was entered):

```
Public Property Get Silly() As Variant

End Property


Public Property Let Silly(ByVal vNewValue As Variant)

End Property
```

After this code is generated, you also need to do the following:

1. In both procedures, replace the Variant keyword with the
desired property type.

2. You must add at least one statement to the Property Get procedure that sets the return value. For example:

```
Silly = m_Silly
```

3. Usually, you'll need some module variable in which to store property data. Declare this as a private variable in the module's Declarations section, using whatever type is appropriate for the property. (Here, I've assumed an integer property.)

```
Dim m_Silly As Integer
```

●─NOTE────────────────────────────────

You can also declare a property by just adding a Public variable declaration in the Declarations section. However, this approach provides less flexibility.

36. How Do I Define an Interface?

An interface is a set of property and method definitions without function code. You can define an interface by opening and compiling an ActiveX DLL. This DLL is then used by any class implementing the interface.

1. Open a new project.

2. Select ActiveX DLL as the project type.

3. The project automatically opens a class module for you. Set the Name property of this module to the desired interface name. (For example, ICar.)

4. Define a series of properties and/or methods — but write no statements inside the procedure definitions. (See the example that follows.)

5. From the File menu, choose the Make command. Choose a meaningful name for the .dll file, such as **ICarRefs**. (Before executing this command, it's also a good idea to assign a meaningful internal name for the project, because it will show up later in the References dialog box.)

For example, the following statements declare one property, speed, and one method, accelerate:

```
Public speed As Double

Function accelerate (delta As Double) As Double

End Function
```

37. How Do I Implement an Interface?

If you have a class module, the class can implement an interface if you carry out the following steps.

1. From the Project menu, choose References.
2. Click the Browse button and use the Browse dialog box to choose the ActiveX DLL that defines the interface. You may need to type in the .dll name yourself. (Note: the next time you use this command, the .dll project name will be added to the list in the References dialog box.)
3. At the beginning of the class module declarations, include an Implements statement specifying the name of an interface to implement. (If you want to implement multiple interfaces, use one of these statements for each interface.) For example:

```
Implements ICar
```

4. For each method declared in the interface, write a procedure definition. Include the interface name and underscore (_) as a prefix to the procedure name. For example, you might implement the accelerate method as follows:

```
Private m_speed As Double

Public Function ICar_accelerate(delta As Double) _
  As Double
     m_speed = m_speed + delta
     ICar_accelerate = m_speed
End Function
```

5. For each property declared in the interface, write Property Get and Property Let procedures. Include the interface

name and underscore (_) as a prefix to the property name.
For example, you might implement the speed property as
follows:

```
Public Property Get ICar_speed() As Double
    ICar_speed = m_speed
End Property

Public Property Let ICar_speed(ByVal newval As _
Double)
    m_speed = newval
End Property
```

38. How Do I Use an Interface?

To use an interface, your project should first include reference
information for the interface, as described in the previous section.

When you refer to a class directly, you can refer to interface
methods and interface properties, but you must spell them out.
Specifically, this means you must include the *interface_* prefix. For
example, if the Auto class implements the ICar interface, you use
the ICar_ prefix when referring to ICar members:

```
Dim a As New Auto

a.ICar_speed = 50
new_speed = a.ICar_accelerate(25)
```

But you can also refer to an object by using a variable with an
interface type. This changes how you refer to the interface properties and methods. With a variable of interface type, you drop
the *interface_* prefix.

For example, you can write a function that takes an interface
as a type.

```
Sub run_car(car As ICar)
    car.speed = 100
    new_speed = car.accelerate(23)
    Debug.Print "new speed is " & new_speed
End Sub
```

The object passed as an argument to this procedure can be of any class, as long as that class implements ICar. New classes can be developed in the future that work with this function, as long as they, too, implement ICar. Because the class implements this interface, it is guaranteed to support speed and accelerate.

Custom (ActiveX) Controls

This section covers all the major aspects of creating an ActiveX control, from opening a control class module to creating a Toolbox icon.

39. How Do I Create a Custom Control?

To start creating a custom control, add a control module (.ctl) to a Standard EXE project:

1. Open the Project menu.
2. Choose Add User Control.
3. When offered a choice of items, choose User Control. (Note: After the control module is created, you can return to this screen to run the User Control Interface Wizard, which is useful in adding properties.)
4. Immediately rename the module by setting the Name property. This becomes the control's class name.

Because you're working in a Standard EXE project, you can test the control as often as you need to by switching to a form and drawing the control onto it. Visual Basic requires you to close the control's designer window before you draw the control on a form.

After you've finished developing, testing, and debugging the control, you can start an ActiveX Control project and add the module to that project. From there, you can compile the code to produce an .ocx file.

40. How Do I Paint a Control's Interface?

The same code is used by Visual Basic to draw the control at both run time and design time. The kind of code you need to write depends on how you create your interface.

- If you place graphical elements on the control by using child controls, you'll need to move and resize these controls in the UserControl_Resize event procedure.

- If you create the look of the control by using graphics drawing methods, you'll need to call these methods in the UserControl_Paint event procedure.

12

From inside a control class, the special UserControl object is always used to refer to the control's internal events and properties, regardless of the class name. The UserControl members help define the control's behavior. Most of these events and properties are never seen directly by the user of the control, unless you expose them.

41. How Do I Add an Event?

Creating an event for a control class is a simple two-step process:

1. In the Declarations section of the control class, declare the event using the following syntax. (Tip: To get to Declarations, select (General) in the left list box in the Code window, and (Declarations) in the right list box.)

   Event event_name([argument_list])

2. Somewhere in the control class code, you must raise the event in response to some situation. To raise an event, call the RaiseEvent statement:

   RaiseEvent event_name [(actual_args)]

You can expose both standard and custom events this way. For example, the following code defines a custom event, ClickArea, and raises it in response to the control being clicked.

```
Event ClickArea(region As Integer)

Private Sub UserControl_MouseDown(Button As Integer, _
  Shift As Integer, X As Single, Y As Single)

  Dim region As Integer

  If X > Y Then
     If X + Y > 0 Then region = 1 Else region = 2
```

```
Else
    If X + Y > 0 Then region = 4 Else region = 3
    End If
    RaiseEvent ClickArea(region)
End Sub
```

The UserControl object always has special meaning within a control class; it refers to the control's internal events and properties. Here, the code responds to the internal MouseDown event.

42. How Do I Add a Property?

You can follow these steps to add a property to a control class, or you can use the ActiveX Control Interface Wizard. To add a property directly:

1. Add a property to the control class, using the Property Get and Property Let procedures as explained in Question 35. Unless you're exposing an internal property, you'll probably need to declare a module variable to store the value.

2. In the Property Let procedure, use the PropertyChanged statement to flag that the property value has changed. Also, if the property affects the display, add a Refresh statement to force a repaint. For example, for a sample property named myProp:

```
PropertyChanged "myProp"
Refresh
```

3. In the UserControl_ReadProperties event procedure, call the PropBag.ReadProperty method to read the value of the control. The arguments include property name and default value. The value should be assigned to whatever location you use to store the data.

```
m_myProp = PropBag.ReadProperty("myProp", def_val)
```

4. In the UserControl_WriteProperties event procedure, call the PropBag.WriteProperty method to write the value of the control. The arguments include property name, current setting of the property, and default value.

```
PropBag.WriteProperty "myProp", m_myProp, def_val
```

To use the Wizard to add a property, open the Project menu and choose Add User Control. When offered a choice of items, choose the item labeled VB ActiveX Control Interface Wizard.

43. How Do I Add Color and Other Special Properties?

Follow the steps outlined in the previous section, but give the property one of the special types listed below:

Type	When User Clicks the Item in the Properties Window, Visual Basic Provides the Following Interface
Boolean	The Properties window provides a drop-down list with values True and False.
Font	Clicking the Edit button (...) displays a dialog box for choosing complete font characteristics, including name, size, and attributes.
OLE_COLOR	Clicking the Edit button (...) displays a pop-up window with System and Palette color selection tabs.
OLE_TRISTATE	The Properties window provides a drop-down list with the values 0 – Unchecked, 1 – Checked, and 2 –Gray. This is useful for providing check-box functionality, especially if a check box is a child control in the control class.
Picture	Clicking the Edit button (...) displays a dialog box for choosing a graphics image file.

Note that with the special Picture type, you will have to use the Set statement to transfer values. See Chapter 10 for more information on this special property type.

Also refer to Chapter 10 for information on how to define and use your own list of settings (enumeration) to appear in the Properties window.

44. How Do I Add a Property Description?

After creating a custom property, you can assign or change a description to appear in the Properties window by doing the following:

1. Open the Object Browser (press F2).

2. Select the name of the property in the right side of the window. If you need to, type the name of the property and press Enter to search for the property first.

3. Right-click the property name. When the pop-up window appears, select Properties.

4. A list box appears (shown in Figure 12-5). Enter a description in the list box labeled Description.

5. Click OK.

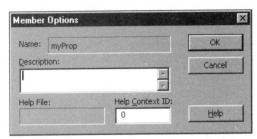

Figure 12-5   *Entering a property description*

Note that if you use the ActiveX Control Interface Wizard to create a property, it automatically gives you an opportunity to add a description as part of the normal process of adding a property.

45. How Do I Create the Control's Icon?

To create and assign a control's Toolbox icon, follow these simple steps:

1. Use a Paint program (such as Microsoft Paint, which comes with Windows) to create a bitmap exactly 16 pixels high by 15 pixels wide. There must not be any extra space. The background should be medium gray.

2. Save the bitmap image in a file in the same directory as the control's project directory.

3. From within the control's class module, set the ToolboxBitmap property to point to this file.

Figure 12-6 shows a sample editing session for a toolbox icon using Microsoft Paint. You may need to adjust zoom, grid, and attributes to get this look. Tip: Use the View menu, Zoom submenu, and Image menus.

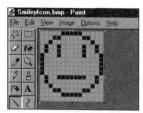

Figure 12-6 *Editing a bitmap for Smiley*

Tables and
Reference Data

Visual Basic 6 in Plain English

The following summary of tasks and other items gives a plain-English description along with the equivalent keyword, so that you can look up exact syntax and examples. Items in the right column are usually statements, functions, methods, or operators, except where otherwise noted. Because many names are overloaded, references to controls and data types are qualified with "control" or "data type".

If you want to...	Use this element
use a *16-bit floating-point* number	`Single` data type
use a *16-bit integer*	`Integer` data type
use a *32-bit floating-point* number	`Double` data type
use a *32-bit integer*	`Long` data type
use an *8-bit integer*	`Byte` data type
select an *abbreviated month name*	`MonthName`
select an *abbreviated weekday name*	`WeekdayName`
get an *absolute value*	`Abs`
lock and share *access to files*	`Open`
allocate an *ActiveX* object	`CreateObject`
add numbers together	`+`
allocate objects	`New`, `CreateObject`
allocate space for a dynamic array	`ReDim`
select between *alternatives*	`OptionButton`, `ListBox` controls
use the *And* operator (logical and bitwise)	`And`
convert *angles* between degrees and radians	`Atn`
draw an *arc*	`Circle`
get an *arc tangent*	`Atn`
pass an *argument* by value or by reference	`ByRef`, `ByVal`
use a variable-length *argument list*	`ParamArray`
create and initialize an *array*	`Array` function
declare and allocate a dynamic *array*	`Dim`, `ReDim`
get the size of an *array*	`LBound`, `UBound`
cycle efficiently through an *array*	`For Each`
use an *array* for binary storage	`Byte`
concatenate an *array of strings*	`Join`
select a subset of strings from an *array of strings*	`Filter`
Declare *array properties*	`Property Get`, `Property Let`
get the *ASCII* value of a character (ANSI)	`Asc`
convert an *ASCII* value to a character	`Chr`
convert *ASCII to and from Unicode*	`StrConv`

If you want to	Use this element
assign an object to an object variable	`Set`
assign value to a character inside a string	`Mid`
get and set file *attributes*	`GetAttr, SetAttr`
create *background graphics* with lightweight controls	`Image, Line, Shape` controls
run a *background routine*	`Timer` control
create arrays of *binary data*	`Byte`
open and close a *binary file*	`Open, Close`
read a *binary file*	`Get`
write to a *binary file*	`Put`
get the *binary value* of a character	`Asc`
display a *bitmap image*	`Image, PictureBox` controls
load and save *bitmap image file*	`LoadPicture, SavePicture`
perform *bitwise operations*	`Not, And, Or, Xor, Eqv, Imp`
execute a *block of statements* conditionally	`If...Then`
use a *Boolean* data type	`Boolean`
get upper and lower *bounds* of an array	`LBound, UBound`
break execution by use of a statement	`Assert, Stop`
use *button controls*	`CommandButton, OptionButton` controls
pass an argument *by reference*	`ByRef`
pass an argument *by value*	`ByVal`
capitalize every word in a string	`StrConv`
add a *caption* to a control that doesn't have one	`Label`
place a *carriage return* in a string	`Chr(13), vbCrLf`
perform a *case-insensitive* string comparison	`StrComp`
convert an ASCII value to a *character*	`Chr`
get a *character from a string*	`Mid`
use a *check box*	`CheckBox` control
choose an expression based on a test value	`Choose`
draw a *circle* using a lightweight control	`Shape` control

If you want to...	Use this element
draw a *circle* using a graphics statement	`Circle`
create an instance of a *class*	`New`, `CreateObject`
get the name of an object's *class*	`TypeName`
clean up resources during object destruction	`Class_Terminate`
close a file	`Close`
use a *collection* class	`Collection`, `Dictionary`
create a *color* value	`RGB`
specify foreground and background *colors*	`BackColor`, `ForeColor`
Cycle efficiently through a *collection*	`For Each`
provide a *command*	`CommandButton` control
compare object variables	`Is`
compare strings	`=`, `Like`, `<>`, `<`, `>`, `<=`, `>=`
compare strings without case sensitivity	`StrComp`
concatenate a series of strings from an array	`Join`
*concatenate string*s	`&`
use *conditional execution* based on a single value	`Select Case`, `Choose`
conditionally execute one or more statements	`If...Then`
connect to a database	`Data`, `ADO Data` controls
write a *constructor* for a class	`Class_Initialize`
group controls by using a *container*	`Frame`, `PictureBox`
convert a variable-length string to a fixed length	`LSet`
convert all occurrences of one substring to another	`Replace`
convert ASCII values to characters	`Chr`
convert characters to ASCII values	`Asc`
convert degrees to radians and vice versa	`Atn`
convert string to uppercase, lowercase, or every word capitalized	`StrConv`
convert to and from Unicode	`StrConv`

If you want to	Use this element
convert to specific data type	CBool, CByte, CCur, CDate, CDbl, CInt, CLng, CSng, CStr, CVar
copy a file	FileCopy, FileSystemObject
use a loop counter	For...Next
get the cube (3rd power) of a number	^
format a number as currency	FormatCurrency
determine if a file is current	FileDateTime
get current date and time	Date, Time, Now
used a customized display format	Format
automate database access for the end user	Data, ADO Data controls
get file date and time	FileDateTime
get current date and time	Date, Time, Now, Timer
extract fields from a Date value	DatePart, Year, Month, Day, Hour, Minute, Second
declare variables	Dim, Static, Private, Public
declare properties	Public, Property Get, Property Let, Property Set
set default command button	CommandButton
set default data type	Deftype
set default lower bounds for arrays	Option Base
define custom (user-defined) types	Type
convert degrees to radians	Atn
delete a file	Kill
write a destructor for a class	Class_Terminate
use a dialog box for quick input or output	InputBox, MsgBox
support directory browsing	DirListBox control
support viewing of directory contents	FileListBox control
read directory contents directly	Dir
display quick output in a dialog box	MsgBox
display dollar-and-cents figures	FormatCurrency
display image by using a control	Image, PictureBox controls
display number in a chosen format	FormatNumber, Format
display percentage figure	FormatPercentage

If you want to...	Use this element
display shape with a lightweight control	`Shape` control
display text in a form or picture box	`Print`
display text in a control that can be edited	`TextBox` control
display text in a non-editable control	`Label` control
divide one number by another	`\, /, Mod`
Embed an OLE *document* on a form	`OLE`
perform *dollar-and-cents* calculations	`Currency, FormatCurrency`
place a *double quotation mark* in a string	`Chr(34)`
convert to and from *double-byte character set* (Unicode)	`StrConv`
round *downward* to nearest integer	`Int`
declare and allocate *a dynamic array*	`Dim, ReDim`
draw figures with lightweight controls	`Line, Shape` controls
draw figures with graphics methods	`Line, Circle, Cls, Pset` methods
draw rectangles and blocks	`Line` method
draw text onto a form or picture box	`Print`
view list of system *drives*	`DriveListBox` control
use a *drop-down list*	`ComboBox` control
drop fraction from a number	`Fix, Int`
drop negative sign from a number	`Abs`
use a *dynamic array*	`Dim, ReDim`
get a close approximation of *e*	`Exp`
enable user to *edit text*	`TextBox`
draw an *ellipse* using a lightweight control	`Shape` control (Oval)
draw an *ellipse* using a graphics statement	`Circle`
use *else-if* logic	`If...Then, Switch`
embed an OLE document in an application	`OLE`
get characters from the *end of a string*	`Right`
detect *end-of-file* condition	`EOF`
end the program immediately	`End`
test for *equality*	`=`

If you want to	Use this element
enable run-time *error handler*	`On Error`
evaluate and act on conditions	`If...Then, Switch`
determine if a number is an *even number*	`Mod`
use bitwise/logical *exclusive OR*	`Xor`
execute a block of statements a set number of times	`For...Next`
execute a block of statements repeatedly	`Do...Loop,` `While...Wend`
get *existing instance* of a class	`GetObject`
exit a loop early	`Exit Do, Exit For`
exit a procedure early	`Exit Function, Exit Sub`
exit the program immediately	`End`
require *explicit variable declaration*	`Option Explicit`
use *exponentiation*	`^; Exp`
extract a character or substring	`Mid`
extract specific fields from a date/time value	`DatePart, Year, Month,` `Day, Hour, Minute, Second`
lock *file access*	`Open`
open and close a *file* for input and output	`Open, Close`
copy a *file* or directory	`FileCopy,` `FileSystemObject`
delete a *file*	`Kill`
load ActiveX object from a *file*	`GetObject`
get and set *file attributes*	`GetAttr, SetAttr`
use *file controls*	`DriveListBox,` `DirListBox, FilesListBox` controls
get *file position*	`Loc`
move *file position*	`Seek`
get *file timestamp*	`FileDateTime`
change *filename*	`Name...As`
get a list of *files* in a directory	`Dir`
filter an array of strings by testing for a substring	`Filter`
find and replace a substring	`Replace`
find a substring within a larger string	`InStr, InStrRev`
get the *first characters* in a string	`Left`

If you want to...	Use this element
declare a *fixed-length string*	`String * N` (declaration)
convert a *fixed-length string* to variable-length string	`LTrim`
use a *flag variable*	`Boolean` data type
use *floating-point* types	`Single, Double`
format a date/time value	`FormatDateTime`
format a number	`FormatNumber`
format a number as currency	`FormatCurrency`
format a number to desired precision	`FormatNumber`
format numbers or dates using customized format	`Format`
format a percentage	`FormatPercentage`
use a *four-byte floating point* number	`Double` data type
use a *four-byte integer*	`Long` data type
drop *fractional portion* of a number	`Fix, Int`
use variables that can hold *fractions*	`Single, Double, Currency` data types
define a *function*	`Function`
generate an event at regular intervals	`Timer` control
generate random numbers	`Randomize, Rnd`
get value of a property specified in a string	`CallByName`
get an existing instance of a class	`GetObject`
get quick input from the user	`InputBox`
respond to class user's *getting a property value*	`Property Get`
use a control for displaying *graphics*	`PictureBox`
use lightweight *graphics controls*	`Image, Line, Shape` controls
use *graphics methods*	`Line, Circle, Cls, Point, Print, Pset, Refresh` methods
test for *greater-than* condition	`>`
test for *greater-than-or-equals* condition	`>=`
group option buttons together	`Frame` control
cycle efficiently through a *group* (collection or array)	`For Each`
collect objects into a *group*	`Collection, Dictionary`
handle run-time errors	`On Error`

If you want to	Use this element
extract *hours* from a date/time value	`DatePart, Hour`
use *if-then* logic	`If...Then, Switch`
display a bitmap *image*	`Image, PictureBox` controls
implement an interface	`Implements`
find the *index* of a substring	`InStr, InStrRev`
test for *inequality*	`<>`
initialize objects of a class	`Class_Initialize`
initialize an array	`Array` function
get quick *input* from the end user	`InputBox`
input a field from a text file	`Input #`
input a line of text from a text file	`Line Input #,` `FileSystemObject`
input data from a binary file	`Get`
insert *OLE objects* into a form	`OLE`
get an existing *instance* of a class	`GetObject`
allocate an *instance* of a class	`Dim, New, CreateObject`
use *integer data types*	`Byte, Integer, Long` data types
use *integer division*	`\`
get *integer portion* of a number	`Fix, Int`

use *international settings* in data formats	`FormatCurrency,`
	`FormatDateTime,`
	`FormatNumber,`
	`FormatPercent`

use the *inverse tangent* function	`Atn`
join a series of strings from an array	`Join`
join strings together	`&`
create a *label* for a control that doesn't have one	`Label` control
use *large floating-point* numbers	`Double` data type
use *large integers*	`Long` data type
get the *last characters* in a string	`Right`
find the *last occurrence* of a substring	`InStrRev`
trim *leading spaces*	`LTrim`
leave a loop early	`Exit Do, Exit For`
leave a procedure early	`Exit Function, Exit Sub`
left-justify a string	`LSet`
get the *leftmost characters* in a string	`Left`

If you want to...	Use this element
get the *length of a file*	`LOF, FileLen`
get the *length of a string*	`Len`
get the *length of an array*	`LBound, UBound`
test for a *less-than* condition	`<`
test for a *less-than-or-equals* condition	`<=`
draw a *line* with a lightweight control	`Line`
place a *linefeed character* in a string	`Chr(10), vbCrLf`
input or output a *line of text* from a file	`Line Input #, Print #,` `FileSystemObject`
link and embed documents	`OLE` control
use a *list-box control*	`ListBox, ComboBox` controls
list directory contents	`FileListBox` control, `Dir`
load an ActiveX object from a file	`GetObject`
load bitmap image file	`LoadPicture`
load a rich-text-format (RTF) file	`LoadFile`
get a *logarithm*	`Log`
perform *logical and bitwise* operations	`Not, And, Or, Xor, Eqv, Imp`
use the *long floating-point* type	`Double` data type
use a *loop structure* for control flow	`Do...Loop, For...Next,` `For Each, While...Wend`
loop through an array or collection	`For Each`
use a *loop variable*	`For...Next`
get the *lower bound* of an array	`LBound`
set default *lower bounds* for arrays	`Option Base`
convert letters to *lowercase*	`LCase`
mask out bit values	`And`
get *maximum index* of an array	`UBound`
define a *method* in a class module	`Sub, Function`
get characters from the *middle of a string*	`Mid`
get *minimum index* of an array	`LBound`
extract number of *minutes* from a date/time value	`DatePart, Minute`
use *modular division*	`Mod`
work with *money*	`Currency` data type, `FormatCurrency`
extract *month* from a date/time value	`DatePart, Month`
get name of a *month* from number	`MonthName`

If you want to	Use this element
move file position	Seek
move files and directories	FileSystemObject
use *multiline text boxes*	TextBox control
enable *multiple selection*	ListBox, FileListBox controls
multiply numbers	*
change the *name of a file*	Name...As
get a *natural logarithm*	Log
use logical or bitwise *negation*	Not
determine if a number is *negative*	Sgn
place a *newline* in a string	Chr(13), vbCrLf
get a random *number*	Rnd
get the *numeric value* of a character	Asc
assign an *object* to an object variable	Dim, Set
compare two *object variables*	Is
allocate *objects*	New, CreateObject
initialize *objects*	Class_Initialize
determine if a number is an *odd number*	Mod
embed an *OLE document*	OLE control
use a *one-byte* integer	Byte data type
open a file for input and output	Open, FileSystemObject
output a quick message to the end user	MsgBox
output data to a binary file	Put
output a field of text to a text file	Write #
output a line of text to a text file	Print #, FileSystemObject
output text to a form or picture box	Print
display an *oval*	Shape control
pad a string with trailing spaces	LSet
specify a *pattern for filenames* to match	FileListBox control, Dir
compare string to a *pattern with wildcards*	Like
format number as a *percentage*	FormatPercentage
get a close approximation of *pi (π)*	Atn
display a *picture*	Image, PictureBox controls

If you want to...	Use this element
get file *position*	Loc
move file *position*	Seek
determine if a number is *positive*	Sgn
post a quick message to the user	MsgBox
raise a number to a specified *power*	^
round to a specified degree of *precision*	Round
preserve the value of a variable between calls	Static
preserve values in an array while resizing	Preserve
print to current form, printer, or Immediate window	Print
print text in a text file	Print #
send output to system *printer*	Printer object
define a *procedure*	Sub
define a *procedure returning a value*	Function
prompt end user for a response	InputBox, MsgBox
access a *property* named in a string	CallByName
declare a *property* within a class	Public, Property Get, Property Let, Property Set
respond to the user's setting a *property value*	Property Let
return a *property value*	Property Get
place a *quotation mark* inside a string	Chr(34)
convert degrees to *radians*, and vice versa	Atn
raise a number to a power	^
raise the number *e* to a power	Exp
get a *random number*	Rnd
set a seed for *random-number generation*	Randomize
open a *random-access file*	Open
read from a *random-access file*	Get
write to a *random-access file*	Put
go to record number in a *random-access file*	Seek
read directory contents	Dir

If you want to	Use this element
read data from binary or random-access file	`Get`
read a string from the console	`InputBox`
read a text file a field at a time	`Input #`
read a text file a line at a time	`Line Input #,` `FileSystemObject`
determine if a file is *read-only*	`GetAttr`
use *real-number types*	`Single, Double` data types
get the *record number* of current file position	`Loc`
move file position to the specified *record number*	`Seek`
define a *record type*	`Type`
access *records* in a database	`Data`, ADO Data controls
read and write *records of a random access file*	`Get, Put`
draw a *rectangle* with a lightweight control	`Shape` control
draw a *rectangle* using a graphics method	`Line` method
get *remainder* from division	`Mod`
remove a file	`Kill`
rename a file	`Name...As`
force an immediate *repaint*	`Refresh`
repeat a character a specified number of times	`String function`
replace a substring	`Mid`
replace all occurrences of a substring by another	`Replace`
resize a dynamic array	`ReDim`
resume execution after an error	`On Error`
return a property value	`Property Get`
reverse the characters in a string	`StrReverse`
load and save a *rich-text-format (RTF)* file	`LoadFile, SaveFile`
get the *rightmost characters* in a string	`Right`
display a *rounded square* with a lightweight control	`Shape` control
round downward	`Int`

If you want to...	Use this element
avoid *rounding errors*	Currency
use *rounding functions*	Int, Fix, Round
handle *runtime errors*	On Error
save a bitmap image file	SavePicture
save a rich-text-format (RTF) file	SaveFile
display a number in *scientific notation*	Format
use a *scrollbar control*	HScrollBar, VScrollBar controls
use a control with built-in *scrollbars*	TextBox, ListBox, ComboBox controls
search for a substring	InStr, InStrRev
extract number of *seconds* from a date/time value	DatePart, Second
get number of *seconds since midnight*	Timer function
set random-number *seed*	Randomize
select strings from an array of strings	Filter
enable multiple *selection*	ListBox, FileListBox controls
print to a *sequential text file*	Print #, FileSystemObject
read a field at a time from a *sequential text file*	Input #
read a line at a time from a *sequential text file*	Line Input #, FileSystemObject
write to a *sequential text file*	Write #, FileSystemObject
respond to a class user's *setting a property*	Property Let
set file attributes	SetAttr
use the *short display format* for date and time values	FormatDateTime
determine positive or negative *sign*	Sgn
use a *sixteen-bit floating point* number	Single data type
use a *sixteen-bit integer*	Integer data type
get the *size of an array*	LBound, UBound
get the *size of a file*	LOF, FileLen
get the *size of a string*	Len
adopt *sorted order* in a list box	Sort property (ListBox, ComboBox)

If you want to	Use this element
repeat *spaces* a specified number of times in a string	`Space`
embed *special characters* in a string	`Chr`
get the *square root* of a number	`Sqr`
display a *square* with a lightweight control	`Shape` control
display a *square* with a graphics method	`Line` method
square a number	`^`
get a *string* from the end user	`InputBox`
get *string length*	`Len`
compare *strings*	`=, Like, <>, <, >, <=, >=`; `StrComp`
concatenate *strings*	`&, Join`
define and use a *structure* type	`Type`
extract a *substring*	`Mid`
replace all occurrences of a *substring* within a larger string	`Replace`
suspend execution	`Assert, Stop`
switch between blocks based on a test value	`Select Case`
view list of *system drives*	`DriveListBox` control
determine if a file is a *system file*	`GetAttr`
take the square root of a number	`Sqr`
use the inverse *tangent function*	`Atn`
write a *termination procedure* for objects of a class	`Class_Terminate`
test for equality	`=`
test for inequality	`<>`
use a control to display *text*	`Label` control
print *text* directly on a form or picture box	`Print`
use strings of *text*	`String` data type
open a *text file*	`Open, FileSystemObject`
print to a *text file*	`Print #`
read one field at a time from a *text file*	`Input #`
read one line at a time from a *text file*	`Line Input #,` `FileSystemObject`

If you want to...	Use this element
write to a *text file*	`Write #,` `FileSystemObject`
get a *TextStream object*	`FileSystemObject`
use a *thirty-two-bit floating point* number	`Double` data type
use a *thirty-two-bit integer*	`Long` data type
get current *time*	`Time, Now` functions
extract *time of day* from a date/time value	`DatePart`
format a *time of day* value	`FormatDateTime`
get *time of last change* to a file	`FileDateTime`
store *time values*	`Date` data type
trap runtime errors	`On Error`
use *trigonometric* functions	`Atn, Cos, Sin, Tan`
trim leading spaces from a string	`LTrim`
trim trailing spaces from a string	`LTrim`
truncate floating-point to integer	`Int, Fix`
truncate string	`Left`
use a *two-byte floating point* number	`Single` data type
use a *two-byte integer*	`Integer` data type
get an expression's *type*	`TypeName`
determine if two expressions are *unequal*	`<>`
convert to and from the *Unicode character set*	`StrConv`
get the *upper bound* of an array	`UBound`
convert letters to *uppercase*	`UCase`
declare a *user-defined type*	`Type`
pass an argument by *value*	`ByVal`
create a *variable-length argument list*	`PamArray`
declare *variables*	`Dim, Static, Private,` `Public`
display a *warning message*	`MsgBox`
extract the *weekday* from a date/time value	`DatePart, WeekdayName`
use a *while loop*	`Do...Loop, While...Wend`
write data to a binary or random-access file	`Put`

If you want to	Use this element
write a field at a time to a text file	`Write #`
write a line at a time to a text file	`Print #,` `FileSystemObject`
write text on a form or picture box	`Print`
extract the *year* from a date/time value	`DatePart`

Visual Basic 6 A – Z

This feature provides a chapter cross-reference for the keywords appearing in Part II and some appearing in Chapter 5, arranged alphabetically. Look up the element you want to find in the left-hand column, and then turn to the chapter given in the right-hand column to get complete syntax information, along with relevant examples.

Element	Chapter
Abs	Chapter 21
Add Watch	Chapter 22
And	Chapter 14
Array	Chapter 5
Asc	Chapter 20
Assert	Chapter 22
Atn	Chapter 21
Boolean	Chapter 13
Byte	Chapter 13
Call stack	Chapter 22
CallByName	Chapter 17
CheckBox	Chapter 15
Choose	Chapter 17
Chr	Chapter 20
Circle	Chapter 4
Class_Initialize	Chapter 16
Class_Terminate	Chapter 16
Clear All Breakpoints	Chapter 22
Close	Chapter 18
Cls	Chapter 4
Collection	Chapter 16
ComboBox	Chapter 15
CommandButton	Chapter 15
Cos	Chapter 21
CreateObject	Chapter 16
Currency	Chapter 13
Data	Chapter 15
Date	Chapter 13
Debug toolbar	Chapter 22
Dictionary	Chapter 16
Dim	Chapter 16
Dir	Chapter 18
DirListBox	Chapter 15
Do...Loop	Chapter 17
Double	Chapter 13
DriveListBox	Chapter 15

Element	Chapter
InStr	Chapter 20
InStrRev	Chapter 20
Int	Chapter 21
Integer	Chapter 13
Is	Chapter 14
IsArray	Chapter 5
Join	Chapter 20
Kill	Chapter 18
Label	Chapter 15
LBound	Chapter 5
LCase	Chapter 20
Left	Chapter 20
Len	Chapter 20
Like	Chapter 14
Line control	Chapter 15
Line method	Chapter 4
Line Input #	Chapter 18
ListBox	Chapter 15
LoadPicture	Chapter 4
Loc	Chapter 18
Locals window	Chapter 22
LOF	Chapter 18
Log	Chapter 21
Long	Chapter 13
LSet	Chapter 20
LTrim	Chapter 20
Mid	Chapter 20
Mod	Chapter 14
MonthName	Chapter 20
MsgBox	Chapter 19
Name...As	Chapter 18
New	Chapter 16
Not	Chapter 14
Object	Chapter 13
OLE	Chapter 15
On Error	Chapter 17

Element	Chapter
Open	Chapter 18
Option Base	Chapter 5
OptionButton	Chapter 15
Or	Chapter 14
PictureBox	Chapter 15
Preserve	Chapter 5
Print	Chapter 19
Print #	Chapter 18
Private	Chapter 16
Property Get	Chapter 16
Property Let	Chapter 16
Property Set	Chapter 16
PSet	Chapter 4
Public	Chapter 16
Put	Chapter 18
Quick Watch	Chapter 22
Randomize	Chapter 21
ReDim	Chapter 5
Refresh	Chapter 4
Replace	Chapter 20
Right	Chapter 20
Rnd	Chapter 21
Round	Chapter 21
RTrim	Chapter 20
Run command	Chapter 22
Run to Cursor	Chapter 22
SavePicture	Chapter 4
ScrollBar	Chapter 15
Seek	Chapter 18
Select Case	Chapter 17
Set	Chapter 16
Set Next Statement	Chapter 22
SetAttr	Chapter 18
Sgn	Chapter 21
Shape	Chapter 15
Show Next Statement	Chapter 22

Element	Chapter
Single	Chapter 13
Space	Chapter 20
Sqr	Chapter 21
Step Into	Chapter 22
Step Over	Chapter 22
StrComp	Chapter 20
StrConv	Chapter 20
String	Chapter 13
String (function)	Chapter 20
StrReverse	Chapter 20
Sub	Chapter 17
Sub (in a class module)	Chapter 16
Switch	Chapter 17
Tan	Chapter 21
TextBox	Chapter 15
Timer	Chapter 15
Toggle Breakpoint	Chapter 22
TypeName	Chapter 16
Type	Chapter 13
UBound	Chapter 5
UCase	Chapter 20
Variant	Chapter 13
VScrollBar	Chapter 15
Watch window	Chapter 22
WeekdayName	Chapter 20
While...Wend	Chapter 17
Write #	Chapter 18
Xor	Chapter 14

Data Types

This chapter consists of a summary of data types, followed by in-depth descriptions, a section on data conversion, and a section on declaring variables.

Summary of Data Types

Table 13-1 gives an overview of all data types supported in Visual Basic 6.

Table 13-1 *Summary of VB Data Types*

Type	Description	Range (Approximate in Some Cases)
Variant	The default type; can contain any kind of data other than user-defined types; this includes arrays and object references	See String, Date, and Double

Continued

Table 13-1   *Continued*

Type	Description	Range (Approximate in Some Cases)
Byte	8-bit unsigned value	0 to 255
Integer	16-bit integer	−32768 to 32767
Long	32-bit integer	±2 billion (10^9)
Single	16-bit floating-point	±3.4 × 10^{38}
Double	32-bit floating-point	±1.8 × 10^{308}
String	Character string; contains text	2-billion character limit
Boolean	Value that holds True or False	False, True
Currency	Fixed-point fractional quantity	±10^{15}, with four digits of precision
Date	Date and time stamp	January 1, 100 to December 31, 9999
Object	Generic object reference; must be set before use	NA

Description of Data Types

The sections under this heading provide more information on the standard data types.

Variant

A variable of type Variant can hold any kind of data other than a user-defined type. This means a variable of type Variant can contain an array or object reference, as well as more conventional data such as a string, number, or a Date value. The Variant data type was introduced in Version 2.0 of Visual Basic, and it replaces Single as the default data type. (See also the section on the Date type.)

This type is convenient because it lets you use variables as strings, date/time values, or numbers, without declaring them or worrying about their type. You can even assign a digit string to a Variant and then use it as a number.

```
V = "5"
Print 7 − V   ' This prints 2.
```

But note that this behavior is no longer unique to Variant data types, because Visual Basic 6.0 supports automatic conversion between strings and numbers. See the section "Data Conversion" later in this chapter.

13

●─NOTE

Because variants are ambiguous, it's necessary to use the dedicated string-concatenation operator (&) if you want to concatenate strings, rather than the plus sign (+).

Variables of type Variant can have one of three special values, described in Table 13-2.

Table 13-2 *Special Values for Variant Type*

Value	Description
Empty	Indicates that the variant has not been assigned a value. Empty is distinct from 0 and zero-length strings (" "), although the variant assumes one of those values if used in an expression.
Null	Associated with database applications; Null indicates missing data. If a Null value is used as an operand in any expression, the result of the expression is always Null.
Error	Indicates that an error has occurred. No error-handling routines are triggered by the assignment of Error; you have to test for Error directly.

Visual Basic provides several support functions for use with these values, including IsEmpty and IsNull, which are simple Boolean tests, and CVErr.

Byte

Byte is a simple integer type. The range is 0 to 255. If the unary minus sign is applied to a Byte value, Visual Basic converts it to type Integer so that it can hold a negative quantity. Default value is 0.

The main purpose of the Byte type is to prevent data from automatic conversions. For example, strings may be corrupted in any operation in which Visual Basic converts between ASCII and Unicode. This happens when reading and writing to files, as well as calling DLLs and object methods. To protect data from conversion, store it in an array of type Byte before passing it.

Integer

The Integer type is the standard 16-bit (2-byte) integer. The keyword Integer is slightly confusing because it is not the only integer type. Byte and Long are both integer types (sometimes called *integral*). Integers cannot contain fractions but are more efficient to use than floating-point numbers. Default value is 0.

The range of Integer is –32768 to 32767. The type is signed and uses the two's complement format for representing negative numbers.

Long

Long is similar to the Integer type but is a 32-bit (4-byte) integer. It therefore has a much bigger range. Default value is 0.

The range of Long is exactly –2,147,483,648 to 2,147,483,647. The type is signed and uses the two's complement format for representing negative numbers.

Single

Single is a 16-bit (2-byte) floating-point type, using the IEEE standard. The range is $\pm 3.402823 \times 10^{38}$. It supports six digits of precision to the right of the decimal point. Default value is 0.0.

When converting back and forth between decimal and binary fractions, some loss of accuracy occurs. For this reason, Currency may be preferable for dollar-and-cents calculations.

Single was the default data type in Visual Basic 1.0 and even earlier versions of Basic. (In fact, if you go far enough into ancient history, it was the only data type supported in Bill Gates' first version of Basic!) These days, there is rarely any reason to use Single — except maybe when storing floating-point numbers on disk when space is at a premium.

Floating-point values can be represented as simple decimal expressions (15.33) or in the scientific format *mmm*E*eee*. You can also use lowercase "e".

```
1.533E1      ' 1.533 times 10 to the 1st power
7.901e5      ' 7.901 times 10 to the 5th power
```

Double

`Double` is the preferred floating-point type. It is a 32-bit (4-byte) value using the IEEE standard. `Double` has the biggest range and precision of all the standard types. The range is $\pm 1.79769313486232 \times 10^{308}$. It supports 14 decimal digits of precision to the right of the decimal point. Default value is 0.0.

When converting back and forth between decimal and binary fractions, some loss of accuracy occurs. For this reason, `Currency` may be preferable for dollar-and-cents calculations.

Floating-point values can be represented as simple decimal expressions (15.33) or in the scientific format *mmm*D*eee*. You can also use lowercase "d". The use of "D", rather than "E", ensures the data is stored internally as `Double`, regardless of how big or small it is.

```
1.533D1      ' 1.533 times 10 to the 1st power
7.901d5      ' 7.901 times 10 to the 5th power
```

String

The standard `String` type creates variable-length character strings. Visual Basic supports many useful string-manipulation functions for use with strings. See Chapter 20 for more information. See also Chapter 14 for use of the string-concatenation operator (&). Default value is the empty string (""). Maximum length is approximately 2-billion characters.

```
Dim S1 As String
S1 = "Enter your name here."
```

You can also declare fixed-length strings. Although you would not often use them in ordinary code, fixed-length strings are sometimes necessary when reading and writing data to a file with fixed-length records or working with databases. The syntax for declaring a fixed-length string is shown here:

```
Dim string_variable As String * length
```

Data assigned to a fixed-length string may need to be padded or truncated, which Visual Basic does automatically. Strings are padded with trailing spaces as needed. Note that in form and class-module declarations, fixed-length strings must not be declared public.

Maximum length of a fixed-length string is 64K.

Boolean

A Boolean holds one of two values: True or False. Default value is False. Visual Basic is slightly skewed in this area, because of its need to be backward compatible. Early versions of Basic treated a Boolean value as just another integer, in which the reasonable values were –1 (true) or 0 (false).

In theory, you can use type Boolean wherever you can use an integer and vice-versa. But in some cases, a Boolean acts differently. If you assign any nonzero value to a Boolean, the amount is converted to True, which is equal to –1.

The best policy is to treat a Boolean as distinct from other kinds of integers. One use for a Boolean variable is to control a loop. In the following example, the end condition is detected in the middle of the loop, instead of the top or bottom.

```
Dim flag As Boolean
flag = True
While flag
    ' Do some stuff…
    If EndCondition Then flag = False
    ' Do some more stuff…
Wend
```

Currency

The Currency type stores fractional quantities in fixed-point format. It stores up to fifteen digits to the left of the decimal point and four to the right. Sign is stored separately, so it can represent both positive and negative numbers. Default value is 0.

You may often hear that floating-point formats introduce rounding errors. The reason may not be immediately obvious. Here's why: With floating-point, fractions are entered and displayed in decimal radix, but internally *stored* in binary radix. There is necessarily a conversion between decimal and binary fractions, which frequently involves loss of data due to rounding. (If you doubt this, try it with a number like 0.7.)

The Currency type largely avoids these errors by using an assumed decimal point. A Currency variable is really a 64-bit integer, but each unit, stored internally, represents $1/10,000$. Thus, the number 2.777 is stored internally as 27,770 units.

13

Date

The Date type can store a date, time of day, or both. This type is frequently used in database applications, where one of the columns may contain a timestamp, and in file operations. You can get the current date and time yourself by using the Date and Time functions. Note that Date is both a type and a function, which is potentially confusing; Visual Basic distinguishes them by context.

```
Dim dt1 As Date, dt2 As Date, dt3 As Date
dt1 = Date
dt2 = Time
dt3 = Date + Time
Print "Current date is "; dt1
Print "Current time is "; dt2
Print "Current date and time is ": dt3
```

One of the reasonable operations you can perform on date/time values is to compare them. For example, the following statements always result in printing "True", because some time elapses between the first and second statements.

```
dt1 = Date + Time        ' Capture date/time.
Print dt1 <= Date + Time  ' Compare to a moment ago.
```

You can use the Now function to get the same result as Date + Time.

```
dt1 = Now            ' Capture date/time.
Print dt1 <= Now     ' Compare to a moment ago.
```

In evaluating a Date value, you may find the following functions helpful: Year, Month, Day, Hour, Minute, and Second each of which takes a Date value and returns the appropriate number. Also useful is the DatePart function, which takes both a Date value and a part specifier (such as "yyyy" for year or "h" for hours - see online Help for DatePart for a list of all these specifiers). The function returns a number in every case. For example:

```
Print "Current month is " & Month(Now)
Print "Current year is " & DatePart("yyyy", Now)
Print "Current hour is " & DatePart("h", Now)
```

Dates can run from January 1, 100 to December 31, 9999. Any time of the day can be stored.

Object

The Object type is a generic type that can represent an object of any class. To successfully use this type, you need to understand a number of concepts. Refer to Chapter 8 for a starting point, or Chapter 16.

As a data type, all object variables are implemented as 32-bit (4-byte) addresses in Visual Basic 6.0. If you're a C programmer, you can best understand an object variable as a pointer without the pointer syntax. (To you C + + programmers, this is a *reference variable*.) Of course, *pointer* is a nasty word to Visual Basic people, so you won't find it in the official documentation.

For advanced programmers, there is one tip that may be useful: Use the Object keyword only when the class is unknown or will change over time. For most object variables, declaring with a specific class, such as TextBox, Collection, a project class module, or a project form, is self-documenting and enables early binding. This kind of binding is more efficient. See Chapter 8 for more information on early and late binding.

Automatic Data Conversion

Automatic conversion between integers and floating-point has been around forever. Conversion between numeric and string values is a relatively new feature of Visual Basic, which used to require the use of Val, Str, or similar functions.

Conversion from numeric (integer or floating-point) to string is automatic and reliable. When you assign a number to a string, the string gets the standard text representation of the number. Automatic conversion is also triggered when you use a number in any context that expects a string — for example, the `AddItem` method.

```
Dim x As Double, s As String
x = 1.507
s = x                    ' s gets "1.507"
List1.AddItem (2 * X)    ' Add "3.014" to list
```

Conversion from string to numeric is trickier, because the string must contain a correct digit string or a run-time error occurs. In some cases, `Val` is still useful; it skips over white spaces and ignores non-numeric characters in converting a string.

```
Dim n As Double
n = "123.4"              ' Valid digit string
n = Val("123 45. 7")     ' Valid use of Val
n = "123 44. 8"          ' ERROR: extra spaces
```

As long as a digit string contains a valid numeral, it can be used anywhere a number is expected. Note that the following performs addition, not string concatenation (which requires `&`).

```
n = n + "12"
```

As an exercise, you might try to figure out why the following statements produce different results:

```
Print n + "1" & "2"      ' Hint: "+" has precedence
Print n + ("1" & "2")
```

Explicit Data Conversion

Sometimes you need control over precisely how a piece of data is stored. This is often the case when you are working with databases and files with fixed-length records. To explicitly convert a value, use one of the functions listed in Table 13-3. Each of these functions takes one argument — which can be an expression of any basic type.

The conversion must not result in an illegal value. For example, converting a Long to an Integer is only valid if the value is in the Integer range.

Table 13-3 *Conversion Functions*

Function	Converts to
CBool	Boolean (converts all nonzero values to True = -1)
CByte	Byte
CCur	Currency
CDate	Date
CInt	Integer
CLng	Long
CSng	Single
CStr	String (generates standard text representation)
CVar	Variant
CVErr	Error (takes an error number as argument)

Note that all Error values have type Variant.

Implicit Variable Declaration

Variable declaration is best done with the Dim statement. This is called *explicit declaration*, and it is good.

```
Dim I As Integer, name As String
```

More to support backward compatibility than for any other reason, Visual Basic supports the type-definition suffixes. Tacking one of these characters to the end of a variable name determines the variable's type. Table 13-4 lists the suffixes.

Table 13-4 *Type-Definition Suffixes*

Suffix	Data Type
$	String
%	Integer

Suffix	Data Type
&	Long
!	Single
#	Double

13

Another way to declare a variable's type without using the Dim statement is to place a Deftype statement in a form or module Declarations section. These statements include DefBool, DefByte, DefInt, DefLng, DefCur, DefSng, DefDbl, DefDate, DefStr, DefObj, DefVar. When using any of these statements, specify a letter or range of letters. Any variable name that starts with one of the letters automatically gets that type, unless a type-definition suffix or Dim statement overrides the type. For example:

```
DefInt A-Z   ' Set integer as default type
```

If you do not set a default type, Variant is the default for all variables.

Operators

This chapter consists of a summary of all operators, followed by information on specific operators.

Summary of Operators

Table 14-1 gives an overview of all VB6 operators. In the syntax column, *num*, *expr*, *str*, *obj*, and *int* stand for number, expression, string, object, and integer, respectively. The precedence level determines the order in which operators are evaluated; operators with higher precedence levels (such as level 1) are evaluated before operators with lower precedence levels (such as level 8). Where precedence level is the same, operators are evaluated left to right.

Table 14-1 *Summary of VB Operators*

Precedence	Operator	Description	Syntax
1	^	Exponentiation	*num* ^ *num*
2	-	Arithmetic negation	- *num*
3	*, /	Multiplication and division	*num* * *num*, *num* / *num*
4	\	Integer division	*num* \ *num*
5	Mod	Modular division	*num* Mod *num*
6	+, -	Addition and subtraction	*num* + *num*, *num* - *num*
7	&	String concatenation	*str* & *expr*, *expr* & *str*
8	=	Equality	*expr* = *expr*
8	<>	Inequality	*expr* <> *expr*
8	<	Less than	*expr* < *expr*
8	>	Greater than	*expr* > *expr*
8	<=	Less than or equal	*expr* <= *expr*
8	>=	Greater than or equal	*expr* >= *expr*
8	Like	Pattern matching	*str* Like *pattern*
8	Is	Object reference	*obj* Is *obj*
9	Not	Logical negation	Not *int*
10	And	Logical And	*int* And *int*
11	Or	Logical inclusive Or	*int* Or *int*
12	Xor	Logical exclusive Or	*int* Xor *int*
13	Eqv	Logical equivalence	*int* Eqv *int*
14	Imp	Logical implication	*int* Imp *int*

In the case of the logic operators (level 9 to level 14), each integer expression, *int*, can be a normal integer type or a Boolean, such as the result of a comparison. (Booleans are actually a subtype of integer.) If both the operands are Boolean, the logic operators help specify a logical condition, just as you would expect. If the operands are non-Boolean, the logic operators function as bitwise operators. For example, And can mask out bits. Booleans and non-Booleans should generally never be combined. The last section in the chapter explains more about these operators and bitwise operations.

Advanced Operators

The use of many of the operators in Table 14.1 should be obvious, but some are either unique to Visual Basic, have special features, or have less obvious uses. The rest of the chapter consists of short sections on the following operators and categories of operators:

- Integer division (\)
- Modular division (Mod)
- String concatenation (&)
- Comparison operators, Like, and Is
- Logic (bitwise) operators

Integer Division

If you look at Table 14.1, you'll see that Visual Basic supports two kinds of division. The first kind is listed next to multiplication (precedence level 3); this is standard, or floating-point, division (/). At precedence level 4 is integer division (\), which is similar, except that it automatically rounds off operands and truncates results, dropping the fractional part, if any.

Standard (floating-point) division produces the result you would usually expect. For example:

```
result1 = 1 / 2       ' Result is 0.5
result2 = 1.5 / 2.5   ' Result is 0.6
result3 = 299 / 100   ' Result is 2.99
```

Integer division first rounds each operand using the following rule: If the fractional part is half-way between two integers, it rounds up for odd numbers (1.5 rounds to 2) and down for even numbers (2.5 also rounds to 2). Otherwise, the number is rounded to the nearest integer. Any fraction in the results is truncated, which means that 0.99 is truncated to 0, for example.

Integer division yields the following results:

```
result1 = 1 \ 2        ' Result is 0
result2 = 1.5 \ 2.5    ' Result is 1
result3 = 299 \ 100    ' Result is 2
```

Modular Division

Modular division returns the remainder portion of a division operation — that is, the amount left over from a division. It is often used in conjunction with integer division, which ignores the remainder. But modular division is also useful by itself.

The following pairs of operations return dividend and remainder:

```
dividend  = 9 \ 2       ' Result is 4
remainder = 9 Mod 2     ' Result is 1

dividend  = 14 \ 5      ' Result is 2
remainder = 14 Mod 5    ' Result is 4
```

The Mod operator provides an easy way to determine if a number is odd or even. The result of the operation in the following example is always 0 if the second operand, 2, divides evenly into the first, the number you're testing.

```
If N Mod 2 = 0 Then Print "N is Even"
```

The Mod operator rounds its operands just as integer division does. See the previous section for more information on rounding.

String Concatenation

The string-concatenation operator (&) replaces the use of the plus sign (+) for joining strings. Although the plus sign can still be used that way, the newer concatenation operator (&) is better because it is unambiguous. This is important in a language like Visual Basic 6, with its support of the Variant data type.

One of the advantages of using this operator is that you can use it to combine strings with other expressions. The result is always a string. In fact, you can use & with *any* two operands, and they will always be converted to strings and then concatenated.

For example:

```
Dim y As Integer, c As Integer, s1 As String
y = 5
c = 100
s1 = "I am " & y & " years old. I can count to " & c
```

The string, s1, now contains the following:

```
I am 5 years old. I can count to 100
```

You can also use this operator to just concatenate two strings. If the operator is used with a `Variant` operand, that operand is interpreted as a string. In contrast, the plus sign performs string concatenation only if both operands are an unambiguous string type.

14

Comparison Operators, Like, and Is

All the comparison operators, including `Like` and `Is`, are at the same precedence level (level 8). When more than one is used in an expression without parentheses, the operators are resolved right to left. This group of operators includes equality (=), greater-than (>), less than (<), and similar operators.

All these operators compare two expressions and produce either `True` or `False`. They are therefore used with control structures, such as `If` and `While`, which require a conditional expression.

With most of these operators — all except `Like` and `Is` — any two expressions may be compared as long as they are the same basic type. All numeric expressions (whether integer or floating-point) can be compared to each other. All strings can be compared to each other. As explained in the note at the end of the next section, string comparisons are case sensitive by default.

The Like Operator

This operator is a variation on string comparison. It tests two strings for equality, with a twist: The second string can contain a pattern.

```
Boolean_result = string Like pattern_string
```

The *pattern_string* is like any other string, except that if special characters occur, they are given the special meanings shown in Table 14-2. A pattern string does not *have* to have these characters. All of them are optional.

Table 14-2 *Special Characters for Like*

Symbol	What This Matches
?	Any one character. ("A?" matches "Aa", "Ax", and "A1", but not "Art".)
*	Any group of zero or more characters. ("B*d" matches any string beginning with "B" and ending in "d".)
#	Any one digit. ("###" matches "123", "439", and "777".)
[*list*]	Any one character that appears in the list.
[!*list*]	Any one character that does *not* appear in the list.

The *list* can be a simple list of characters: For example, "[aeiou]" matches any lowercase vowel. The list can also include a range of characters. The expression "[a-mA-M]" matches any letter in the first half of the alphabet.

To match an *actual occurrence* of one of the characters ?, *, or #, enclose it in brackets. For example, "Ab[?]" matches "Ab?" but not "Abx".

Chapter 11 shows an example of use of the Like operator with the Recordset.Find method. Like is often used in database operations.

●─NOTE────────────────────────────

All string comparisons, including those for Like, are affected by the issue of case sensitivity. The Option Compare Binary statement specifies a case-sensitive order based strictly on the binary values of the character set. Option Compare Text specifies a case-insensitive order, so that "A" and "a" are equivalent. The default is Option Compare Binary (case sensitive). These statements can only appear in the Declarations section of a form or module.

The Is Operator

The Is operator compares two object variables and returns True if they refer to the same object in memory. This is not a comparison of contents. For example, in the following code, A Is B returns True.

```
Set A = B        'A now refers to the same object
If A Is B Then
```

```
        Print "A and B refer to the same object"
End If
```

Suppose you have two different objects, represented by the variables C and D, with identical contents. In this case, C Is D returns False no matter what the contents are. To test contents, you may need to write a special method for that purpose.

● NOTE

You must set your object variables to refer to objects before they can be used with the Is operator.

14

Logic (Bitwise) Operators

The logic operators are used for both Boolean and bitwise operations. There is no confusion as long as you keep the two contexts separate.

In logical (Boolean) expressions, these operators combine the results of different comparisons to produce a complex conditional. You can also combine them with Boolean properties such as Visible.

```
If a = b And c > d Then DoSomething
If sum < 100 Or count >= limit Then DoSomethingElse
If Not Text1.Visible Then Text1.Visible = True
```

Here the logic operators do exactly what you'd expect. The only caveat is that it is unsafe to use the shortcuts C programmers are famous for — combining a Boolean with a non-Boolean value, for example.

The other use for logic operators is in bitwise operations. All the operators compare each corresponding bit in one operand to the corresponding bit in the other operand, according to the rules in Table 14-3.

Of these operators, Not is the only unary operator (Figure 14-1). It works on just one operand, and it produces a result that reverses the setting of each bit in the operand.

Table 14-3 *Rules for Logical (Bitwise) Operators*

Operator	Set a Bit to 1 in the Result If and Only If
Not	The corresponding bit in the (single) operand is 0.
And	Both of the bits in the operands are 1.
Or	Either of the bits in the operands is 1.
Xor	Either, but not both, of the bits in the operands is 1.
Eqv	The bits in the operands have the same value.
Imp	The bit in operand1 is 0 or the bit in operand2 is 1.

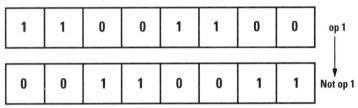

Figure 14-1 *Sample effect of the Not operator*

All the other logic operators work on two operands, comparing the two corresponding bits for each position. Figure 14-2 shows the result that each would produce on two sample operands.

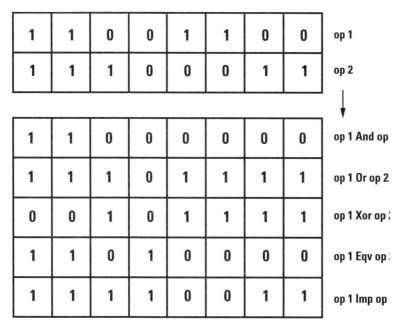

1	1	0	0	1	1	0	0	op 1
1	1	1	0	0	0	1	1	op 2

1	1	0	0	0	0	0	0	op 1 And op
1	1	1	0	1	1	1	1	op 1 Or op 2
0	0	1	0	1	1	1	1	op 1 Xor op :
1	1	0	1	0	0	0	0	op 1 Eqv op :
1	1	1	1	0	0	1	1	op 1 Imp op

Figure 14-2 *Sample effect of binary logic operators*

●—NOTE

If you want to use the logic operators to do bitwise operations, remember that their precedence is low regardless of how they are used. You may need to use parentheses.

Strangely, the logic operators work in both contexts without change. In fact, they do precisely the same operation in both cases, because True and False are defined so that bitwise operations support a Boolean result. True and False are defined as all 1's and all 0's, respectively. Therefore, the operators repeat the same operation in every bit position. Given True and False inputs, the result is always either True or False.

The encoding of all 1's for True results in an integer value of –1.

15

Summary of Standard Controls

This chapter consists of a summary of each control, including a brief description, a picture, and a summary of important properties and events. Each section describes methods in those cases where use of the methods are critical to the basic operation of the control.

The controls are presented here in alphabetical order:

CheckBox	Line
ComboBox	ListBox
CommandButton	OLE
Data	OptionButton
DirListBox	PictureBox
DriveListBox	ScrollBar (vertical and horizontal)
FilesListBox	Shape
Frame	TextBox
Image	Timer
Label	

CheckBox   Check box control

A check box (class CheckBox) provides a simple yes/no selection mechanism. It is different from an option button, which works as part of a group.

Important Properties

The Caption property provides a built-in label for the check box. Aside from Caption, the most important property is the Value property, which has three values: 0 – Unchecked, 1 – Checked, and 2 – Grayed.

The Grayed setting is a neutral state that can be set programmatically. Although this state looks similar to the state of being disabled, the effect is not the same. If the control is actually disabled — by setting the Enabled property to False — the user cannot click the check box. Setting Value to 2 – Grayed does not prevent the user from interacting with the control; it is merely a way of indicating an intermediate state, usually before the user has made a choice. It is very Zen: It is not yes and it is not no.

Important Events

Any change to the state of the Value property results in the Click event. The Click event is triggered when the user clicks the check box on ("checking" the control) as well as clicking it off ("unchecking" the control). If you change Value programmatically, this also triggers a Click event. Within the procedure, test the Value property to determine whether the control has been checked or unchecked.

ComboBox   Combo box control

A combo box control (class ComboBox) provides three variations on the standard list box. None of these support multiple selection.

Important Properties and Methods

The Style property can be set to 0 – Dropdown Combo, 1 – Simple Combo, or 2 –Dropdown List. 0 is the default. It may be easiest to think of the combo box control as three controls in one.

15

Appearance	User Can Enter Text	User Must Select From List
List always visible	ComboBox, Style 1	List box
Drop-down list	ComboBox, Style 0 (default)	ComboBox, Style 2

The Text property specifies a string containing the current selection. See ListBox control for a description of the AddItem and RemoveItem methods, which work with all combo boxes as well as list boxes. Combo boxes also support the Sorted property.

Important Events

If the Style property is set to 0 or 1, the combo box supports the Change event. This event is triggered when a change is made by direct entry of text. All styles of combo box support the Click event, when a selection is made from a list. Combo boxes with styles 0 or 1 should respond to both.

CommandButton | Command button control

A command button (class CommandButton) is the standard control for providing a direct command, such as OK or Cancel.

Important Properties

The Caption property specifies the button's text, which is typically a command name. The Visible and Enabled properties are Boolean properties controlling visibility and user access, respectively. The basic use of a command button requires little setting of properties, although some provide useful advanced features.

You can set the Style property to 1 – Graphical at design time. This lets you control exactly what the button displays at any time by setting the Picture, DownPicture, and DisabledPicture image properties.

Other useful properties that can be set at design time include Default and Cancel. When Default is set to True, the button gets a Click event whenever the user presses Enter — regardless of which control on the form previously had the focus. When Cancel is set to true, the button gets a Click event whenever the user presses Esc.

Important Events

Use the Click event to respond to the user clicking on the button. In most cases, this is the only event procedure you need to write for a command button. Note that setting a command button's Value property to True triggers the Click event.

Data	**Database access control**

A data control (class Data) enables the user to browse through a database. It is usually linked to other controls bound to it through their DataSource property.

Important Properties

To enable operation of the control, first set its DatabaseSource and RecordSource properties:

Property	Description
DatabaseName	Set this first. This property specifies the name of a database file, (such as Nwind.mdb, which comes with Visual Basic).
RecordSource	This property specifies the name of one of the tables (or other components) from the database specified in DatabaseName.

After these two properties are set, you can bind other controls — typically text boxes — by setting each control's DataSource and DataField properties. Set DataSource to the name of your Data control. Then set DataField to one of the column names; Visual Basic provides a convenient drop-down box with all the columns listed.

Data controls support a number of other useful properties. One of these is Connect, which specifies a database type. Another is ReadOnly, which, if set to True, prevents users from making changes to the database.

Important Methods

The control's Recordset property supports many useful methods of its own. Several of the Recordset methods move the record position within the table: MoveFirst, MoveLast, MovePrevious, and MoveLast. Other Recordset methods support modification of the database: AddNew, Delete, Update, and Refresh.

DirListBox   Directory list box control

A directory list box (class `DirListBox`) provides a specialized list box for browsing the file system. It is intended to be used with `DriveListBox` and `FileListBox` controls.

Important Properties

15

The most important property for a directory list box is the `Path` property. The `Path` setting for a directory list box contains the path name of the current directory. The control automatically displays a file hierarchy above this directory as well as one level of child directories below it. The end user selects the current directory by double-clicking it.

Setting `Path` is similar to a change-directory command. For example, setting `Path` with a simple drive letter tells the control to switch drives (comparable to the effect of `CD C:` in DOS). Any time you *get* the value of `Path`, it returns the complete directory name, including both drive letter and file path.

Important Events

For a directory list box, you usually only need to write code to connect it to a file list box. The following code provides the connection between two controls, `Dir1` and `File1`:

```
Private Sub Dir1_Change()
    File1.Path = Dir1.Path
End Sub
```

DriveListBox

Drive list box control

A drive list box (class `DriveListBox`) provides a drop-down list of drives on the system. It is intended to be used with `DirListBox` and `FileListBox` controls.

Important Properties

This control supports one all-important property: `Drive`, a string property. This property contains the current drive letter followed by a colon (for example, c:). When you set this property, only the first letter of the string is significant, and case doesn't matter.

Important Events

For a drive list box, you usually only need to write code to connect it to a directory list box. The following code provides the connection between two controls, `Drive1` and `Dir1`:

```
Private Sub Drive1_Change()
    Dir1.Path = Drive1.Drive
End Sub
```

This code assigns the drive letter (for example, c:) to the `Path` property of the directory list box. Setting `Path` causes the directory list box to switch to the specified drive. (See `DirListBox`).

FileListBox   File list box control

A file list box (class `FileListBox`) provides a simple list of files for a specified directory and (optionally) filename pattern such as *.txt" or *.exe.

Important Properties

Two of the important properties for this control are `Path` and `FileName`, both string properties available at run time only. You can set `Path` with a drive letter, directory path, or both. Changing `Path` specifies a new directory to be displayed. When you get the value of `Path`, it always returns the complete path to the file list box's current directory, including drive letter.

The `FileName` property contains an empty string if no file is selected. If a file is selected, `FileName` returns the filename without directory path. You can get the complete filename with path by using the following code:

```
If Right(File1.Path, 1) <> "\" Then s = "\"
theFile = File1.Path & s & File1.FileName
```

You can set `FileName` with a filename, drive letter, directory, or pattern, triggering the appropriate event. `Pattern` is a string property determining what files to display.

The file list box supports the `MultiSelect` property. When this property is set to `True`, use the `List`, `Selected`, and `ListCount` properties to get selections. See `ListBox`.

Important Events

To respond to a user choice, write an event procedure for `DblClick`. Assignment of a valid name to the `FileName` property also triggers the `DblClick` event. Other useful events include `PathChange` and `PatternChange`.

Frame	Frame control

A frame control (class Frame) provides a mechanism for grouping other controls. This can be for visual clarity, grouping option buttons, or for creating a group of controls that can be easily moved as a unit.

Important Properties

Setting the BorderStyle property to 0 – None has the effect of making the frame invisible at run time, including the caption, if any. The default value is 1 – Fixed Single. Note that a frame can be useful even if not visible.

The frame control comes with a built-in label, which is set with the Caption property. The Appearance property has a default setting of 1 – 3D but can be set to 0 – Flat.

Important Events

A frame is not often used for responding to events, although it does recognize a number of common events, such as Click.

Special Usage Tips

To place controls in the interior of a frame, first create the frame and then draw controls onto the frame using the drag-and-draw approach. If a frame moves, it takes with it only those controls that were drawn on it. However, for option buttons to be grouped by a frame, it is only necessary that the option buttons be completely inside the interior of the frame.

15

Image	Lightweight image control

An image control (class Image) provides a simple bitmap image to place in the background graphics of its container (form, picture box, or frame). It has some features in common with a picture box, but it is less flexible and uses fewer resources.

Important Properties

The Picture property specifies a bitmap to load an image from. When you attempt to set this property at design time, Visual Basic provides a dialog box for choosing a bitmap file. (Note that to clear the image, highlight the word (Bitmap) and press Del.)

The Stretch property is another useful property for controlling appearance. If Stretch is set to True, and if the picture is smaller than the control's area, then the picture is stretched to fill the space. Regardless of the value of Stretch, if the picture is bigger than the control's area, the control's area is automatically expanded to fit, downward and to the right; the top-left corner is fixed.

The Enabled property, if set to False, turns off the ability of the control to respond to user events.

Important Events

Although an image control cannot respond to all the events that a picture box can respond to, it does recognize some events — most notably Click and DblClick.

Label	**Label control**

A label control (class Label) provides a one-line, non-editable description. This is useful for labeling other controls that do not have their own built-in label.

Important Properties

The most important property for a label control is the Caption property, which specifies the text to be displayed. Typically, this is the only part of the control the user sees.

The label control is simple, but it has some special features. Setting the Border control to 1 draws a visible border around the control's area.

Setting the BackStyle property to 0 – Transparent enables background graphics to show through; otherwise the label's area blocks out what's in the background. The default setting of this property is 1 – Opaque. As with the line, shape, and image properties, a label is basically part of the background graphics. If one of the other standard controls overlaps the label's area, the label appears to be "underneath" the control, regardless of BackStyle.

Important Events

Surprisingly, the label control recognizes a number of events, although it cannot get focus. You can respond to the Click event, for example, and the Change event is triggered whenever the caption is changed by the program.

15

Line | Line drawing control

A line control (class Line) provides an easy way to draw lines in the background graphics of a form, picture box, or frame at design time.

Important Properties

Line controls support a small number of properties for modifying appearance, including BorderColor, BorderStyle, and BorderWidth. Visible is a useful Boolean property.

The DrawMode property determines how the line interacts with the background to produce pixels. The default is 13 – Copy Pen, which does what you would usually expect: It draws the line while ignoring the background. Potentially useful is 7 – Xor Pen, which applies an exclusive OR operation on the pen and background pixels. What makes this useful is that applying Xor twice restores the original background, making a line erasable.

The line's endpoints are controlled by the X1, Y1, X2, and Y2 properties. All these can be set at design time or run time.

Tips on Usage

Line and shape controls are always associated with the background of some container. If you want to place a line control in a frame or picture box container, you must first create the container and then draw the line control onto that container. A line control appears behind other controls (unless that control is the container), because the line is a part of background graphics. It behaves much like output of Visual Basic graphics statements. However, it is automatically redrawn

Events

Line and shape controls cannot get the focus and do not recognize any events. All mouse events in the line's area go to the container.

ListBox
List box control

A list box control (class ListBox) provides a simple drop-down list of strings. Optionally, a list box can support multiple selection. See also ComboBox.

Important Properties

The MultiSelect property is an integer property that can be set to 1 – Simple or 2 – Extended. If MultiSelect is turned off by being set to 0 (the default setting), the currently selected item is stored in the Text string property. If multiple selection is enabled, you'll need to use the List, Selected, and SelCount properties. List is an array of strings that holds all the list box items. Selected is an array of Boolean values, in which an element is True if the corresponding item in the list box is selected. These arrays and the list box are all zero-based. SelCount returns the number of selected items. (For examples, see Chapter 6.)

There are a number of other useful properties for list boxes, including Sorted. When set to True, this property causes items to be automatically maintained in alphabetical order. The ListCount property returns the total number of items in the list.

Important Methods

The AddItem method provides the only way to initialize list box contents. Each call takes one string argument and, optionally, an index indicating where to insert the item. A good place to do this initialization is in Form_Load. RemoveItem takes a single integer argument. Both methods use zero-based indexes.

Important Events

The most important events are Click and DblClick. The DblClick event indicates a definite choice; Click can be triggered by the user scrolling through the list with arrow keys.

OLE	OLE container control

The OLE container control (class OLE) enables you to place data from another application into a Visual Basic form.

Important Properties

This control supports a number of unique properties. For complete information, consult online Help. Three of the most important are Class, SourceDoc, and SourceItem, which together determine what is embedded or linked.

The Class property specifies what application the OLE data is taken from. A sample setting is Word.Document.8, which has the form *app.doctype.version*. The SourceDoc property specifies the filename of the document; this is left blank if the OLE control is being used to create a new document. Finally, the SourceItem property — which is often left blank — is useful in some cases for specifying part of a document. The notation used is specific to the application. With Excel, a range of cells may be specified with a setting such as R1C1:R5C5.

No code is required to create a functioning OLE container. The Class and SourceDoc properties are set automatically when you use the Insert Object dialog box at design time. This dialog box comes up when you create the OLE control. You can also activate it by right-clicking to get the control's pop-up menu, and then choosing Insert Object.

Important Methods and Events

Some of the important methods for this control are Copy, Paste, Delete, and DoVerb. The Close method closes the OLE object.

Events are not always used with OLE controls. However, a number are recognized, including Click, DblClick, Validate, and Updated. Be careful about responding to Click and DblClick, because at run time, the user clicks the document to edit it.

OptionButton   Option button control

An option button (class OptionButton) indicates a selection from two or more alternatives. Unlike check boxes, option buttons are designed to work as part of a group; selecting an option button deselects the other buttons in the group.

Important Properties

15

Physical grouping determines how option buttons are related. All buttons in the same container (usually, a frame or picture box) are part of the same group. You can create a frame and then draw option buttons inside it. Also, all the option buttons drawn directly onto a form, and not inside another container, constitute a group. All this is done by drawing the controls at design time, without coding or property setting; why do you think it's called *Visual* Basic?

As with other controls, the Caption property specifies text for the built-in label of the button. Other properties provide advanced ways of controlling the button's appearance. If you set the Style property to 1 – Graphical, you can set the Picture, DownPicture, and DisabledPicture image properties to give the button a customized look.

The all-important Value property specifies whether the control is actually selected or not. It has only two values: True or False.

Important Events

Use the Click event to respond to the user selection of the option button. In addition, any time the Value property is set to True, the Click event is triggered. Note that (in contrast to check box behavior) the Click event is only triggered when the control is selected. Going to the unchecked state does not trigger this event.

PictureBox   Picture box control

A picture box (class `PictureBox`) provides a graphical area with maximum flexibility. You can use it, like a form, to draw to at run time or as a container for other controls, including option buttons, shapes, lines, and multiple images.

Important Properties

A picture box differs from an image control in that the picture box is a fully functional container for other controls, as well as a separate window. A picture box can contain several image controls, for example, but the converse is not true.

Nevertheless, both types of controls support the `Picture` property for setting a bitmap to load an image from. When you attempt to set this property at design time, Visual Basic provides a dialog box for choosing a bitmap file. (Note that to clear the image, highlight the word (Bitmap) and press Del.)

At run time, you can access a picture box's `Image` property to get a bitmap of everything drawn onto the control, including pictures, shapes, and graphics statement output. This property can then be assigned to another picture box's `Picture` property, something you would need to do if you've turned `AutoRedraw` off and are restoring the image from a buffer.

```
Private Sub Form_Paint()
    Picture1.Picture = pctBuffer.Image
End Sub
```

Important Events and Methods

In addition to support `Click` and `DblClick`, picture boxes recognize many of the same events that forms do, including the `Paint` and `Resize` events.

Picture boxes support all the same graphics drawing methods that forms do, including `Print`, `Line`, `Circle`, `Cls`, and `Refresh`.

| **ScrollBar** | **Horizontal and vertical scrollbars** |

Scrollbar controls (class names HScrollBar and VScrollBar) provide a scrollbar mechanism that you can interact with programmatically. Although they come in two versions — horizontal and vertical — the properties and events are the same for both.

Important Properties

By themselves, scrollbar controls do nothing but provide a way of displaying a value to the user and letting the user set that value. It is your responsibility to translate that value into an action, if any (for example, moving through a bitmap or a document).

The Min and Max properties establish the meaning of the scrollbar range. For example, Min and Max settings of 0 to 100 mean that every position on the scroll bar represents some value between these numbers — 50 being the half-way point. On horizontal controls, Max corresponds to the rightmost point; on vertical controls, it corresponds to the point nearest the bottom of the screen. You can reverse these directions by assigning a higher value to Min than to Max.

The Value property specifies the position of the scrollbar indicator, relative to Min and Max. Setting it causes the indicator to move; getting its value gives the indicator's current position. Other useful properties include Enabled, which when set to False blocks user interaction; and LargeChange, which sets the amount that Value moves when the user clicks on the bar on either side of the indicator.

Important Events

The two interesting events for scrollbars are Change and Scroll. The choice of which to respond to is important. If the user grabs the scrollbar, moves it around, and releases it, this triggers just one Change event. But the same action generates many Scroll events. Use Scroll only when you want constant updating during scrollbar movement.

Shape	Shape drawing control

A shape control (class Shape) provides an easy way of creating background graphics (rectangle, square, circle, or oval) of a form, picture box, or frame at design time.

Important Properties

The most interesting property for this control is Shape (same as the class name), which determines which shape is drawn. It can be set at design time and run time. The values are 0 – Rectangle, 1 – Square, 2 – Oval, 3 – Circle, 4 – Rounded Rectangle, and 5 – Rounded Square.

The FillStyle, FillColor, and BackStyle properties all affect how the shape is filled in. A BackStyle property setting of 0 – Transparent enables other background graphics to show through. A setting of 1 – Opaque causes the interior of the shape to block out any background graphics drawn earlier. The default is Transparent.

Tips on Usage

Line and shape controls are always associated with the background of some container. If you want to place a shape control in a frame or picture box container, you must first create the container and then draw the shape control onto that container. A shape control appears behind other controls (unless that control is the container), because it's a part of the background graphics. It behaves much like output of Visual Basic graphics statements. However, it is automatically redrawn.

Events

Line and shape controls cannot get the focus and do not recognize any events. All mouse events in the shape's area go to the container.

TextBox   Text box control

A text box control (class TextBox) provides a standard Windows text box. The user can enter and edit text in this control unless you prevent it (by setting Enabled to False).

Important Properties

The Text property is a string containing the contents of the text box. If you set this property, the new setting replaces the entire contents. If you get the value of this property, the contents are returned in a single string. With multiline text boxes, all the contents are returned along with carriage-return/newline pairs (vbCrLf) to separate lines.

The Multiline property, if True, causes the text box to support multiple lines of text. Another important design-time property is Scrollbars, which may be set to 0 – None, 1 – Horizontal, 2 – Vertical, and 3 – Both. These settings produce built-in scrollbars, not to be confused with ScrollBar controls. Setting Enabled to False prevents the user from editing text, but does not change the appearance of the text box.

Several properties deal with selected text and are available at run time only. The SelText property is a string containing the selected (highlighted) text. Setting this property replaces all selected text, or inserts new text at the insertion point if no text is selected. SelStart indicates where the selection or insertion point begins; it is a zero-based index into the text. SelLength indicates number of characters selected.

Important Events

Any change to the contents triggers the Change event. The KeyPress event gives the added capability of intercepting keystrokes: Changing the value of the Keyascii argument changes the character just typed. Changing the value to 0 cancels the keystroke.

Timer   Timed interval control

A timer control (class `Timer`) lets you write code to be executed at regular intervals.

Important Properties

The timer control is the simplest of the standard controls in terms of its structure. The only property unique to this control is the `Interval` property, which specifies the interval of time between events. This is an integer property specifying time in milliseconds. A value of 500, for example, means that the `Timer` event (see "Important Events" section that follows) is triggered every half second. A value of 100 means that the event is triggered every tenth of a second.

The timer supports the `Top` and `Left` properties, but these have no meaning at run time. Timers are visible only at design time, and then only for convenience. Timers have no graphical component at run time.

The `Enabled` property has a specific function with regard to timers: When `Enabled` is set to `False`, it blocks the timer from triggering events. It has no connection to the user.

Important Events

Whenever the time period set in `Interval` elapses, it triggers a `Timer` event. This is the only event supported. The name of this event is the same as the class name of the control (`Timer`), which should confuse you only for a short interval.

16

Object Keywords and Tools

Whether you consider Visual Basic object oriented or merely object based, objects and classes are a big part of the language these days. Visual Basic now supports nearly all the features of object-oriented languages. The major omission is that it still does not support subclassing. In spite of that, polymorphism is made possible through late binding and through the use of interfaces, compatible with COM.

Almost all the object-oriented features of Visual Basic 6.0 are inherited from Version 5. One of the new features is the ability to use CreateObject to get type information from a remote machine on the network.

This chapter reviews the object-oriented tools available to you. For an introduction to the concepts, see Chapter 8.

This chapter consists of the following major topics:

- Keywords: object variables
- Keywords: class modules
- Testing an object's type
- The object browser

- Interfaces
- Collection objects
- Dictionary objects

Keywords: Object Variables

The keywords in this section, summarized in Table 16-1, enable you to create and set individual objects.

Table 16-1 *Keywords Used with Object Variables*

Keyword	Description
Dim and related keywords	Can be used to declare object variables, optionally allocating an object with New
Set statement	Assigns an object to an object variable
New operator	Allocates a new object
CreateObject function	Allocates a new ActiveX object
GetObject function	Returns a reference to an existing ActiveX object or allocates an ActiveX object associated with a file

Using Dim to Declare Object Variables

The Dim statement, when used to create an object variable, has the following syntax. The brackets indicate that the use of New is optional.

    Dim varname As [New] classname

The *classname* is either Object , an intrinsic class, or the name of a class module in the project. If New is used, then an object of the specified type is allocated and assigned to *varname*. If New is omitted, then *varname* must later be set to an actual object before being used.

For example, the following Dim statement allocates an object and assigns it to objVar:

    Dim objVar As New myClass

But in the next example, the first statement declares objVar without allocating an object to which it refers. The second statement, Set, allocates the actual object and assigns it. The effect of these two statements is the same as the one statement in the previous example.

```
Dim objVar As myClass
Set objVar = New myClass
```

You can also declare an object variable by using the generic Object type. Such a variable can be assigned an object of any class. However, using this approach causes property and method references to be late bound and therefore less efficient.

```
Dim objVar As Object
Set objVar = New myClass
```

16

●—**NOTE**————————————————————————————————

Other data-declaration statements, including Public, Private, and Global, can be used to declare object variables, just as Dim can. All the same considerations apply.

Set	**Object assignment**
	statement

The Set statement assigns an object reference to an object variable. Except in the case of Nothing, this has the effect of making an object variable refer to an actual object in memory. Until an actual object is assigned to it, an object variable cannot be used to refer to properties or methods.

There are several ways to use the Set statement:

```
Set var1 = New classname
Set var1 = var2
Set var1 = Nothing
Set var1 = CreateObject(strClass [, strMachine])
Set var1 = GetObject([strPathname] [,strClass])
```

Continued

The first syntax allocates a new object in memory of type *classname* and assigns it to *var1*. For example, the following statement allocates a new Collection object.

```
Set anObjVar = New Collection
```

The second syntax sets *var1* to refer to the same object that *var2* does. This does not copy object contents, which you might expect. Instead, there is still only one copy of the object, but now two variables refer to it. Note that this statement is legal only if the variable on the right side of the equal sign (=) has an object assigned to it.

```
Set anotherObjVar = anObjVar
```

The third syntax releases the connection between the object variable and the object it refers to. Note that when the number of references to an object go to zero, it is automatically deleted, freeing up memory.

```
Set anObjVar = Nothing
```

The CreateObject and GetObject functions are used for getting ActiveX objects. The details of using these functions are covered in upcoming sections.

New	**Allocation operator**

The New operator allocates an object in memory and returns a reference to the object. The class name immediately following New specifies the object type.

New *classname*

The *classname* must be an intrinsic type or the name of a class module in the project. Allocating an ActiveX object requires the use of CreateObject or GetObject rather than New. For the use of New in context, see the previous two sections.

Notice that New can be used in at least two principal contexts: It can be used in the same statement that declares an object variable, and it can be used in a Set statement. For example, here New is used in data declarations:

```
Dim theColl As New Collection
Static carl As New Auto      ' Auto is a class module
```

Here New is used with the Set statement:

```
Set theColl2 = New Collection
```

In either case, the effect of New is the same: to create an object of specified type, which is then assigned to some object variable.

CreateObject   Create application object function

The CreateObject function allocates an ActiveX object in memory and returns a reference to it. The function is used in a statement with the following syntax. The brackets indicate that *strMachine* is optional.

Set *varname* = **CreateObject(**strClass [, strMachine]**)**

Here, *strClass* is a string that contains the name of an object. The string has the following form, in which *appname* is the name of an application and *class* is a specific object type.

"appname.class"

An ActiveX object can come from Visual Basic Scripting classes or from an application (such as Excel) that supports ActiveX. You can also allocate ADO database classes this way. (See Chapter 11 for more information on ADO.) For example:

```
Dim file As Object, dict As Object, xlss As Object
Set file = CreateObject("Scripting.FileSystemObject")
Set dict = CreateObject("Scripting.Dictionary")
Set xlss = CreateObject("Excel.Sheet")
Set conn = CreateObject("ADODB.Connection")
```

The optional *strMachine* argument is a string containing the name of a remote server. The server name is associated with the public share of the server. For example, if the share is "\\theServer\public," then *strMachine* should contain the text "theServer".

Continued

● **NOTE**

This ability to specify a remote machine as server is a new feature in Visual Basic 6.0.

GetObject	Get reference to object function

The GetObject function returns a reference to an existing object or an object associated with an existing file. The function has the following syntax.

```
Set var1 = GetObject([strPathname] [,strClass])
```

Here *strPathname* and *strClass* are both strings containing a filename and a class name, respectively. The filename can be a complete path.

This syntax, in effect, provides four different versions of the function. Each does something different.

Syntax	Description
GetObject(*strPathname*, *strClass*)	Loads the file and returns an object of the specified class.
GetObject(*strPathname*)	Loads the file. ActiveX automation determines what type of object is returned.
GetObject("", *strClass*)	Creates an instance of the class and returns a reference.
GetObject(, *strClass*)	Returns a reference to an existing instance of the class. If no instance exists, the function generates an error.

If *StrClass* is omitted, ActiveX automation determines what kind of object is returned. For example:

```
Dim myXLS As Object
Set myXLS = GetObject("c:\Excel\MYSPREAD.XLS")
```

If *StrClass* is included as an argument, it uses the same *app-name.class* format used with CreateObject. For example:

```
Dim mySpread As Object
Set mySpread = GetObject(, "Excel.Application")
```

Note that this version returns a currently active instance of `Excel.Application`. If no instance can be found, it generates an error.

Keywords: Class Modules

Defining an object type in Visual Basic is as easy as creating a class module. To define a class, open the File menu and choose Add Class Module.

The name of the module determines the class name: Use the Project window to select the class module, and then use the Properties window to set the `Name` property.

Table 16-2 summarizes the keywords that can be used to implement properties and methods in a class module.

Table 16-2 *Keywords Used with Class Modules*

16

Keywords	Description
`Public`	Declares a simple property. (This is mutually exclusive with the use of `Property Get`, `Set`, and `Let`.)
`Function` , `Sub`	Declares a method.
`Property Get`	Returns a property value to object user.
`Property Let`	Lets user of object set a property value.
`Property Set`	Same as `Property Let`, except that it is used with properties that are objects.
`Class_Initialize`	Called when an object is created.
`Class_Terminate`	Called just before object is destroyed.

Declaring Properties with Public

The simplest properties are those that the object user sets and gets directly. Such properties don't do anything special — they just hold a value. To create such a property, just declare it with `Public` in the class module's Declaration section.

```
Public Address As String   ' Creates Address property
Public Amount As Integer    ' Creates Amount property
```

Suppose that these declarations are placed in a class module named myClass. Now, any object of type myClass automatically has read/write access to properties named Address and Amount. For example:

```
Dim theObj As New myClass
theObj.Address = "1600 Penn Ave"
theObj.Amount = 100
```

If you want a property to do more than just passively hold data, you'll need to write Property Get and Property Let procedures. In that case, you won't be able to declare a variable of the same name; usually, you'll declare a private variable with a different name to hold the actual data. (See "Property Get Procedure" for an example.)

Declaring Methods with Function and Sub

All Function and Sub procedures declared in a class module are Public by default and therefore define methods. A method must be accessed through *object.method* syntax from other modules. For example, suppose you have the following declaration in the module myClass:

```
Sub display(s As String)
  '...
End Sub
```

This creates a display method. To call it from outside the class module, it's necessary to first create an object:

```
Dim theObj As New myClass
theObj.display "Hello"
```

To declare a procedure that is not a method, modify the declaration with Private or Friend. A Private procedure is not accessible to other modules. This is appropriate for procedures that are for internal use only.

A procedure declared with Friend is accessible to other modules, but is not called with the *object.method* syntax. A Friend procedure is a standard procedure that just happens to reside in a class module.

The `Public`, `Private`, and `Friend` keywords are all modifiers that appear in front of `Function` or `Sub` in the first line, if used at all.

Property Get	Return property value procedure

Use a `Property Get` procedure to return the value of a property. This procedure is called when the user of an object (an instance of the class module) gets the property's value.

```
Print theObject.prop1    ' Calls Property Get prop1
```

This approach is not compatible with declaring the property as a public variable, as described earlier. If you write a `Property Get` procedure, you should also write a `Property Let` or `Property Set` procedure for the same property, unless it is read-only.

A `Property Get` procedure has the following syntax. The brackets indicate that the `As` clause is optional, but you should include it unless your property's type is the same as the default type. This use of `As type` specifies the property's type. The *args* are optional; you can employ them to create property arrays, using any kind of index(es).

Property Get *propname* [(*args*)] [**As** *type*]
  statements
End Property

The *statements* can include the following special statements:

Syntax	Description
propname **=** *value*	Required, except in the case of object properties. At least one such statement must be placed in the procedure. This statement sets the property value until overridden by another statement.
Set *propname* = *object*	Required for properties that are objects.
Exit Property	Optional. This statement enables you to exit early.

Continued

The following example creates a read/write string property named Upstring. It uses a Property Let procedure as well as Property Get. This property has the special feature of always returning uppercase letters. The actual data is stored in m_Upstring, a private variable.

```
Dim m_Upstring As String   ' This stores the data.

' This is called when user gets the value.
'
Property Get Upstring As String
    Upstring = UCase(m_Upstring)
End Property

' This is called when user sets the value.
'
Property Let Upstring(ByVal newstring As String)
    m_Upstring = newstring
End Property
```

Property Let	Respond to new value procedure

Use a Property Let procedure to respond to a new property setting. This procedure is called when the user of an object (an instance of the class module) sets the property value.

```
theObject.prop1 = newval   ' Calls Property Let prop1
```

This approach is not compatible with declaring the property as a public variable, as described earlier. If you write a Property Let procedure, you should also write a Property Get procedure for the same property, unless it is write-only.

A Property Let procedure has the following syntax. The brackets indicate that the As clause is optional, but you should include it unless your property's type is the same as the default type. This use of As *type* specifies the property's type. The *args* are optional; you can use them to create property arrays, using any kind of index(es).If *args* are used, they must match the corresponding argument list in Property Get exactly.

```
Property Let propname ([args,] ByVal newval [As type])
    statements
End Property
```

The statements can include the special End Property state-ment for exiting early. There are no required statements.

For an example, see the previous section, "Property Get Procedure."

Property Set   Assign object property procedure

A Property Set procedure is the same as a Property Let proce-dure, except that it is used with properties that are embedded object references. Property Set is called when a user of a class-module object attempts to assign a new object to the property.

```
' theObject is an instance of the class module,
'  prop1 is an embedded object
'
Set theObject.prop1 = obj    ' Call Property Set prop1
```

You may not wish to let the user of the object reassign what object your property refers to. In such a case, make the property read-only by not writing a Property Set procedure. The user of the object will still be able to modify the embedded object's contents.

A Property Set procedure has the following syntax. The brackets indicate that the As clause is optional, but you should include it unless relying on the default type.

```
Property Set propname (newval [As type])
    statements
End Property
```

The statements can include the special Exit Property state-ment for exiting early. There are no required statements.

The following example shows an object property with Property Get and Property Set procedures. The actual object is a collection declared as theColl, and the property name is mycol-lection. Class_Initialize is used here to ensure that there is an

Continued

actual object to refer to, in case the class user refers to
object.mycollection without first setting it.

```
Dim theColl As Collection

Property Get mycollection As Collection
    Set mycollection = theColl
End Property

Property Set mycollection(newObj As Collection)
    Set theColl = newObj
End Property

Private Sub Class_Initialize
    Set theColl = New Collection
End Sub
```

16

Class_Initialize — Initialize class procedure

The Class_Initialize procedure, if present, is automatically
called immediately after an object of the class is allocated, but
before anything else happens. (For you C + + fans, this is the
equivalent of a constructor.) It's a useful place to set initial values
for any and all properties, as well as performing any other initialization you might need. The Class_Initialize procedure has the
following syntax:

```
Private Sub Class_Initialize()
    statements
End Sub
```

For example, the following procedure initializes a couple of
variables and allocates a new Collection object.

```
Private Sub Class_Initialize()
    n = 1
    aString = "xxx"
    Set aBunchOfStuff = New Collection
End Sub
```

Class_Terminate — Terminate class procedure

The Class_Terminate procedure, if present, is automatically called just after the decision has been made to terminate an object but before it is deleted from memory. (For you C++ fans, this is the equivalent of a destructor.) You can do any cleanup here you feel is necessary. The Class_Initialize procedure has the following syntax:

```
Private Sub Class_Terminate()
    statements
End Sub
```

Usually, there isn't much reason to write a Class_Terminate procedure, because Visual Basic automatically cleans up most kinds of resources for you. One possible use is to print a diagnostic, so that you know when an object was in fact destroyed. Another is to close an open file.

```
Private Sub Class_Terminate()
    Debug.Print "class myClass: terminating now."
    Close #1
End Sub
```

Testing an Object's Type

The TypeName function returns a string containing the name of a variable's type:

```
TypeName(varname)
```

In the case of simple data types, the string returned may contain a name such as "Integer", "Long", "Double", "String", and so on. In the name of an object variable, the string contains the name of the specific object type assigned to it, if any. For example:

```
Dim theObj As Object
Set theObj = New myClass
Debug.Print TypeName(theObj)   ' Prints "myClass"
```

The use of `TypeName` allows you to test an object before calling its methods. For example:

```
Sub handleObject(obj As Object)
    If TypeName(obj) = "myClass" Then
        ' Call myClass methods
    End If
    '...
End Sub
```

Another way to test object variables is to use the `Is` operator, which determines if two variables refer to the same object in memory (see Chapter 14).

The Object Browser

16

Pressing F2 displays the Object Browser. You can also display the browser by choosing the Object Browser command from the View menu. Figure 16-1 shows a sample session with the Object Browser. The left side displays classes and types. The right side displays several kinds of class members: constants, methods, and properties, each kind identified by a different icon.

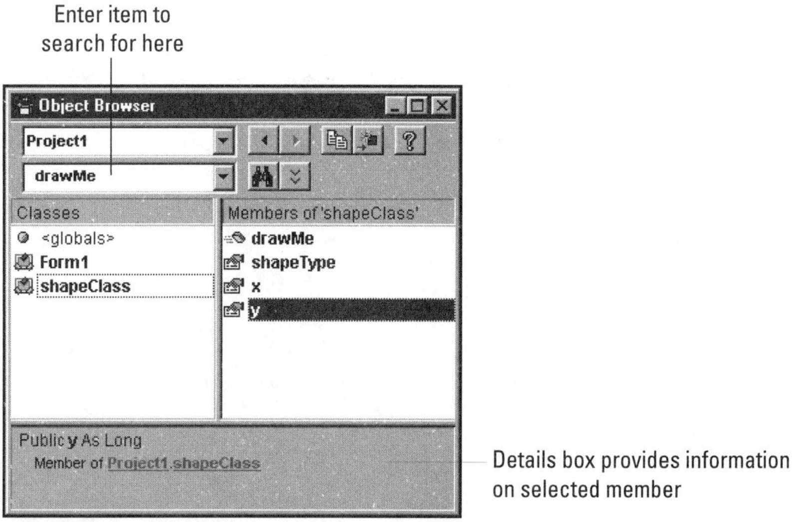

Enter item to
search for here

Details box provides information
on selected member

Figure 16-1 *The Object Browser*

Mostly, the use of the Object Browser is self-explanatory, but the browser has a couple of features that might not be obvious at first.

The Details box appears at the bottom of the Object Browser and provides type information for whatever item (class or member) is selected. For constants, the value is displayed. The first text box in the upper-left corner selects the library. The second text box can be used to search for a specific member (constant, method, or property). To use this text box, type a name and press Enter. The button containing the two arrows can be used to close the Search Results pane afterward.

To go directly to the definition of a class member, double-click the name. Doing so displays the Code window.

Interfaces

In the Visual Basic environment, you can both define and implement interfaces. An *interface* is like a contract: By implementing an interface you agree to support a certain list of properties and/or methods. Visual Basic interfaces are fully compatible with interfaces used by Microsoft's Component Object Model (COM).

Class modules can implement interfaces. A class that implements one interface can implement others, and it can have other properties and methods. Any number of classes can implement the same interface. Each provides its own code for all the interface methods.

Interfaces are polymorphic, which is one of the reasons they are useful. *Polymorphism* is one of the most advanced concepts in object-oriented programming. Basically, it means that in the following code, the exact type of theObj doesn't have to be known until run time:

```
Sub doShape(theObj As IShape)
    '...
    theObj.display 100, 200
End Sub
```

Why is this interesting or useful? Because any number of different classes can provide their own version of IShape_display, and this procedure will work with any of them. You can even develop a new class in the future and pass it to doShape, without having to recompile the module containing doShape.

By convention, names of interfaces start with the letter "I."

Defining an Interface

An interface can be provided by Component Object Model (COM) tools, such as the MkTypeLib utility. You can also define an interface from within Visual Basic itself. To define an interface, follow these steps:

1. Open a new project.
2. Select ActiveX DLL as the project type.
3. The project automatically opens a class module for you. Set the Name property of this module to the desired interface name. (For example, ICar.)
4. Define a series of properties and/or methods — but write no statements inside the method declarations. (See the example that follows.)
5. From the File menu, choose the Make command. Choose a meaningful name of the .dll file, such as **ICarRefs**. (Before executing this command, it's also a good idea to assign a meaningful internal name for the project, because it will show up later in the References dialog box.)

For example, the following statements declare one property, speed, and one method, accelerate:

```
Public speed As Double

Function accelerate (delta As Double) As Double

End Function
```

To implement the interface, first switch to a new project.

Implementing an Interface

Once an interface is defined in an ActiveX DLL and then compiled, you can use the interface definition in other projects. The first thing you will want to do is create at least one class that implements the interface. An *implementation* of an interface provides code for all the properties and methods declared in the interface.

After switching to a new project, you can gain access to the interface definition by doing the following:

1. From the Project menu, choose References.
2. Click the Browse button.
3. Use the Browse dialog box to choose the DLL that contains the interface declarations. If necessary, enter the name of the DLL in the text box yourself.

Any class can implement an interface, providing its own code for items declared in that interface. The Declarations section of the class module must contain the following statement:

Implements *interfacename*

For example:

```
Implements ICar
```

For each method declared in the interface, provide a procedure named *interface_method*, where *interface* is the interface name.

Sub *interface_method(arglist)*
    statements
End Sub

Or, if it is a Function method:

Function *interface_method(arglist)* **As** *type*
    statements
End Function

For each property in the interface, you must provide Get and Let procedures as follows. Use of Get and Let procedures is required, regardless of how the property was declared in the interface.

Property Get *interface_propname* **As** *type*
    statements
End Property

Property Let *interface_propname(ByVal RHS As type)*

```
    statements
End Property
```

Consider the following declarations for the ICar interface:

```
Public speed As Double

Function accelerate (delta As Double) As Double

End Function
```

The following code provides a possible implementation of ICar:

```
    Implements ICar
Dim mySpeed As Double

Property Get ICar_speed As Double
    ICar_speed = mySpeed
End Property

Property Let ICar_speed(ByVal RHS As Double)
    mySpeed = RHS
End Property

Function ICar_accelerate(delta As Double) As Double
    mySpeed = mySpeed + Delta
    if mySpeed < 0 Then mySpeed = 0
    Icar_accelerate = mySpeed
End Function
```

Using the Implementation

Interface methods and properties can be used in two ways. When an object is referred to by an ordinary object variable, you access methods and properties by their full name, including the *interface_* prefix. For example:

```
Dim hotrod As New Auto
hotrod.ICar_speed = 100
```

```
spd = hotrod.ICar_accelerate(25)
```

However, when you refer to an object through a variable of interface type, you drop the *interface_* prefix for methods and properties. For example:

```
Sub run_car(car As ICar)
    car.speed = 100
    new_speed = car.accelerate(23)
    Debug.Print "new speed is " & new_speed
End Sub
```

This procedure, run_car, will work on any object of any class that implements the ICar interface. This makes the procedure polymorphic, because there is no limit to the number of different classes that can be used with this procedure. Each such class provides its own implementation — that is to say, its own procedure-definition code — for the ICar members, speed and accelerate. This procedure will work with any classes implementing ICar, now or in the future.

Much of the benefit of this system lies in its reliability. Because the argument, car, implements the ICar interface, it is guaranteed to support speed and accelerate.

● NOTE

Code that uses an interface as a variable or argument type must occur in a project that understands that interface. For any project, you can add a reference to the DLL defining the interface, as described at the beginning of the previous section.

An interface type cannot be used to allocate an object. You therefore cannot use it as an argument to New or to CreateObject. You can, however, allocate an object of some class that implements the interface, and then assign that object to an interface variable. For example, suppose that Auto is a class that implements ICar. You can allocate an object, assign it to an interface variable, and then use that variable to refer to interface methods and properties. For example:

```
Dim cars(10) As ICar
Dim a As New Auto
cars(1) = a
a.speed = 50
```

Collection Objects

The `Collection` class is an intrinsic Visual Basic class that supports building of collections. Each item in a collection can have any type and can be accessed by a one-based index or an optional key. Collections are a good deal more flexible than arrays; for one thing, they can grow without limit.

An alternative to the `Collection` class is the `Dictionary` class, which in some ways is more flexible but requires keys for every item. I describe the `Dictionary` class in the next section.

Table 16-3 summarizes the common syntax of each `Collection` method. The `Add` method actually has a more complex syntax, which I describe later.

Table 16-3   *Collection Class Methods*

Common syntax	Description
`obj`.`Add` `item` [, `key`]	Adds an item of any type to the collection. The optional *key* argument is a string containing a key (a unique identifier). This method also supports the optional *before* and *after* arguments, described later in this section.
`obj`.`Count`	Returns the current number of items.
`obj`.`Item(`*index* | *key*`)`	Returns an item, using either a one-based index number (*index*) or a string containing a key. The latter technique only works if the item was assigned a key when added.
`obj`.`Remove` *index* | *key*	Removes specified item, using same argument syntax accepted by the `Item` method.

Here is an example of code that creates a simple collection:

```
Dim myStuff As New Collection
myStuff.Add 12.5
myStuff.Add "Now is the time."
myStuff.Add aDate

For i = 1 To myStuff.Count
```

```
      Print myStuff.Item(i)
Next i
```

The For loop can be replaced with a For Each loop. (See Chapter 17 for more information on this syntax.)

```
For Each i in myStuff
   Print i
Next i
```

The Add method can use a more complex syntax. You can optionally specify a position at which to insert the new item by using *before* or *after* (but not both).

```
obj.Add item, [key], [before], [after]
```

The *before* argument, if included, specifies a target item by using either a one-base index (if numeric) or a key (if a string). The method inserts the new item just before the target item. The *after* argument works the same way but inserts the new item just after the target item.

As with most Basic functions and statements, commas are argument-field separators: You can use multiple commas to skip arguments, and you don't use them after the last argument. For example:

```
myStuff.Add 27, , 5      ' Insert in 5th position
myStuff.Add 35, , , 1    ' Insert just after 1st item
```

Dictionary Objects

A Dictionary object provides a more advanced version of a collection. It has useful methods that the intrinsic Collection class does not have, but it also requires that every item have a key. This makes Dictionary objects a little more specialized, because extensive use of keys does not fit every situation. Dictionary objects are good, nice, and well mannered. Collection objects let you fly by the seat of your pants.

Dictionary objects work with For Each loops, just as Collection objects do. The previous section gives an example of For Each.

16

One slight drawback of Dictionary is that it is part of the Visual Basic Scripting classes and therefore requires use of the CreateObject function. For example:

```
Dim myStuff As Object
Set myStuff = CreateObject("Scripting.Dictionary")
```

Table 16-4 describes the Dictionary class methods. In each case, *key* is a string containing a key, not an index.

Table 16-4   *Dictionary Class Methods*

Method Syntax	Description
obj.Add *key, item*	Adds specified item, which may be of any type. The *key* argument is a string containing a unique identifier.
obj.Exists(*key*)	Returns True if specified *key* is in use.
obj.Items	Returns an array of type Variant, containing all the items.
obj.Keys	Returns an array of type Variant, containing all the keys.
obj.Remove(*key*)	Removes item, specified by key, and returns the item.
obj.RemoveAll	Removes all items in the collection.

The properties of the Dictionary class are equally important. Table 16-5 describes these properties.

Table 16-5   *Dictionary Class Properties*

Property Syntax	Description
obj.CompareMode	Integer property. If set to 1 (vbTextCompare), all searches for keys ignore case. Default setting of 0 is case-sensitive.
obj.Count	Integer, read-only property. Specifies number of items.

Property Syntax	Description
obj.**Item**(*key*)	Accesses item by using key contained in the string argument, *key*. This is a read/write property, so you can associate a new item with the specified key.
obj.**Key**(*key*)	If a string is assigned to this property, it replaces the old key with the new key specified. This enables you to keep the same item but assign it a new key. Remember that keys must be unique.

The following code shows a relatively simple use of a Dictionary object. The code first creates and initializes a Dictionary object, empAges, and then uses a loop to print out all keys next to their values. Note that keys must be unique, but items can be repeated. Here the names "SteveB", "BillG", and "BrianO" are all keys.

```
Dim keysArray() As Variant

Dim empAges As Object
Set empAges = CreateObject("Scripting.Dictionary")

empAges.Add "SteveB", 41
empAges.Add "BillG", 41
empAges.Add "BrianO", 35
keysArray = empAges.Keys
For i = 0 To empAges.Count - 1
    Print keysArray(i),
    Print empAges.Item(keysArray(i))
Next i
```

Control Structures

The term *control structure* refers to a set of keywords that enable you to take different actions, depending on conditions at run time. Table 17-1 lists most of the current Visual Basic control structures; the others are mentioned in the text that follows.

This is a fairly large group — a testament to how Basic has evolved over the years. But there are still more. Several keywords are supported for the sake of backward compatibility. These include GoSub...Return, On...GoSub, and On...GoTo. Unless you're programming in the Stone Age, you don't have much reason to use these. There's also that old standby, GoTo. GoTo is mostly unnecessary, because of the availability of many forms of Exit. If you must use GoTo, be sure to give it a labeled statement as a target. Here's an example of GoTo use that is equivalent to a Do...Loop statement:

```
topOfLoop: If i>n Then Exit Sub
'...
GoTo topOfLoop
```

Table 17-1 *Summary of Control Structures*

Control Structure	Description
CallByName	Responds to a method or property name in a string
Choose	Returns a value from an ordered list of values
If...Then	Conditional execution, with optional Else and ElseIf
Do...Loop	Repeats a loop; similar to While...Wend, but more flexible
For...Next	Executes a set of statements a specific number of times
For Each...Next	Executes a set of statements once for each element in a group (array or collection)
Function	Defines a Function procedure (returns a value)
On Error	Enables a run-time error handler
Select Case	Conditional execution based on testing a single value
Switch	Returns a value by testing a series of conditions; a compact form of If...Then...Else
Sub	Defines a Sub procedure (does not return a value)
While...Wend	Repeats a loop while a condition is true; see also Do...Loop

Another group sometimes classed as control structures include those used for basic program operation: DoEvents, End, and Stop. DoEvents yields processor time to other programs until everything else on the system has gotten a chance to run; it's a good idea to do this periodically if you're doing something that's highly calculation-intensive. End terminates execution. Stop acts as a breakpoint if the program is running in the development environment; otherwise it terminates execution.

The `Call` and `Declare` statements are useful for calling Windows API routines and other DLLs. `Call` has a simple syntax:

```
Call name(arglist)
```

Several control structures create properties for class modules and ActiveX controls. These include `Property Get`, `Property Let`, and `Property Set`. I cover these in Chapter 16, as well as in Chapter 8.

CallByName	Property or method access (VB6)

The `CallByName` keyword is one of the slickest new features of Visual Basic. It lets you access a method or property named by a string. The string can be constructed at run time, which opens up some interesting possibilities.

One use for `CallByName` is to enable the end user to enter the name of a property at run time and manipulate its values directly. Another probably more practical use is to enable databases to maintain references to properties of objects.

The `CallByName` keyword has two versions: function and statement. The function version is used when there is a return value. In the function version, *calltype* is either vbGet or vbMethod:

```
CallByName(object, procedurename, calltype, arguments)
```

In the statement version, *calltype* is either vbLet, vbSet, or vbMethod:

```
CallByName object, procedurename, calltype, arguments
```

In both versions, *object* is a reference to a form, control, or other object. *procedurename* is a string containing a property or method name. *calltype* is vbGet, vbLet, vbSet, or vbMethod. The *arguments* contain a property setting in the case of vbLet or vbSet. They contain method arguments in the case of vbMethod.

17

Continued

For example, you can get the value of a named property by using a *calltype* of vbGet.

```
propname = InputBox("Enter property name:")
v = CallByName(Form1, propname, vbGet)
MsgBox "The property value is " & v
```

You can set a value for most properties by using a *calltype* of vbLet. (Properties that refer to an embedded object require vbSet.)

```
propname = InputBox("Enter property name:")
v = InputBox("Enter new value:")
CallByName Form1, propname, vbLet, v
```

You can call a method by using a *calltype* of vbMethod. For example, the following code fragment calls the Move method with arguments of 0, 0.

```
CallByName Form1, "Move", vbMethod, 0, 0
```

17

Choose	**Select value from list**

The Choose function returns a value from a list of values. One way to think of Choose is as a compact version of Select Case. The syntax of this function is as follows:

Choose(*index*, *value* [, *value*]...)

This syntax indicates that *index* is followed by one or more values: at least one, but up to any number. Each occurrence of *value* has type Variant, which means you can supply strings, numbers, or dates. The action of the function is to select a *value* based on *index*, which is a 1-based index into the list. For example, if index is 2, the Choose function returns the second *value*.

Here is a simple example that gives a feel for the flavor of Choose:

```
theString = Choose(n, "one", "two", "three")
Print theString
```

Here, theString is assigned the string "one", "two", or "three", depending on the value of n. If n is less than 1 or greater than the number of entries (three in this case), Choose returns Null.

If...Then

Conditional branching statement

The If...Then statement has two versions: single-line and multi-line. In the multiline version, you must use End If.

If *condition* **Then** *statement*

If *condition* **Then**
    statements
End If

In both versions, *condition* is a Boolean (true/false) value. Technically, it can be any numeric value, but problems can arise if you don't use a Boolean. The following things qualify as a Boolean: the results of comparisons (such as test for equality, =), Boolean properties, variables of type Boolean, and Booleans combined through logic operators.

For example, the following condition combines two comparisons through the logic operation And:

If x > 0 And x <= 100 Then Print "x is in range"

In the multiline version, *statements* is a series of zero or more statements. It is completely valid to have just one statement, or even none, if you choose.

With the single-line version, it's possible to execute multiple statements by using the colon (:). In the following example, if doSwitch is True, Visual Basic executes all three of the statements after Then. If doSwitch is False, none of those statements are executed.

If doSwitch Then temp = a : a = b : b = temp

Continued

Both versions can have optional ElseIf and Else clauses. Here, the brackets indicate optional items. If followed by ellipses (...), an item can be repeated any number of times. What this means in this case is that you can use ElseIf as many times as you want.

```
If condition Then statement [ElseIf condition Then _
    statement]... [Else statement]
```

```
If condition Then
    statements
[ElseIf condition Then
    statements]...
[Else
    statements]
End If
```

In the following example, a series of three conditions are tested. If all three of the tests fail, this implies that fahren_temp is equal to 100 or more.

```
If fahren_temp < 60 Then
    Print "Too cold."
ElseIf fahren_temp < 80 Then
    Print "Just right."
ElseIf fahren_temp < 100 Then
    Print "Too hot."
Else
    Print "Way too hot!"
End If
```

●—NOTE

The syntax can get a little tricky, because ElseIf is one word, whereas End If is two. However, if you mistype End If as one word, Visual Basic will cheerfully correct it for you. Note that a single-word ElseIf is provided for a good reason; Else If (two words) is perfectly legal but creates the need for an additional, matching End If.

Do...Loop

Conditional looping statement

The Do...Loop statement is a flexible control structure designed to replace the While...Wend statement from BASICA. Do...Loop does everything that While...Wend does, and it offers the option of early exit. Although there are a number of Do...Loop variations, they share one basic idea: Execute a group of statements as long as some condition is true (or false, if Until is used).

Do...Loop has several forms, which (to be kind), I've separated into different syntax summaries. First, you can write a Do loop that tests a condition at the top. Here, the braces indicate that you use either While or Until, but not both.

Do {**While** | **Until**} *condition*
    statements
Loop

The *statements* are one or more statements. Exit Do may be one of these statements; usually, Exit Do appears within an If statement, if it appears at all. When executed, Exit Do transfers control to the first statement after Loop.

In this context, While and Until have a similar purpose, but Until negates the Boolean (true/false) value. Until is the same as While Not.

The second form of this statement tests the condition at the bottom of the loop, guaranteeing that the statements are executed at least once, even if the *condition* is false (zero value):

Do
    statements
Loop {**While** | **Until**} *condition*

There is even a third form that omits the condition altogether. This, at least on the surface, creates an infinite loop.

Do
    statements
Loop

17

Continued

With this form, the use of Exit Do is practically a requirement. The statements execute over and over, until the loop exits.
In the following example, this form is used to calculate a factorial:

```
i = 1
Do
    If i > n Then Exit Do
    fact = fact * i
    i = i + 1
Loop
```

This example has the condition (i > n) at the top, and is
therefore a good candidate for Do While or Do Until. Here is the
Do While version, which is cleaner than the previous example:

```
i = 1
Do While i <= n
    fact = fact * i
    i = i + 1
Loop
```

The Do Until version reverses the condition:

```
i = 1
Do Until i > n
    fact = fact * i
    i = i + 1
Loop
```

17

For...Next	Looping statement with counter

The For...Next statement uses a loop counter to execute a group
of statements a specific number of times. The loop counter should
be a numeric variable — usually an integer — and is often referred
to within the loop itself.

For loops have the following syntax. Here the brackets indicate optional items. The placeholders named *start* and *end* are numeric values (constants or variables) that specify where to start and stop the loop.

```
For counter = start To end [Step increment]
    statements
Next [counter]
```

The *statements* are one or more statements; these may include Exit For statements. Exit For is used infrequently, but it's sometimes useful as a way of bailing out early. Usually, Exit For appears within an If statement, if it appears at all.

The Step *increment* clause, which is optional, allows you to specify how much the counter increases after each execution of *statements*. This amount can be negative — but in such a case, *end* must be smaller than *start*. More often than not, specifying *increment* isn't necessary, because it defaults to 1.

If you've never seen this control structure before, it's easy enough to understand by looking at a trivial example.

```
Print "Now let's count from 1 to 100!"

For i = 1 To 100
    Print i & " ";
Next
```

The Print statement gets executed a hundred times. The loop sets i to 1, increments i by 1 each time, and stops executing when i is greater than 100.

The example from the previous section is another good place to use a For loop. The Do While version had the following code:

```
i = 1
Do While i <= n
    fact = fact * i
    i = i + 1
Loop
```

Continued

Notice the use of the variable i, which starts at 1 and then goes to an ending value, n. This makes the statement a good candidate for a For loop, with i as the loop counter. The following code does the same thing as this Do While loop, but look how much more compact it is.

```
For i = 1 To n
    fact = fact * i
Next
```

● **NOTE** ─────────────────────────────────

This For loop is slightly inefficient. The starting condition could be changed to cut down on execution time without affecting the final result. This is left as an exercise.

Some old-line Basic purists (you know who you are!) insist on including the loop counter in the Next statement. This is really only necessary when you have nested loops — when, for example, you are initializing multidimensional arrays — but it is never wrong. (I just get lazy in the simple cases.) Here is the two-dimensional-array case, where you need it for clarity.

```
Dim i As Integer, j As Integer, mat As Long(23, 27)
For i = 1 To 23
    For j = 1 To 27
        mat(i, j) = 0
    Next j
Next i
```

For Each...Next	Looping statement for groups

The For Each...Next statement is similar to the standard For...Next, but instead of using a loop counter, it cycles through every element in a group automatically. The group in this case may be an array or a collection. Collections include Collection and Dictionary objects, as well as the collections returned by FileSystemObject methods and certain ADO classes. (You can also create custom collection classes, as long as you give them an enumerator; see the Stack class in Chapter 8 for details.)

In the following syntax, the brackets indicate that the use of element after Next is optional.

```
For Each element In group
    statements
Next [element]
```

The *statements* can include an optional Exit For statement. Usually, Exit For appears within an If statement, if it appears at all.

The loop variable, element, must have Variant type if *group* is an array, and Object type if *group* is a collection. (However, a variant can assume the Object type.) Within the *statements*, you can refer to element, which in this context means "the current member of *group*." You can get the value of element, although assignments to it have no effect.

A simple example should help to make the mechanics of For Each clear. Note that in the following code, the variable i has no prior connection to the array arr. Yet within the For loop, i serves as a stand-in for elements such as arr(0) and arr(1).

```
Dim arr(2) As Integer, i As Variant
arr(1) = 25
arr(2) = 50


For Each i In arr
    Print i
Next
```

This code, when executed, prints out the following results on the current form:

```
0
25
50
```

There are three elements (unless Option Base is in effect), because one of the elements is arr(0).

Function	**Procedure definition with return value**

The Function keyword defines a procedure that returns a value. The most obvious use for a Function procedure is to perform some calculation, but a function can do anything that a Sub procedure can do. In many respects, Sub and Function procedures are similar. Note, however, differences in how they are called, discussed later in this section.

The syntax for a Function procedure definition is shown below. Brackets indicate an optional item.

```
[modifiers] Function name [(arglist)] [As type]
    statements
End Function
```

The *statements* consist of one or more statements, and include the following special statements:

17

Statement	Description
Exit Function	Optional. This statement enables you to exit early.
name = return_value	Required. At least one such statement must be placed in the function declaration. This statement fixes the return value, until overridden by another such statement.

Here is a sample declaration of a Function procedure. Note the use of *name = return_value*.

```
Function fact(n As Integer) As Long
    Dim i As Integer
    fact = 1
    For i = 1 To n
        fact = fact * i
    Next
End Function
```

Function Procedure Modifiers

The *modifiers* section of a procedure has the following syntax:

[**Public** | **Private** | **Friend**] [**Static**]

This syntax indicates that you can include one of the three keywords Public, Private, or Friend, but no more than one. The Static keyword is separate and can be included whether or not you include one of the first three. The following table describes the meaning of each keyword.

Keyword	Description
Public	Procedure is available to procedures in all modules. This is the default.
Private	Procedure is available only to procedures in the same module.
Friend	Used in a class module. Procedure is available to all modules, but does not create a method, as Public procedures do.
Static	All the procedure's local variables are automatically declared Static, meaning they retain value between calls.

Function Return Type

Functions have return types, just as variables do, and the rules for determining the type are basically the same. For example, you can create a function that has the default type.

```
DefInt A-Z     'Declare integer as default type.


Function returnAnInt(first, second)
    ' Put some statements here...
End Function
```

Here, both the function itself (returnAnInt) and the two parameters (first, second) have the default type, Integer. The function's type determines what type of value it is valid to return.

Continued

Other ways to declare the return type include use of a type-definition suffix and the As clause. The following example uses As:

```
Function returnAStr(first, second) As String
    ' Put some statements here...
End Function
```

The returnAStr function must indeed return a string, and the arguments have the default type.

The Argument List

Visual Basic has grown to support flexible argument syntax. Typically, an argument list contains just a series of argument names (*parameters* or *formal arguments*), along with optional As clauses to identify their types.

```
Function getAChar(n As Integer, char As String)...
```

An argument list is made up of zero or more argument declarations, with the arguments separated by commas if there is more than one. The following syntax summarizes all the possibilities for an individual argument declaration. Brackets indicate optional items. As mentioned earlier, only the argument name is strictly required.

```
[modifiers] argname[( )] [As type] [= default_value]
```

The *modifiers* for an argument include the following: Optional, ByVal, ByRef, and ParamArray. Optional indicates that during a procedure call, the argument can be omitted. If used, the Optional argument must be the last in the argument list, or else all the arguments that follow it must be declared Optional as well.

ByVal and ByRef cause passing by value and passing by reference, respectively. These are mutually exclusive. Passing by reference, which is the default, means that the procedure can change the value of a variable passed to it in this argument slot. (Constants and complex expressions can be passed by reference; in that case, what the procedure actually receives is a reference to a temporary variable that ultimately gets discarded.)

The ParamArray keyword is explained at length in Chapter 5. It is mutually exclusive with Optional. If ParamArray is used in the argument list, no argument can use Optional.

The rest of the syntax is fairly self-explanatory. The parentheses, if included, indicate that an array is expected. (See Chapter 5

for an example.) The *default_value* is used in conjunction with
Optional. If the argument is omitted during a call to the procedure, it gets assigned *default_value* during execution.

Calling the Function

As in most other computer languages, when you call a function in
Visual Basic, you enclose the argument list in parentheses —
unless there are no arguments. (If there are no arguments, you
can omit the parentheses entirely.) This is noticeably different
from the way you call a Sub procedure; in that case, the argument
list is never enclosed in parentheses unless used with Call.

Regardless of how internally complex a Function procedure is,
it always returns a single value. A function call must be used
within a larger statement, either a simple assignment or something more complex. For example:

```
amt = fact(5)
n = fact(5) + 10
Print "The factorial of 6 is "; fact(6)
```

17

On Error	Enable error routine statement

The On Error statement enables an error handling routine. Such a
routine is not a separate procedure or structured block, but a sub-
section of a procedure identified by a label. (See example for clari-
fication.) In this way, Visual Basic is less structured than C++,
but still provides a usable error handling capability. If you do not
have an error handler enabled, any run-time error causes immediate termination of the program.

The On Error statement has three variations, but by far the
most commonly used is the following syntax:

On Error GoTo *label*

The *label* can also be a line number, but I don't recommend
using line numbers under any circumstance. Generally, *label* is a
statement label. Such a label is created by putting a label name in
column 1 and following the name by a colon (:).

Continued

For example, the following code enables an error handler identified by the statement label ErrHandler.

```
Function doCalc(x, y, z) As Double
    On Error Goto ErrHandler
    x2 = x * x
    doCalc = (x2 * y) / z
    Exit Function

ErrHandler:
    MsgBox "Error occurred:" & vbCrLf & _
     Err.Description
    doCalc = 0
End Function
```

A typical run-time error in this situation might be a "divide by zero" error, which normally would halt the program.

17

This example, simple though it is, illustrates some key points about error handlers. First, although the error handler is identified by a statement label (ErrHandler), it acts almost like a separate routine. The effect of a run-time error is to transfer execution to the first line after the label; execution proceeds normally after that. Here, the Exit Function statement is used to prevent the flow of control from reaching the handler if there is no error.

Another important point is that after an error has occurred, you can take advantage of the predefined Err object. Err.Description is a string that provides a description of the error that just occurred. Err.Number returns the system error number, and Err.Source is a reference to the object that generated the error.

The On Error statement also supports the following syntax:

```
On Error GoTo 0      ' Disable error handler in this
                     '  procedure.

On Error Resume Next ' After error, resume execution
                     '  in the statement following
                     '  the one causing the error.
```

The On Error Resume Next statement causes execution to proceed to the statement immediately after the one that caused the error, just as it would normally. This is almost the same as ignoring the error. If you use this version of On Error, you should periodically test Err.Number to see if an error has occurred.

| **Select Case** | Select alternative statement |

The Select Case statement is an alternative to If...Then that is somewhat more compact and easier to read. Select Case can be used when the program logic depends on a single test value, either numeric or string.

The statement has the following syntax. Brackets indicate optional items, and items followed by ellipses can be repeated any number of times. This means that you can have multiple occurrences of Case expressionlist.

```
Select Case testexpression
    [Case expressionlist
        statements]...
    [Case Else
        statements]
End Select
```

When the Select Case statement is encountered, the first thing that Visual Basic does is evaluate *testexpression*, a numeric or string value. It then examines each occurrence of Case *expressionlist* until an *expressionlist* matches the test value. When a match is found, the corresponding statements are executed. Each *statements* consists of zero or more statements.

The easiest way to understand Select Case is to first look at an If...Then statement that tests a particular variable. For example:

```
If x = 1 Then
    DoRoutine1
ElseIf x = 2 Then
    DoRoutine2
ElseIf x = 3 Then
```

Continued

```
      DoRoutine3
Else
      DoDefaultRoutine
End If
```

The following Select Case statement does the same thing.

```
Select Case x
   Case 1
      DoRoutine1
   Case 2
      DoRoutine2
   Case 3
      DoRoutine3
   Case Else
      DoDefaultRoutine
End Select
```

The syntax for *expressionlist* is highly flexible. The *expressionlist* can be a simple value, a range of values, an expression of the form Is > value (in which another comparison operator can be substituted for >), or a list of any of these combined with commas. For example:

```
Case 5, 7, 9          ' Match 5, 7, or 9
Case "a"              ' Match "a"; strings only
Case "a" To "d"       ' Match strings in this range
Case 20 To 30         ' Match any value from 20 to 30
Case Is > 100         ' Match any value > 100
Case 5, 20 To 300, Is > 100
```

In the second and third cases in this example, the test value must be a string; in the other cases, it must be numeric. The comments explain most of these cases. In the third case, the test value matches if it is anywhere in the sort order between "a" and "d"; this includes strings such as "aardvark" and "boy". In the last case, the test value matches if it has the value 5, a value between 20 and 30, inclusive, or any value greater than 100.

Switch — Compact conditional statement

The Switch function evaluates a series of conditions and returns the corresponding value as soon as a true (nonzero) condition is found. Switch provides a compact version of If...Then...Else, just as Choose provides a compact version of Select Case.
The syntax of this function is as follows:

```
Switch(condition, value [, condition, value]...)
```

What this syntax means is that you can include any number of condition/value pairs, but there must be at least one. Here is a simple example that gives a feel for the flavor of Switch:

```
s = Switch(n = 1, "one", n = 2, "two", n = 3,"three")
Print s
```

In this example, s is assigned the string "one", "two", or "three", depending on the value of n. Both Switch and all of the arguments have type Variant, so that it is flexible with regard to types. If none of the conditions are true, Switch returns Null.

Sub — Procedure definition

The Sub keyword defines a procedure that does not return a value. The absence of a return value makes Sub procedure syntax a little simpler than Function syntax, but most of the same rules apply. One of the important differences is that unlike functions, Sub procedures are always called with no parentheses around the argument list.
The syntax for a Sub procedure definition is shown below. Brackets indicate an optional item.

```
[modifiers] Sub name [(arglist)]
    statements
End Sub
```

Continued

The *statements* consist of one or more statements. These can include the optional Exit Sub statement, which causes an early exit from the procedure. As with other Exit statements, Exit Sub usually appears inside an If statement if it appears at all.

Here is a sample Sub procedure declaration:

```
Sub repeatChar(n As Integer, char As String)
    Dim i As Integer
    For i = 1 To n
        Print char;
    Next
End Sub
```

Sub Procedure Modifiers

The *modifiers* section of a procedure has the following syntax:

[**Public** | **Private** | **Friend**]   [**Static**]

This syntax indicates that you can include one of the three keywords Public, Private, or Friend, but no more than one. The Static keyword is separate and can be included whether or not you include one of the first three.

See the section "Function," earlier in this chapter, for a description of each of these keywords.

The Argument List

Visual Basic has grown to support flexible argument syntax. In the most typical case, an argument list contains just a series of argument names (*parameters* or *formal arguments*), along with As clauses to identify their type.

```
Sub repeatChar(n As Integer, char As String)...
```

An argument list is made up of zero or more argument declarations, with the arguments separated by commas if there is more than one. The following syntax summarizes all the possibilities for each argument declaration. Brackets indicate optional items. As mentioned earlier, only the argument name is strictly required.

[*modifiers*] *argname*[**( )**] [**As** *type*] [= *default_value*]

The *modifiers* for an argument include the following:
Optional, ByVal, ByRef, and ParamArray. See the section
"Function," earlier in this chapter, for a description of each of
these keywords and the rest of the argument-declaration syntax.

Calling the Sub Procedure

A call to a Sub procedure forms a complete statement. In keeping
with Basic statement syntax, no parentheses should appear
around the argument list (although parentheses may of course be
used in calculating an individual argument). Here are two examples of a Sub procedure call.

```
repeatChar 5, "A"
repeatChar (1 + amt) / 2, "b"
```

There is one exception to this syntax: If you use a Sub procedure call with the Call statement, then there are parentheses
around the argument list.

While...Wend	**Conditional looping statement**

The While...Wend statement executes a group of zero or more
statements repeatedly, just as the Do...Loop statement does.
However, While...Wend is less flexible and does not support any
Exit statement for ending the loop early.
The syntax of this statement is as follows:

```
While condition
    statements
Wend
```

As long as *condition* is true (nonzero), the *statements* are
executed.
This control structure is not really encouraged anymore by
the people who design Visual Basic, because it is less flexible than
Do...Loop. It is supported for the sake of backward compatibility.
However, if all you need is simple While logic, the truth is that
this version works perfectly well in most cases.

Continued

Here is the factorial example, coded with `While...Wend`:

```
i = 1
While i <= n
    fact = fact * i
    i = i + 1
Wend
```

17

Keyword Summary: File System

Interacting with the file system is one of the areas in which Visual Basic 6.0 provides new features not found in Version 5.0. You can continue to use the traditional functions and statements for reading, writing, and searching for files. But you can also use the new FileSystemObject methods, which provide an improved programming model for many file operations. (Note, however, that they do not yet support binary or random-access file I/O.)

The set of file-oriented keywords is large, so I've broken them down into a series of subgroups. The last section introduces the new FileSystemObject capabilities.

- **General File I/O.** This includes old file-system keywords necessary for reading and writing files generally: Open, Close, EOF, LOF.

- **Sequential Text Mode.** This includes keywords for reading and writing to text files, including Input #, Write #, and Line Input #.

- **Random and Binary Modes.** This includes keywords specific to random-access and binary I/O modes, such as Get, Put, and Seek.

- **General File Commands.** This includes the older keywords that perform some major operation, such as Dir, which lists directory contents; and Kill, which deletes a file.

- **The FileSystemObject Model.** This new class and its related classes (File, Folder, Drive, TextStream) provide enhanced capabilities for interacting with the file system and accessing text files. Performing operations on entire directories ("folders") is much easier with this model than with the older keywords. The only drawbacks are that these classes require a little understanding of objects and you can't yet use them for random or binary I/O.

General File I/O

Before you do any reading or writing with the traditional file-system keywords, you first need to open a file. You should also close a file when you're no longer working on it. Table 18-1 describes the keywords concerned with opening and closing files, as well as EOF and LOF, which are generally useful.

Table 18-1   *General File I/O Keywords*

Keyword	Description
Open statement	Opens a file for reading or writing
Close statement	Closes one or more files
EOF function	Returns True if the end of the file has been reached
LOF function	Returns the length of a currently open file

Visual Basic provides a couple of related keywords that are usable, if somewhat superfluous. The FreeFile function returns an unused file number. The Reset statement closes all open files, just as Close without arguments does.

Open   File open statement

Before you read or write to any file, you need to open it. The Open statement has the following syntax. Brackets indicate optional items.

```
Open pathname For mode [Access access] [lock] _
As [#]filenumber [Len=reclength]
```

Every Open statement must specify a *pathname* and a *filenumber*. The *pathname* is a string containing a filename, which can optionally include a complete directory path. The *filenumber* can be any number in the range 1 to 511, inclusive, but it must be a number currently unused by other files. This number is used later to identify the file.

To open a file for sequential text I/O, specify *mode* as Append, Input, or Output. The other, optional fields can be ignored.

```
Open filename1 For Input As #1
Open filename2 For Output As #2
```

You can also open a file with *mode* as Binary, in which case you need to specify an *access* value: either Read, Write, or Read Write.

```
Open binaryFilename For Binary Access Read As #3
```

Finally, you can open a file with *mode* as random-access (Random), in which case you must specify a record length. Random mode is similar to Binary mode, except that random-access files have built-in record length and automatically have read/write access.

```
Open randomFilename For Random As #4 Len=recLength
```

The record length is usually the size of a user-defined type, created with the Type statement. For example:

```
Type EmployeeRecType
    empID As Integer
    empSSN As Long
    empName As String * 20
End Type
```

Continued

```
Dim empRec As EmployeeRecType
Open randomFilename For Random As #5 Len=Len(empRec)
```

The *lock* argument determines whether other processes have access to the file while you have it open. This argument can be Shared, Lock Read, Lock Write, or Lock Read Write.

Close	Close file statement

The Close statement closes a specified file that is currently open. The statement has the following syntax:

Close [*filenumber*]

You can also use Close to close multiple files:

Close [*filenumber*] [, *filenumber*]...

The brackets indicate that *filenumber* is optional. If it is omitted, then all open files are closed. Each *filenumber* can optionally have a # prefix. The *filenumber* is the integer that was used to open a file. For example, the following statements open and close a file:

```
Open "MYFILE.DAT" For Input As #1
' Do some stuff with the file...
Close #1
```

EOF	Detect end-of-file function

The EOF function is a Boolean function that returns True if the end of file has been reached. It has the following syntax:

EOF(*filenumber*)

The *filenumber* is the integer that was used in the Open statement to identify the file.

The action of the function is simple. It looks at the next byte of input and sees if any more bytes are available. If not, it returns True. Note that testing for the EOF condition does not automatically protect against all errors. It returns True only if the previous operation *has read all the way up to the very end of the file*. If you are using Line Input # or random access mode, you can safely assume that the last successful read will take you to the end of the file and no further. With binary mode, you may need to use the Loc and LOF functions to determine how much to read.

The following example reads in each line of a file opened as #1, converts it to uppercase, and writes it out to a file opened as #2.

```
Do Until EOF(1)
    Line Input #1, strInput
    Print #2, UCase(strInput)
Loop
```

LOF   Length-of-file function

The LOF function returns a Long integer value containing the length — from beginning to end — of a currently open file. It has the following syntax:

LOF(*filenumber*)

Here *filenumber* is the integer that was used in the Open statement to identify the file. The FileLen function is similar to this function, but FileLen takes a complete path name. Usually, it is more convenient to use LOF. The following example gets the length of an open file identified by the number 3:

```
Open "AFILE.DAT" For Input As #3
'...
fileLength = LOF(3)
```

The LOF function always returns length in bytes, even in the case of random-access files.

Sequential Text Mode (Input, Output, Append)

Once you open a text file, you can read or write to it either as a stream of text (like the console under DOS) or as a series of discrete data fields. In either case, all numeric and other expressions are represented in text form in the file.

Table 18-2 describes the keywords that support these operations. Note that you can perform almost the same operations with the FileSystemObject model.

Table 18-2 *Sequential Text Keywords*

Keyword	Description
Input # statement	Reads input from one or more data fields; should be used with Write #
Line Input # statement	Reads line-oriented text
Print # statement	Writes line-oriented text
Write # statement	Writes variables as discrete data fields; should be used with Input # statement

18

In addition, the Width # statement is occasionally useful for setting a text-line width. The Input and InputB functions (not to be confused with the Input # statement) can be used to read in a specified number of characters, regardless of where line breaks and other delimiters occur. See online Help for descriptions.

Input #	Read fields from text file statement

The Input # statement (not to be confused with the Input function) reads from one or more fields of text. The data should have been created earlier with the Write # statement. The Input # statement has the following syntax:

```
Input #filenumber, variable [, variable]...
```

The brackets and ellipses (...) indicate that you must include at least one variable, but you can have any number of variables after that. The *filenumber* is required; this is an integer that was used in the Open statement to identify the file.

Each *variable* is a simple variable of primitive or user-defined type. Arrays and object variables are not legal in this context, although individual elements of arrays are. To work correctly, each *variable* should have an appropriate type for the corresponding data field. Note that the Write # statement outputs data fields using the same format that Input # recognizes.

The following example reads an integer and two strings:

```
Open "c:\myfile.txt" For Input As #1
Input #1, n, str1, str2
```

Line Input #	Read line from text file statement

The Line Input # statement reads an entire line of a text file and returns it as a single string. After getting the string, you can use string keywords to parse and analyze the string as appropriate (see Chapter 20). The function has the following syntax:

Line Input #*filenumber, stringvar*

Here *filenumber* is the integer that was used in the Open statement to identify the file, and *stringvar* is a variable of Variant or string type. The action of the statement is to read up to the first carriage return (Chr(13)) or carriage-return/linefeed pair (Chr(13) & Chr(10)). These characters are not returned as part of the string.

This statement works well with files created with the Print # statement. Print # writes lines of text output and terminates them with carriage returns.

The following example reads in each line of a file opened as #1, converts it to uppercase, and writes it out to a file opened as #2.

```
Open filename1 For Input As #1
Open filename2 For Output As #2
```

Continued

```
Do Until EOF(1)
    Line Input #1, strInput
    Print #2, UCase(strInput)
Loop
```

Print #   Write line to text file statement

The Print # statement enables you to write a line of text to a file, just as you would write to the console (under DOS) or to the Immediate window, a form, or a picture box with the Print method. Print # has the following syntax:

Print #*filenumber* [, *items*] [;|,]

The brackets indicate that the *items* are optional. If they are omitted, the statement just writes a carriage return. The *items* can include any number of expressions; the statement prints out the appropriate string representation of each. For example:

```
Print #1, "The value of x is "; x
```

As with the Print method, you can separate multiple *items* with commas and semicolons. If there's a comma between two items, the second begins at the next tab column (also called a *print zone*). If there's a semicolon, the second item begins at the very next space.

A comma or semicolon after the last item is significant, because it prevents the statement from writing a carriage return at the end of the line. In the following example, all the output is printed on the same line of text:

```
Open "c:\myfile.txt" For Output As #1
Print #1, "The value of x is ";
Print #1, x
```

The default behavior is for Visual Basic to write a carriage return after each and every call to Print #.

The *items* can include any of the following:

expression	' Print string representation
Tab(*n*)	' Advance to column position n
Spc(*n*)	' Insert n spaces

See the section "The Print Method" in Chapter 19 for additional examples and details.

Write #	**Write fields to text file statement**

In contrast to the Print # statement, the Write # statement writes out data in discrete fields of text. Among other things, this allows you to write out a series of strings. The file can later be opened for input, and the Input # statement can be used to read the strings, without having to determine where one ends and the next one begins. However, when later using the Input # statement to read back the data, you should know what kind of data to expect.

The Write# statement has the following syntax:

Write #*filenumber, expression* [, *expression*]...

The brackets and ellipses (...) indicate that you must have at least one expression, but you can have any number of expressions after that. The *filenumber* is required; this is an integer that was used in the Open statement to identify the file.

The following example writes an integer and two strings:

```
Open "c:\myfile.txt" For Output As #1
Write #1, 5, "This is a string", "This is another"
```

Random and Binary Modes

The random-access and binary modes support almost the same keywords, so I deal with both of these modes here. There are some differences in how these work, however, due to observance of a fixed-length record structure in random-access mode. For example, writing in random-access mode always writes up to the next record boundary, padding if necessary.

Use random-access mode if you want to deal with a file that is entirely made up of fixed-length records. Use binary mode if you need maximum flexibility. In binary mode, you can examine any file, and no data translation is performed for you.

Table 18-3 describes the keywords supporting random and binary mode.

Table 18-3   *Random and Binary Mode I/O*

Keyword	Description
Get statement	Reads data from file to specified variable, optionally specifying file position at which to read
Loc function	Returns current file position.
Put statement	Writes data to file, optionally specifying file position at which to write
Seek statement	Moves to specified record or byte offset within the file
Seek function	Does the same thing as Loc

With binary mode, you can also use the Input function (not to be confused with the Input # statement). The Input function returns the specified number of bytes as a string. With both random-access and binary mode, you can use Lock and Unlock to protect a range of records from other processes; this is useful in multiprocess environments.

When using Get and Put with random-access files, you should rely on a user-defined type to define a record. You should not attempt to read or write more than one record at a time. And to keep matters simple, you should use fixed-length strings and arrays, rather than variable-length ones, within the user-defined type. Otherwise, matters can quickly get complicated. For a fuller description of how Visual Basic implements reading and writing of specific types, see online Help for Get and Put.

The Type statement is used to declare a user-defined type. See the example for the Open statement earlier in this chapter.

Get

Read data from file statement

The Get statement reads data from the file into a variable. This statement is the converse of Put. The exact amount of data read depends on the variable's type. The Get statement has the following syntax, in which *filenumber* is the integer used to identify the file when it was opened.

```
Get [#]filenumber, [recordnum], varname
```

The brackets indicate optional items. You can omit *recordnum*, but the two commas must always be present. If *recordnum* is omitted, the statement reads from the current file position. The *recordnum* is a record number, in the case of random-access mode; or a byte position, in the case of binary mode. In both cases, the beginning of the file is record number 1.

With random-access mode, *varname* should share the file's underlying record type. Get always reads an entire record. For example:

```
Dim empRec As EmployeeRecType
Open randomFilename For Random As #1 Len=Len(empRec)
Get #1, ,empRec
```

With binary mode, Get reads directly from the file with no structure imposed. Remember that the type of *varname* controls exactly how much data is read. In the case of strings and arrays, Get reads raw data and does not expect a string or array descriptor. (This matches Put behavior.) The size of the string or array determines how much data to read. If the string is a variable-length string, the number of characters read is equal to the current number of characters in the string.

For example, one way to use Get with binary files is to use an array of type Byte. The following example reads exactly 100 bytes:

```
Dim lotsaBytes As Byte(1 To 100)
Open binFilename For Binary Access Read As #2
Get #2, ,lotsaBytes     ' Read 100 bytes
```

Continued

● NOTE ───

Be careful about reading and writing `Variant` types directly to the file. When getting a `Variant`, Visual Basic first reads two bytes that indicate the string or numeric format. You're better off avoiding variants in file I/O, except within user-defined types. Also note that object variables cannot be directly read or written to files.

Loc	Get file position function

The `Loc` function returns the current file position. It has the following syntax, in which *filenumber* is the integer used to identify the file when it was opened.

`Loc(`*filenumber*`)`

The number returned is a `Long`. (The maximum file size for this function is therefore two gigabytes!) This number represents a record number, in the case of random-access mode; or a byte position, in the case of binary mode. The beginning of the file is record number 1.

The following example stores the current location in a variable, n:

`n = Loc(1)`

Put	Write data to file statement

The `Put` statement writes the value of an expression directly to the file. This statement is the converse of `Get`. The exact amount of data written depends on the expression's type. The `Put` statement has the following syntax, in which *filenumber* is the integer used to identify the file when it was opened.

`Put [#]`*filenumber*`, [`*recordnum*`],` *expression*

The brackets indicate optional items. You can omit *recordnum*, but the two commas must always be present. If *recordnum* is omitted, the statement writes to the current file position. The *recordnum* is a record number, in the case of random-access mode; or a byte position, in the case of binary mode. In both cases, the beginning of the file is record number 1.

With random-access mode, *expression* should share the file's underlying record type. Put always writes an entire record. For example:

```
Dim empRec As EmployeeRecType
Open randomFilename For Random As #1 Len=Len(empRec)
'
' Assign values to empRec...
' Then write to file.
'
Put #1, ,empRec
```

With binary mode, Put writes values directly to the file with no structure imposed. In the case of strings and arrays, Put writes the elements only; it does not write a string or array descriptor. (This matches Get behavior.) The size of the string or array determines exactly how much data to write.

For example, in the following code, Put writes exactly 100 bytes:

```
Dim lotsaBytes As Byte(1 To 100)
Open binFilename For Binary Access Write As #2
Put #2, ,lotsaBytes      ' Write 100 bytes
```

●—**NOTE** ————————————————————————————————

Be careful about reading and writing Variant types directly to the file. When writing out a Variant, Visual Basic first writes out two additional bytes to indicate the string or numeric format. You're better off avoiding variants in file I/O, except within user-defined types. Also note that object variables cannot be directly read or written to files.

Seek	Move file position
	statement

The Seek statement moves the current file position. It has the following syntax, in which `filenumber` is the integer used to identify the file when it was opened.

    Seek [#]filenumber, recordnum

The brackets indicate the `filenumber` prefix (#) is optional. The `recordnum` is a record number, if the file is open for random-access mode; or a byte position, if the file is open for binary mode. In both cases, the beginning of the file is record number 1.

The following example moves the current file position of file #1 to record number 50. In the case of binary files, this is byte position 50, at offset 49 from the beginning of the file.

    Seek #1, 50

18

Seek	Get file position function

The Seek function does the same thing as the Loc function, returning current file position. It's not clear why the designers of Visual Basic felt they needed this duplication.

    Seek(filenumber)

General File Commands

This section summarizes the traditional keywords for general searching and manipulation of the file system — in other words, the keywords in this section do not involve reading and writing to the files. Table 18-4 lists these keywords. Note that most of the same operations can be performed with the new FileSystemObject model.

Table 18-4 *Summary of General File Commands*

Keyword Syntax	Description
`Dir [(pathname , [attributes])]`	Returns first matching filename if path is specified. Subsequent calls to `Dir` with no arguments return the next matching filename. The `pathname` can include pattern characters * and ?. Empty string indicates no match.
`FileDateTime(pathname)`	Returns a `Date` value for time of last modification to specified file.
`FileLen(pathname)`	Returns length of specified file as a `Long`.
`GetAttr(pathname)`	Returns attributes as a set of flags.
`SetAttr pathname, attributes`	Sets attributes for specified file.
`FileCopy sourcefile, destfile`	Copies `sourcefile` to `destfile`; each can include a path specification.
`Kill pathname`	Deletes specified file or file pattern.
`Name oldname As newname`	Renames file, `oldname`, to `newname`; each can include a path specification.

In the case of `Dir` syntax, brackets indicate optional items. The first call to `Dir` usually specifies a pattern; subsequent calls to `Dir` (with no argument) look for the next filename matching the pattern. For example, following code prints out all files matching `"*.TXT"` in the current directory.

```
s = Dir("*.TXT")
Do While s <> ""
    Debug.Print s
    s = Dir
Loop
```

In each statement, a `pathname` can include a simple filename or a complete path name. In the case of `Dir` and `Kill`, the `pathname` can optionally include pattern-matching characters * and ?.

The GetAttr function and SetAttr statements represent *attributes* as an integer containing several bits that serve as flags for various on/off conditions. Table 18-5 lists the bit-flag constants and their corresponding values. To create an *attributes* argument, add together all the bit flags that apply. For example, to set attributes to be both read-only and hidden, add vbReadOnly and vbHidden:

```
SetAttr filename, vbReadOnly + vbHidden
```

To decode *attributes*, test them against one or more constants. For example, to determine if vbDirectory is on (indicating that the file is actually a directory or folder), test an *attributes* value by using And to test it against vbDirectory:

```
condition1 = (GetAttr(filename) And vbDirectory) <> 0
```

Table 18-5 *Attribute Values for File Commands*

Constant	Value
vbNormal	0
vbReadOnly	1
vbHidden	2
vbSystem	4
vbDirectory	16
vbArchive (file has changed since last backup)	32

The FileSystemObject Model

The FileSystemObject class is a new feature of Visual Basic. You can use an object of type FileSystemObject to do many of the same things that you can do with the traditional file-system keywords described earlier in this chapter. There are several differences between use of this class and the traditional file commands:

- The high-level FileSystemObject methods can do nearly everything the traditional keywords can do, and in some cases a good deal more. In particular, the methods let you move or copy entire directories, which is difficult to do with the traditional keywords.

• Some of the methods lend support for creating, extracting, and manipulating filenames; you can even generate unused names for temporary files.

• Some of the `FileSystemObject` methods return other object types: `File`, `Folder`, `Drive`, and `TextStream`. Each of these has many useful methods and properties of its own. (On the whole, this system is a better way to organize all the file-interaction capabilities.)

• Binary and random file I/O are not yet supported for `FileSystemObject`. You can, however, read and write to text files with the `TextStream` class.

To perform file operations under this model, you first need to create an object of type `FileSystemObject`. You only need one such object. The following statement shows how:

```
Dim f
Set f  = CreateObject("Scripting.FileSystemObject")
```

You can, of course, give the object any name you choose. Here, I've picked the name `fso`. Once the object is created, you can use it to call any number of `FileSystemObject` methods. Table 18-6 summarizes all the `FileSystemObject` methods. For more information on any given method, see online Help.

With these method names, keep in mind that *folder* means essentially the same thing as *directory*. Basically, *directory* is the old name reminiscent of MS-DOS. The word *folder* is the new and improved name for Windows 95 and beyond — no new capabilities are involved; the name's just supposed to conjure up the warm-and-fuzzy feeling of a graphical user interface. Also, remember that brackets indicate optional items and that all these methods must be prefixed with a reference to an object of type `FileSystemObject`.

18

Table 18-6 *Summary of FileSystemObject Methods*

FileSystemObject Method	Description and Syntax
BuildPath	Returns a string formed by concatenating *path* and *filename* and inserting a backslash (\\) if needed. **BuildPath(** *path*, *filename***)**
CopyFile	Copies *src* file to *dest* file. If *src* contains wild-cards, or *dest* ends in a backslash (\\), *dest* is assumed to be a folder. If false, *overwrite* prevents existing files from being overwritten. **CopyFile** *src*, *dest* [,*overwrite*]
CopyFolder	Copies *src* folder to *dest* folder. *src* can contain wildcard characters. (See MoveFolder.) If false, *overwrite* prevents existing folders from being overwritten.**CopyFolder** *src*, *dest* [,*overwrite*]
CreateFolder	Creates indicated folder, if possible; if successful, it returns the name. **CreateFolder(** *foldername***)**
CreateTextFile	Returns a TextStream object after opening a text file for reading and writing. If true, *overwrite* enables overwriting of an existing file. If true, *unicode* creates the file as a Unicode file. **CreateTextFile(** *filename* [,*overwrite*] [,*unicode*]**)**
DeleteFile	Deletes indicated file; a range of files can be specified by using wildcard characters. If true, *force* enables deletion of read-only files. **DeleteFile** *filespec* [,*force*]
DeleteFolder	Deletes indicated folder and all its contents; a range of folders can be specified by using wildcard characters; if true, *force* enables deletion of read-only folders. **DeleteFolder** *folderspec* [,*force*]
DriveExists	Returns True if specified drive exists. *drivespec* is a short string containing a drive or a complete path specification. **DriveExists(** *drivespec***)**

18

FileSystemObject Method	Description and Syntax
`FileExists`	Returns `True` if specified file exists. *filename* can contain a relative or complete path specification. **FileExists(** *filename***)**
`FolderExists`	Returns `True` if specified folder exists. *foldername* is a relative or complete path specification. **FolderExists(** *foldername***)**
`GetAbsolutePathName`	Returns a string containing a complete path specification. *pathspec* can be a relative path or a path containing special characters, such as "c:*.*\stuff" or ".." **GetAbsolutePathName(** *pathspec***)**
`GetBaseName`	Returns a string containing the base name of indicated file. File doesn't necessarily have to exist. **GetBaseName(** *filename***)**
`GetDrive`	Returns a `Drive` object. *drivespec* can is a string containing a drive letter, a path specification, or a network share. **GetDrive(** *drivespec***)**
`GetDriveName`	Returns a string containing the drive letter in the specified path name. **GetDriveName(** *path***)**
`GetExtensionName`	Returns a string containing the file extension. File doesn't necessarily have to exist. **GetExtensionName(** *filename***)**
`GetFile`	Returns a `File` object. *filespec* can contain a path specification. **GetFile(** *filespec***)**
`GetFileName`	Returns the filename portion from a path specification. **GetFileName(** *pathspec***)**
`GetFolder`	Returns a `Folder` object. *folderspec* can contain a relative or complete path specification. **GetFolder(** *folderspec***)**
`GetParentFolderName`	Returns a string naming the parent folder to the indicated *path* specification. **GetParentFolderName(** *path***)**

18

Continued

Table 18-6 *Continued*

FileSystemObject Method	Description and Syntax
GetSpecialFolder	Returns one of three Folder objects; *folder-spec* can be WindowsFolder, SystemFolder, or TemporaryFolder. **GetSpecialFolder(** *folderspec***)**
GetTempname	Returns a string containing a randomly generated, unique filename or folder name. **GetTempname**
MoveFile	Moves *src* file to *dest* location. If *src* contains wildcards or *dest* ends in a backslash (\), *dest* is assumed to be a folder. This method can be used to simply rename a file. **MoveFile** *src, dest*
MoveFolder	Moves *src* folder to *dest* location. If src contains wildcards or *dest* ends in a backslash (\), *dest* is assumed to be an existing folder under which to add new folder(s). Otherwise, *dest* is the name of a folder to create. **MoveFolder** *src, dest*
OpenTextFile	Returns a TextStream object after opening an existing text file for reading or appending (default is ForReading). If *create* is True, this method can create a new file. See online Help for description of other arguments. **OpenTextFile(** *filename* [,*iomode*] [,*create*] [,*format*]**)**

Once you create an object of type FileSystemObject, you can use it to perform general operations on the file system and to get other objects, each of which corresponds to a more specific entity — Drive, Folder, File, and TextStream.

● **NOTE**

Remember that the term *folder* is synonymous with *directory*.

The following example demonstrates how to use the FileSystemObject class in obtaining other types of objects. In this code, assume that driveletter, folderspec, filespec1, filespec2, and filespec3 are all strings. Assume that the other variables have type Object or Variant.

```
Set f = CreateObject("Scripting.FileSystemObject")
Set drv = f.GetDrive(driveletter)
Set fol = f.GetFolder(folderspec)
Set fil = f.GetFile(filespec1)
Set inf = f.OpenTextFile(filespec2)
Set outf = f.CreateTextFile(filespec3)
```

The File and Folder classes support approximately the same set of properties, which are listed in Table 18-7. These classes also support a small set of methods, which essentially duplicate some of the FileSystemObject methods. The properties do most of the work for File and Folder classes.

Table 18-7 *Summary of File and Folder Properties*

File/Folder Property	Description
Attributes	Integer containing a set of attribute flags. (See Table 18-5.) Read/write, although some attributes are read-only.
DateCreated	Date value specifying when the item was created.
DateLastAccessed	Date value specifying when the item was last accessed.
DateLastModified	Date value specifying when the item was last modified.
Drive	Drive object corresponding to the file or folder.
Files (folders only)	Collection of child File objects.
IsRootFolder (folders only)	Boolean value that is True if the item is a directory root, such as C:\.
Name	String containing name of item (no path). Read/write.
ParentFolder	Folder object for parent of item.
Path	String containing directory path of item.
ShortName	String containing a name fitting the old 8.3 format.
ShortPath	String containing a path fitting the old 8.3 format.

18

Continued

Table 18-7 *Continued*

File/Folder Property	Description
Size	Long integer specifying size in bytes. For folders, this is size of all child files and folders, counted recursively.
SubFolders (folders only)	Collection of child Folder objects.
Type	String containing a brief descriptive phrase (for example, "Text Document" for files ending in .TXT).

You can use these properties to get a number of different attributes for a file or folder. For example, the following code prompts the user for a file specification (a filename with or without path) and then prints out data about the file. Note that the code lacks error handling for the case of file not found, which you may want to add on your own.

```
DefStr A-Z

Private Sub Form_Click()
    Dim f As Object, fil As Object

    Set f = CreateObject("Scripting.FileSystemObject")
    filespec = InputBox("Enter file specification")
    Set fil = f.GetFile(filespec)
    strName = fil.Name
    strSize = fil.Size
    strCreate = fil.DateCreated
    strAccess = fil.DateLastAccessed
    strModify = fil.DateLastModified
    s = "Name: " & strName & vbCrLf & _
    "Size: " & strSize & vbCrLf & _
    "Time created: " & strCreate & vbCrLf & _
    "Time last accessed: " & strAccess & vbCrLf & _
    "Time last modified: " & strModify
```

18

```
    MsgBox s
End Sub
```

The Folder class supports the same properties, as well as
some others. The Files property (note that it is plural) returns a
collection you can use to print out directory contents. For example, the following code prints out the contents of the root directory on the C drive.

```
Private Sub Form_Load()
    Dim f As Object, fold As Object
    Dim filesColl As Object, fil As Object

    Set f = CreateObject("Scripting.FileSystemObject")
    Set fold = f.GetFolder("C:\")
    Set filesColl = fold.Files
    For Each fil In filesColl
        s = s & fil.Name & "    "
    Next
    MsgBox "Root directory contents: " & vbCrLf & s
End Sub
```

18

Similarly, the SubFolders property returns a collection of child
Folder objects. Because each of those Folder objects has its own
SubFolders collection, you can use it to search folders recursively.

With a Files and SubFolders collection, you should use the
For Each control structure to step through the collection, as
shown in the previous example. These collections do not support
all the Collection class methods. You can, however, access the
Count property of these collections.

A Drive object corresponds to a system drive, either local or
remote. The Drive class properties, shown in Table 18-8, enable
you to access information about the given drive. There are no
Drive methods.

Table 18-8 *Summary of Drive Properties*

Drive Property	Description
AvailableSpace	Integer value in bytes.
DriveLetter	One-character string containing drive letter.

Continued

Table 18-8 *Continued*

Drive Property	Description
DriveType	Integer having one of the following values: 0 – Unknown, 1 – Removable, 2 – Fixed, 3 – Network, 4 – CD-ROM, 5 – RAM Disk.
FileSystem	String containing "FAT", "NTFS", or "CDFS".
FreeSpace	Integer value in bytes. Usually the same as AvailableSpace.
IsReady	Boolean value returning True if drive is ready to be accessed.
Path	String containing drive letter, such as "C:".
RootFolder	Folder object for root directory on drive.
SerialNumber	Long integer containing serial number used to uniquely identify a drive.
ShareName	String containing network share name; empty for local drives.
TotalSize	Integer value in bytes.
VolumeName	String containing volume name. Read/write.

18

Finally, you can use TextStream objects to sequentially read or write to specified text files. In Visual Basic 6.0, there are no FileSystemObject classes for reading and writing to binary or random-access files.

For example, the following code creates a new text file and writes to it. This example calls the WriteLine method of the TextStream object, outf.

```
Set fso = CreateObject("Scripting.FileSystemObject")
Set outf = fso.CreateTextFile("c:\myfile.txt", True)
outf.WriteLine "This is the first line."
outf.WriteLine "This is the second."
outf.Close
```

If you want to read an existing file, then first create a TextStream object by calling OpenTextFile, which opens a file that already exists. You can then read input. The following example reads all the lines of the file by calling the ReadLine method and checking AtEndOfStream, a Boolean property.

```
Set fso = CreateObject("Scripting.FileSystemObject")
Set inf = fso.OpenTextFile("c:\myfile.txt")
Do Until inf.AtEndOfStream
    Debug.Print inf.ReadLine
Loop
inf.Close
```

Table 18-9 summarizes all the TextStream methods. Some of these return a value and must be used like functions. In the syntax column of Table 18-9, *textf* is a TextStream object, *n* is an integer, and *stringOuput* is a string expression.

In addition to supporting these methods, TextStream objects support the following properties: AtEndOfStream, AtEndOfLine, Column, and Line. The first two are Boolean properties. The second two contain the column number and line number, respectively, of the current file position. All four are read-only properties.

● **NOTE** ────────────────────────────────────

To write string representations of numeric values with the Write and WriteLine methods, just give the value as an argument. Visual Basic automatically converts numbers and other basic types (dates, Booleans) to string format in such cases.

18

Table 18-9   *TextStream Methods*

Keyword Syntax	Description
textf.**Close**	Closes the associated file
textf.**Read**(*n*)	Returns a string containing the next *n* characters in the file
textf.**ReadAll**	Returns a string containing entire contents of the file
textf.**ReadLine**	Returns a string containing contents up to the next newline character
textf.**Skip** *n*	Skips over next *n* characters
textf.**SkipLine**	Skips past the next newline character
textf.**Write** *stringOutput*	Writes *stringOutput* to the file
textf.**WriteBlankLines** *n*	Writes *n* newline characters
textf.**WriteLine** *stringOutput*	Writes *stringOutput* and appends a new line character

Keyword Summary: General I/O

Visual Basic supports several keywords for general input and output — by which I mean input and output not directly involving files or properties. Remember that input and output can be handled in other ways: using controls and customized dialog boxes, for example. In fact, a well-designed Visual Basic program usually includes these user-interface elements.

Still, the keywords in this chapter can be convenient, especially for simple programs and code fragments where you want to see quick results. Table 19-1 describes these keywords.

Table 19-1   *General I/O Keywords*

Statement/Function	Description
InputBox function	Gets a string from the user. The function displays a dialog box with a prompt string you specify and waits for user response.
MsgBox function	Displays a dialog box with a message you specify. The function returns a number indicating what button the user clicked.
MsgBox statement	Displays a dialog box just as the MsgBox function does, except that you don't deal with a return value. Because this version is a statement, no parentheses appear around the argument list.
Print method	Prints one or more expressions to a graphical object. The default object is the current form.

The rest of this chapter provides a fuller description of each of these keywords.

● **NOTE**

You may notice that InputBox lacks the string type suffix ($), even though it returns a string. This is a change from some older versions. Visual Basic built-in functions no longer require type suffixes. For backward compatibility, however, both InputBox and InputBox$ are accepted.

19

InputBox   Input function

The InputBox function is convenient way to grab some ad-hoc input. It has the following syntax. The brackets indicate optional items. Note that InputBox is a function returning a string, so you can only use it as part of a larger statement (such as an assignment).

```
InputBox(prompt [,title][,default][,x][,y] _
   [,helpfile, context])
```

Note that if you include *helpfile*, you must include *context*, and vice versa.

As with most Visual Basic argument syntax, commas are used as argument separators, and you can use multiple commas to skip over arguments. The *prompt* argument is required. But you can, for example, skip over *title* and *default*, which are optional, and include the *x* and *y* arguments.

```
inputStr = InputBox("Enter a string:", , , 100, 200)
```

Here, 100 and 200 are assigned to the arguments *x* and *y*, respectively, whereas the arguments *title* and *default* are skipped.

Table 19-2 describes the arguments to InputBox.

Table 19-2   *Arguments to InputBox*

Argument	Description
prompt	Prompt string. Limit is approximately 1,024 characters. This string can be made multi-line by including carriage-return/ linefeed pairs (Chr(13) & Chr(10)). This is the only required argument.
title	String to display on input-box title bar.
default	Default response. This is text that appears in the text box and will stay there until the user edits it or deletes it.
x, y	Position of dialog box, in twips, relative to edge of the screen.
helpfile	String containing the name of the help file.
context	Number identifying the help context of this dialog box, within the help file.

19

The InputBox dialog box, when displayed, always provides an OK button and a Cancel button (see Figure 19-1). If the user presses Enter or clicks OK, the InputBox function returns whatever was in the dialog's text box. If the user clicks Cancel, the InputBox function returns an empty string.

An easy way to use InputBox is to include a prompt string and omit the rest of the arguments. This is perfectly legal, but the title bar will contain the name of the application, and nothing more. For example, here is a simple use of InputBox:

Continued

```
Dim inputStr As String
inputStr = InputBox("Enter something, anything...")
```

This example displays the input box shown in Figure 19-1.

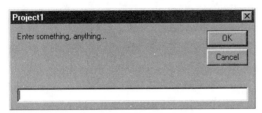

Figure 19-1 *Sample InputBox dialog box*

The following, slightly more sophisticated example includes the first three arguments (*prompt, title, default*), but omits the rest.

```
Dim s As String
s = InputBox("Enter something.", "Input box", "silly")
```

Figure 19-2 shows the resulting InputBox dialog box.

Figure 19-2 *InputBox dialog box with title and default*

●—**NOTE**

If you want numeric input, you have a number of choices. You can use the Val function, which converts string input to numeric; assign the input string to a Variant type; or rely on Visual Basic's automatic conversion of string data to numeric. The drawback of the latter method, however, is that the string must be a correctly formulated digit string, with no non-numeric input.

MsgBox   Display message function

The MsgBox function displays a string, waits for the user to click a button (typically the OK button), and then goes away. This sounds like a simple operation. It often is, but MsgBox supports a number of optional features, such as indicating whether the user clicked OK, Cancel, Yes, No, or some other button.

MsgBox has the following syntax. The brackets indicate optional items. Note that MsgBox is a function returning a number, so you can only use it as part of a larger statement (such as an assignment).

MsgBox(*prompt* [,*buttons*][,*title*][,*helpfile*, *context*])

This syntax should be taken to imply that if you include *helpfile*, you must include *context*, and vice versa.

As with most Visual Basic argument syntax, commas are used as argument separators, and you can use multiple commas to skip over arguments. The *prompt* argument is required. But you can, for example, skip over *buttons*, which is optional, and include the *title* argument.

```
n = MsgBox("Sorry, it didn't work.", , "Error msg")
```

Most of the arguments are straightforward. The *prompt* argument is a string up to approximately 1,024 characters in length. Typically, *prompt* is a message string and is the main reason for the existence of the MsgBox dialog box. You can create multiline text by embedding the *prompt* string with carriage-return/linefeed pairs (Chr(13) & Chr(10)).

●—NOTE ───────────────────────────────────

The Visual Basic constant vbCrLf is a convenient way to represent the two-character string Chr(13) & Chr(10).

The *title* argument is the optional title of the dialog box. The default value is the name of the application.

The *helpfile* and *context* arguments form a link to an optional help topic; *helpfile* is a string specifying the help file name, and *context* is a number identifying the help context within that file. To use a help topic, you also need to add vbMsgBoxHelpButton to the *buttons* argument (in addition to whatever *buttons* flags you are using).

19

Continued

I discuss the meaning of MsgBox return values later, in the section "Returning from the MsgBox."

Supplying the Buttons Argument

The *buttons* argument is actually a complex series of flags. The easiest way to use it is to treat it as a combination of four distinct groups. Make one selection from each group (considering 0 the default in each case), note the constants, and then add them up. The groups describe the following: buttons to display, icon style, selection of default button, and modality.

Use at most one number from the first group to determine what buttons to display. Note that OK and Cancel are triggered by the user pressing Enter and Esc, respectively.

Symbolic Constant	Value	Buttons Displayed
vbOKOnly	0	OK
vbOKCancel	1	OK and Cancel
vbAbortRetryIgnore	2	Abort, Retry, and Ignore
vbYesNoCancel	3	Yes, No, and Cancel
vbYesNo	4	Yes and No
vbRetryCancel	5	Retry and Cancel

Use at most one number from the second group to determine what icon to display in the MsgBox dialog box, if any. (For no icon, use 0.)

Symbolic Constant	Value	Icon Displayed (Exact Depiction May Vary in Different Countries)
vbCritical	16	Critical message (a red "X")
vbQuestion	32	Warning query (a question mark)
vbExclamation	48	Warning message (a yellow caution sign with "!")
vbInformation	64	Information message (a large, low-ercase "i")

19

Use at most one number from the third group to determine what button is the default — that is, which button has the focus when the dialog box appears.

Symbolic Constant	Value	Default Button
vbDefaultButton1	0	First (leftmost)
vbDefaultButton2	256	Second
vbDefaultButton3	512	Third
vbDefaultButton4	768	Fourth

Use at most one number from the fourth group to determine modality of the dialog box. The word *modality* just means that the dialog box blocks the user from doing anything else as long as it is displayed.

Symbolic Constant	Value	Description of Modality
vbApplicationModal	0	The user cannot use the rest of the application before responding to the dialog box, but he or she can switch to other applications.
vbSystemModal	4,096	The user cannot do anything else before responding to the dialog box.

Finally, there are some miscellaneous button values that are not mutually exclusive with anything else. You can use as many or as few of these values as you choose.

Symbolic Constant	Value	Description
vbMsgBoxHelpButton	16,384	A Help button is added to the dialog box.
vbMsgBoxSet-Foreground	65,536	The dialog box's window becomes the foreground window.
vbMsgBoxRight	524,288	Message text is right aligned.
vbMsgBoxRtlReading	1,048,576	In Hebrew and Arabic systems, the text reads left to right.

19

To produce a value for the *buttons* argument, select all the constants that apply, and then add them together. The following MsgBox example employs this simple technique.

Continued

```
Dim btn As Long, msg As String, n As Integer
msg = "I think you broke it."
btn = vbRetryCancel + vbDefaultButton2 + vbCritical
n = MsgBox(msg, btn, "ERROR")
```

Figure 19-3 shows what the resulting dialog box looks like.

Figure 19-3 *MsgBox example*

Returning from the MsgBox

With the MsgBox function, you must always do something with the value returned, even if all you do is store it in a variable. Often, however, the value is useful. The following table shows the meaning of MsgBox return values.

Symbolic Constant	Value	The User Clicked This Button
vbOK	0	OK
vbCancel	1	Cancel
vbAbort	2	Abort
vbRetry	3	Retry
vbIgnore	4	Ignore
vbYes	5	Yes
vbNo	6	No

For example, the following code ends the program if the user clicks Yes.

```
n = MsgBox("End the program?", vbYesNo)
If n = vbYes Then End
```

MsgBox

Display message statement

The MsgBox statement is the same as the MsgBox function, except that you ignore the return value. In addition, because it is a statement, you don't use parentheses around the argument list. Parentheses around a single argument are legal, but not necessary.

The statement version of MsgBox is more convenient when all you want to do is display a message and nothing more.

```
MsgBox "We come in peace."
MsgBox "That was a wise choice.", , "Quick msg"
```

The statement version is especially convenient when you're writing a short program and all you want to do is get quick feedback on a value at run time.

```
MsgBox "The value of x is " & x
```

Aside from the fact that the return value is ignored and no parentheses are needed, the MsgBox statement is the same in every respect as the MsgBox function, and it supports all the same arguments. See the previous section for more information.

Print

Text output method

19

Strictly speaking, there is no longer any PRINT (or even Print) statement. It's been replaced by the Print method. During the dark days of Visual Basic 1.0, this sentence produced panic in many a business programmer: "You mean I have to use a *method*?" But this scary word — *method* — just means that you can choose to use Print in a number of places. You can print to any forms and picture boxes you may have, as well as the Immediate window or the system printer.

Here is the Print method syntax:

```
[object.]Print [items] [;|,]
```

Continued

The brackets indicate optional items. If the *object* reference is omitted, Print sends its output to the current form — that is, the form to which the code is attached — or, if the statement is entered in the Immediate window, Print sends output to that window

Where can you send Print output? The following table summarizes the ways you can use the method. There's no new syntax here; this just elaborates on the kind of object you can print to. Yes, it's yet another table!

Form of Print	Description
Print *items*	Prints to the current form or window.
Debug.Print *items*	Prints to the Immediate window. This window is only visible when a program is run within the development environment. Using Print this way can be a convenient way to show diagnostics as a program is running.
Printer.Print *items*	Sends output to the system's default printer. The printer is not engaged until a page advances or the program ends (flushing the printer buffer). The Printer.NewPage method can be used to advance a page.
object.Print *items*	Prints to specified *object*. This can be a named form or picture box, or a reference to one of these through an object variable.

In all of these cases, *items* is one or more expressions and/or other items, described later. You can have no items at all, in which case all the method does is advance to the next print line:

```
Print
Picture1.Print
```

You can separate multiple *items* with commas and semicolons. If a comma appears between two items, the second item begins at the next tab column (also called a *print zone*). If a semicolon appears between two items, the second item begins at the very next space.

```
Print "The value of x is "; x
```

A comma or semicolon after the last item is significant, because it prevents the statement from printing a carriage return at the end of the line. In the following example, all the output is printed on the same line:

```
Print "The value of x is ";
Print x
```

The default behavior is for Visual Basic to advance to the next line after each and every call to the Print method.

The *items* can include any of the following:

```
expression     ' Print string representation
Tab(n)         ' Advance to column position n
Spc(n)         ' Insert n spaces
```

The keywords Tab and Spc can be used to determine how many spaces to advance before printing the next expression. Tab(n) advances to an absolute column number; but if this position has already been passed, Print advances to the next line and then moves to the column position.

```
' The statement advances an extra line before "more"
'
Print Tab(30); "Here is a string."; Tab(20); "more"
```

● NOTE

For a form or picture box, print output is sent to the current drawing coordinates, a location determined by the CurrentX and CurrentY properties. You can set these properties before printing to a form or picture box. In determining how to set these, you may find the form methods TextWidth and TextHeight useful. TextHeight is particularly useful, because it gives you the number of units in a line of text in the current font. The Cls method resets CurrentX, CurrentY to 0, 0.

Concatenation vs. Multiple Expressions

At first glance, string concatenation and printing multiple expressions on a line appear to be equivalent. For example:

```
Print "This is your name: "; yourname
Print "This is your name: " & yourname
```

Continued

But printing multiple expressions can result in spaces being inserted, because the Print method guarantees that spaces surround consecutive numerals. Concatenation, on the other hand, never inserts spaces.

```
Print 5; 6     ' Prints " 5 6"
Print 5 & 6    ' Prints "56"
```

Print Statement vs. Other Text Output

In Visual Basic, there are several ways to put words on the screen. One way is to set a Text or Caption property in a control that displays text. This has the effect of replacing all of the text. In contrast, Print has the effect of advancing to the next space, tab position, or line; it does not replace existing text. If you want to replace all the text on a form or picture box, you need to first use the Cls method. For example:

```
Form1.Cls
Form1.Print yourname, myname
```

When you use the Print method, you can specify the coordinates for where you want the next line of text to print. To set these coordinates, use the CurrentX and CurrentY properties.

Another way to place text on a form or picture box is to position a label control on the object at design time. The label can be moved or changed at run time.

19

Keyword Summary: Strings

One of the strengths of Visual Basic has always been its string-handling capabilities, which apply to variables of type `String` as well as quoted strings. These features are even more convenient in recent versions, due to automatic conversion between strings and other types. In addition, Version 6.0 adds eleven new string functions.

Remember that you can use the string-concatenation operator (`&`) to join strings. The overloaded plus operation (`+`) is also supported for strings for the sake of backward compatibility. However, `&` is much more reliable.

```
Dim s1 As String, s2 As String, s3 As String
s1 = s2 & s3
```

See Chapter 14 for more information on the concatenation operator (`&`).

Visual Basic 6.0 includes many string functions that were not present in Version 5.0; in fact, this is one of the main areas in which the differences between Versions 5.0 and 6.0 are most noticeable. Table 20-1 lists all the new string-handling functions, followed by Table 20-2, which lists the old functions and statements.

Why new string functions? One notable feature here is the availability of a number of new formatting functions (FormatCurrency, FormatDateTime, FormatNumber, and FormatPercent) intended to largely replace the old Format function. The new functions are simpler and easy to use; moreover, they provide more international portability, because — without any special coding on your part — they automatically use the regional settings for displaying numbers.

Table 20-1   *New String Functions in Visual Basic 6.0*

Keyword	Description
Filter function	Searches strings in an array to find strings that contain the specified substring. Results are returned as another string array.
FormatCurrency function	Returns a string containing a formatted number, including dollar sign ($).
FormatDateTime function	Returns a string containing a formatted date and/or time.
FormatNumber function	Returns a string containing a formatted number.
FormatPercent function	Returns a string containing a formatted percentage.
InStrRev function	Returns the position of a substring within a larger string, or 0, if not found. Same as InStr (see Table 20-2), but it starts search at right end of string.
Join function	Returns a string that results from concatenating a series of strings in an array.
MonthName function	Returns a string containing the name of a month.
Replace function	Replaces all occurrences of a target string with a replacement string, and returns results.
StrReverse function	Returns string that is the reverse of its argument.

20

Keyword	Description
WeekdayName function	Returns a string containing the name of a weekday.

Table 20-2 lists common functions and statements inherited from Version 5.0 (although most have been around much longer than that). After this table, I mention a few remaining keywords that see use only rarely.

Table 20-2   *Common String Keywords in Version 5.0*

Keyword	Description
Asc function	Returns the numeric ASCII value of the first character.
Chr function	Converts an ASCII value into a one-length character string.
Format function	Returns a formatted string.
InStr function	Returns position of a substring within a larger string, or 0, if not found.
LCase function	Returns a string after converting to all lowercase.
Left function	Returns the *n* leftmost characters.
Len function	Returns the length of a string.
LSet statement	Left-justifies a substring into a larger string, padding with spaces on the right.
LTrim function	Returns a string without leading spaces.
Mid function	Returns a specified portion of a string.
Mid statement	Similar to the Mid function, except that you replace the specified portion of the string. Mid appears on left side of assignment (=) with this version of the keyword.
Right function	Returns the *n* rightmost characters.
RTrim function	Returns a string without trailing spaces.
Space function	Returns a string containing *n* spaces.

20

Continued

Table 20-2 *Continued*

Keyword	Description
StrComp function	Compares two strings (optionally case-insensitive) and returns –1, 0, or 1, depending on result.
StrConv function	Performs specified conversion and returns the results.
String function	Returns a string contain n repeated characters.
UCase function	Returns a string after converting to all uppercase.

Other string keywords include RSet, Str, and Trim. RSet, which right-justifies text within a larger string, is seldom used. The Str function is supported for backward compatibility, but it is largely unnecessary. Visual Basic automatically converts numbers to their string representation where needed (which is the action of Str).

Finally, some of the functions have "binary" versions, such as AscB, ChrB, InStrB, LenB, and MidB. The use of these is a little obscure; they would only become relevant in a situation where you had copied binary data into a string, by use of the Chr or ChrB function, and you were concerned about the effect of potential ASCII/Unicode conversions in international settings. In these cases, the binary versions ensure that the string operation treats each byte as an individual character, regardless of whether Unicode is in use.

20

● NOTE

You may notice that the functions in this chapter lack the string type suffix ($), even those that return a string. This is a change from some older versions. Visual Basic built-in functions no longer require type suffixes. For backward compatibility, however, the string suffix is accepted for all intrinsic functions that return a string.

The rest of this chapter consists of sections on the functions and statements listed in both Table 20-1 and Table 20-2.

Asc

ASCII value from string function

The `Asc` function returns the numeric ASCII value of the first character in a string. The function has the following syntax:

```
Asc(string)
```

This function is useful when you want to deal with characters as binary values rather than as text. In the following example, the code converts a string into a series of values in a `Byte` array.

```
Dim byteArr() As Byte
ReDim byteArr(Len(theString))

For i = 1 To Len(theString)
    ch = Mid(theString, i, 1)
    byteArr(i) = Asc(ch)
Next
```

Each iteration of this loop uses the `Mid` function to get a single character from a specified position of the string. The `Asc` function then converts the character into a numeric value.

Chr

Character from ASCII function

20

The `Chr` function, which is roughly the inverse of `Asc`, converts a numeric ASCII value into its one-character string equivalent. The `Chr` function has the following syntax:

```
Chr(numvalue)
```

The `Chr` function has many uses, not the least of which is to help you embed characters that are difficult to code using the normal string nomenclature. For example:

```
strQuote = Chr(34)          ' dbl quote mark (")
strCR = Chr(13)             ' carriage return
```

Continued

```
strLF = Chr(10)                    ' linefeed
strCRLF = Chr(13) & Chr(10)  ' CR/LF pair

multLine = "First line" & strCRLF & "Second line"
```

●—NOTE
Visual Basic predefines some useful character strings for you, including `vbCrLf`, which is equivalent to `strCRLF` in the preceding example.

Filter	String filter function (VB6)

The `Filter` function searches an array of strings and returns all those that contain a specified substring. Alternatively, you can use it to return those strings that do not contain the substring. The selected strings are returned in another array.

The function has the following syntax. Brackets indicate optional items. If you use *compare* but not *include*, use commas to indicate the skipped argument. (See example.)

Filter(*strArray*, *substring*, [, *include*] [, *compare*])

Here *strArray* is the array of strings to be searched. This must be a one-dimensional array. By default, the function searches for strings that contain at least one occurrence of *substring*, a string argument. If the *include* argument is used and set to `False`, the function searches for strings that do not contain *substring*.

The optional *compare* argument can be used to determine what constitutes a match. If *compare* has the default value of 0, the function does case-sensitive comparisons. But if it has the value 1 (`vbTextCompare`), the function does case-insensitive comparisons.

The selected strings are returned in an array. To receive this array, you need to declare a variable-length array of strings, as demonstrated in the following example.

```
Dim sa(3) As String, found() As String
sa(0) = "Brian"
sa(1) = "Rob"
```

```
sa(2) = "Joe"
sa(3) = "Barb"
found = Filter(sa, "B", , vbTextCompare)

For Each i In found
    Print i
Next
```

This example prints the following strings:

```
Brian
Rob
Barb
```

Format	Format string function

The `Format` function returns a string produced by placing a numeric or date/time value into a customized format. Numeric formats include such features as printing leading or trailing zeros, specifying where to round, and use of the thousands separator (,).

● **NOTE**

Although `Format` is still useful in some situations, it can mostly be replaced by new functions such as `FormatNumber` and `FormatDateTime`. The new functions are not only easier to use, but also have the advantage of automatically conforming to regional settings on each computer.

The function has the following syntax. The brackets indicate that the format string is optional.

Format(*expression* [,*formatString*])

The `Format` function supports two other optional fields that let you specify the first day of the week and the first week of the year. The use of these is rare, so I omit them here.

If you omit *formatString*, the function returns the standard string representation of *expression*. This is roughly the same action as the `Str` function, except that `Str` inserts a blank space in front of positive numbers.

Continued

The *formatString* uses characters such as #, 0, and the decimal point (.), among others, to represent a numeric format. # represents a digit position; using 0 is the same as #, except that use of 0 will print a trailing or leading zero and # will not. For example:

```
s = Format(15.5, "###.00")     ' s gets "15.50"
```

Digits to the right of the decimal point (either # or 0) indicate how many digits to print before rounding. For example:

```
s = Format(15.889, "###.##")   ' s gets "15.89"
```

Another convenient feature of **Format** is the use of a comma (,) as the thousands separator. For example:

```
s1 = Format(24500, "####.0")   ' s1 gets "24500.0"
s2 = Format(24500, "#,###.0")  ' s2 gets "24,500.0"
```

There are many other fine points in the use of format strings. In particular, you can use the letter **E** to indicate use of scientific notation. You can also design a customized format for dates and times. For a complete description, see the online Help topic "Format Function" and then click **See Also**.

FormatCurrency	Format as currency function (VB6)

The **FormatCurrency** function returns a string displaying a formatted dollar-and-cents amount. The input can be any numeric expression; it does not necessarily have to be type **Currency**. The formatted string contains a dollar sign ($), optional parentheses for negative numbers, and specified digits to the right of decimal point, among other features.

The function has the following syntax. Brackets indicate optional items. Use commas to indicate skipped arguments.

```
FormatCurrency(num, [,digits] [,useLeadingDigit] _
  [,useParens] [,useGrouping])
```

Here *num* is the numeric expression to be formatted. The optional *digits* argument specifies the number of digits to print to the right of the decimal point. If this provides less precision than needed to print the full number, the function rounds up or down as appropriate. If *digits* is omitted, the function uses the default in the regional settings.

The other three arguments each have three possible settings: `vbTrue` (-1), `vbFalse` (0), and `vbDefault` (-2). In each case, the default is determined by regional settings if the argument is omitted.

The *useLeadingDigit* argument determines whether a leading digit is used for quantities between –1.0 and 1.0; for example, printing .33 as $0.33 rather than $.33.

The *useParens* argument determines whether negative numbers are placed in parentheses: for example, printing –10.55 as ($10.55) rather than -$10.55.

The *useGrouping* argument determines whether the comma is used as a thousands-place separator. If this argument is set to `True`, the regional settings are used to determine exactly how digits are grouped.

The following examples show some possible results.

```
Print FormatCurrency(.5, 2, vbTrue)     ' Prints $0.50
Print FormatCurrency(.5, 3, vbFalse)    ' Prints $.500
Print FormatCurrency(2.777, 2)          ' Prints $2.78
Print FormatCurrency(-12, 1,, vbTrue)   ' Prints ($12.0)
```

FormatDateTime	**Format date or time function (VB6)**

20

The `FormatDateTime` function returns a string representing a date or time, formatted according to one of several different ways. The function has the following syntax. The Brackets indicate that *formatNum* is optional. If omitted, `vbGeneralDate` is used.

FormatDateTime(*datetime* [,*formatNum*])

Here *datetime* is an expression of type `Date`, which can contain a date, time, or date/time combination. The *formatNum* has one of the values shown below. Note that most of the formats below vary depending on regional settings.

Continued

Constant/Value	Value	Description
vbGeneralDate	0	Displays date portion, if any, in short format and time-of-day portion, if any, in long format
vbLongDate	1	Displays date portion in long format
vbShortDate	2	Displays date portion in short format
vbLongTime	3	Displays time-of-day portion in long format
vbShortTime	4	Displays time-of-day portion in short, 24-hour format (hh:mm)

For example:

```
Print FormatDateTime(Date, vbLongDate)
```

On my computer, this statement printed the following:

```
Thursday, June 18, 1998
```

FormatNumber	**Format number function (VB6)**

The FormatNumber function returns a string displaying a number rounded to a specified degree of precision, optional parentheses for negative numbers, and other features. This function is similar to FormatCurrency and FormatPercent, and can usually serve as a more convenient version of the Format function.

The function has the following syntax. Brackets indicate optional items. Use commas to indicate skipped arguments.

```
FormatNumber(num, [,digits] [,useLeadingDigit]_
  [,useParens] [,useGrouping])
```

See the FormatCurrency function for a description of each argument. The following examples show the function in use.

```
Print FormatNumber(.5, 2, vbTrue)    ' Prints 0.50
Print FormatNumber(.5, 3, vbFalse)   ' Prints .500
Print FormatNumber(2.777, 2)         ' Prints 2.78
Print FormatNumber(-12, 1,, vbTrue)  ' Prints (12.0)
```

FormatPercent
Format as percentage function (VB6)

The `FormatPercent` function returns a string displaying a number as a formatted percentage. First it multiplies the number by 100 and then it tacks on a percent symbol (%). The function also supports the same formatting operations as `FormatCurrency` and `FormatNumber`, including rounding to a specified degree of precision and optional parentheses for negative numbers.

The function has the following syntax. Brackets indicate optional items. Use commas to indicate skipped arguments.

```
FormatPercent(num, [,digits] [,useLeadingDigit] _
  [,useParens] [,useGrouping])
```

See the `FormatCurrency` function for a description of each argument. The following examples show the function in use.

```
Print FormatPercent(.5, 2)            ' Prints 50.00%
Print FormatPercent(.005, 1, vbFalse) ' Prints .5%
Print FormatPercent(.005, 1, vbTrue)  ' Prints 0.5%
Print FormatPercent(-.75, 0,, vbTrue) ' Prints (75%)
```

InStr
Substring search function

The `InStr` function conducts a search for a substring inside a larger string and returns the first position in which the substring is found. If the substring is not found, it returns 0. (String positions are one-based, so that the first position in a string is position 1.)

The function has the following syntax. Brackets indicate optional items:

```
InStr([start,] string, substring [, compare])
```

The optional *start* argument specifies what position of *string* to start the search in. The search moves right, so characters to the left of *start* are never searched. Note that regardless of *start*, the return value is always relative to the beginning of *string*.

Continued

The optional *compare* argument is an integer that modifies how the search is carried out. A setting of 1 (**vbTextCompare**) specifies a case-insensitive text comparison. A setting of 0 (the default), specifies a strict binary-value comparison, which is case-sensitive.

The following example searches for any occurrence of the target word "the".

```
searchString = InputBox("Enter string:")
p = InStr(searchString, "the")
If p > 0 Then Debug.Print "The word <the> was found."
```

The next example counts the occurrences of the word "the". This is a more complex example. Notice that as repeated occurrences of "the" are found, p increases in value by at least 1. This keeps the search moving to the right.

```
p = 0
numFound = 0
searchString = InputBox("Enter string:")
Do
    p = InStr(p + 1, searchString, "the")
    If p > 0 Then
        numFound = numFound + 1
    End If
Loop While p > 0
Debug.Print "NumFound = " & numFound
```

20

InStrRev	**String search function (VB6)**

The InStrRev function performs the same action as InStr, but instead of searching left to right, it starts at the end of the string and searches left. Note that the order of the arguments is different.

InStrRev(string, substring [,start] [, compare])

Join — Concatenation function (VB6)

The Join function returns a single string that is the concatenation of a series of strings. All the input strings are contained in the same array argument. The function has the following syntax:

```
Join(strArray [,delimiter])
```

Here *strArray* is the array containing all the input strings. The optional *delimiter* argument is a string of zero or more characters to print between each string in *strArray*. If *delimiter* is omitted, the function uses the default value of a single blank space (" "). You can choose to specify an empty string (""), which causes only the input strings to be placed in the result.

The following example shows how these arguments work:

```
Dim sa(4) As String
sa(0) = "This"
sa(1) = "Is"
sa(2) = "How"
sa(3) = "It"
sa(4) = "Looks"
Debug.Print Join(sa, " ")
Debug.Print Join(sa, "***")
Debug.Print Join(sa, "")
```

The last three lines produce the following output:

```
This Is How It Looks
This***Is***How***It***Looks
ThisIsHowItLooks
```

LCase — Lowercase function

The LCase function converts a string to all lowercase and returns the result. It does not affect the original string, which stays as it is. It also does not affect non-letter characters or characters that are already lowercase.

Continued

The function has the following syntax:

```
LCase(string)
```

For example, consider the following code:

```
aString = "I used to work for NASA."
Debug.Print LCase(aString)
```

This example prints the following string:

```
i used to work for nasa.
```

Left   Leftmost characters function

The `Left` function returns a string containing a specified number of characters on the left side of its string argument. In other words, it returns the first *n* characters. The function has the following syntax:

```
Left(string, n)
```

The function returns the *n* leftmost characters; if *n* is greater than the length of the string, `Left` returns the whole string. If *n* is zero, it returns an empty string.

Consider the following example:

```
aString = "The good, bad, ugly fish."
Debug.Pring Left(aString, 8)
```

This prints the following string:

```
The good
```

Len   String length function

The `Len` function returns the length of a string. It has the following syntax:

```
Len(string)
```

This function has many uses. Here it's used to dimension a byte array large enough to hold all the bytes in a string.

```
Dim byteArr() As Byte
ReDim byteArr(Len(theString))
```

The `Len` function can also be used with other types. In cases other than string expressions, the `Len` function returns the storage size of the expression's type, in bytes.

LSet   Left-justify statement

The `LSet` statement performs an assignment that left-justifies a string of text inside a larger string of text. It's most often used to copy data from a variable-length string to a fixed-length string. The statement can also be used to copy data between user-defined types. The `LSet` statement has two forms:

LSet *stringVar* = *stringExpr*
LSet *userTypeVar1* = *userTypeVar2*

In the first form, the string expression, *StringExpr*, is copied to the string variable *StringVar*. If *StringExpr* is shorter than *StringVar*, the data is left-justified and padded with trailing spaces. If *StringExpr* is longer, the statement copies only as many characters as already exist in *StringVar*.

For example, the following code copies six characters and pads the data with four trailing spaces:

```
Dim fixStr As String * 10
LSet fixStr = "blobby"    ' fixStr gets "blobby    "
```

The other use for `LSet` is to copy between variables of user-defined type.

```
Dim emprec1 As empRecType, emprec2 As empRecType
'
' Assign values to emprec2...
'
LSet emprec1 = emprec2
```

LTrim

Trim leading spaces function

The `LTrim` function returns a string without leading spaces. It has the following syntax:

```
LTrim(string)
```

For example:

```
' After this operation, the string s gets
'  "the words you say   "
'
s = LTrim("     the words you say   ")
```

Mid

Extract substring function

The `Mid` function — along with its cousin, the `Mid` statement — provides the ability to perform many different string operations. `Mid` returns a string containing a selected portion of a target string, specified by position and length. The function has the following syntax. Brackets indicate that *length* is an optional argument.

```
Mid(string, start [,length])
```

The function copies data from the *string* argument, beginning in the position denoted by *start*. A *start* value of 1 refers to the first position in the string.

The optional *length* argument indicates how many characters to get. If *length* is omitted or is greater than the remaining string size, the function simply copies all the characters from *start* onward.

The following examples demonstrate how the `Mid` function works:

```
aString = "It was a good, good year."
s = Mid(aString, 1, 6)    ' s gets "It was"
s = Mid(aString, 4, 1)    ' s gets "w"
s = Mid(aString, 21)      ' s gets "year."
```

Mid	Replace substring statement

Whereas the `Mid` function returns a portion of a target string, the `Mid` statement *replaces* the selected portion of an existing string. It never changes the size of the target string. In this version, the `Mid` keyword appears on the left of the equal sign (=, which in this context is an assignment operator).

`Mid(stringVar, start [,length]) = newString`

The arguments *start* and *length* have the same meaning they do for the `Mid` function. If *length* is omitted, this statement selects all remaining characters in *stringVar*, beginning at position *start*. String positions are one-based, so that the first character is position 1.

If the selected portion of *stringVar* is shorter than *newString*, the function uses only part of *newString*. For example, if the selected portion of *stringVar* is three characters long, the `Mid` statement uses only the first three characters of *newString*.

If the selected portion of *stringVar* is longer than *newString*, then *newString* is left-justified within the specified *stringVar* area.

The following examples should help clarify how these principles work:

```
s = "Good car."
Mid(s, 1, 1) = "B"        ' s = "Bood car."
Mid(s, 4, 1) = "ttt"      ' s = "Boot car."
Mid(s, 6) = "strap"       ' s = "Boot stra"
Mid(s, 2, 3) = "lip"      ' s = "Blip stra"
Mid(s, 2, 5) = "oop"      ' s = "Boop stra"
```

20

MonthName
Get month name function (VB6)

The `MonthName` function returns a string containing the name of a month, specified by a number from 1 to 12. The function has the following syntax. Brackets indicate that the second argument is optional.

MonthName(*month*, [*useAbbreviation*])

Here *month* is an integer and *useAbbreviation* is a `Boolean` value. If *useAbbreviation* is `True`, the function returns the abbreviation of the month name. The default setting for this argument is `False`.

The following example prints out the abbreviated names of all the months, in order:

```
For i = 1 To 12
    Debug.Print MonthName(i, True) & " ";
Next
```

This prints out the following in the Immediate window:

```
Jan Feb Mar Apr May Jun Jul Aug Sep Oct Nov Dec
```

In conjunction with `MonthName`, you may find the `DatePart` function useful in extracting the month portion of a date. In the following example, a call to `Date` returns the current date; `DatePart` extracts the month portion as a number, which in turn is passed to `MonthName`.

```
Print "The current month is ";
Print MonthName(DatePart("m", Date))
```

Here's sample output of this code:

```
The current month is June
```

20

Replace	**Replace substring function (VB6)**

The `Replace` function returns a string containing a version of a source string (*strSource*) in which a series of replacements have been made. The function itself does not modify the source string (although assignment could have this effect, of course).

The function has the following syntax. Brackets are used to indicate optional arguments. Use commas to indicate skipped arguments. (See example.)

```
Replace(strSource, strFind, strNew [,start] [,count]
[,compare])
```

The first three arguments, which are all required, are strings. The first, *strSource*, is the string to be searched. The *strFind* and *strNew* arguments indicate the target string and the string to replace it with, respectively. The function finds each occurrence of *strFind* and replaces it with *strNew*. Note that using an empty string for *strNew* is perfectly valid; in such a case, the function simply removes all occurrences of *strFind*.

The other arguments, which are all optional, are integers. The *start* argument specifies a one-based starting position. (1 means start with the first character.) The *count* argument specifies the maximum number of substitutions to perform; the default value of –1 causes the function to make all possible substitutions.

The *compare* argument modifies how matches are made. The default value of 0 (`vbBinaryCompare`) indicates case-sensitive comparisons. Setting the argument to 1 (`vbTextCompare`) indicates that uppercase and lowercase letters are equated.

For example, the following code carries out case-insensitive substitutions:

```
bigString = "The blue-haired girl had Blue eyes."
Print Replace(bigString, "blue", "red", , , 1)
```
This prints out the following:
```
The red-haired girl had red eyes.
```

Right   Rightmost characters
                                                    function

The `Right` function returns a string containing a specified number of characters on the right side of its string argument. In other
words, it returns the last *n* characters of the string. The function
has the following syntax:

```
Right(string, n)
```

The function returns the *n* rightmost characters; if *n* is
greater than the length of the string, `Right` returns the whole
string. If *n* is zero, it returns an empty string.
Consider the following example:

```
aString = "The good, bad, ugly fish."
Debug.Pring Right(aString, 10)
```

This prints the following string:

```
ugly fish.
```

RTrim   Trim trailing spaces
                                                    function

The `RTrim` function returns a string without trailing spaces. This
function is potentially useful with assignments from a fixed-length
string to a variable-length string, because fixed-length strings frequently have trailing spaces. (This is often relevant to random-
access file operations.) See also `LSet`.
The `RTrim` function has the following syntax:

```
RTrim(string)
```

For example:

```
' After this operation, the string s gets
'    "    the words you say"
'
s = RTrim("    the words you say    ")
```

20

Space — Repeat spaces function

The `Space` function returns a string that consists of a specified number of spaces. This function is sometimes useful as a way of creating a string of a specific length. (Such an operation is never necessary for fixed-length strings, but it can be useful for variable-length strings.) The function has the following syntax:

```
Space(n)
```

The function returns a string with *n* spaces. For example, the following code prints 20 spaces between "now" and "then":

```
Print "now" & Space(20) & "then"
```

StrComp — Compare strings function

The `StrComp` function compares two strings and returns a number indicating which is behind or ahead in alphabetical order — or whether they are the same. You can achieve the same results with the standard comparison operators (>, <, =, and so on) except for one difference: `StrComp` lets you specify whether or not the comparison is case-sensitive.

The function has the following syntax. The brackets indicate that *compare* is optional.

```
StrComp(string1, string2 [, compare])
```

If *string1* is earlier in alphabetical order than *string2*, the function returns –1. If the strings are the same, the function returns 0. If *string1* is later in alphabetical order, the function returns 1.

The optional *compare* argument determines case-sensitivity. If *compare* is set to 1 (**vbTextCompare**), the comparison is case-insensitive, so that "The", "the", and "THE" are all considered the same. If *compare* is set to 0 (**vbBinaryCompare**), the default, the comparison is a straight comparison of binary values, so that uppercase letters are all earlier in the order than lowercase letters.

Continued

The following example demonstrates how these arguments work:

```
Print StrComp("ax", "boy")   ' Prints -1
Print StrComp("A", "a")      ' Prints -1
Print StrComp("A", "a", 1)   ' Prints 0
```

StrConv   Convert string function

The `StrConv` function performs any of a number of different conversions, and returns the string result. The function has the following syntax:

StrConv(*string, conversionType*)

The *conversionType* is an integer that can have any of the following values. This is a partial list.

Symbolic Constant	Value	Description
vbUpperCase	1	Convert letters to all-uppercase.
vbLowerCase	2	Convert letters to all-lowercase.
vbProperCase	3	Capitalize the first letter of every word.
vbUnicode	64	Convert from local character set to Unicode.
vbFromUnicode	128	Convert from Unicode to the local character set.

20

The function also supports some other *conversionType* values that are specific to certain international character-set translations. See online Help for complete details.

You can, if you choose, combine a value from the first three rows with one of the values from the last two. For example:

```
s = StrConv(aString, vbUpperCase + vbUnicode)
```

String	**Repeat character function**

Like the `Space` function, the `String` function returns a string that consists of a specified number of characters. The difference is that with `String`, you specify the character you want repeated, as well as the number of repetitions.

The function has the following syntax:

`String(n, char)`

The function returns a string with *n* occurrences of the specified character. Usually, *char* is a string with one character, but it can also be a numeric value, in which case it is interpreted as an ASCII value. If *char* is a string longer than one character, the function uses the first character in that string.

For example, the following code prints 20 asterisks (*) between "now" and "then":

`Print "now" & String(20, "*") & "then"`

StrReverse	**Reverse string function (VB6)**

The `StrReverse` function returns a string that is the reverse of its argument. The function has the following syntax:

`StrReverse(stringExpression)`

For example, the following code reverses a well-known palindrome:

`Debug.Print StrReverse("Madam, I'm Adam")`

This prints out the following string:

`madA m'I ,madaM`

UCase   Uppercase string function

The UCase function converts a string to all uppercase and returns the result. It does not affect the original string, which stays as it is. It also does not affect non-letter characters or characters that are already uppercase.

The function has the following syntax:

UCase(*string* **)**

For example, consider the following code:

```
aString = "I used to work for NASA."
Debug.Print UCase(aString)
```

This example prints the following string:

```
I USED TO WORK FOR NASA.
```

WeekdayName   Day of week function
                                                          (VB6)

The WeekdayName function returns a string containing the day of the week, specified by a number from 1 to 7. The function has the following syntax. Brackets indicate optional arguments; use commas to indicate a skipped argument.

WeekdayName(*day* [, *abbreviate*] [, *firstDayOfWeek*] **)**

Here *day* is an integer and *abbreviate* is a **Boolean** value. If *abbreviate* is **True**, the function returns the abbreviation of the weekday. (See example.) The default setting for this argument is **False**.

The optional *firstDayOfWeek* argument specifies which of the seven days of the week is considered to be the first; the value of *day* is interpreted relative to this setting. The default value is 1 (Sunday). You can also specify 0, which means use the system default.

The following example prints out the abbreviated names of the weekdays, in order:

```
For i = 1 To 7
    Debug.Print WeekdayName(i, True) & " ";
Next
```

This prints out the following:

```
Sun Mon Tue Wed Thu Fri Sat
```

In conjunction with WeekdayName, you may find the DatePart function useful in extracting the day of the week from a date value. In the following example, a call to Date returns the current date; DatePart extracts the weekday portion as a number from 1 to 7, which in turn is passed to WeekdayName.

```
Print "The current day is ";
Print WeekdayName(DatePart("w", Date))
```

Here's sample output of this code:

```
The current day is Thursday
```

20

Keyword Summary: Math

21

Visual Basic 6.0 supports mathematical functions inherited from previous versions, along with one new function: Round, which rounds a number to a specified degree of precision. The Visual Basic math functions include support for standard trigonometric, logarithmic, random-number, and rounding functions. Although not every trigonometric function is directly supported, it is fairly easy to derive other functions from the ones supported here: Atn (arctangent), Cos, Sin, and Tan.

Almost all the mathematical keywords are intrinsic functions. One statement, Randomize, is used with the Rnd function. If you are doing math, you should also check out Chapter 13. Operator support for advanced math operations includes the exponentiation operator (^), integer division (\), and the Mod operator, in addition to the standard operators for addition, subtraction, multiplication, and floating-point division. Table 21-1 summarizes the mathematical functions and statements.

Table 21-1 *Math Functions and Statements*

Keyword	Description
Abs function	Returns absolute value
Atn function	Returns the arctangent
Cos function	Returns the cosine
Exp function	Raises the number *e* to the specified power and returns the result
Int function	Returns the integer portion of a number
Fix function	Rounds down to nearest integer, even if negative
Log function	Returns the natural logarithm (base *e*) of the argument
Randomize statement	Starts a random number sequence; used with Rnd
Rnd function	Generates a random number between 0 and 1.0
Round function	Rounds a floating-point number to nearest integer and returns the result
Sgn function	Returns –1, 0, or 1, depending on sign of argument
Sin function	Returns the sine
Sqr function	Returns the square root
Tan function	Returns the tangent

Abs	Absolute value function

21

The **Abs** function returns the absolute value of its argument. It has the following syntax:

Abs(*num*)

Here, *num* is any numeric expression. The function returns exactly the same type as it was passed. For example, **Abs** returns a **Long** if *num* is a **Long**.

The absolute-value function changes negative numbers to positives, but otherwise leaves the amount unchanged. For example:

```
Print Abs(12.5)    ' This prints "12.5"
Print Abs(-12.5)   ' This also prints "12.5"
```

Atn	Arctangent function

The **Atn** function returns the arctangent of its argument. It has the following syntax:

Atn(*num*)

Here, *num* is any numeric expression. The function returns a value of type **Double**. This value represents an angle in radians; it is always in the range $-\pi/2$ to $\pi/2$.

The arctangent function is the inverse of the tangent function (**Tan**). An arctangent takes as input the ratio of side A to side B of a right triangle, and it returns the angle (in radians) between the hypotenuse and side B, where A is the side opposite the angle and B is the side that, together with the hypotenuse, forms the angle.

The following example demonstrates the use of the **Atn** function in a couple of ways. First, it uses the formula **Atn(1) * 4** to get the value of π (()), which is generally useful with trig functions. It then prompts the user for two lengths, calculates the arctangent, and displays the results in degrees by using the conversion factor $180/\pi$.

Continued

21

```
Dim pi As Double, a As Double, b As Double
pi = Atn(1) * 4
a = InputBox("Enter length of side A:")
b = InputBox("Enter length of side B:")
angle = Atn(a / b) * 180 / pi
s = Format$(angle, "##.##")
n = MsgBox("The angle is " & s & " degrees.")
```

Cos — Cosine function

The Cos function returns the cosine of its argument. It has the following syntax:

Cos(*num*)

Here, *num* is any numeric expression. The function returns a value of type Double. The result is in the range –1 to 1.

The argument *num* expresses an angle in radians. To convert from degrees to radians, multiply by the factor pi/180. You can use the Atn function to get the closest approximation to pi (approximately 3.141593) in the range of the Double data type.

```
Dim Pi As Double, nDeg As Double, nRad As Double
pi = Atn(1) * 4
nDeg = InputBox("Enter angle in degrees: ")
nRad = nDeg * pi / 180
n = MsgBox("The cosine is " & Cos(nRad))
```

Exp — Exponential function

The Exp function returns the mathematical value *e*, raised to a specified exponent. It has the following syntax:

Exp(*num*)

Here, *num* is any numeric expression. The function returns a value of type Double.

21

The `Exp` function should not be confused with the more general exponentiation operator (^), which allows you to specify any numeric expression as the base. See Chapter 13 for more information on this operator.

One of the more obvious uses of the `Exp` function is to obtain the value *e* itself:

```
e = Exp(1)
```

Fix	Truncate to integer function

The `Fix` function returns the integer portion of a numeric expression. It has the following syntax, in which *num* is any numeric expression.

```
Fix(num)
```

Unlike the `Int` function, `Fix` returns the integer portion of the number, regardless of sign. For example:

```
Debug.Print 5.9    ' Prints "5"
Debug.Print -5.9   ' Prints "-5"
```
See also `Int` and `Round`.

Int	Round down to integer function

The `Int` function returns the highest integer that is less than or equal to a specified number. It has the following syntax, in which *num* is any numeric expression.

```
Int(num)
```

Unlike the `Fix` function, `Int` always rounds downward, even in the case of negative numbers. For example:

```
Debug.Print 5.9    ' Prints "5"
Debug.Print -5.9   ' Prints "-6"
```

See also `Fix` and `Round`.

| **21** | **Log** | **Natural logarithm function** |

The Log function returns the natural logarithm of a specified number. (The natural logarithm uses the mathematical value *e* as the base.) The function has the following syntax:

Log(*num*)

Here, *num* is any numeric expression. The function returns a value of type Double. You can use the Log function to get a logarithm for any base, as demonstrated in the following function.

```
Function logB(base, num)
    logB = Log(num) / Log(base)
End Function
```

| **Randomize** | **Set random seed statement** |

The Randomize statement starts a new sequence of random numbers to be generated with the Rnd function. If you are working with random numbers, you should call Randomize at least once, at the beginning of the program.

The statement has the following syntax. The brackets indicate that *seed* is optional.

Randomize [*seed*]

The optional *seed* argument is a numeric expression. If *seed* is omitted, Randomize uses the system time. In practice, you should almost always omit *seed*. The exception would be if you wanted to generate the same series of numbers every time, for testing purposes.

The following example shows typical use of Randomize and Rnd. This code generates three random numbers.

```
Randomize
r1 = Rnd
r2 = Rnd
r3 = Rnd
```

| Rnd | Generate random number function | 21 |

The `Rnd` function returns a random number as a floating-point value between 0.0 and 1.0. The function has the following syntax. The brackets indicate that the argument, along with the parentheses, is optional.

`Rnd[ (num) ]`

If *num* is less than 0, `Rnd` starts a new sequence of numbers using *num* as the new seed. If *num* is 0, `Rnd` returns the last random number generated. If *num* is any positive number or is omitted, `Rnd` returns the next random number in the sequence.

To get reasonable random numbers for most purposes, call `Randomize` at least once before calling `Rnd` for the first time. Omit arguments in both cases.

```
Randomize
r = Rnd
```

An alternative method is to use an argument for `Rnd`, but give the system time as the *seed* argument:

```
r = Rnd(Timer)
```

The number returned by `Rnd` is a `Single` value between 0 and 1. (In practice, neither 0 nor 1 is ever returned, since the odds of generating either 0 or 1 precisely is infinitesimal.) To translate this value into a random integer, multiply by n, where n is the maximum value desired, and round downward. Then add 1.

The following example demonstrates this technique; `randN` is a function returning a random number from 1 to n, where n is the argument. For example, `randN(3)` can return 1, 2, or 3.

```
Function randN(n As Variant) As Integer
    Randomize
    randN = 1 + Int(Rnd * n)
End Function
```

21

Round	Round number function (VB6)

The Round function, which is new in Visual Basic 6.0, lets you round a fractional number to a specified degree of precision. You can achieve similar results with the Format function, but the Round function returns a number, not a string. Unlike the Int and Fix functions, you can use the Round function to round to the nearest integer, rather than truncating.

The Round function has the following syntax. The brackets indicate that the second argument is optional:

Round(num [, digits]**)**

If *digits* is used, it specifies a number of digits to the right of the decimal point. The function rounds to the specified digit, looking one additional digit to the right to see if it should round up or down. (See example.) If *digits* is omitted, the function rounds to the nearest integer.

For example:

```
Print Round(5.7)        ' Prints "6"
Print Round(5.3335)     ' Prints "5"
Print Round(5.3335, 1)  ' Prints "5.3"
Print Round(5.3335, 3)  ' Prints "5.334"
```

The advantage of this function is that it enables you to round a number to specified precision before it is used in calculation, rather than after, as is the case with the Format function.

Sgn	Get sign function

The Sgn function returns the sign (positive or negative) of its argument. It has the following syntax, in which *num* is any numeric expression:

Sgn(num**)**

The function returns –1 for negative numbers, 0 for zero, and 1 for positive numbers.

Sin	Sine function

The Sin function returns the sine of its argument. It has the following syntax:

```
Sin(num)
```

Here, *num* is any numeric expression. The function returns a value of type Double. The result is in the range –1 to 1.

The argument *num* expresses an angle in radians. To convert from degrees to radians, multiply by the factor pi/180. You can use the Atn function to get the closest value to pi (approximately 3.141593).

```
Dim pi As Double, nDeg As Double, nRad As Double
pi = Atn(1) * 4
nDeg = InputBox("Enter angle in degrees: ")
nRad = nDeg * pi / 180
n = MsgBox("The sine is " & Sin(nRad))
```

Sqr	Square root function

The Sqr function returns the square root of its argument. It has the following syntax, in which *num* is any numeric expression:

```
Sqr(num)
```

The function returns a result of type Double. Not surprisingly, the function generates a run-time error if you specify a negative argument.

21 | Tan
Tangent function

The Tan function returns the tangent of its argument. The tangent of an angle is the ratio of two sides A and B of a right triangle, given the specified angle between side B and the hypotenuse. The function has the following syntax:

Tan(*num*)

Here, *num* is any numeric expression. The function returns a value of type Double.

The argument *num* expresses an angle in radians. To convert from degrees to radians, multiply by the factor pi/180. You can use the Atn function to get the closest value to pi (approximately 3.141593).

```
Dim pi As Double, nDeg As Double, nRad As Double
pi = Atn(1) * 4
nDeg = InputBox("Enter angle in degrees: ")
nRad = nDeg * pi / 180
n = MsgBox("The tangent is " & Tan(nRad))
```

Debugging
Commands

"In run mode, no one can hear you scream."

—Billg Ates, ace programmer

The very first product I worked on for Microsoft was the CodeView debugger, which was, for many programmers, revolutionary in its day. The most useful features of the debugger are now a part of the Visual Basic environment. About the only thing you can't do now that you could do with old debuggers is dump absolute memory addresses, and with a high-level language, you should never need to do that anyway.

In some respects, the current debugging commands and features (inherited from Version 5.0) are superior to CodeView's in terms of quick access and ease of use. This is certainly true of Visual Basic, which lets you examine data values by simply moving the mouse pointer over a variable.

This chapter describes debugging features in several major areas.

- General debugging features
- Commands on the Debug menu
- Debugging commands on the View menu
- Debugging and the flow of events
- Final thoughts

22

General Debugging Features

Debugging a program means analyzing a program while it's actually running so that you can figure out how and why something went wrong. No one understands your own programming code better than you do. Therefore, the best aid you can have in debugging is to have effective tools and know what they do. But for those so inclined, there are some good texts which explain debugging principles in some depth. I'd suggest you try *Visual Basic 6 Bible,* by Eric Smith, Valor Whisler, and Hank Marquis (IDG Books Worldwide, 1998).

In Visual Basic, a debugging session begins by entering break mode by one of several ways:

- Run the program (press F5), and then press Ctrl + Break.
- Set a breakpoint (press F9), and then run the program.
- Add a watch expression that breaks on a condition, and then run the program.
- Insert a **Debug.Assert** or **Stop** statement into the code; this provides a programmatic breakpoint.

Although all these methods work as a way of entering break mode, the last three are more reliable. The problem with pressing Ctrl + Break is that if the application is waiting for a user response, execution will not stop on one of your program's statements, and you won't be able to trace execution. The Immediate window, however, will still work.

Figure 22-1 summarizes the ways in which you can move between design, run, and break modes. Note that you always start in design mode.

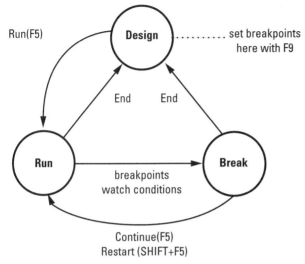

Figure 22-1 *Relationship of design, run, and break modes*

Most of the commands involved here (Start, Break, and End) are available on the Run menu. They are also available in Visual Basic's main toolbar. Figure 22-2 shows the three buttons — Start, Break, and End — available on the main toolbar for controlling program execution.

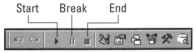

Figure 22-2 *Start, Break, and End on the main toolbar*

Managing the Watch Window

There are a few general principles of debugging, and one in particular is especially helpful. This principle is *"debug data, not code,"* a mantra sometimes heard in the halls at Microsoft. When an error occurs, the source is most often a variable with a bad value. The variable may have gone out of bounds, been incorrectly initialized, or been assigned a value you never expected. For example, the logic error in the following loop is the failure to initialize the value of `fact` to 1. Because `fact` starts off at 0, it never increases in value.

```
Function fact(n As Integer) As Integer
   For i = 1 To n
      fact = fact * i
   Next
End Function
```

In this case, the error could be detected by watching what happens to the value of `fact`. Once you saw that `fact` was always 0, you'd quickly understand that it was lacking the following statement:

```
fact = 1    ' Insert at beginning of the function
```

One of the important debugging tools in Visual Basic is therefore the Watch window, which not only lets you view data, but also lets you use expressions to stop execution, just like a breakpoint. This can be very helpful, because frequently you are not interested in a particular line of code as much as in finding *which* line of code caused some data to get the wrong value.

There are two ways to add an expression to the Watch window, which can be done either in design or break mode.

- Choose the Add Watch command from the Debug menu, and then enter any expression you like.

- Highlight a variable or expression in the Code window, and press Shift + F9 to execute the Quick Watch command. This instantly adds a watch expression. If you then want to make this expression into a break condition, choose the Edit Watch command (Ctrl + W).

When the `Add Watch` dialog box is displayed, as shown in Figure 22-3, it lets you specify several kinds of watch expressions. All watch expressions display their current value in the Watch window. But you can also specify watch expressions that break when `True` or break when any change occurs in their value. An example of the former would be n > 100. In such a case, n might be the highest acceptable value, and you want to stop execution at precisely the point where n gets too high.

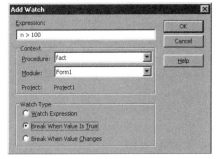

Figure 22-3   *The Add Watch dialog box*

As watch expressions accumulate, they appear in the Watch window. This window is easy to maintain. To delete a watch expression, make sure the item is highlighted and then press Del. To change an expression, highlight the item and choose the Edit Watch command (Ctrl + W).

Figure 22-4 shows an example of each of the three kinds of watch expressions, in this order: simple watch, break when changed, and break on condition. The icon to the left of each item indicates which kind of watch expression that item is.

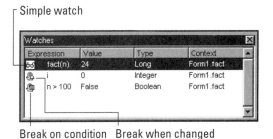

Simple watch

Break on condition   Break when changed

Figure 22-4   *The Watch window*

Getting Instant Data Values

Once you're in break mode, you can get fast feedback on the value of variables and expressions. It's not always necessary to use the Watch window.

To view the value of a variable while in break mode, move the mouse pointer over the variable and leave it there. (The mouse pointer appears as an insertion point, a large "I".) The variable must appear in the current procedure or a procedure on the call stack. Visual Basic responds by displaying a small box, underneath the pointer, showing the value.

To view the value of an expression, highlight the expression in the Code window and leave the mouse pointer over the highlighted area. The expression must be in an active procedure (on the call stack) and the expression cannot contain any procedure calls. Thus, you can view the value of (amount + 5) / d, but not fact(n).

Figure 22-5 shows an example of how Visual Basic displays quick feedback on values.

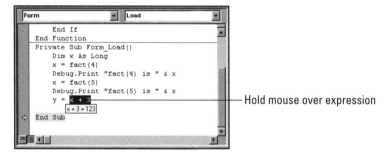

Hold mouse over expression

Figure 22-5   *Quick feedback on data values*

Breaking with the Assert Method

Yet another way to break execution is to use the Assert method. Place a Debug.Assert statement any place you think a program-logic error is likely to occur. The Assert method has the following syntax:

Debug.Assert *booleanExpression*

If *booleanExpression* is False, Visual Basic halts execution and enters break mode. For example, the following statement halts execution if n is greater than upwardLimit:

```
Debug.Assert n <= upwardLimit
```

One advantage of using Assert is that when you are finished debugging and go to build a stand-alone executable, you do not

need to strip `Assert` statements from your code to improve efficiency. The Visual Basic compiler automatically skips over them.
The following statement is the equivalent of a breakpoint, except it is not controlled by menu commands:

```
Debug.Assert False
```

Commands on the Debug Menu

Usually, all the commands on the Debug menu are enabled when you're in break mode. The exception is when the Code window is not visible or the line containing the cursor is not visible; in that case, commands relating to the cursor line are disabled.

Some of the commands (such as the Watch-expression commands and Toggle Breakpoint) are available in design mode as well as break mode. None are enabled in run mode. Remember that the Run and View menus also contain commands useful in debugging.

Table 22-1 summarizes the commands on the Debug menu.

Table 22-1 *Commands on the Debug Menu*

Command	Shortcut Key	Description
Step Into	F8	Executes next statement, stepping into procedure call if applicable
Step Over	Shift+F8	Executes next statement
Step Out	Ctrl+Shift+F8	Executes to the end of current procedure
Run to Cursor	Ctrl+F8	Executes until cursor line is reached
Add Watch		Brings up `Add Watch` dialog box
Edit Watch	Ctrl+W	Edits current item in the Watch window
Quick Watch	Shift+F9	Adds selected expression to Watch window
Toggle Breakpoint	F9	Sets or removes breakpoint from cursor line

Continued

22

Table 22-1 *Continued*

Command	Shortcut Key	Description
Clear All Breakpoints	Ctrl+Shift+F9	Clears all breakpoints, if any
Set Next Statement	Ctrl+F9	Sets current statement to cursor line
Show Next Statement		Displays current line if not currently visible

Step Into	**Debug menu command**

The Step Into command executes the current statement, stepping into a procedure if the statement involves a procedure call. It does not step into a procedure if the current statement is not a procedure call or source code for the procedure is not in the project. (Step Into, therefore, does not enter intrinsic functions.) When you enter a procedure with Step Into, the Code window displays that procedure and highlights the first line.

For example, in Figure 22-6, the Step Into command causes execution to step into the Function procedure, func2.

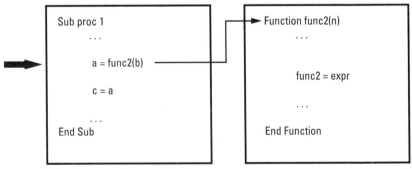

Figure 22-6 *Example of Step Into command*

The shortcut key for Step Into is F8. The access key is I, so that you can access it through Alt + D + I. You can also click the command from the Debug toolbar.

Step Over | Debug menu command

The Step Over command executes the current statement. Unlike the Step Into command, Step Over executes a procedure call as a single statement. (If the current statement is not a procedure call, the action of Step Into and Step Over is the same.) Step Over stays inside the same procedure declaration until the last line is reached, in which case it "pop outs" into the calling procedure, if there is one.

For example, in Figure 22-7, the Step Over command executes the statement a = func2(b) as one unit and sets the next statement at the line c = a. Contrast this with Figure 22-5.

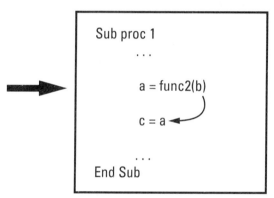

Figure 22-7 *Example of Step Over command*

The shortcut key for Step Over is Shift + F8. The access key is O, so that you can access it through Alt + D + O. You can also click the command from the Debug toolbar.

22

Step Out — Debug menu command

The Step Out command executes to the end of the current procedure. Execution stops at the statement immediately after the call to the current procedure. For example, if the current procedure is `proc1`, the next line to be executed is the statement following the call to `proc1`.

The shortcut key for Step Out is Ctrl + Shift + F8. The access key is U, so that you can access it through Alt + D + U. You can also click the command from the Debug toolbar.

Run to Cursor — Debug menu command

The Run to Cursor command continues execution, stopping when the line containing the cursor is reached. (The simplest way to move the cursor is to click on a line.) The effect is the nearly the same as setting a breakpoint and then running. The difference is that `Run to Cursor` does not set a permanent breakpoint. Also, note that `Run to Cursor` does not override any existing breakpoints, so execution might not reach the cursor line.

The shortcut key for Run to Cursor is Ctrl + F8. The access key is R, so that you can access the command through Alt + D + R

Add Watch — Debug menu command

The Add Watch command brings up the Add Watch dialog box. You can use that dialog box to add a watch expression to the Watch window. See the section "Managing the Watch Window" earlier in the chapter, for more information on watch expressions. Note that if all you want is a simple watch expression (one that does not involve breaking execution), you can usually add the expression faster by using Quick Watch.

The access key for this command is A, so that you can access the command through Alt + D + A.

Edit Watch
Debug menu command

The Edit Watch command is similar to Add Watch: It brings up
the Add Watch dialog box. The difference is that Edit Watch modifies the current item in the Watch window; it does not add a new
watch expression. By default, the Edit Watch command selects
the first item in the Watch window for editing if no other item has
been selected.

The shortcut key for this command is Ctrl + W. The access key
is E, so that you can access the command through Alt + D + E.

Quick Watch
Debug menu command

The Quick Watch command adds the currently selected expression in the Code window, if any, to the Watch window. The selected expression is the highlighted expression. If you haven't
highlighted any expression in the Code window yet, Quick Watch
is disabled. See the section "Managing the Watch Window" earlier
in the chapter, for more information on watch expressions.

The shortcut key for Quick Watch is Shift + F9. The access key
is Q, so that you can access the command through Alt + D + Q. You
can also click this command on the Debug toolbar.

Toggle Breakpoint
Debug menu command

The Toggle Breakpoint command sets or clears an individual
breakpoint. (A statement with a breakpoint automatically stops
the program when it is about to be executed, switching the Visual
Basic environment into break mode.) If the line containing the
cursor does not have a breakpoint, this command sets one. If the
line already has a breakpoint, this command clears it.

When a statement line has a breakpoint, it is identified with
red highlight and a circle icon to its right. Figure 22-8 shows an
example of two breakpoints.

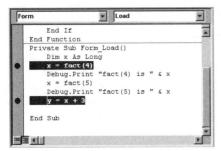

Figure 22-8 *Debugging session with two breakpoints*

The shortcut key for Toggle Breakpoint is F9. The access key is T, so that you can access the command through Alt + D + T. You can also click the command on the Debug toolbar.

Clear All Breakpoints	Debug menu command

The Clear All Breakpoints command is self-explanatory. If there are any breakpoints, this command clears them all. See the previous section for a discussion of breakpoints.

The shortcut key for Clear All Breakpoints is Ctrl + Shift + F9. The access key is C, so that you can access the command through Alt + D + C.

Set Next Statement	Debug menu command

The Set Next Statement command can be used to skip over an arbitrary number of statements or to reset execution to a previous line. You should use this command with care, because it disrupts the logical flow of the program. To use the command, first move the cursor to the desired line (for example, by clicking that line) and choose the command. Visual Basic then sets the line as the current statement. When execution resumes, this line will be the next to be executed.

The shortcut key for Set Next Statement is Ctrl + F9. The access key is N, so that you can access the command through Alt + D + N.

Show Next Statement	Debug menu command

The Show Next Statement command ensures the current statement is displayed. (Despite the name, this command has little to do with Set Next Statement.) The command is most likely to be useful when you are scrolling through large amounts of code and the current statement is no longer in view. In addition, if the Code window is no longer visible, the command displays the Code window and brings it to the foreground.

The access key for this command is X, so that you can access the command through Alt + D + X.

Debugging Commands on the View Menu

The View menu of the development environment supports several commands that are useful in debugging. Most of these are enabled at all times, although the Call Stack command is enabled only during break mode.

Table 2-2 summarizes these commands. Note that these comprise only a subset of the View menu. The Toolbars command is at the very bottom of the menu.

Table 22-2 *Debugging Commands on the View Menu*

Command	Shortcut Key	Description
Immediate Window	Ctrl+G	Displays the Immediate window
Locals Window		Displays the Locals window, which shows values of all local variables in whatever procedure is executing

Continued

22

Table 22-2 *Continued*

Command	Shortcut Key	Description
Watch Window		Displays the Watch window
Call Stack	Ctrl+L	Displays the call stack, which shows a list of all currently executing procedures
Toolbars		Can be used to display the Debug toolbar

Immediate Window   View command

The `Immediate Window` command displays the Immediate window, which is probably familiar to you if you've used Visual Basic before. There are two main ways to use the window:

- Move the cursor to the window, enter a statement such as `Print X`, and press Enter. (Note that while in the window, you can use the question mark, `?`, as shorthand for `Print`; Visual Basic will expand `?` into `Print` as soon as you press Enter.)
- Print to the window from the program by inserting `Debug.Print` statements.

The shortcut key for the Immediate Window command is Ctrl + G. The access key is I, so you can also access the command through Alt + V + I.

Locals Window   View command

The Locals Window command displays a Locals window, which hangs around until closed but displays different data depending on what procedure you are in. Whenever code is executing inside a procedure, the Locals window displays a list of all arguments and local variables for the procedure, along with their values. Figure 22-9 shows a sample Locals window.

Click to display property settings

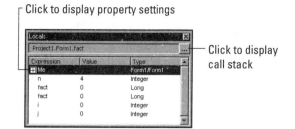

Click to display
call stack

Figure 22-9 *The Locals window*

In addition to displaying variables and arguments, the Locals window has a couple of special features. First, there is an item named Me that, when clicked, expands into a list of current property settings for the form. (If there are controls, you can browse setting for controls as well, by clicking Me.) Also, by clicking the button with ellipses (...), you display the call stack.

The access key for the Locals Window command is S, so you can access the command through Alt + V + S. You can also click this command on the Debug toolbar.

Watch Window   View menu command

The Watch Window command displays the Watch window, which (unlike the Locals window) shows the value of selected Watch expressions — expressions you've added to the window yourself. For more information on the Watch window, see the section "Managing the Watch Window" earlier in this chapter.

The access key for the Watch Window command is H, so you can access the command through Alt + V + H.

Call Stack

View menu command

The Call Stack command displays the current call stack. This command is available during break mode only. A call stack shows all the procedures that are currently executing, in reverse order in which they were called. Any procedure that has yet to return is in the call stack. For example, suppose you have an event procedure `Form_Click`, which called a `Sub` procedure named `doCalc`, which in turn called function `func1`. All three would be listed on the call stack, in this order: `func1`, `doCalc`, and `Form_Click`.

An interesting use of the call stack is with recursive functions. For example, the factorial function, `fact`, can be written so that it calls itself recursively. Figure 22-10 shows a call stack for a program in which `Form_Load` calls `fact`, which in turn calls itself.

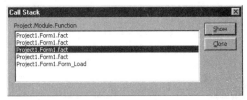

Figure 22-10   *The call stack*

If you click the Show button in this window, it displays the Code window and uses a green arrow to indicate the last line executing in the selected procedure. Double-clicking a procedure name within this window has the same effect. The Locals window, if open, will then show current values for that particular procedure call.

The shortcut key for the Call Stack command is Ctrl + L. The access key is K, so you can also access the command through Alt + V + K. You can also click this command on the Debug toolbar.

●─**NOTE**────────────────────────────────────

Unlike the other debugging windows, the call stack is a modal window, which means you have to close it before doing anything else in the development environment.

Toolbars (Debug)   View menu command

The Toolbars command brings up any of several toolbars. One of these is the Debug toolbar, which is useful to have hanging around if you're going to do a lot of debugging. As a toolbar, it floats in front of ordinary windows; the Debug toolbar can become annoying if it blocks the view of something you'd rather see. Therefore, you'll want to drag the toolbar to some unused or unobtrusive area of the screen. You can even attach it to the main toolbar, if you want, or to the left or right edge of the screen. (This is called *docking* the toolbar.)

Figure 22-11 shows the Debug toolbar. It contains a number of the most useful debugging commands from the Run, Debug, and View menus.

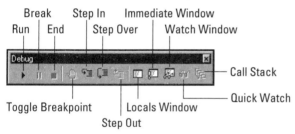

Figure 22-11 *The Debug toolbar*

Debugging and the Flow of Events

Most of the time, user events and debugging actions are sufficiently separate that no conflicts occur. In a few cases, however, the same actions used to control the environment can overlap with the very events your program is handling, and debugging conflicts are possible.

Conflicts due to event handling arise in the following situations:

- When you break inside a MouseDown event procedure, the development environment intercepts further mouse actions until run mode resumes — by which time the mouse button will have been released. (In theory, it's possible to avoid this problem by holding the mouse button down and stepping through with keystroke commands, but this is too cumbersome to be practical.)

Consequently, the program never gets a MouseUp event. This is a problem if your code needs to respond to both MouseDown and MouseUp events.

- Similarly, when you break inside a KeyDown event procedure, the development environment intercepts further keystroke actions. Consequently, the program never gets a KeyUp event. This is a problem if your code needs to respond to both KeyDown and KeyUp events.

- When you break inside a Timer event (associated with the Timer control), the system stops generating further Timer events. As a result, the behavior of the Timer control will not reflect run-time conditions, which typically rely on events at regular intervals.

In all of these situations, you may have to rely on placing Debug.Print statements into the program code rather than taking advantage of high-level debugging commands. Use of Debug.Print is often less convenient, but it has the advantage of not interfering with the flow of events in any way. As soon as a Debug.Print statement is executed, the Immediate window is displayed and you can see the output of these statements at the same time as the program runs.

Debug.Print uses the Print method; see Chapter 19 for Print method syntax.

Final Thoughts

Debugging can't be taught any more than programming can. You learn some tools and building blocks, but then it's up to you to build a structure. Of course, with debugging it's more detective work than carpentry. You follow the data (your evidence) and you use it to track down the guilty party — your lines of code being the suspects. At least 99% of debugging is detection. It's hard work, but it's a great feeling when you finally discover the reason behind a problem, because then fixing it is easy. Sometimes you want to hit your head, simulating the feeling of Newton when the apple struck.

It's been said that debugging is like trying to follow a worm through an apple, watching it weave its way around the core and the bruises, an explorer in a strange land. (Okay, maybe no one said that, but I'm saying it now.) The worm may gnaw itself a labyrinth, but ultimately, it can't get away. As the Clown character says in Shakespeare's *Antony and Cleopatra*, I wish you joy of the worm.

22

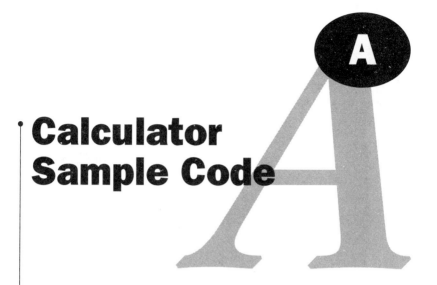

Calculator Sample Code

The following code implements the Calculator application described near the end of Chapter 5. See that chapter for a picture of the user interface, which includes a text box named `Readout` and an array of command buttons named `Keys`.

Although this code is sufficient to create a usable calculator application, it can be further enhanced in a number of ways. For example, you could write a `KeyPress` event procedure for the `Keys` array; the appropriate action would be to respond as if the corresponding key was pressed (no matter which button had the focus.) For example, typing "1" would cause the same action as clicking the button labeled "1".

The code supports a command button with the caption "C". This creates a Clear key, which is useful to have. You can enhance the application by adding such a button to the interface.

```
' This application has a text box named Readout
' Application also has an array of command buttons
'   named Keys; each has a different caption
```

```
Dim op1 As Double, op2 As Double    ' operands
Dim pendingOp As String             ' old operation
Dim opPendingFlag As Boolean     ' Is operation pending?
Dim newEntryFlag As Boolean      ' Start new entry?
Dim decimalPresent As Boolean    ' Is a dec. pnt present?

' Keys_Click: get key that was pressed and take
' appropriate action.
'
Private Sub Keys_Click(Index As Integer)
    Dim cap As String
    cap = Keys(Index).Caption
    Select Case cap
        Case "0" To "9"
            doNum cap
        Case "/", "*", "-", "+", "="
            doOp cap
        Case "."
            doDec
        Case "C"
            opPendingFlag = False
            Readout.Text = ""
    End Select

End Sub


' doNum: If newEntryFlag is true, start new entry
'   with number that was pressed. Else, append number.
'
Sub doNum(cap As String)
    If newEntryFlag Then
        decimalPresent = False
        newEntryFlag = False
        Readout.Text = cap
    Else
```

```
        Readout.Text = Readout.Text & cap
    End If
End Sub


' doOp: If operation is pending, store readout num
' in op2 and carry out op1 op op2. Else, store
' readout in op1. Finally, set pending operation
' to current key and enable newEntryFlag.
'
Sub doOp(cap As String)
    If Not opPendingFlag Then
        op1 = Readout.Text
        opPendingFlag = True
    Else
        op2 = Readout.Text
        Select Case pendingOp
            Case "/"
                op1 = op1 / op2
            Case "*"
                op1 = op1 * op2
            Case "-"
                op1 = op1 - op2
            Case "+"
                op1 = op1 + op2
            Case "="
                op1 = op2
        End Select
        Readout.Text = op1
    End If
    newEntryFlag = True
    pendingOp = cap
End Sub


' doDec: If new entry, start entry with dec. point.
' Else if decimal not present, append dec. point.
'
```

```
Sub doDec()
    If newEntryFlag Then
        decimalPresent = True
        newEntryFlag = False
        Readout.Text = "."
    ElseIf Not decimalPresent Then
        decimalPresent = True
        Readout.Text = Readout.Text & "."
    End If
End Sub
```

Stack Class

The following code presents the completed `Stack` class described in Chapter 8. This class provides examples of methods, properties, and passing along an enumerator, which enables objects of the class to work with the `For Each` statement. For a description of each of these features, see Chapter 8.

```
' Private data member, theColl: data is actually
'   stored in this collection.

Private theColl As New Collection

' Push and Pop methods defined here.
'
Sub Push(Item As Variant)
    theColl.Add Item
End Sub
```

```
Function Pop() As Variant
   Dim i As Integer
   i = theColl.Count
   If i > 0 Then
      Pop = theColl.Item(i)
      theColl.Remove i
   Else
      Pop = Null
   End If
End Function


' The procedures that follow implement Item as a
'   read/write property taking an argument (index).
'   Property GET lets class user get value: procedure
'   returns Item(n) to the class user by calling Item
'   method in Collection. Property LET responds to user
'   assigning a value to an item by adding a new item
'   and deleting the old.
'
Public Property Get Item(ByVal index As Long) _
 As Variant
    Item = theColl.Item(index)
End Property

Public Property Let Item(ByVal index As Long, _
 ByVal newval As Variant)
    theColl.Add newval, , index
    theColl.Remove index + 1
End Property


' The following procedure implements Count as a
'   read-only property. Class user can GET value of
'   this property but not set it.
'
Public Property Get Count() As Integer
    Count = theColl.Count
```

```
End Property

' NewEnum: return the collection's enumerator, so
'  that Stack class works with For Each.
'  Note that the procedure ID must be set to -4.
'
Public Function NewEnum() As IUnknown
    Set NewEnum = theColl.[_NewEnum]
End Function
```

ASCII
Character Table

The following table lists the first 128 ASCII character codes and the printable characters they correspond to. If no character is shown next to a number, Windows does not support that ASCII character.

00		26		52	4	78	N	104	h
01		27		53	5	79	O	105	i
02		28		54	6	80	P	106	j
03		29		55	7	81	Q	107	k
04		30		56	8	82	R	108	l
05		31		57	9	83	S	109	m
06		32	(space)	58	:	84	T	110	n
07		33	!	59	;	85	U	111	o
08	BKSP	34	"	60	<	86	V	112	p
09	TAB	35	#	61	=	87	W	113	q
10	LF	36	$	62	>	88	X	114	r
11		37	%	63	?	89	Y	115	s
12		38	&	64	@	90	Z	116	t
13	CR	39	'	65	A	91	[	117	u
14		40	(	66	B	92	\	118	v
15		41	)	67	C	93	]	119	w
16		42	*	68	D	94	^	120	x
17		43	+	69	E	95	_	121	y
18		44	,	70	F	96	`	122	z
19		45	-	71	G	97	a	123	{
20		46	.	72	H	98	b	124		
21		47	/	73	I	99	c	125	}
22		48	0	74	J	100	d	126	~
23		49	1	75	K	101	e	127	
24		50	2	76	L	102	f		
25		51	3	77	M	103	g		

Index

Symbols

, 326, 331, 337, 360
!, 357
', 42
."," 136
#, 357, 364
$, 356, 462
%, 356
&, 60, 61, 326, 331, 337, 351, 357,
     360, 362–363, 473
', 59–60
(), 61, 72
*, 333, 360, 364
+, 61, 324, 360, 362
,, 471
-, 360
/, 360
;, 470, 471

=, 116, 326, 328, 337, 360
?, 61, 364. *See also* Print method
[], 432
^, 329, 334, 337, 360
(_), 42

A

Abs function, 324, 328, 500, 501
Accelerate method, 312
Active Server pages, 168
ActiveX, 17
    BigX control, 224–225
    Boolean values, 317
    classes and, 219
    click events, 227–229
    color, 317
    creating, 12–13, 229–231, 314

Continued

Continued

Continued

my2cents.idgbooks.com

Register This Book — And Win!

Visit **http://my2cents.idgbooks.com** to register this book and we'll automatically enter you in our fantastic monthly prize giveaway. It's also your opportunity to give us feedback: let us know what you thought of this book and how you would like to see other topics covered.

Discover IDG Books Online!

The IDG Books Online Web site is your online resource for tackling technology — at home and at the office. Frequently updated, the IDG Books Online Web site features exclusive software, insider information, online books, and live events!

10 Productive & Career-Enhancing Things You Can Do at www.idgbooks.com

1. Nab source code for your own programming projects.

2. Download software.

3. Read Web exclusives: special articles and book excerpts by IDG Books Worldwide authors.

4. Take advantage of resources to help you advance your career as a Novell or Microsoft professional.

5. Buy IDG Books Worldwide titles or find a convenient bookstore that carries them.

6. Register your book and win a prize.

7. Chat live online with authors.

8. Sign up for regular e-mail updates about our latest books.

9. Suggest a book you'd like to read or write.

10. Give us your 2¢ about our books and about our Web site.

You say you're not on the Web yet? It's easy to get started with IDG Books' *Discover the Internet*, available at local retailers everywhere.